The Security Handbook

The Security Handbook

Second Edition

Philip P. Purpura, CPP

An Imprint of Elsevier

Amsterdam · Boston · London · New York · Oxford · Paris
San Diego · San Francisco · Singapore · Sydney · Tokyo

Butterworth-Heinemann is an imprint of Elsevier.

Copyright © 2003, Elsevier. All rights reserved.

Library of Congress Cataloging-in-Publication Data
Purpura, Philip P.
    The security handbook / Philip P. Purpura.—2nd ed.
      p. cm.
    Includes bibliographical references.
    ISBN-13: 978-0-7506-7438-6 ISBN-10: 0-7506-7438-5
    1. Private security services—Handbooks, manuals, etc. 2. Private security services—United States—Handbooks, manuals, etc. I. Title.

HV8290 .P88 2003
363.28'9'068—dc21
2002027946
ISBN-13: 978-0-7506-7438-6
ISBN-10: 0-7506-7438-5
British Library Cataloguing-in-Publication Data
A catalogue record for this book is available from the British Library.

The publisher offers special discounts on bulk orders of this book. For information, please contact:

Manager of Special Sales
Elsevier
200 Wheeler Road
Burlington, MA 01803
Tel: 781-313-4700
Fax: 781-313-4882

For information on all Butterworth-Heinemann publications available, contact our World Wide Web home page at: http://www.bh.com

10 9 8 7 6 5 4

Printed in the United States of America

Figures courtesy of Delmar Publishers are used with permission.

This book is dedicated to the United States and its allies, to the victims of terrorism, and to the millions of military, public safety, and security personnel who strive to create a safe and secure world.

Contents

Preface

The Security Handbook is designed for introductory courses on security and as a foundation for training entry-level security officers. This book also serves as a refresher for more experienced officers, supervisors, and managers.

Because of an increasingly dangerous world, more businesses and institutions are looking to security personnel for protection against numerous threats. Violence in the workplace, internal theft, burglary, terrorism, cybercrime, accidents, and fires are some of the many events causing serious losses. This book describes many threats and countermeasures, and the role of security officers as participants in protection efforts. During their career, security officers are likely to be involved in many protection challenges. Through an understanding of threats and countermeasures, a security officer will be better prepared to deal with serious incidents and perform in a competent, professional manner. With public police, fire, and other emergency services strained to the limit, private security will continue to increase in importance.

The second edition of *The Security Handbook* has been thoroughly updated with newer concepts, laws, statistics, and strategies of protection. Many resources have been researched to improve this book as listed in the references for each chapter. Reviewer feedback and suggestions played a role in increasing the objectivity of this book and the variety of topics enclosed. New photos and illustrations have been added.

The attack against the United States on September 11, 2001 brought with it a new era of security. There is no more "business as usual." Security personnel are on the front lines against enemies of the United States, its citizens, and its allies. Our cherished freedoms have enabled the enemy to infiltrate our boarders. Security personnel must train for worse case scenarios, prevent losses by remaining vigilant, "work smarter," and expect the unexpected.

The reader will find several features in this book designed to assist him or her in understanding the theory and reality of security work.

- Each chapter begins with an outline and behavioral objectives to guide the reader.
- Key terms are defined and basic information presented before moving on to more advanced topics.
- Numerous examples, illustrations, and figures help to relate theory to practice.
- Boxed-in cases present security situations that further illustrate the reality of the field.

- This second edition includes a new feature, "What If" scenarios, to assist the reader in understanding decision making and action as a security officer. This feature offers suggestions, helps to avoid costly mistakes, and improves professionalism.

- Also new to the second edition are Web addresses that provide direction for additional information.

- At the end of each chapter, objective questions serve as a review and test of knowledge, and applications enable the reader to apply the information acquired from the chapter.

- This book can also serve as a basic supplemental reference for: state mandated training; security officer certification examinations such as the Certified Protection Officer (CPO) program sponsored by the International Foundation for Protection Officers; and the Certified Protection Professional (CPP) examination sponsored by the American Society for Industrial Security.

Section 1 of the book introduces the private security industry. Chapter 1 emphasizes the history and development of private security. Chapter 2 covers the business, functions, and professionalism of private security, as well as industry problems and solutions. Section 2, "Security in Action," stresses the important areas in which security is involved, namely, customer service and public relations, crime prevention and physical security, post assignments and patrol, communications and reporting writing, law, arrest, and self-defense and weapons. Section 3 covers the serious threats facing businesses and the role security plays in combatting losses. Topics include internal losses, retail loss prevention, safety and fire protection, medical emergencies, and special problems. The final section, Section 4, helps the reader to enter and advance within the security profession.

Acknowledgments

I would like to thank the many people who contributed to this second edition. Gratitude goes to my wife, Amyie, for her assistance, and to my family for their patience. I am thankful to the many security practitioners and librarians who provided a wealth of information to support the contents of this book. The hardworking editorial team at Butterworth-Heinemann, including Mark Listewnik and Jennifer Rhuda are to be recognized for their talents and skills in publishing this book. I am grateful for the team effort, among so many people, for without it this book could not be published.

Author's Notice to the Reader

The reader is reminded to seek additional sources of information, and training, prior to performing security duties. By reading one book, an individual is not ready to assume the role of a security practitioner. Proper training and supervision are vital to any security effort. Certain topics are particularly important for training programs prior to duty assignments. These topics include arrest law and procedures, self-defense, firearms, safety and fire protection, and emergency first aid. In-class and hands-on training complement each other and are necessary to produce well-trained, professional security personnel.

Supervisors and managers are also reminded that security planning requires the consideration of numerous variables such as the following: business need; corporate culture; individual rights; local, state, and federal laws; and insurance requirements. Seek competent legal counsel.

The reader is warned to consider and adopt all safety precautions from this source and others and to avoid potential hazards. The reader assumes all risks in connection with the subject matter of this book. The author and publisher shall not be held liable for any damages resulting, in whole or in part, from the readers' use of, or reliance upon, this material.

About the Author

Philip P. Purpura, Certified Protection Professional, is a college educator, consultant, expert witness, and writer. He began his security career in New York City and held management and proprietary and contract investigative positions. He also worked with a public police agency. Mr. Purpura is the author of three other security textbooks: *Security & Loss Prevention: An Introduction*, fourth edition (Butterworth-Heinemann, 2002), *Retail Security and Shrinkage Protection* (Butterworth-Heinemann, 1993), and *Modern Security and Loss Prevention Management* (Butterworth-Heinemann, 1989). He also wrote *Police and Community: Concepts and Cases* (Allyn & Bacon, 2001), *Criminal Justice: An Introduction* (Butterworth-Heinemann, 1997), and numerous articles in journals, magazines, and newsletters. He has served as a contributing editor to three security periodicals. Mr. Purpura holds an Associate degree in Police Science from the State University of New York at Farmingdale, and Bachelor's and Master's degrees in Criminal Justice from the University of Dayton and Eastern Kentucky University, respectively. He has also studied in several foreign countries. He serves on the American Society for Industrial Security Council on Academic Programs. Presently, in South Carolina, he is Director of the Security Training Institute and Resource Center and Coordinator of the Security for Houses of Worship Project.

SECTION
I

INTRODUCTION

1

Historical Development of Security

CHAPTER OUTLINE

OBJECTIVES

After studying this chapter, you will be able to:

- Define security and loss prevention.
- List the benefits of studying the history of security.
- Explain how early tribes and civilizations protected themselves.

- Describe methods of protection used during the Middle Ages.
- Summarize the contributions made to public and private protection in England during the eighteenth and nineteenth centuries.
- Discuss the evolution of security in America.
- Describe the growth of private security companies in America.
- Summarize how the railroads, labor unrest, and wars influenced private security.
- Describe the development of security from the Cold War to today.
- Discuss the history of security devices.

Introduction

Although this book focuses on security, you will find information on law, safety, fire protection, business, psychology, and report writing, among other topics. If security professionals are to provide protection in our complex world, they must develop various skills and become knowledgeable of the many disciplines that assist security. This is the essence of the modern, professional security officer.

Basic Definitions

We will discuss two of the basic definitions and a key strategy in the security industry. This brief explanation will provide a foundation as you begin your study of security.

Security

Security can be defined as those methods that promote a safe and protected environment so people can pursue their daily activities. The primary purpose of security is to protect *people* and *property*. Examples of security methods are security officers, locks, fences, and intrusion alarms. Security is not foolproof but without it people and property become more vulnerable to crime and other losses.

Loss Prevention

Loss prevention is an emerging concept in the security field. Basically, loss prevention takes security several steps further by applying a broader range of methods to protect people and property. Loss prevention not only emphasizes traditional security methods (e.g., security officers, locks) but also safety and fire protection. Crimes, fires, and accidents are the major targets of loss prevention.

Loss prevention actually originated in the insurance industry. During the nineteenth century, excessive fire losses (due to so many wooden buildings) and rising insurance premiums caused people to act. The answer was to take steps to prevent fire, such as the prohibition of wooden chimneys. This reduced losses and insurance premiums.

Prevention

Prevention is a key strategy in the security and loss prevention field. Prevention involves methods that reduce the chances of a loss occurring and associated expenses. Crime prevention, fire prevention, and accident prevention all aim to avert loss events. Prevention strategies are numerous and limited only by our imagination. Simple examples are installing a fence to prevent burglaries, establishing a no smoking policy to prevent fires, and requiring workers to wear safety glasses to prevent eye injuries.

Also, modern security and loss prevention draw on many fields of study to answer protection problems. Business management, psychology, and information technology are examples of the many fields studied by security professionals who seek solutions and strategies to protection problems.

History

Now, we will explain the history of security. First, we will list the benefits of studying the history of security, then focus on England since much of our legal system and several security strategies are derived from this country.

Benefits of Studying the History of Security

We should study the history of security because:

- We learn of the origins of the profession and how it developed.
- We can see how gaps in security and safety within society were filled by the private sector.
- We learn of noted practitioners and their challenges, failures, and successes.
- Security in the past can be compared to security in the present to note areas of improvement and areas requiring improvement.
- We learn how security services and devices have been controlled and regulated.
- We learn of the interaction of private and public police over time.
- History repeats itself. We should strive to avoid the mistake of the past and continue with successes.
- We can learn how social, economic, political, and technological forces have impacted security over time.
- The past assists us in understanding the present and it offers us a foundation to anticipate future events.

Figure 1-1   Caves for protection.

Early Civilizations

Security has a long history dating back to the origin of human beings. Cave dwellers devised various forms of security to protect themselves and their property from other tribes and wild animals. By living above the ground along cliffs, rolling a large rock in front of their caves, or using fire at entrances, early tribes were afforded some protection, Figure 1-1. Prehistoric Pueblo Indians, who lived in present-day Colorado, used ladders to access their cliff dwellings. These ladders could be pulled in for protection. Another early strategy was to build dwellings on sunken pilings or platforms on lakes. Access required a boat or a drawbridge that placed enemies at a disadvantage.

One of the most amazing security systems, and the longest structure ever built, is the Great Wall of China. Construction began in the 400s B.C. and continued until the 1600s A.D. Thousands of laborers were needed for the project as it was being constructed. The Chinese built the wall to protect their northern border from invaders. It has a total length of about four thousand miles and is twenty-five feet in height. Forty-feet-tall watchtowers are located every 100 to 200 yards, Figure 1-2.

Essentially, all these forms of protection can be classified as *physical barriers*. Today, physical barriers, such as fences, walls, and water, are still used.

Another earlier strategy of protection was to live in protected communities where security was a shared responsibility. This strategy promoted cooperative efforts and cohesion. Organized protection began to evolve. At the same time, hostility occurred within and among tribal groups. Early justice required retaliatory punishment. Revenge in the form of flaying, burning, stoning, and exposure to wild animals was common. In fact, human branding and mutilation served as the first criminal record. From this primitive justice evolved the "blood feud" where family members of a victim sought revenge. These prolonged clashes would often destroy entire families.

Figure 1-2   Great Wall of China.

To stop this destructive revenge, disputes began to be settled with property. Thus began civil justice—restitution and damages paid for wrongdoing.

With the introduction of farming and raising of livestock, protection demands increased. And, as land became a valuable asset, security and social order became important to preserve prospering economic conditions. The earliest record of laws to protect people and property is traced to the *Laws of Hammurabi*, King of Babylon (1900 B.C.). These laws, engraved in an eight foot pillar, covered responsibilities of the individual to the group, private dealings between individuals, and retributive penalties (i.e., "eye for an eye").

As civilization advanced politically and economically so did the need for protection. The ancient Greek city-states (about 600 B.C.) consisted of the municipality and the surrounding territory with a centrally located fortress built on a hill. For example, Sparta was a city-state obsessed with war and the need for self-protection. Spartan males lived under military discipline from the age of seven when they were taken from their parents and taught reading, music, running, and fighting. Adult males lived in the barracks until they were thirty, though they could marry when they were twenty. Life was harsh in Sparta.

These city-states created what is considered the first police force, although responsibility rested with citizens. The Greek government, at that time, did not consider local policing to be a state responsibility. Army units were used for governmental law enforcement. Also, a secret police was organized to protect the government from subversion.

During the time of Christ, Caesar Augustus, emperor of ancient Rome, established a police force. The major objective of this force was to protect the life and property of the emperor. From this force emerged *urban cohorts* to keep peace in the city. Later, policing and firefighting were conducted by the nonmilitary *Vigiles*. Modern day coordinated patrolling and crime prevention began with this unit. Rome also created the *Vigilantes*, a secret unit to protect the state.

England

Many customs and laws of the United States originated from England. Likewise, policing innovations and techniques and methods of protection were also transported from England to the new world.

THE MIDDLE AGES The period of history between the fifth and fifteenth centuries is called the Middle Ages. This period lies between ancient and modern times. During this period, after the destruction of the ancient Greek and Roman empires, *feudalism* developed in Europe. Overlords provided food and safety to those people who worked the land and were bound to it. A system of castles with moats and drawbridges provided security, Figure 1-3. In fact, security required registration, licensing, and a fee. Following a long civil war over access to the throne, King Henry II of England who reigned from 1154 to 1189 destroyed more than a thousand unlicensed castles built during the war.

Those people who migrated to England from the mainland of Europe brought the principle of communal responsibility for protection. Groups of ten families, or *tithings*, were formed to maintain peace and share protection duties. All members were responsible for the good behavior of each member. At the same time, the *Frank-Pledge* system spread from France where the king demanded citizens swear to maintain the peace. Also, this system focused on shared responsibility and mutual protection.

A dramatic change in justice and protection in England occurred in 1066 when William, Duke of Normandy (France), conquered England. King

Figure 1-3   Castle.

William assumed ownership of all the land in England and divided the country into fifty-five military districts called *shires.* An army officer was assigned to each district and given the title of *reeve.* Through history the *shire-reeve* became the modern day sheriff. King William decided that shire-reeves should not try cases of persons arrested. Thus, a traveling judge was sent to hear cases. This was the forerunner of today's circuit judge and the separation of law enforcement and the judiciary. Also during this time, another position created to assist the reeves was *constabuli,* meaning keeper of the stable. Since travel and fighting were done on horseback, this job was very important. Today, the term *constable* denotes someone with special police powers. Finally, King William also promoted the concept that a crime was an offense against the *state.* This was different from the earlier concept where a crime was an offense against the *individual.*

The feudal system began to change significantly when the despised King John was forced to sign the *Magna Charta* in 1215. This document guaranteed basic civil and political liberties to both people and nobles. Local control was restored to the communities of England. A clear separation was established between national and local government. This resulted in local decision making over many security matters.

By 1250 the tithing system had decreased in efficiency to the point where individual service was used only when called upon. To improve protection, King Edward I issued the *Statute of Westminster* in 1285 that established a systematic police and justice system. The *watch and ward* organized town watchmen to patrol at night (watch) to assist the constables who worked during the day (ward). Watchmen arrested at night and transferred arrestees to the constables in the morning. All men had to serve on the watch or face punishment in the stocks. Community responsibility for policing had surfaced again in history. In fact, the word "*cop*" originated from *civilian on patrol.* Among the security measures employed under this system were the closing of gates (of walled towns) between sunset and sunrise, and the restricting of men living in the suburbs (i.e., the beginning of the curfew idea). This act also established the position of *bailiff* who was required to check on all strangers every fifteen days. Today, bailiffs are officers of the court. Assistants to bailiffs were called *sergeants.* This period also saw the registration of prostitutes and the restriction of their trade to certain parts of cities known as *red-light districts.*

The *hue and cry* was an integral part of the watch and ward. If an offender were resisting arrest or fleeing, the watchman called for help and all citizens were required to respond. To reinforce citizen participation, the Statute of Westminster established the *assize of arms* that required all males between fifteen and sixty years to maintain a weapon in their home.

The Statute of Westminster played a significant role in promoting law and order. However, the huge movement of people into the cities of England as commercial activity and world trade expanded, prompted the need for increased protection. Merchants were greatly dissatisfied with the increasing crime rate, and the middle class was rebelling against the compulsory watch.

Deputies were hired to replace those who could pay them, but adequate protection was still lacking. Merchants were forced to pay for private police to guard their businesses, investigate crimes, and recover stolen property. In 1663, King Charles II provided a thousand watchmen or "bellmen" to patrol from sunset to sunrise. They were inefficient and became a target of English humor through such terms as "Charlies" (i.e., reference to the king) and the "shiver and shake watch."

THE EIGHTEENTH CENTURY During the eighteenth century, the Industrial Revolution brought a massive influx of people into the cities to work in factories. Urban blight and an awful crime rate created a chaotic situation in large cities such as London. With no organized police force, citizens carried arms for self-protection. Private police were hired to protect people and property. When street riots got out of control, the military was called.

History records several individuals whose efforts were aimed at reducing the crime problem in England. In 1749 Henry Fielding published the first great social novel entitled *Tom Jones*. This realistic book depicted the hard-drinking, hard-riding country squires and the toughs of London slums. Fielding, who was a magistrate, knew firsthand the characters he portrayed. He also struggled for social and criminal reform and conceived the strategy to prevent crime through police action. His ideas included a foot patrol to make streets safer, a mounted patrol for the highways, and the famous *Bow Street Runners*. The Bow Street Runners are often referred to as the first detective unit, since they quickly moved to the scene of crimes for immediate investigation.

THE NINETEENTH CENTURY At the beginning of the nineteenth century, several different police and protection agencies existed. Besides the Bow Street Runners, the merchant police was a private force that guarded businesses; the parochial police offered protection within a parish; the watches and wards provided civilian patrol, and the Thames River police protected the waterfront.

Despite these protection efforts, crime continued to rise as cities produced great slums. The courts sentenced offenders to long prison terms and banished them to America or Australia. At one time, there were 160 crimes punishable by death. During one month over forty persons were hung each day. Since crime was out of control, citizens increased their self-protection efforts. The unlicensed privilege to bear arms took hold. To protect homes, various traps were used. Wolf traps, for example, were placed inside doors and windows to catch thieves.

To deal with the horrendous crime problem, Sir Robert Peel introduced into Parliament the Metropolitan Police Act in 1829. He argued for a single police system in London composed of professionals that would be carefully selected and thoroughly trained. At the same time, he realized the police could never be effective if the laws were wide in scope and harsh in penalty. To gain public support and respect, he reduced penalties and abolished the death sentence for over one hundred offenses. Peel's recommendations were accepted by Parliament. He was selected to lead the new police force. Thus, a revolution in law enforcement began that reaches to modern policing. In fact, today police officers in England are called "Bobbies," named after Sir Robert Peel.

Strategies evolving from the Peelian reform movement that still exist today include the prevention of crime, the distribution of crime news, the deployment of personnel by time and area, proper training, and good appearance.

Although Peel emphasized crime prevention soon after organizing the London Metropolitan Police, his personnel were so preoccupied with investigations and arrests that prevention became less of a priority. And the need for private security did not wane, even though legislation was passed establishing police forces throughout England.

Evolution of Security in America

As settlers migrated to America they brought the English system of protection. This system included collective action and the use of watchmen. During the westward expansion, frontier settlements required protection from Indians and bands of criminals. Often, a central fort was built so settlers could seek refuge more secure than their farms when an alarm was sounded, Figure 1-4.

During the 1600s, several cities established a "watch." However, like their English counterparts, many were inept. Their status was further tarnished because of the practice of sentencing those convicted of minor offenses to serve on the watch. In the Northeast, the office of constable became appropriate for growing communities whereas the sheriff served the needs of a rural South. Most areas of early America simply had inadequate protection and a growing crime problem. The situation grew worse because of limited budgets, poor selection and training, and corruption. As in England, before the nineteenth century, protection lacked uniformity and consistency. As a result, private individuals and businesses were forced to obtain their own protective services.

During the 1800s several cities—Detroit, Chicago, Philadelphia, San Francisco, and Los Angeles—established paid public police forces. New York

Figure 1-4   Early American fort.

City and other police forces adopted the Peelian principles. Federal law enforcement agencies were also organized. The U.S. Post Office established an investigative arm in 1828 and the U.S. Treasury Department did the same in 1864. The U.S. Department of Justice, created in 1870 and responsible for enforcing most federal criminal laws, borrowed agents from the Treasury Department and relied on part-time private detectives. In 1908 the Department of Justice formed the Bureau of Investigation that became the FBI in 1924, headed by J. Edgar Hoover. But even with many law enforcement agencies organizing on the local, state, and national levels, crime was overwhelming. As a result, private security services were still in demand.

Other Nations Contributed to the Development of Security

Besides England and the United States, other nations played a role in the development of security methods through history. We read that early Greek and Roman civilizations devised various forms of protection. The French, under King Louis XIV, during the 1600s, promoted crime prevention through preventive patrol and street lighting. Asian investigative methods used psychology to elicit confessions.

Private Security Grows in America

Allan Pinkerton, who was a cooper (maker of barrels) by trade, settled in Chicago from Scotland. He became interested in law enforcement and made a career change by becoming a deputy sheriff. In 1843 he was appointed Chicago's first detective. Seven years later, he formed his own private security company, Pinkerton National Detective Agency, that provided security to various business clients. Although developing public police agencies were limited by jurisdiction, Pinkerton was able to investigate and apprehend offenders through several states. Thus, his popularity soared. During the Civil War, President Lincoln summoned Pinkerton to Washington to establish an intelligence network for Union forces, Figure 1-5. Following the war, Pinkerton became more famous by capturing train robbers. Today, Pinkerton Service Corporation is a subsidiary of Securitas, based in Stockholm, Sweden.

Another historical figure in the growth of private security in the United States is William J. Burns. He was a former Secret Service investigator who headed the Bureau of Investigation. In 1909 he formed the William J. Burns Detective Agency that became the sole investigating agency for the American Bankers Association, Figure 1-6. Today, Burns International Services Corporation is a subsidiary of Securitas.

As the West expanded in the 1800s so did the risk of transporting valuables, such as gold. In 1850 Henry Wells joined with William Fargo and

Figure 1-5 Major Allan Pinkerton, President Lincoln, and General John A. McClellan, Antietam, MD, October 1862. Courtesy: National Archives.

established American Express, which operated east of the Missouri River. Two years later, Wells Fargo was formed to service the market west of the Missouri River. Since the freight transportation business was so dangerous, "shotgun riders" and detectives were necessary. Today, Wells Fargo is a division of Burns International Services Corporation.

In 1859 Washington Perry Brink established a freight and package delivery service in Chicago. Brink also concentrated on the protection of valuables in transit. A milestone was reached when this firm carried a payroll of the Western Electric Company in 1891. Brink's business of transporting valuables expanded throughout the country. As holdups became more threatening and after two of Brink's men were killed in a robbery, the armored

Figure 1-6 In 1910, William J. Burns, the foremost American investigator of his day and the first director of the government agency that became the FBI, formed the William J. Burns Detective Agency.

truck was born in 1917. Today, this company is the largest armored truck service in the world and a subsidiary of the Pittston Company.

Railroad Police

Many people do not realize the power of the railroads, especially during the nineteenth century. This was the era of the "robber barons," when massive corporate organizations formed secret agreements to eliminate competition. Several railroad companies used their power in transportation to acquire large portions of certain industries, such as coal, kerosene, and furnaces. Farmers bitterly complained that railroad monopolies charged outrageous prices to ship their grain. Although Congress passed the Sherman Antitrust Act in 1890 to curb monopolies, railroads became one of the most hated industries, thus were subject to violence. In fact, those individuals who violently attacked and robbed railroads were regarded as folk heroes—Jesse James, the Younger brothers, and the Dalton brothers. It was Jesse James who devised the idea of using dynamite to wreck a train before robbing it. His gang first used this dangerous technique in Iowa on July 21, 1873.

Because of public law enforcement's limited capabilities and problems of jurisdiction, several states enacted legislation permitting railroads to organize security forces with full police powers. This enabled railroad security personnel to pursue criminals and make arrests. Those who attacked railroad passengers, workers, or property could be assured that the railroad police would respond. By 1914 there were about 14 thousand railroad police in America. During World War I, they were deputized by the federal government to help prevent sabotage.

Labor Unrest

The history of private security should include the unfortunate violence between workers and strikebreakers. During the latter part of the nineteenth century, the forming of union organizations gained momentum. Businesses responded by developing strategies to deal with unruly workers. Many companies obtained the services of the Pinkerton Agency or other security firms. Confrontations occurred at several industrial sites. In 1892, the Homestead, Pennsylvania Carnegie Steel plant was involved in a bloody fight where three Pinkerton security men and five workers died. The Pinkertons were outnumbered and surrendered before the plant was occupied by troops sent by the governor. Bad publicity and a Congressional investigation resulted in a law prohibiting the employment of private detective agencies by the government.

The Ford Motor Company also had a history of violent confrontations. Henry Ford was staunchly opposed to unions. What came to be known as the Bridge Fight at the Ford River Rouge plant in 1937 resulted in the brutal beating of union officials by Ford security men. Reporters were also beaten and had their cameras smashed but were able to salvage some pictures that appeared across the nation. The publicity was awful for Ford and sales slumped. Finally, Ford recognized the union.

Security During the Two World Wars

Fear from enemies abroad and from within during World Wars I and II prompted government and industry to take steps aimed at protection against sabotage and espionage. Vital industries, transportation networks, and utilities were among those targeted for increased security.

Following World War I, Prohibition occupied public law enforcement resources in the unsuccessful war against the illegal manufacture and distribution of alcohol. Consequently, fewer public police were available for private sector security needs. The Great Depression initially dulled the expansion of the private security industry as the economy slumped. However, as labor unrest spread, protection needs increased.

World War II was a benefit to the need for security. With enemies across both oceans, and after the Japanese attacked Pearl Harbor in 1941, the United States clamored for intense protection of its people and industries. The federal government stipulated, as today, that before awarding a national defense contract, a comprehensive security program was required to protect classified information and materials and to prevent espionage and sabotage. The government also granted the status of auxiliary military police to over

200,000 industrial security personnel who guarded more than ten thousand industrial sites.

The Growth of Security after World War II

Following World War II, more people in business and government began realizing the importance of private security to protect people and property. In 1950 the Korean conflict and the cold war increased security needs. The fear of communism spreading throughout the world also intensified concern for protection. In 1952 the Department of Defense formalized security requirements for defense contractors to protect classified information and materials and to prevent espionage and sabotage.

When the turbulent 1960s arrived, many people thought revolution in America was imminent. Several situations facing our nation were the Vietnam War, protests, the civil rights movement, three political assassinations—President John Kennedy, Senator Robert Kennedy, and Martin Luther King, Jr.—increased heroin use, and FBI statistics showing a significant rise in crime. These turbulent times acted as a magnet in attracting and expanding private security. Many businesses and institutions realized that public police had limited resources and could not adequately respond to the tremendous demands for law and order.

By the time the 1970s arrived, the Vietnam War had caused the defense industry to expand, which required tight security. Also, political violence, as a form of protest, and terrorism were increasingly being directed at corporations and institutions. And crime rates grew worse as insurance companies continued to provide discounts to policyholders who installed security systems. Compounding the public safety problems were the citizen tax revolts where residents in many locales wanted relief from high taxes. Public safety agencies had more to do with less resources. Therefore, many businesses and institutions turned to private security to fill the gap. *Private Security and Police in America: Hallcrest Report*, a well-known study completed in 1985, said, "The forces that accelerated growth in the late 1970s will continue to affect private security in the 1980s, including fear of crime, declining law enforcement resources in the public sector, and the protective initiatives of citizens, neighborhoods, businesses, and institutions."

The events of the last decade of the twentieth century, namely the first bombing of the World Trade Center, the bombing of the Murrah Federal Building in Oklahoma City, the war against Iraq, the crimes resulting from the expansion and use of the Internet and computers, the increased value of proprietary information, and the attention to violence in the workplace illustrated the threats to be expected in the coming years.

A New Century with Challenges

Not long into the twenty-first century, on September 11, 2001, terrorist attacks with hijacked airliners killed about 5,000 people by leveling the World Trade Center towers and destroying part of the Pentagon. These bold, surprise attacks, subsequent bio-terrorism, and the war in Afghanistan, show the difficult challenges facing the world in this new century. A re-thinking of defense and security strategies will meet these threats and provide a safer world. (More on these topics in Chapter 14.)

Security professionals are on the front lines facing, not only the threat of terrorism, but other threats such as a variety of crimes, fire, accidents, and disasters. At the same time, the "watchmen" and "guard" are yielding to the professional security officer who is more educated, better trained, and knowledgeable of numerous security and loss prevention strategies.

Development of Security Devices

Although personnel are the backbone of protection efforts, various security devices and systems provide additional safeguards. Archeological digs of primitive tribes have uncovered canine remains near those of humans. It is likely that guard dogs, with their keen sense of smell, are a very old form of alarm notification. The ancient civilizations of China and Egypt equipped doors with primitive keyed locks. Pegs were used to slide down into a door to secure it. A special notched board was required to raise the pegs high enough to clear the door. Early Egyptians constructed locked vaults deep inside huge pyramids that illustrated the concept of "protection-in-depth," a modern strategy used at banks. The ancients of Israel used bright lights and loud noises to scare intruders. Gideon, a Jewish warrior king, instilled fear in a large invading force by blowing three hundred trumpets and waving three hundred torches. The Romans used the sensitive hearing and squawking of geese to warn of an approaching army.

During the 1700s, British inventors assembled the first mechanical burglar alarm system to protect doors. It was a set of chimes linked to a door lock. Therefore, burglars defeated the system by cutting the cord between the lock and the chimes.

In 1852 Augustus R. Pope filed a patent for an electromagnetic alarm consisting of an electric bell activated by a falling weight or uncoiling of a spring when a door or window was opened. Six years later the famous pioneer of alarm protection, Edwin Holmes, bought Pope's patent and formed the first private company that provided alarm protection. It is interesting to note that initially Holmes had a difficult time selling the idea of electronic security. People found it hard to believe that a bell could be rung on the second floor of a home when a door or window was opened on the first floor. To convince potential customers, Holmes went door-to-door with a scale model of a home containing his alarm system. For his clients, Holmes connected colored tabs to a wired panel in the customer's home so the resident could identify which door or window activated the alarm. For wealthier customers, a clock was attached to the system that automatically disconnected the alarm in the morning. During the 1880s when the electric light was invented, Holmes added this feature to illuminate the house during an alarm. By this time the central station monitoring of alarm systems had emerged. In other words, instead of the alarm notifying only the resident or business person, it was also monitored at a central station so police or security personnel could be dispatched. Holmes Protection Group, Inc., was acquired by ADT Security Services, Inc., at the end of the twentieth century.

CHAPTER REVIEW

A. Multiple Choice

1. Early civilizations used what type of security strategy that is still used today?
   a. taut wire
   b. physical barriers
   c. shrubbery
   d. fire

2. The earliest record of laws to protect people and property is traced to the
   a. Laws of Hammurabi.
   b. feudal system.
   c. Code of Caesar Augustus.
   d. Magna Charta.

3. Many of the customs and laws of the United States originated from
   a. Germany.
   b. France.
   c. Spain.
   d. England.

4. This individual became Chicago's first detective, went on to form a security company, and established an intelligence network for Union forces during the Civil War.
   a. Allan Pinkerton
   b. Washington Perry Brink
   c. William Fargo
   d. Augustus R. Pope

5. Which of the following events had the most harmful impact on the growth of private security in America?
   a. railroads
   b. labor unrest
   c. World War I
   d. World War II

B. True or False

1. Loss prevention not only emphasizes traditional security methods but also safety and fire protection.

2. There are only a few security and loss prevention methods that are truly foolproof.

3. During the Middle Ages, as today, security required registration, licensing, and a fee; King Henry II destroyed more than one thousand unlicensed castles.

4. Both World Wars I and II had a minimal impact on private security growth because most protection officers were fighting overseas.

5. The ancient civilizations of China and Egypt equipped doors with primitive keyed locks.

Applications

Application 1A

What security strategies applied prior to the 1900s are still applied today?

Application 1B

Research a large security company in your area. Trace the history of the company. Prepare a report.

Application 1C

How do you think security has changed since the September 11, 2001 terrorist attack on the United States?

2

Security: Business, Functions, and Professionalism

CHAPTER OUTLINE

OBJECTIVES

After studying this chapter, you will be able to:

- Discuss the business of security.
- Explain the services and functions of the security industry.
- Explain the advantages and disadvantages of contract security officers.
- Explain the advantages and disadvantages of proprietary security officers.
- List and explain at least three security industry problems and solutions.
- Explain why security is a profession.
- Discuss the code of ethics for both private security employees and private security management.

The Business of Security

The security industry is a multibillion-dollar business. Every decade seems to bring an increased need for security services. Violence in the workplace, computer crime, and terrorist attacks (Figures 2-1 and 2-2) are examples of why there are greater demands for the protection of people and assets.

Figure 2-1   The twenty-first century has brought with it serious terrorist threats to the United States and other countries and the need for enhanced security. Courtesy: Wackenhut, Inc.

Figure 2-2 Twenty-first century terrorist attacks have changed our approaches to homeland defense, security, and safety for our citizens and property.

At the end of the last century, research of the private security industry by the National Institute of Justice, U.S. Department of Justice, showed that private security is clearly the nation's primary protective resource, outspending public law enforcement by 73 percent and employing $2\frac{1}{2}$ times the workforce. During 2001 the Bureau of Justice Statistics listed private security employees at between 1.2 to 1.4 million. There were 531,496 full-time employees of local police departments, of which 420,000 were sworn personnel. Sheriffs' departments had 263,427 full-time employees, including 175,000 sworn personnel. State and federal police had 59,000 and 70,000 sworn officers, respectively. Annual spending for police was about $58 billion.

The Security Industry Association, the trade group that represents security businesses, reported that projected revenues of security-related manufacturers and service providers for the United States and Canada during 2000 would be about $103 billion. Major categories, with revenues in billions of dollars, were: manufacturers of electronic security systems ($37.2), contract security officer services ($21.5), proprietary security ($16), alarm companies ($14), private investigators ($4.6), and armored car ($1.3).

The Freedonia Group, a Cleveland-based market research firm, published *World Security Services* to report that the world market for private security services grew 8.3 percent annually from 1989 to 1999 and will grow 8.4 percent annually through 2004, approaching $100 billion. By 2009 revenues are expected to be $150 billion. In the United States such revenues are projected at $40 billion in 2004 and $59 billion in 2009. (The Freedonia study emphasizes revenues from "security services" whereas the Security Industry Association study is broader and includes manufacturers of electronic security systems.) The Freedonia study noted that contractual security officer services will remain the largest segment of the market and benefit from the outsourcing of public and proprietary protection; however, growth will be hindered by more affordable electronic security systems. The report stated that six large companies account for 18 percent of global revenues. They are: Securitas, Secom, Brinks, Tyco, Group 4 Falck, and Wackenhut. The larger companies have been acquiring the smaller firms at a record pace since the 1980s when, in the United States, there were 10,000 contract security officer firms, 26,000 investigative firms, and 10,000 alarm installation firms.

Security Services and Functions

Just about all businesses, institutions, and organizations require protection. Examples are numerous and include retail businesses, industrial facilities, transportation terminals, airports, nuclear plants, office and apartment buildings, banks, schools, hospitals, museums, libraries, hotels, and sport facilities. Each location has unique needs.

At the same time, the basic functions performed by security officers at different locations are similar. These functions involve the following:

1. The protection of people and assets.
2. The prevention of crimes, fires, and accidents.
3. The placement of officers on patrol or stationary posts.

4. Access control.
5. Observing and reporting.

The following describes major security services and functions.

Security Officer Services

The strategic deployment of security officers is a major security strategy. There are many diverse skills required in security work that only humans can perform. No single device or system can practice good public relations, direct traffic, operate a vehicle, evaluate an incident, take notes, make an arrest, testify, and so forth. Security officers are assigned to fixed posts usually for access control. Or they may be required to patrol the premises to make periodic inspections of crucial locations, such as doors, safes, chemical containers, boilers, and so forth.

Contract Security Compared to Proprietary Security

Management is often confronted with the decision to use either contract or proprietary (in-house) security. The *Report of the Task Force on Private Security* lists advantages and disadvantages of each.

CONTRACT SECURITY OFFICERS The advantages of contract security officers include:

- Usually cost less than in-house security.
- Screening, hiring, training, and supervision are handled by contractor.
- More or fewer officers can be supplied as needed.

The disadvantages of contract security officers include:

- High turnover.
- Officers often have multiple jobs because of the low pay. This can lead to fatigue.
- Applicant screening, training, supervision, and liability insurance may be inadequate.

PROPRIETARY SECURITY OFFICERS The advantages of proprietary security officers include:

- Knowledgeable of the particular business because of permanent employment.
- Loyalty.
- More control of officers because they are inside company structure.
- Better communications.

The disadvantages of proprietary security officers include:

- More expensive than contract security (i.e., salary, benefits, uniforms, equipment, and training).
- Officers may become too familiar with workers to be effective.
- Officers may side with union or strike.

Comparison of Private Security and Public Police

	PRIVATE SECURITY	PUBLIC POLICE
Employed by:	Businesses, Institutions, Private Concerns	Government
Serve:	Businesses, Institutions, Private Concerns	The Public
Supported by:	Businesses, Institutions, Private Concerns	Tax Dollars
Basic Strategy:	Prevent Crime	React to Crime and Arrest
Legal Authority:	Citizen Arrest Powers	Greater Arrest and Search Powers

The above generalizations contain exceptions. Government units sometimes contract with security firms to save money. Also, public police serve the public primarily. However, depending on available time and resources, public police may become involved in the investigation of crimes in businesses. Sometimes, public police, under a special grant, may install and service robbery alarms at high crime businesses. Although public police are arrest oriented and have traditionally reacted to crimes following each reported offense, the strategy of prevention is being applied more often. Private security, on the other hand, is generally prevention oriented although some businesses place an emphasis on arrests. Public police usually possess greater arrest powers than security officers. However, depending on the state, security officers may possess arrest powers equal to the public police but only on the protected property.

Investigative Services

When a serious incident occurs, an investigator may be dispatched to gather facts. A factual account of an incident helps management in making decisions. The circumstances surrounding an accident, for example, may cause management to implement safety measures. Or an investigation of theft may result in discharge, arrest, and improved security.

Several types of investigators exist. As with security officers, private sector investigators can be proprietary (in-house) or contract. There are advantages and disadvantages of each, similar to security officers. Proprietary investigators are usually well versed on the unique needs and characteristics of their employer. This knowledge is a great aid during investigations. On the other hand, contract investigators can be less expensive. These investigators are especially useful for undercover investigations to infiltrate employee groups involved in theft and illegal drugs. By using a contract investigator, a client company does not have to decide where to place the investigator within the company after the investigation.

Another way to classify investigators is public and private. The public police detective serves the public and investigates such crimes as murder, rape, robbery, burglary, and larceny. Depending on public police resources, they may or may not have the time to investigate minor cases of theft and drug abuse in businesses. Consequently, private sector investigators are employed. Once a private sector investigator puts together a case, the prosecutor often requires solid evidence (confession or witnesses) before the case is prosecuted. In more serious cases on the premises, including murder, rape, robbery, and arson, public police involvement is assured once these crimes are reported.

Private sector investigators perform various functions beyond criminal and accident investigations. They may gather information concerning: a job applicant's background, the financial health of a company, an insurance claim, a lawsuit, a divorce, or a missing person. Private investigators, as popularized on television, handle many of these types of cases. Corporate, proprietary investigators are less likely to investigate missing persons or divorce cases.

Alarm Monitoring and Response Services

Intrusion detection systems are comprised of sensors on protected property that are connected to a remote central station where numerous locations are monitored for alarms. When an alarm is triggered, security officers are dispatched or public police are notified. Because of the high rate of false alarms from intrusion detection systems, connections of these systems to police departments has become an annoyance to police. Consequently, the private sector has filled the void for a profit. Central station alarm systems also monitor smoke and fire, conditions in manufacturing, temperature, flooding, and other vital signs, such as water pressure for sprinkler systems (for fire protection).

Armored Car and Courier Services

This security service provides protection of valuables during transportation by using armored vehicles and armed security officers. Money, securities, jewelry, precious metals, art, and other valuable items are transported by this service. Courier services are distinguished from armored car services by the use of quick delivery, lightweight vehicles, and often the transportation of less valuable items.

Other Services

Additional services provided by security firms include:

- Consulting to expose vulnerabilities and to suggest remedies.
- Training to upgrade and professionalize security forces.
- Detection of deception (paper-and-pencil honesty tests, polygraph).
- Drug detection and countermeasures.
- Bodyguard services.
- Canine patrols.
- Technical services to detect listening devices (i.e., bugs, taps on telephones).
- Private vault storage for valuables.

Industry Problems and Solutions

Although the security industry has sustained considerable growth, problems have developed over the years. One avenue to study security industry problems and solutions is to discuss major research reports on this industry.

Rand Report

Business and government leaders have realized that the growing private security industry is an ally of the criminal justice system in preventing and controlling crime. With this thinking in mind, the U.S. Department of Justice provided financial support for the production of important research reports. In 1972 the *Rand Report* became the first major study of private security. Many people in the security industry were displeased with the research results. However, it is important to bring industry problems into the open so solutions can be found. Results cited were poor training and abuses of authority by security officers. Solutions focused on the licensing of security businesses and the registering of personnel. This report noted that "the typical private guard is an aging white male, poorly educated, usually untrained, and very poorly paid." Today, this is not true.

Report of the Task Force on Private Security

The next major research project, again supported by the U.S. Department of Justice, was the *Report of the Task Force on Private Security* in 1976. This was the first national effort to set standards and goals to improve the effectiveness of the security industry. Emphasis was placed on licensing security businesses, selecting and training uniformity, registering personnel, cooperating with public police, establishing a code of ethics, and promoting professionalism.

Private Security and Police in America: The Hallcrest Report

In 1985 another research report was published called *Private Security and Police in America: The Hallcrest Report.* Hallcrest Systems, Inc., completed this research that was funded by the U.S. Department of Justice. This report focused research on three major areas: (1) the contributions of both public police and private security to crime control, (2) the interaction of these two forces and their level of cooperation, and (3) the characteristics of the private security industry. This report noted that the security industry had improved since the earlier research reports. For example, the typical security officer was more likely to be younger (thirty-one to thirty-five years). Also, half of all security officers had completed at least some college level work.

Hallcrest Report II

The Hallcrest Report II—Private Security Trends: 1970 to the Year 2000 was released in 1990. This report provided a comprehensive study of security trends observed and predicted up to the twenty-first century. Hallcrest Report II showed changes in the security industry since the first Hallcrest Report. Among these changes was an increase use of contract security and systems as in-house security declined slightly. Since Hallcrest I there had been an increase in the number of private security employees, from one million to 1.5 million, with one million employed in contract security and one-half million in proprietary security. Security officers are younger, better educated, and represent greater numbers of women and minorities.

Hallcrest II predicted that a growing crime problem will face corporate America. Such crimes include drug trafficking and drug use in businesses, computer crime, and fraud of all kinds. The cost of crime to U.S. businesses was $67 billion in 1980, $114 billion in 1990, and was estimated to reach $200 billion by the year 2000.

When Hallcrest I and II are compared, it is interesting to note that some persistent problems are very difficult to solve within the security industry. Problems still exist with the quality of security officers, especially concerning low pay, high turnover, and inadequate screening and training. Another persistent problem is the huge waste of public resources that are spent responding to false alarms.

Security industry problems and preferred solutions discussed in the above reports are covered next. These problems still persist today, however, efforts are continuing toward improvements.

Problem
Limited cooperation exists between public police and private security in crime prevention efforts.

Recommendations

1. Businesses should share their security expertise with merchants and civic groups.
2. Both public police and private security should cooperate in making the public aware of self-help crime prevention strategies.

Problem

Longstanding obstacles to interaction and cooperation continue to exist between public police and private security.

Recommendations

1. Cooperation.
2. Police should appoint a high-ranking officer to foster communications.
3. Joint task forces should be established to investigate serious losses in the private sector.

Problems

1. Many security firms use uniforms, badges, and equipment similar to police departments.
2. Numerous small firms are susceptible to failure due to inadequate business skills.

Recommendations

1. Security uniforms should be clearly different from those of public police.
2. Statewide licensing should be required for contract personnel, investigation, and alarm firms.

Problem

Recruitment, selection, pay, and training vary widely among private security organizations.

Recommendations

1. States should enact legislation to permit private security companies to access criminal history records to improve the applicant selection process.
2. Minimum training levels should be required for all security personnel.
3. Training records should be routinely inspected by the state.
4. Certification programs should be prepared to increase professionalism and to set objective guidelines for setting wage scales.

Problem

Limited public police resources to combat crime.

Recommendations
1. Transfer some responsibility for minor crimes to private security.
2. Select services that might be performed by private security for a lower cost.

Problem
False alarms (for burglary or robbery) are as high as 90 percent in many communities, constituting 10 to 12 percent of public police calls-for-service.

Recommendations
1. Cooperation among users, alarm companies, and police.
2. Standardized training, testing, and licensing for alarm installers/technicians.
3. Local government false alarm control ordinances.

An example of how industry problems have been reduced include meetings for over a decade among the International Association of Chiefs of Police (IACP), the National Sheriffs' Association, and the American Society for Industrial Security (ASIS). This communication has resulted in, for instance, the IACP Private-Sector Liaison Committee, *Private Security Officer Selection, Training and Licensing Guidelines*. As we begin the twenty-first century, cooperative efforts must continue in an effort to enhance the resources and capabilities of each sector. Suggested areas of cooperation are: sharing data, information, and technology; sharing expertise in combating fraud, cybercrime, and terrorism; and shared training.

Although attempts have been made through Congress to pass a national law to regulate the security industry and improve training (e.g., H.R. 2092, *The Private Security Officers Quality Assurance Act of 1995*), no national law exists. However, states have improved background checks of security officer applicants and training.

Improving the Security Industry

There are several ways to improve the security industry. Before we explain security as a profession, three issues will be covered: licensing and registration, the false alarm problem, and privatization.

Licensing and Registration

Government licensing and registration of the security industry is controversial, especially with those who favor government deregulation. At the same time, consumers of security services should be afforded protection. What if a convicted felon decides to begin a security business or applies for a security position? A mechanism is needed to screen undesirables from the industry.

Some of the negative factors resulting from a few people in the industry include:

deceptive advertising and sales	false imprisonment
lack of insurance	illegal searches
poor screening and training	misuse of authority and weapons
unnecessary use of force	numerous lawsuits

Both the *Report of the Task Force on Private Security* and the *Hallcrest Reports* favored regulation of the security industry. The *Report of the Task Force on Private Security* recommended the following:

- The private security industry should be regulated by each state.
- Regulation can be achieved by requiring licensing of contract security companies and by requiring the registration of all those security personnel within these businesses. Personnel included contract security officers, private investigators, armored car personnel, and alarm system technicians.

Most states have legislation regulating the security industry. Each state varies as to the agency that handles security regulation and the specific requirements for licensing. City and county governments are also involved in the regulation process. This causes some problems for security companies that have contracts among numerous jurisdictions and states.

The False Alarm Problem

A persistent problem that causes friction between public police and the private sector is false alarms. It is generally agreed that over 95 percent of all alarm response calls received by public police are false alarms. However, the definition of *false alarm* is subject to debate. It often is assumed that, if a burglar is not caught on the premises, the alarm was false. Police do not always consider that the alarm or the approaching police could have frightened away a burglar.

The Task Force and Hallcrest Reports discussed the problem of false alarms. Many police agencies nationwide continue to spend millions of dollars each year in personnel and equipment to respond to these calls. For example, in 1998 Indianapolis police responded to 29,651 false alarms expending 20,460 hours of police time. For decades municipalities and the alarm industry have tried various solutions. Police agencies have selectively responded or not responded to alarms. City and county governments have enacted false alarm control ordinances that require a permit for an alarm system and impose fines for excessive false alarms. The industry claims that 80 percent of the problems are caused by the end-users. It continues its education campaign while trying a multitude of strategies, such as offering a class for repeat offenders instead of a fine, setting standards of exit delay at no fewer than 45 seconds and entry times of at least 30 seconds, and audio and video verification of alarms. Since the industry is installing 15 percent more systems each year, these efforts must continue.

The Issue of Privatization

Privatization is the contracting out of government programs, either wholly or in part, to for-profit and not-for-profit organizations. There is a growing interdependence of the public and private sectors. A broad array of services are provided to government agencies by businesses. For crime control efforts, we see private security patrols in residential areas, private security officers in courts and other government buildings, and private prisons. In the future we will see more and more services previously performed by public police performed by the private sector. Examples are alarm response, traffic enforcement, preliminary investigations of minor crimes, and transportation of prisoners. Business people attract government leaders when they claim that they can perform services more efficiently and at a lower cost than the public sector.

Critics of privatization argue that crime control by government is rooted in constitutional safeguards and crime control should not be contracted to businesses. Use of force and searches by the private sector, punishment in private prisons, and liabilities of governments and contractors are examples of the thorny issues that face privatization.

The Security Profession

The security and loss prevention field has reached the status of a profession. If we look to other professions as models, we see the following in each as we see in the security and loss prevention profession: a history, body of knowledge, and theory recorded in books and periodicals; associations that promote advancement of knowledge, training, certification, and a code of ethics; standards; and programs of higher education that prepare students for the profession.

Theoretical Foundations

The challenges of security and loss prevention in a complex world has created an intense search among security practitioners to seek answers to protection problems. Many fields of study offer answers for the practitioner. An example is the work of Oscar Newman that is the bedrock of many security designs worldwide. He argued that informal control of criminal behavior can be enhanced through architectural design (e.g., fences, lighting) that creates "defensible space" and changes residents' use of public places while reducing fear.

The field of criminology also helps us to improve security. One theory, known as routine activities theory, stresses that some people engage in regular or routine activities that increase their risk of victimization. Three factors must occur for victimization under this theory: (1) an attractive target; (2) a motivated offender; and (3) the absence of "guardianship" (e.g., nearby people who can protect an intended victim). Corporate security and executive protection programs can benefit from this theory and related research.

Employee theft and embezzlement are huge problems for businesses. Criminologist Donald Cressey's formula offers insight into causes and preventive measures. The formula is: motivation + opportunity + rationalization = theft. Motivation comes from, for instance, the need to satisfy a drug problem. An opportunity occurs when security is lax. A rationalization is an excuse (e.g., "everybody else is stealing").

This snapshot of various theories is a beginning point from which to build improved security. And, the social sciences are by no means the only disciplines helpful to security and loss prevention. Other helpful fields include law, marketing, accounting, fire science, safety, and risk management.

Security Periodicals and the Web

There are many security periodicals (i.e., magazines, journals, and newsletters) published by a variety of associations and organizations. Periodicals serve as a platform for not only the theoretical foundation of the security and loss prevention field but also to introduce readers to new developments, security strategies and technology, law, and a host of other topics. What follows are noted periodicals in this field.

Security Journal is published by Perpetuity Press United Kingdom and supported by the American Society for Industrial Security Foundation. The editorial staff is from the United States and the United Kingdom. The journal publishes articles on a variety of topics on the latest developments and techniques of security management. Articles include findings and recommendations of independent research. Two other journals from this publisher are: *Risk Management: An International Journal* and *Crime Prevention and Community Safety: An International Journal.* Website: www.perpetuitypress.co.uk.

Journal of Security Administration is a scholarly semi-annual journal that presents excellent articles on a variety of security topics. It is affiliated with the Security and Crime Prevention Section of the Academy of Criminal Justice Sciences. Website: www.wiu.edu/users/mfkac/jsa/.

Security Management is a monthly magazine published by the American Society for Industrial Security. Each issue contains a wealth of informative articles on a broad range of topics written by experienced security professionals. It is the best general security periodical. Website: www.asis.com.

Protection News, published by the International Foundation of Protection Officers, is a newsletter containing current trends of the security industry and it covers topics on life-safety and the protection of property. Its website has an excellent "security surfer" with links to numerous security associations and organizations and related periodicals. Website: www.ifpo.org.

An alternative to the above "security surfer" is a good search engine. By typing school security, health care security, bank security, computer security, or whatever type of security, you will be introduced to the many specializations in this discipline. And, each specialization is likely to have an association, an agenda of objectives to advance the profession, training, certification, and a periodical.

Security Associations

Several security associations exist to promote professionalism and improve the security field. One major association is the International Foundation for Protection Officers. Besides the magazine cited above, the IFPO offers training and the Certified Protection Officer (CPO) and Certified Security Supervisor (CSS) programs. This association has done much to improve the professionalism of security officers.

Another major security association is the American Society for Industrial Security. Besides the magazine cited above, the ASIS has a membership over 30,000, it is the leading general organization of protection executives and specialists, and it offers courses, seminars, and a certification program for the Certified Protection Professional (CPP).

Other associations and the certification provided include the Academy of Security Educators and Trainers, offering the Certified Security Trainer (CST) and the Association of Certified Fraud Examiners, offering the Certified Fraud Examiner (CFE).

The National Association of Security and Investigative Regulators contains members who are state employees involved in the licensing and regulation of the private security industry. This group promotes effective regulation and enforcement, assists in training and education, and influences legislation. Most states are represented in the membership. The group's website (www.nasir.org) lists state licensing information for security officers, armored car officers, private investigators, and electronic security companies.

The National Association of Security Companies represents the private security industry and its membership includes large contract security companies. Its goals are to monitor proposed state and federal legislation that might affect the quality or effectiveness of private security services, upgrade standards within the industry, and foster uniformity of regulation throughout the United States.

Figure 2-3   Professionalism is strengthened through training.
Courtesy: Wackenhut, Inc.

Training

Numerous research reports and other publications have pointed to the need
for more and improved training of personnel in the security industry (Figure
2-3). Training of all security officers prior to assignment should be required
by law in all states. The Task Force Report and the Hallcrest Reports stress
the need for improved recruitment, selection, pay, and training within the
security industry.

The Hallcrest Report II noted that the typical uniformed security officer
receives an estimated four to six hours of training before assignment.
However, security training varies widely. In essence, what we have seen following these national reports and recommendations is an industry that
needs to do more to help professionalize the industry and security personnel. Unfortunately, we have seen changes resulting from many lawsuits
claiming negligent security. Fear of such litigation motivates the industry to
change. On the bright side, there are many security service companies that
are professional, set high standards for themselves, and have improved the
industry. It is hoped that these companies continue to set an example to be
followed by others.

Topics for security training that have been included in proposed federal
legislation during the 1990s are:

- Law of arrest, search, and seizure.
- Safety and fire protection.
- First aid.
- When and how to notify public authorities.
- Employer policies.
- Report writing.
- Fundamentals of patrolling.
- Use of equipment.
- Deportment and ethics.
- Crowd control.

Code of Ethics

A code of ethics is an essential part of professionalism. It guides behavior through standards of conduct. Practitioners obtain a perspective of their behavior by studying a code of ethics. The security industry is not immune from unethical practices such as:

- Contract security services billing clients for hours not worked.
- Sales of unnecessary and outdated security systems.
- Investigative reports that are deliberately exaggerated.
- Investigations unnecessarily prolonged for profit.

Naturally, all professions are subject to unethical practices, often by a few individuals. Such unethical behavior reflects on the whole profession, and unethical practices are costly to business. If consumers of security services and systems are repeatedly subjected to unethical practices, various negative consequences are possible, such as complaints, bad publicity, loss of business, lawsuits, and increased government regulation. Thus, a code of ethics promotes moral behavior and it is an asset to business. The same is true for in-house security organizations. In other words, once management loses respect for security, the personnel and budget are doomed. The *Report of the Task Force on Private Security* stated that "A code of ethics should be adopted and enforced for private security personnel and employers.

CODE OF ETHICS FOR PRIVATE SECURITY EMPLOYEES   The Code of Ethics for Private Security Employees (see page 39) is important for you to understand. It contains guidelines to improve professionalism.

CODE OF ETHICS FOR PRIVATE SECURITY MANAGEMENT   The Code of Ethics for Private Security Management (see page 40) is also important for you to understand. Obviously, all security officers have a supervisor. This code can be your first step in understanding your supervisor's responsibilities. In turn, this knowledge may lead to better communication and cooperation between you and your supervisor. Also, you may someday be in a management position as you advance in your career.

The Web is a rich source of information on ethics. The Corporate Social Responsibility Resource Center for Business Ethics (www.bsr.org/resourcecenter) focuses on many topics such as ethics training, competitive intelligence, corruption and bribery, "cyberethics" challenges, defense industry initiative on ethics, and what a variety of corporations are doing. The Markkula Center for Applied Ethics (www.scu.edu/Ethics/) provides training and educational tools to heighten ethical awareness and improve ethical decisions.

WHAT IF?

As a Security Officer, What Do You Do if You Are Assigned to a Stationary Post at a Shipping and Receiving Dock and a Truck Driver Asks You to "Look the Other Way" for $500?

Because security officers are charged with the protection of people and property, and because they are the major line of defense against criminals, they will be targeted by criminals to compromise security. A security officer who is approached by someone with the above proposition is dealing with a criminal. Whatever they say is likely to be a lie and their ulterior motives may not be obvious. As a security officer, "what do you think this criminal is up to?" The criminal could be planning one of a wide variety of criminal acts, from stealing merchandise to planting a bomb to kill you and the rest of the people in the building. Since you may be dealing with a dangerous criminal with accomplices, try to find a safe location to contact dispatch. Another possibility is that this encounter is an integrity test to check on your trustworthiness.

Security officers face challenges in their day-to-day duties. They need guidelines for their decisions. Here are guidelines to consider:

- Does the decision violate law, a code of ethics, or company policy?
- What are the short-term and long-term consequences of your decision for the organization you work for and yourself?
- Is there an alternative course of action, that is less harmful?
- Are you making a level-headed decision, rather than a decision based on emotions?
- Would your family support your decision?
- Would your supervisor and management support your decision?

Code of Ethics for Private Security Employees

In recognition of the significant contribution of private security to crime prevention and reduction, as a private security employee, I pledge:

    I. To accept the responsibilities and fulfill the obligations of my role: protecting life and property; preventing and reducing crimes against my employer's business, or other organizations and institutions to which I am assigned; upholding the law; and respecting the constitutional rights of all persons.

    II. To conduct myself with honesty and integrity and to adhere to the highest moral principles in the performance of my security duties.

    III. To be faithful, diligent, and dependable in discharging my duties, and to uphold at all times the laws, policies, and procedures that protect the rights of others.

    IV. To observe the precepts of truth, accuracy, and prudence, without allowing personal feelings, prejudices, animosities or friendships to influence my judgments.

    V. To report to my superiors, without hesitation, any violation of the law or of my employer's or client's regulations.

    VI. To respect and protect the confidential and privileged information of my employer or client beyond the term of my employment, except where their interests are contrary to law or to this Code of Ethics.

    VII. To cooperate with all recognized and responsible law enforcement and government agencies in matters within their jurisdiction.

    VIII. To accept no compensation, commission, gratuity, or other advantage without the knowledge and consent of my employer.

    IX. To conduct myself professionally at all times, and to perform my duties in a manner that reflects credit upon myself, my employer, and private security.

    X. To strive continually to improve my performance by seeking training and educational opportunities that will better prepare me for my private security duties.

(Source: Report of the Task Force on Private Security, Washington, DC: U.S. Government Printing Office, 1976)

Code of Ethics for Private Security Management

As managers of private security functions and employees, we pledge:

I. To recognize that our principal responsibilities are, in the service of our organizations and clients, to protect life and property as well as to prevent and reduce crime against our business, industry, or other organizations and institutions; and in the public interest, to uphold the law and to respect the constitutional rights of all persons.

II. To be guided by a sense of integrity, honor, justice, and mortality in the conduct of business; in all personnel matters; in relationships with government agencies, clients, and employers; and in responsibilities to the general public.

III. To strive faithfully to render security services of the highest quality and to work continuously to improve our knowledge and skills and thereby improve the overall effectiveness of private security.

IV. To uphold the trust of our employers, our clients, and the public by performing our functions within the law, not ordering or condoning violations of law, and ensuring that our security personnel conduct their assigned duties lawfully and with proper regard for the rights of others.

V. To respect the reputation and practice of others in private security, but to expose to the proper authorities any conduct that is unethical or unlawful.

VI. To apply uniform and equitable standards of employment in recruiting and selecting personnel regardless of race, creed, color, sex, or age, and in providing salaries commensurate with job responsibilities and with training, education, and experience.

VII. To cooperate with recognized and responsible law enforcement and other criminal justice agencies; to comply with security licensing and registration laws and other statutory requirements that pertain to our business.

VIII. To respect and protect the confidential and privileged information of employers and clients beyond the term of our employment, except where their interests are contrary to law or to this Code of Ethics.

IX. To maintain a professional posture in all business relationships with employers and clients, with others in the private security field, and with members of other professions; and to insist that our personnel adhere to the highest standards of professional conduct.

> X. To encourage the professional advancement of our personnel
>   by assisting them to acquire appropriate security knowledge,
>   education, and training.
>
> *(Data source: Report of the Task Force on Private Security, Washington, DC: U.S.*
> *Government Printing Office, 1976)*

Standards

As with licensing and registration, security standards have been controversial.
It can be argued that the security industry will become more professional
through standards and that an organization will have a much stronger
defense if it is sued by a victim claiming inadequate security. To illustrate,
suppose hotel security standards are formulated and followed by that industry. Hotel security standards may specify, for example, that all hotels should
have adequate lighting, locks, and security patrols. Hotels adhering to these
standards are more likely to be safer and withstand a lawsuit for inadequate
security after a crime incident on the premises.

The Security Law Institute in Washington, DC, has formulated security
standards that can be used by businesses and the court system. Furthermore,
the *Report of the Task Force on Private Security* issued standards for the security
industry as discussed earlier.

There are those who argue against standards because it is impossible
to standardize protection with so many diverse businesses, even in the same
industry. Each business is unique. For example, there are many types of
hotels that are located in numerous types of environments. Those against
standards also cite costs. Another problem is the different opinions of diverse
courts concerning what is adequate security. What is acceptable in one state
may not be sufficient elsewhere. The formulation of acceptable standards is
a difficult process. However, losses from a negligence suit for inadequate
security can cause a business to fail.

Although standards for security programs at businesses are not fully
developed and accepted, standards for security and safety hardware have
existed for many years. During the 1920s, for example, Underwriters
Laboratory (UL), an independent testing organization, worked with insurers
to establish a rating system for alarm products and installations. This system
assists insurance agents in setting premiums for customers. An alarm
company may show customers that its service is of a higher standard than a
competitor's. UL has various listings, and it requires that an alarm company
advertise its listing specifically. What a company has to do to obtain a listing
as a central station burglar alarm company differs widely from what it has to
do to be listed as a residential monitoring station; providing fire-resistant
construction, backup power, access controls, and optimal response time following an alarm are a few examples (UL; www.ul.com; 1285 Walt Whitman
Rd., Melville, NY 11747-3081; Tel.: 631-271-6200).

Consumers, in general, are more familiar with UL as an organization promoting the electrical safety of thousands of retail products. Companies pay a fee to have UL test their products for safety according to UL standards. The famous UL label often is seen attached to the product.

Another organization producing standards is the *National Fire Protection Association* (NFPA). This group has established standards for fire protection equipment and construction that have been adopted by government agencies in the form of codes, in addition to companies manufacturing products. Beginning in 1898, in cooperation with the insurance industry, the NFPA has produced standards covering sprinklers, fire hoses, and fire doors, among other forms of fire protection (NFPA; www.nfpa.com; 1 Batterymarch Park, Quincy, MA 02269-9101; Tel.: 617-770-3000).

The *American Society for Testing and Materials* (ASTM), organized in 1898, has grown into one of the largest voluntary standards development systems in the world. ASTM is a nonprofit organization providing a forum for producers, consumers, government, and academia to meet to write standards for materials, products, systems, and services. Among its 132 standards-writing committees are committees that focus on security, safety, and fire protection (ASTM; www.astm.org; 100 Barr Harbor Dr., West Conshohocken, PA 19428; Tel.: 610-832-9500).

The *American National Standards Institute* (ANSI), organized in 1918, is a nonprofit organization that coordinates U.S. voluntary national standards and represents the United States in international standards bodies such as the International Organization for Standardization. ANSI serves both private and public sectors in an effort to develop standards that exist in all industries, such as safety and health, information processing, banking, and petroleum (ANSI; www.ansi.org; 11 West 42nd St., New York, NY 10036; Tel.: 212-642-4900).

The *International Organization for Standardization* (with the initials of ISO) is a worldwide federation of national standards bodies from about 130 countries, one from each country. It is a nongovernmental group based in Geneva, Switzerland, established in 1947 and with the purpose of promoting standardization globally to facilitate the international exchange of goods and services. Its agreements are published as International Standards (ISO) (www.iso.ch).

Besides standards, there are city, state, and federal codes to follow. Among federal agencies are regulations set by the U.S. Congress through the *Occupational Safety and Health Act* (1970) and the *Americans with Disabilities Act* (1990), both of which are covered later.

Some security standards focus on uniform standards of protection for specific industries, as seen at banks through federal law; at airports through the Federal Aviation Administration (FAA); and at companies with a U.S. Department of Defense (DOD) contract.

Facility security standards, in some form and coverage, also exist at U.S. colleges under federal law, at health care facilities under accreditation requirements, and at some convenience stores under state or local laws. Specific types of security characterize these different industries. Unfortunately, many types of businesses and institutions have no uniform standards of protection (for example, retail businesses, hotels, restaurants, office buildings, and manufacturing plants).

The controversy concerning standards will continue, as will lawsuits involving negligent security. Those organizations that maintain professional security programs and personnel will set an example to be followed.

CHAPTER REVIEW

A. Multiple Choice

1. The world market for security services grows about what percent each year?
   a. 2%
   b. 45%
   c. 8%
   d. 12%

2. The basic strategy of private security is to
   a. make arrests.
   b. prevent crime.
   c. conduct searches and seizures.
   d. assist public police.

3. How many security personnel work in the private sector?
   a. over one million
   b. 500,000
   c. 350,000
   d. 150,000

4. This research report was the first national effort to set standards and goals to improve the effectiveness of the security industry.
   a. *Rand Report*
   b. *Report of the Task Force on Private Security*
   c. *Warren Commission Report*
   d. *Hallcrest Report*

5. Which of the following is not an avenue to improve the security profession?
   a. a code of ethics
   b. industry standards
   c. arming all security officers after training
   d. licensing and registration

B. True or False

1. A federal law exists that has helped to improve the professionalism of the security field through the screening of job applicants and requiring 80 hours of training.

2. Compared with contract officers, a major advantage of proprietary security officers is reduced costs.

3. Both private security officers and public police are supported by tax dollars.

4. UL, NFPA, and OSHA are involved in setting standards useful in the security, safety, or fire protection field.

5. Contract investigators are especially useful for undercover investigations.

Applications

Application 2A

Invite guest speakers to lecture and answer questions on the business, functions, and professionalism of security.

Application 2B

Which area of the security field interests you for employment?

Application 2C

You have been a uniformed security officer for three years. About a year ago you became a supervisor with training responsibilities. You are also an active member of a local police-security council that meets monthly to foster closer working relations. The president of the council asks you to develop a plan to improve police-security cooperation at all levels in the city. What are your specific plans that you will present to the council?

Application 2D

As a uniformed security officer how would you handle the following situations?

- Another security officer says that you can leave two hours early during second shift and she will "punch you out."
- A security officer that you work with shows you how to make the required physical inspections around the plant without leaving your seat.
- During the holidays, a group of coworkers planning a party on the premises, ask you if you want to contribute to a fund to hire a stripper/prostitute.
- You are testifying in court, in a shoplifting case and the defense attorney asks you to state whether you ever took your eyes off of the defendant when the incident occurred. The case depends on you stating that you never lost sight of the defendant. You actually lost sight of the defendant once. How do you respond?
- Your employer offers you free training on a state-of-the-art security system, but you will have to work later each day for a few weeks for no extra pay.

- Your best friend wants you to provide a positive recommendation for him when he applies for a job where you work, even though he has an arrest record.

- You see your supervisor take company items and put them in the trunk of her vehicle.

- A contract security officer fails to show up for first shift. You hear the contract security manager tell the client that the replacement officer has been screened and trained. You know this is false.

- Your employer is violating environmental laws. You know that if the government learns of the violations, your company will be unable to financially survive criminal and civil action and pollution controls. You will certainly lose your job.

- While reviewing CCTV video footage, you see your boss inappropriately touching a coworker who recently filed a sexual harassment suit against the boss who vehemently denied the allegations. You placed the pin-hole lense camera in the office supply closet to catch a thief, not expecting to see your boss touching the coworker. No one knows of the placement of the camera and the video footage, except for you. Your boss has been especially helpful to your career.

- You are testifying in a case of alleged negligent security concerning the retail store where you are employed. The plaintiff's attorney asks you if any security surveys were ever conducted at the store where the murder occurred. You know that a survey conducted a short time prior to the murder showed the need for increased security at the store. Such information would secure a victory for the plaintiff. You are also aware that your supervisor and his boss already testified that no security survey was conducted prior to the murder. What is your response to the question?

SECTION 2

SECURITY IN ACTION

3

Customer Service and Public Relations

CHAPTER OUTLINE

OBJECTIVES

After studying this chapter, you will be able to:

- Define customer service, marketing, and public relations.
- Explain the importance of customer service, marketing, and public relations.
- Discuss verbal and nonverbal communication.
- Explain at least ten guidelines to improve job performance.
- Describe the importance of human relations.

- List and explain the five categories and questions that are strategies for understanding yourself.
- Explain the significance of diversity.
- Explain the strategies of security officer appearance.
- Describe public police and private security cooperation.
- Explain how a security officer should handle the media.

Customer Service

Customer service is defined as those activities performed by employees that simplify the purchase of services or products. Employees provide customer service by applying their knowledge and skills of a service or product, offering resources and support, acting in a courteous manner, and creating a pleasant and beneficial experience for the customer. Employees must work to succeed at customer satisfaction through quality service. Otherwise, a business will not survive and jobs will be lost. Customer satisfaction can lead to repeat business and new business. Simply put, customers who are pleased, tell other people.

Marketing is a word often used in the business world to describe research of customers to find out their needs and to develop products and services to be sold at a profit. The key to marketing is to know customers and what they want. The "cola wars" serve as an example of companies in competition to satisfy customer needs by offering a variety of cola drinks such as regular, diet, caffeine-free, diet caffeine-free, and so forth. In the security field, whether we are speaking of a security service company or a proprietary (in-house) security department, customers are of the utmost importance (Figure 3-1). Well-managed companies are customer driven through constant contact with customers who provide insights that direct the company.

All security personnel must realize, just like employees of other businesses, that loyal customers must be created and retained. At the same time, for security officers to operate effectively, they must have the confidence, respect, and support of customers who should be made to feel that they are important. Also, customers should be made aware that they are receiving value from the services being offered. Manning and Reece note the following in *Selling Today*: "In a world of increased global competition and narrowing profit margins, customer retention through value-based initiatives can mean the difference between increasing or eroding market share." Value, for example, can be in the form of a report to a client of the accomplishments of security. However, all security officers can show value through a smile, friendly tone, helping hand, or by asking, "How can I help you?"

From a marketing perspective, key questions that must be asked frequently of customers are: Were you satisfied with the service? In what ways can the service be improved? If a security business or proprietary security organization is not able to answer these questions and seek improvements, loss of business and turnover of personnel are likely. Because the issue of

Figure 3-1 Customer service while protecting people and property.
Courtesy: Wackenhut, Inc.

customer service is so important, management often conducts surveys of customers by using a questionnaire or by conducting interviews.

How does the individual security officer fit into customer service and marketing? Every security officer is part of a team charged with the duty to find out the needs of customers, report these needs to supervisors, work to solve problems, and offer the best possible services with the utmost courtesy. These efforts promote positive customer relations and strengthen business ties. What follows here are specific methods and techniques to accomplish these objectives.

Public Relations

From a business point-of-view, *public relations* involves communications and relationships with many internal and external publics to create an image for a service, product, or organization. Publics include customers, stockholders, employees, the general public, government, and society. Public relations is a form of business communications integrated into a marketing plan that provides news about new products and services and accomplishments of a business. Communications is done through press releases and feature articles that set the stage for advertising. The following website on public relations offers information on marketing, media relations, case studies, and many other topics: http://publicrelations.about.com/mbody.htm

As discussed in Hess and Wrobleski's *Introduction to Private Security*, "Public relations includes all activities undertaken to bolster image and create good will." Everyone in an organization should practice good public relations. Security officers are involved in public relations through such strategies as a sharp appearance, a positive attitude, and good human relations (the ability to get along with others).

Good public relations sell the company and its product or service. Because security officers are often posted at access points of businesses, outsiders, such as customers, are typically greeted by security officers. Therefore, security officers often become the *first representatives* of a business. We have all probably heard of the saying, "First impressions are lasting." Suppose officers became accustomed to "confronting" customers instead of "greeting" them. Obviously, business may be harmed. Thus, instead of making rudeness contagious, all employees should strive to make courtesy contagious.

Good public relations fosters cooperation by those served by a security organization. Security officers are often placed in the position of restricting people's movements and reminding them about company rules. Many people resent being advised about what they can and cannot do. Historically, Americans have resisted authority while cherishing freedom. When government or management in a business restricts freedom, friction may develop between opposing groups. Security officers, as are public police, are regarded as "symbols of authority." Resistance and disapproval of rules is directed at security even though security may have nothing to do with management directives. Consequently, good public relations becomes more important if security is to gain the cooperation of others.

For instance, suppose a security officer patrolling a parking lot notices an employee pulling into a restricted parking space. The officer then approaches the employee. Good public relations would be destroyed if the officer were to say, "Hey you, where do you think you're parking?" "Can't you read?" A more appropriate statement is, "I would appreciate it very much if you would park at another space, since this space is restricted."

Security officers can improve customer service and public relations by using empathy and offering alternatives to customers. Seek to acknowledge how the customer feels by "putting yourself in their shoes." For example, if an employee is required to drive away from a checkpoint to a new area for parking, apologize for the inconvenience. By offering alternatives, the security officer shows concern and interest in the customer. Example: "I'm sorry that you must park in a new area as we improve security. If you turn left at the entrance, you will find a convenient parking space. Thank you."

Naturally, even when an officer is polite, a negative comment may be returned to the officer. Good public relations should continue even in the face of belligerence. Although extra effort, concentration, and a controlled emotional state are necessary in such a situation, the security officer's job is likely to become easier over time. Refuse to argue with the customer and apologize for the inconvenience. Depending on the situation, ask for an explanation of the problem and emphasize that you will try to help. This approach has a tendency to disarm the customer.

One unprofessional incident between a security officer and an employee reflects adversely on the entire security department. Since no security organization is perfect, human relations mistakes are inevitable. An isolated case of rudeness can momentarily harm public relations efforts. However, continued politeness will overcome temporary setbacks.

The importance of good public relations becomes more apparent when a case becomes difficult to solve or when an emergency occurs. Employees are more willing to provide information to security officers about crimes when security officers are respected. If security officers are viewed as rude and nasty, cooperation is less likely. During an emergency, a crisis atmosphere has a better chance of being resolved if security officers are known to be professionals. Naturally, people will look to security officers for direction during an emergency. Security departments should have clear policies and procedures on public relations, supported by quality training and supervision. Professionalism and good training will pay off.

Verbal and Nonverbal Communication

We have all heard the phrase "actions speak louder than words." The daily activities of security officers send positive or negative messages to others. When greeting the public, talking on the telephone, patrolling, or gathering information for a report, security officers must realize that their actions communicate subtle image about security. Tone of voice, facial expressions, posture, and hand and arm movements are examples of nonverbal communications. In fact, there is considerable agreement that nonverbal communication is more accurate than what a person is saying.

Many of us do not realize how we look, act, and sound. We may have an unpleasant tone of voice, an avoidance of eye contact with those we speak with, or say "um" or "you know" frequently.

Improving Verbal and Nonverbal Communication

One of the best strategies to improve communication is by using audio/visual equipment to record as you participate in a short and simple role-playing exercise of while you complete a five minute presentation on any security topic. For example, role-playing can consist of a security officer stopping an employee (played by another security officer) who forgot his or her identification but still wants to pass an access point that strictly prohibits access without an ID card. Following a few minutes of recording, the tape can be played back. Positive and negative verbal and nonverbal communication can be pinpointed. Suggestions to improve your performance can then be discussed.

Factors to Improve Job Performance

By improving your performance, you will also improve your image as a security officer. The following list provides a frame of reference and some specific things you can do to improve your job performance.

Guidelines

1. Always speak and act in courteous manner even when people are disrespectful. Patience and control show others that you are a professional.
2. Avoid losing your temper and never use profane language.
3. Speak clearly to others.
4. Listen attentively. Good listening skills are essential. Concentrate on what others are saying. Give others an opportunity to fully explain themselves.
5. Maintain eye contact without staring when listening or speaking to others.
6. Avoid long conversations. Sometimes, offenders distract security personnel so a crime can be committed.
7. Be courteous during telephone conversations. To check on your tone of voice, use a tape recorder. Most individuals are surprised when they hear themselves.
8. Always carry a small notebook and a pen to record important information during conversations. A competent security officer knows to not completely rely on memory.
9. Never sleep or use intoxicants when on duty. Smoking or chewing must be done discreetly.
10. Strive to be fair and trustworthy.
11. Develop a positive view of employees and customers as potential aids to security.
12. Avoid a "we versus them" attitude.
13. Do not project an image that security officers are eager to arrest and jail people. Modern security emphasizes prevention.
14. Avoid using excessive police terminology and wearing items such as silver handcuffs as a tie tack or earrings. These symbols may be offensive to others. Rather than alienating people, security should use as many strategies as possible to gain cooperation.

What If?

As a Security Officer, What Do You Do if You Face an Angry Customer?

Employees of service-related businesses sometimes encounter customers who are upset, angry, and difficult to assist. Such customers may state offensive remarks; however, security officers must not take the remarks personally. Officers should realize that the customer is upset and frustrated. The officer must calm the customer, think safety, and help the customer to resolve the problem. The first few seconds of the encounter are crucial. Avoid an escalation of the incident by lowering, rather than raising, your voice and asking for information so you can work toward a solution. Show genuine concern through good listening skills and ask the customer to explain statements you do not understand. Speak in a calm, reassuring tone. If violence is possible from the customer, stand at an angle and step back slightly to protect yourself. Call for backup. You may have to call for a supervisor anyway if the customer demands to see your supervisor. Although these situations are challenging and require professional behavior, the ultimate goals are to solve the problem, salvage the customer, and create a favorable impression of you and your employer in their mind.

Understanding Yourself

Usually, lessons on public relations emphasize appropriate behavior by security officers. However, a critical ingredient is often missing from this training: Officers should learn to understand themselves. One key question is why do we behave the way we do? Actually, everybody should try to learn more about themselves, especially those who have considerable contact with others in their job. Figure 3-2 shows that understanding yourself is the foundation of human and public relations. Thus, before discussing strategies for understanding yourself, the following discussion will explain the importance of human relations. After studying this section, you will be able to list several reasons why human relations and public relations are important and crucial to you in your role as a security officer.

The Importance of Human Relations

Laird and Laird, in their book *Psychology: Human Relations and Motivation*, state that "Whenever two or more persons are together or work together, problems in human relations may arise. . . . every individual—hermits excepted—is surrounded by a sea of human-relations problems. Many of life's difficulties are caused by individuals who botch their human relations."

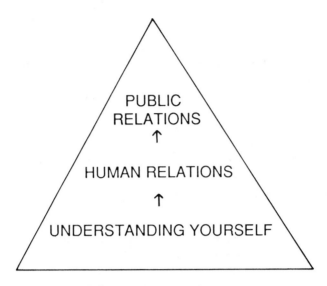

Figure 3-2   The path to quality public relations.

Furthermore, they state that "Although job ability is very important, one must be able to get along with people in order to get ahead. A study of the reasons workers were not promoted revealed that only 10 percent were passed over because of skill deficiencies. Almost 80 percent were held back for reasons of personality and character."

In the book, *Your Attitude Is Showing*, author Elwood Chapman made the following observations:

> Human relations is also knowing how to handle sticky problems when they arise. It is learning how to work with demanding and sometimes unfair supervisors. It is understanding the personality of others and of oneself. It is building sound working relationships in forced associations where things can get touchy. It is knowing how to restore a working relationship that has deteriorated. It is learning how to live with one's frustrations without hurting others. It is building and maintaining relationships in many directions, with many different kinds of people, whether they are easy to get along with or not.

Furthermore, he states that "From the moment you join an organization you assume two obligations: (1) to do a job—the best job you can do in the work assigned to you; (2) to get along with all people to the best of your ability. It is the right combination of these two factors that spells success."

Security officers face a variety of people in many situations as they perform their duties. Whether the duties are routine or involve an emergency, the outcome of incidents depend largely on an officer's human relations skills.

Strategies for Understanding Yourself

To enhance these previous discussions, we now will present some strategies to help you better understand yourself. Within five basic categories, five specific questions are presented and explained to direct you toward self-evaluation.

ATTITUDE *Do you have a positive attitude?* The answer to this question can lead to your success or failure. We all know at least one person who has a negative view about everything and anything. Unfortunately, a negative attitude makes the world look gloomy. This kind of attitude can also spill into a person's career and personal life.

We must remember that every position has unfavorable aspects. If negative feelings persist, then your employer may not be right for you. Therefore, resigning may be the best avenue after finding another more suitable employer.

An attitude can be described as a mental set that causes a person to respond in a characteristic way. Attitude will have an impact on whatever you are involved in—a job task, studying for a test, human relations, an interpersonal relationship, sports, and so forth. A positive attitude can provide enough momentum to produce success. A negative attitude provides fuel for failure. Instead of focusing on the unpleasant things in life and individual shortcomings, concentrate on the pleasant, inspirational things and personal attributes of yourself and others. A positive attitude makes you a happier person. People will like you more because you are pleasant. Your positive attitude is a valuable personal possession that will create rewarding and enjoyable opportunities. This attitude will have a major impact on your future success and life.

COMMUNICATION *Are you a quiet person?* Most people would probably prefer to work with a quiet person than with a person who constantly talks. However, quiet people are often misinterpreted as being aloof and indifferent. Also, they may cause people to feel uncomfortable. Young people are prone to being quiet, especially when they first join an organization. Quiet individuals should try to communicate with as many people as possible. They should say hello, smile, and ask questions. Also, quiet people should respond in a positive manner on a variety of topics. In the beginning, this behavior and communication may be difficult, but these changes will become easier over time. Since many people generally like to engage in conversation, you will be on your way to developing good human and public relations. As a result, your job will become easier because of the many contacts you have developed.

COOPERATION *Do you work at getting along with your boss?* Whatever type of boss you must work with, part of your job is to develop a good working relationship with your boss. First, it is important to try to understand your boss's job. Recall from the previous chapter the Code of Ethics for Private Security Management. This can be the starting point to help you understand your supervisor's job. What are the pressures of the job? What type of supervisor does your boss have? What pressures cause stress for both of you? Expect difficult days on the job. No organization operates smoothly all the time.

Negative attitudes toward authority figures may be transferred to supervisors by subordinates. This may be caused by earlier unfortunate experiences with parents, teachers, and others. Self-analysis and a positive attitude help to correct this problem. For example, ask yourself if you are venting hostility toward your boss. If you are, ask yourself why you are behaving in this manner. After discovering the reason for your behavior, you can change it.

If you have a disagreement with your supervisor, try to talk about it at an appropriate time. The best time to talk is when the working environment is calm. To resolve disagreements or problems, *always* speak to your boss first. Avoid speaking of the situation(s) to others in the workplace, especially your supervisor's boss. Also, remember that some supervisors are difficult to communicate with and can intimidate subordinates. If you find yourself working for such a supervisor, try to work at getting along. If you find this is not possible, it would probably be beneficial for you to find another place to work.

Support your supervisor whenever possible. This behavior is often appreciated and can have a definite impact on your working relationship.

Personnel evaluation systems are never perfect. Each supervisor evaluates personnel differently. Some supervisors may be tough, while other supervisors may be easy. However, when you are evaluated, the best response is to tell your boss that you will work to correct your weaknesses. This reaction shows your maturity and often can lead to a promotion for you.

BEHAVIOR *Do you lose your temper frequently?* Control of anger is vital for job success and a professional image. Although individuals differ as to what makes them angry, a key point is that anger results from our *perception* of situations. When an unfortunate event occurs, individuals make a decision about how they will react. Acting impulsively and yelling are not professional behavior. What a person must do is make a conscious effort to "get a grip on oneself" and remain calm. One technique is to repeatedly say to oneself, "Remain calm!" "Act as a professional!" This takes practice, and a short temper can be corrected like other bad habits.

How Much of Their "Lip" Must Our Security Officers Take?

Some of the workers at our plant can be pretty rough-tongued. How much of their "lip" must our security officers take? We nearly had an arrest last night and I can't blame the officer who was sorely provoked.

Tell the officers to stay calm, despite the provocations. In a similar case, in which an arrest was actually made, a U.S. District Court ordered damages paid.

Said the judge, "It takes strength of character to withstand the abuse heaped on officers as they go about their daily work. This condition should not exist and the urge to support the occasional officer who loses his cool in the face of this type of harassment is very strong." Nonetheless, decided the court, the officer should have ignored the verbal outburst. With no violence threatened, there was no cause for an arrest. (428 F. Supp. 321)

However, in a case where a worker was discharged for verbally harassing a security officer, the dismissal was upheld by an arbitrator. The correct course of action is to report these misconducts to a supervisor for disciplinary action.

(Source: Corporate Security, [New York: Business Research Publications, October 1988], p. 5)

Mental health specialists recommend venting anger in a constructive way. If we repress anger, it can cause physical and emotional problems. If no person is available to talk with, then other methods are helpful, such as having a hobby. Also, sports that involve hitting a ball can be an avenue to vent anger.

In a previous chapter, we discussed the reform efforts of Sir Robert Peel in London during the nineteenth century. He emphasized an important standard that is still appropriate today. He said, "No quality is more indispensable to a policeman than a perfect command of temper; a quiet, determined manner has more effect than violent action."

EDUCATION *Do you believe in lifelong learning?* We all know people who think they know everything. They feel there is no need to learn anything else. Obviously, it is impossible to know everything. However, lifelong learning means that as one goes through life, there are endless information and skills to be learned. Even professionals with many college degrees are in a constant state of learning. In fact, one great tool a person should acquire in their education is to learn how to learn. This entails several skills such as reading comprehension and how to use the Internet and a library.

Security officers should take advantage of training opportunities offered by their employer. Also, security officers should read and study on their own.

College courses and specialized security training programs are also available from various sources. On the job there are often experienced people who have a wealth of practical information. Learn as much as you can from these people. Some of these experienced people will say that you cannot learn security from a book. One of the best avenues is a combination of theories and practices that complement each other. Theories are the foundation of many strategies applied in the real world; and theories help us to understand, use, and evaluate practical experience. When security officers continue to learn, this means they are preparing for new opportunities and refuse to put their potential on the shelf.

Diversity

Another aspect of customer service and public relations is the issue of diversity. *Diversity* encompasses many different dimensions, including sex, race, national origin, religion, age, and disability. The workforce, for example, historically dominated by white men, is being increasingly replaced with workers from diverse backgrounds (Figure 3-3). The 2000 census showed what demographers have long predicted—that the fast-growing Hispanic population would soon become the nation's largest minority group. Numbering about 35 million, at 12.6 percent of the U.S. population of 281 million, these figures are about equal to African-Americans in the United States. The U.S. Bureau of Labor Statistics estimates that, by the year 2005, the U.S. labor force will consist of only 38 percent white, non-Hispanic men. More than half

Figure 3-3 Diversity in the workplace.

of the new entrants into the workplace will be women, the average age of employees will climb, immigrant employees will have language and cultural differences, and as companies become more global, there will be an increasing need to respond to the unique needs of individual employees, including their languages, values, and customs.

In August of 2000, the American Society for Industrial Security (ASIS), held a conference on "Women and Minorities in Security." The conference was noteworthy because this field has been dominated by white males since the beginning. The speakers were straightforward with the challenges facing minorities and the security industry. With an increasingly diverse society, recruitment of women and minorities is essential; however, public and media perceptions of security—often in a negative light—makes recruitment difficult. Women have played an increasing role in the industry, but more needs to be done to recruit more women, African-Americans, and Hispanics.

Diversity facilitates tolerance to different behavioral styles and wider views, which can lead to greater responsiveness to diverse customers. The challenge of diversity is an investment in the future.

Security Officer Appearance

A sharp-looking security officer commands respect. Since security officers typically make frequent short-term contacts with many people, the initial contact is crucial. As stated earlier, "first impressions are lasting." In fact, there is only one opportunity to create a first impression. There is no second chance. An officer's appearance indirectly informs people of the caliber and competence of the security force. In other words, a sloppy officer sends a negative message. On the other hand, an officer who has good posture, wears a neat uniform, speaks clearly, and knows the job, will leave a positive impression on others. Furthermore, during critical events, a neat, professional appearance helps to maintain people's attention and cooperation.

Factors Impacting Appearance

The following points have an impact on appearance.

1. Uniforms should fit properly and be clean and pressed.
2. Uniform ornaments should be neat and aligned properly, while not being excessive.
3. Polished shoes and dark socks to match the uniform enhance appearance.
4. Personal hygiene is important. Neat hair, clean fingernails, and a close shave are examples of good grooming.
5. A healthy diet and regular exercise both improve appearance.
6. Since appearance is so important to a security force, managers and supervisors typically monitor security officers and impose disciplinary action when relevant policies are violated.

Types of Images

Security attire can project two major types of images—visibility and subtlety.

VISIBILITY Visibility represents the standard security uniform that has the capacity to convey professionalism and authority. In fact, increased visibility and a stricter image are projected through traditional uniforms. However, it is important that traditional uniforms do not look similar to those worn by public police. If this happens, mistakes can be made by citizens needing aid and the public police resent such uniforms.

SUBTLETY Subtle attire consists of blazers, sports jackets, dresses, and skirts. A warmer, less threatening, and less authoritarian image is projected. According to Hess and Wrobleski, "These uniforms are most often used by officers who work exclusively indoors, usually in office buildings or institutions such as museums, libraries, and hospitals. The soft look is very low key and will blend in well with a corporate or office environment where an emphasis on security is deemed to be intimidating."

Public Police and Private Security Cooperation

Public police and private security both work toward reducing crime. As stated in the previous chapter, the key differences between public police and private security are that public police are employed by government, serve the public, are supported by tax dollars, and have greater arrest powers. On the other hand, private police serve private businesses who pay for such services. Their arrest powers are limited and prevention is a key strategy.

Public police generally undergo more thorough screening and training processes than security officers. However, this does not mean that cooperative relations have to be avoided. In reality, though, a large portion of public police are critical of private security because of screening and training differences.

Public police and security personnel should maintain positive attitudes toward each other. They should provide mutual assistance whenever possible. Security officers can improve relations by refraining from activities that imply security is acting like public police. Public police should realize the increasing educational level of security personnel revealed by the *Hallcrest Report*.

Cooperative working relationships between public police and private security vary. For example, certain types of information are shared. Police may learn about counterfeiters or bad check passers approaching a business district. Immediately, all businesses and private security personnel are notified. Likewise, a security organization may know the whereabouts of a person wanted by the police and pass this valuable information to authorities. The opening of a new shopping mall may require cooperative planning for traffic control. Labor problems and demonstrations may also require coordination. One of the most important activities requiring cooperation follows an arrest by security. Public police and prosecutors are a necessity as the case progresses through the criminal justice system.

Robert Gallati, in his book *Introduction to Private Security*, makes the following observation. "If there is hostility and tension between the private and public police, only the criminals will benefit and crime rates will continue to rise. If there is an enlightened effort to link both forces to deal with the plague of crime, it may well be that together we can reverse destructive trends. We must work toward gaining greater respect and increasing our capabilities so as to contribute in an optimum manner to the reduction of crime both 'on premises' and 'on the streets'."

The Media

The rule for security officers when confronted with newspaper and television reporters is to state they will have to speak to the officer's supervisor. *Do not say anything else!* Contact your supervisor who will probably direct them to a designated speaker. Most organizations have one person who is skilled in speaking to the media as a company representative. Such an approach coordinates information as it leaves an organization. This prevents several employees from making conflicting statements or releasing proprietary information.

Security officers should realize that media people are like investigators. That is, they persistently search for information. Reporters aggressively pursue stories to sell newspapers and increase their television audience. Therefore, security officers may be subject to manipulation by media representatives. For example, an officer may be asked to comment "off the record" and then discover that sensitive information is published the next day.

CHAPTER REVIEW

A. Multiple Choice

1. The best description of public relations is that it
   a. requires an open door policy to the public.
   b. requires all managers to get along with everybody.
   c. includes all activities undertaken to bolster image and create good will.
   d. can only be obtained through a neat uniform.

2. Which of the following is an incorrect statement concerning public relations?
   a. Security officers must earn respect through good public relations.
   b. It should be practiced more frequently during holidays.
   c. An isolated case of rudeness can momentarily harm public relations.
   d. Good public relations fosters cooperation by those served by security officers.

3. Tone of voice, facial expressions, posture, and hand and arm movements are examples of
   a. proper attire.
   b. public relations.
   c. interpersonal relations.
   d. nonverbal communications.

4. The rule for security officers when confronted with newspaper and television reporters is to
   a. state that they will have to speak to your supervisor.
   b. state only the facts.
   c. say "no comment."
   d. direct them to the local police department.

5. When you have a personnel evaluation, the most appropriate response is to
   a. claim that you are doing your best.
   b. argue for more training to appear interested in learning.
   c. request a new assignment.
   d. inform your boss that you will work to correct weaknesses.

B. True or False

1. Public relations need only be practiced by supervisors and managers.
2. Historically, Americans have resisted authority while cherishing freedom.

3. The Bill of Rights of the U.S. Constitution prohibits security officers from limiting employee access within businesses.

4. Of the two major types of images for security attire, subtlety projects a stricter image.

5. A positive attitude can provide momentum for success, whereas a negative attitude provides fuel for failure.

Applications

Application 3A

As a newly promoted supervisor, you are responsible for five security officers. One security officer is doing a poor job at public relations. She is involved in confrontations with employees in the parking lot at least once a week. From previous work with this security officer, you know that she is overbearing, speaks to people in a condescending manner, and regularly uses profane language. You are considering disciplinary action but you decide to talk with the security officer. What do you say? What are your strategies to solve this problem?

Application 3B

As a proprietary security officer, you notice a large object causing an employee's jacket to bulge as the first shift is leaving the plant. You follow security policy and stop the employee who hands over a company drill. The employee is disciplined but remains on the job. Now, every time you encounter this employee you are called "rent-a-cop" and other derogatory names. You notice that others are doing the same thing, and the situation is getting worse. You are becoming increasingly aggravated by this situation. What do you do?

Application 3C

As a new security officer, you recently completed an in-house, 120-hour training course. Now you are half through a six week on-the-job training program, paired with a master security officer named Larry Webster who is to be promoted to sergeant. During the first three weeks of this field training, you notice Larry speaks to employees and customers in a rude manner. He has also confronted people for speeding in the parking lot when they have not been speeding. Once you saw him take a parking decal off a car and then write a ticket for not having a decal.

One day you are requested by a lieutenant to come to the security office. When you enter the office, the lieutenant states that the security department has received several complaints about Larry Webster. The lieutenant wants to know what is going on. What do you say?

Application 3D

Modify the previous Application 3C to include the following additional information. One day while on the job, you were sure that Webster had been smoking marijuana. Also, you saw him drinking whiskey.

Application 3E

You are a security supervisor and one of your officers, Latasha Jackson, a black female, is upset and tells you that another security officer, Raymond Smith, a white male, had an argument with her and called her a "nigger bitch" in front of two other security officers and a customer. As the supervisor, what action do you take?

4

Crime Prevention and Physical Security

CHAPTER OUTLINE

OBJECTIVES

After studying this chapter, you will be able to:

- Define and explain crime prevention.
- Explain various forms of crime prevention.
- Describe three community crime prevention programs and explain how they can be applied to businesses.
- Explain how management provides a foundation for physical security.
- Illustrate how critical thinking skills are applied to security.
- List and explain at least seven types of physical security methods.

Crime Prevention

Definitions of Crime Prevention

Definitions for crime prevention vary. It can best be described as those strategies designed to keep crime from occurring and reducing the amount of crime. The National Crime Prevention Institute defines crime prevention as "the anticipation, recognition, and appraisal of a crime risk and the initiation of some action to remove or reduce it."

For many years public police have been involved in crime prevention by educating the public about how to prevent crime and protect themselves. Police crime prevention officers use public service announcements and brochures to communicate strategies to prevent burglary, rape, mugging, and so forth. Also, many police departments have crime prevention specialists who visit and evaluate homes and businesses before recommending security methods.

It is important to remember that public police as well as private security personnel have limited resources and are unable to handle the crime problem without assistance. Most communities have between one and three police officers per one thousand residents. The number of private security officers in each business varies. There are usually two or more private security officers per police officer nationwide. For these reasons, employees in businesses and citizens in the community must become knowledgeable about crime prevention and take personal steps to protect themselves.

Forms of Crime Prevention

Crime prevention efforts can take many forms. For instance, public police typically amass assorted crime statistics. An analysis of this information can provide direction for crime prevention efforts for both police and citizens. An analysis of crime statistics for a city may show, for example, that a four block area on the east side of town is subject to numerous burglaries on Mondays and Tuesdays between the hours of 9 A.M. and 3 P.M. With such information, police can assign more officers to this area. Also, residents can be informed about this problem and urged to secure their doors and windows while keeping a watch on their neighbor's homes. Businesses can also apply crime analysis methods. For example, security personnel for a chain of restaurants may notice upon studying the company's crime statistics that robberies are occurring mostly between the hours of 10 P.M. and 11 P.M. on Fridays in urban areas.

Fire departments also campaign for prevention. Fire prevention officers visit businesses and homes to distribute brochures and recommend methods to prevent fire. The installation of smoke detects has been a top priority of many fire prevention programs.

As they do their job, security officers can become involved in prevention activities. To illustrate, suppose a security officer on patrol notices a garbage dumpster located close to a shipping and receiving dock. The security officer should regularly check in and around the dumpster because it is a favorite spot for employee-thieves to hide merchandise before putting it in their automobiles. If employees see the security officer checking the dumpster, then they may be deterred from theft. The security officer can also suggest to his or her supervisor that crime can be prevented if the dumpster is moved to another location. In fact, the security department may have a daily report form where such suggestions are welcome. However, suggestions must be made discreetly. In other words, suggestions must be carefully stated. Remember that you presenting an idea to a supervisor who may or may not be interested.

Crime prevention by security officers serve several functions. It shows that security officers are doing their job and possess the knowledge to reduce crime. By making suggestions to employees, security officers are performing a public relations and educational function similar to what public police do in their crime prevention efforts. Security officers who pinpoint security weaknesses will increase their chances for promotion. Furthermore, security work becomes more interesting when security officers apply their skills to the job.

Security officers should search for problems that, if corrected, can prevent or reduce losses. Examples are numerous and include damaged security equipment, suspicious people, things out of place, fire extinguishers not properly charged, blocked emergency exits, and any type of crime, fire, or accident hazard. Recall from a previous discussion that broader efforts beyond the crime problem that include fire and accident prevention are termed *loss prevention.*

Private security is generally more prevention-oriented than public police. This stems from the traditional after-the-fact police activity of responding to a crime, investigating, gathering evidence, searching for the offender, and making an arrest. Since private security serves business interests, we should always remember that *businesses exist to make a profit.* Consequently, many business executives would rather avoid an arrest situation (if possible) because of the personnel costs and effort to conclude a case. Employees in production may have to be diverted to the criminal case. And, a civil suit can result against the company.

At some businesses, security officers are not permitted to make arrests unless management grants approval. Management's view on this decision varies with the business at hand. Many businesses favor a *prevention* approach where strategies, such as patrolling, access controls, fences, alarms, and so forth, are used to lessen the chances of crime. However, these same businesses should realize that an arrest may be the only alternative in certain situations. Security officers should practice good prevention methods but also be trained and prepared for arrests.

Crime Prevention Programs

Crime prevention strategies can be applied to crime problems in both residential and business communities. Remember the term crime prevention is a broad concept involving many different methods to decrease or prevent crime. The ideas for crime prevention are limited only by our imagination. Let us discuss three residential programs that are also helpful in preventing crimes against businesses.

NEIGHBORHOOD WATCH *Neighborhood watch* exists in many communities, spearheaded by public police departments who organize neighborhood residents to watch each other's homes. Since people living in the same neighborhood are familiar with each other's routines, it is easier to spot unusual activities, such as strange people and vehicles. Neighborhood watch programs promote surveillance by many people and reporting to the police of suspicious activity.

In the workplace, employees should be involved in a "watch," organized by security personnel. With so many threats facing the workplace, the extra "eyes and ears" can improve protection. Another approach to the "watch" is when a group of retailers organize a business watch to protect each other's stores. They can also share information on offenders who write bad checks and shoplift. In addition, the retailers may decide to share the expenses of hiring a security force.

OPERATION IDENTIFICATION *Operation identification* is not as popular as it used to be, however, it still has value in protecting property and solving crimes. Residents engrave valuable property with their driver's license number or other identifying number. If the property is stolen and then recovered, valuables are easier to return to the owner. Also, the prosecutor's case is stronger because marked property in the possession of offenders links them to the crime scene. Those locations participating in operation identification usually display special decals on windows and doors. This makes the premises a less attractive target and prevents crime. Likewise, those who deal in stolen items are less interested in marked property.

In the business sector, marked property helps to identify it as belonging to a particular company. In a case of theft, security personnel must prove that an item is company property, otherwise prosecution will not be successful.

Serial numbers and invisible and unique substances are used to identify company property.

TARGET HARDENING The purpose of *target hardening* is to make property less vulnerable to criminals by using physical security methods. Examples include locks, window protection, alarms, fences, and closed-circuit television (CCTV).

Foundations of Physical Security

Two lessons from the September 11, 2001 terrorist attack on the United States are that we must *critically think about our security methods to improve them* and *we cannot afford to have failures of our imagination of what criminals can do.* At the same time, we should *avoid focusing all of our security attention on terrorism because there are a variety of other risks facing businesses and institutions.* Examples are violence in the workplace, theft, cybercrime, fires, accidents, and disasters.

We begin the coverage of physical security by explaining the management foundation supporting it. This provides us with the "big picture." Then we cover critical thinking so we can maximize security efforts and seek to outwit offenders.

Management

Personnel are the most important component of physical security programs. Besides security officers who are on the "front lines" operating physical security systems, management personnel provide support by planning, budgeting, purchasing, supervising, preparing policies and procedures, hiring, training, and evaluating.

In the planning process for physical security, management may begin with a risk analysis to identify the threats that face the organization. A *risk analysis* consists of a survey of the organization to pinpoint vulnerabilities (e.g., inadequate access controls) and develop plans for improved protection. The survey should tailor its questions to the unique needs of the premises to be protected. The survey may go beyond physical security and include information protection, safety, fire protection, and other risks. Once the security planner has pinpointed the organization's vulnerabilities, a determination is made of the probability, frequency, and cost of each loss. The next step is to use this information to plan and implement countermeasures.

We should not develop "tunnel vision" by thinking that outsiders are the only threat to an organization. It is often said that "the greatest threat is from within." (More about the internal threat in later chapters.) Also, we should not fall into the trap of thinking that physical security is the main avenue to avoid losses. Other strategies of avoiding or reducing losses include hiring quality personnel, training, insurance, and auditing.

Let us take a look at policies and procedures to see how these management functions support physical security. Policies and procedures are communicated to employees through manuals and memos. *Policies* are management tools that control employee decision making and reflect the goals and objectives of management. *Procedures* guide action to fulfill the requirements of policies. As an example, a company policy states that the fence, lighting, and intrusion alarm system surrounding company property must be checked every two weeks. The procedure for this policy requires a team of two security officers to conduct the inspection, complete a checklist form, and provide the form to their supervisor.

Critical Thinking

Critical thinking is a process of thinking that helps us to improve our understanding of the world around us so we can make better decisions. Since highly intelligent offenders confront security personnel periodically, critical thinking provides an extra edge or tool to improve security and safety. Critical thinking also helps us to become an active learner to not only absorb information but to probe and shape knowledge. The critical thinker goes beyond collecting "facts" and memorizing information in an effort to understand causes, motives, and change. Many questions are asked by the critical thinker. Critical thinking requires us to "jump out of our own skin" to see the world from the perspective of others. Although this is not an easy process, we are much better informed prior to our conclusions and decisions.

Critical thinking is not to be used as a tool to open up the floodgates of criticism in the workplace. It is to be applied discreetly to understand the world and to meet challenges with the best possible decisions.

Our world is filled with many efforts to influence our thinking. Examples are the media, advertisers, politicians, educators, and writers. This author is biased just like other writers and within these pages is a North American interpretation of security. Although an effort has been made to write an objective book here, it is impossible for any writer and biases surface. Objectivity is fostered in this book through an introduction to critical thinking skills, boxed topics, a variety of sources, and applications at the end of chapters that bridge theory to practice and ask the reader to make decisions as a professional.

With so much competition seeking to influence us, choices become difficult and confusing. And, as we think through complex challenges, we need a method of sorting conflicting claims, differentiating between fact and opinion, weighing "evidence" or "proof," being perceptive to our biases and those of others, and drawing logical conclusions.

David Ellis suggests a four-step strategy for critical thinking:

Step 1: Understanding the point of view.
- Listen/read/study without early judgment.
- Seek to understand the source's background (e.g., culture, education, experience, and values).

- Try to "live in their shoes."
- Summarize their viewpoint.

Step 2: Seek other views.

- Seek viewpoints, questions, answers, ideas, and solutions from others.

Step 3: Evaluate the various viewpoints.

- Look for assumption (i.e., an opinion that something is true, without evidence), exceptions, gaps in logic, oversimplification, selective perception, either/or thinking, and personal attacks.

Step 4: Construct a reasonable view.

- Study multiple viewpoints, combine perspectives, and produce an original viewpoint that is a creative act and the essence of critical thinking.

Security officers are not being asked here to apply critical thinking skills to day-to-day routine duties or directives from supervisors. Critical thinking should be applied in select situations such as when trying to understand others, when dealing with manipulative and crafty offenders, and when confronted with a variety of information and viewpoints.

Applying Critical Thinking Skills to Security

One avenue to improve physical security is to study the methods used by offenders. This means to "think like a thief." If you were an offender, how would you penetrate or circumvent security? *Forced entry* is a common method used to gain unauthorized access. Windows and doors are especially vulnerable to forced entry. Offenders repeatedly break or cut glass (with a glass cutter) on a window or door and then reach inside to release a lock or latch. To stop the glass from falling and making noise, a suction cup or tape is used to remove or hold the broken glass together. A complex lock may be rendered useless if the offender is able to go through a thin door by using a hammer, chisel, and saw. Forced entry also may be attempted through walls, floors, ceilings, skylights, utility tunnels, sewer or storm drains, and ventilation vents or ducts.

Unauthorized access also can be accomplished *without force*. Wherever a lock is supposed to be used, if it is not locked properly, access is possible. Windows or doors left unlocked are a surprisingly common occurrence. Lock picking or possession of a stolen key or computerized access card renders force unnecessary. Dishonest employees are known to assist criminals by unlocking locks, windows, or doors and by providing keys and technical information. Offenders sometimes hide inside a building until closing and then break out after stealing something. Tailgating is a method where by an intruder blends into a group of entering employees. These sly methods of gaining entry are often referred to as *surreptitious entry*. Use your imagination to think about ways in which offenders may gain unauthorized access.

Consider applying critical thinking skills to the following three models of security. All security strategies can be placed into one of these three categories:

1. It protects people and/or assets.
2. It accomplishes nothing.
3. It helps offenders.

Illustrations of security protecting people or assets are seen when a hospital security officer escorts nurses to their vehicles at night or when a safe proves too formidable for a burglar, who leaves the scene. Security accomplishes nothing when security officers sleep on the job or fail to make their rounds or when alarm systems remain inoperable. Sometimes unknown to security practitioners and those they serve are the security strategies that actually help offenders. This can occur when security officers are poorly screened and they commit crimes. The ordinary padlock is an example of how physical security can assist offenders. An unlocked padlock hanging on an opened gate can invite *padlock substitution* whereby the offender replaces it with his or her padlock, returns, at night to gain access, and then secures the gate with the original padlock. Such cases are difficult to investigate because signs of forced entry may be absent. Fences, another example, often are built with a top rail and supports for barbed-wire that are strong enough to assist and support offenders, rather than the fence and barbed-wire. Also, attractive looking picket fences have been knocked down by offenders and used as ladders. *Security practitioners should identify and classify all security strategies under these models to expose useful, wasteful, and harmful methods.*

Another way to think critically about security is to consider the "five Ds."

Deter. The mere presence of physical security can dissuade offenders from committing criminal acts. Offenders may go elsewhere. What improvements can be made to security to increase the chances that offenders will go elsewhere?

Detect. Offenders should be detected and their location pinpointed as soon as they step onto the premises or commit a violation on the premises. This can be accomplished through observation, CCTV, intrusion sensors, protective dogs, duress alarms, weapons screenings, and hotlines. What methods work best?

Delay. Security is often measured by the time it takes to get through it. *Redundant* (e.g., two fences; two types of intrusion sensors) and *layered* (e.g., perimeter fence, strong doors at buildings) security creates a time delay. Thus, the offender may become frustrated and decide to depart, or the delay may provide time for a response force to arrive to make an apprehension.

Deny. Strong physical security can deny access. A steel door and a safe are examples. Frequent bank deposits of cash and other valuables extend the opportunity to deny the offender success.

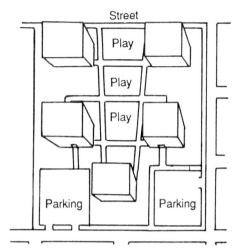

Figure 4-1   Five unmodified apartment buildings.

Destroy: When you believe your life or another's will be taken, you are permitted to use deadly force. An asset (e.g., proprietary information on a computer disk) may require destruction before it falls into the wrong hands.

Physical Security

Crime Prevention Through Environmental Design

During the late 1960s and early 1970s, *Oscar Newman* conducted research into the relationship between architectural design and crime prevention that developed into the concept of *defensible space.* He studied over 100 housing projects and identified design elements that reduce crime (Figures 4-1 and 4-2). For instance, Newman favored the creation of surveillance opportunities through windows for residents and the recognition that the neighborhood surrounding the residential setting influences safety. An essential part of defensible space is to create designs that change residents' use of public places while reducing the fear of crime; this is hoped to have a snowballing effect. Crime prevention through environmental design (CPTED) is applicable not only to public housing but also businesses, industries, public buildings, transportation systems, and schools, among others.

An illustration of how CPTED is applied can be seen with the design of Marriott and other hotels. To make offenders as visible as possible, traffic is directed toward the front of hotels. Lobbies are designed so that people walking to guest rooms or elevators must pass the front desk. On the outside, hedges are emphasized to produce a psychological barrier that is more appealing than a fence. Pathways are well-lit and guide guests away from isolated areas. Parking lots are characterized by lighting, clear lines of sight, and

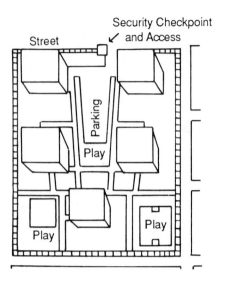

Figure 4-2 Five apartment buildings modified with perimeter fence, central parking, limited access, and security checkpoint.

access control. Walls of the garage are painted white to enhance lighting. On the inside of hotels, the swimming pool, exercise room, vending and laundry areas have glass doors and walls to permit maximum witness potential. One application of CCTV is to aim cameras at persons standing at the lobby desk and install the monitor in plain view. Since people can see themselves, robberies have declined.

Perimeter Security

Perimeter means outer boundary, and it is often the property line and the first line of defense against unauthorized access (Figures 4-3 and 4-4). Building access points such as doors and windows also are considered part of perimeter defenses at many locations. Typical perimeter security begins with a fence and may include locks, alarms, lighting, CCTV, and patrols. To permit an unobstructed view, both sides of a perimeter should be kept clear of vehicles, equipment, and vegetation. This allows for what is known as *clear zones.* Although the least number of entrances strengthens perimeter security, the plan must not interfere with normal business and emergency situations. The perimeter of a building, especially in urban areas, often is the building's walls. A thief may enter through a wall from an adjoining building.

Perimeter security may be classified according to various types of barriers. Post and Kingsbury refer to natural, structural, human, animals, and energy barriers. *Natural barriers* are rivers, hills, cliffs, mountains, foliage, and other features difficult to overcome. Fences, walls, doors, and the architec-

Figure 4-3 Multiple security methods are often applied along a perimeter.

tural arrangement of buildings are *structural barriers*. *Human barriers* include security officers who check people, vehicles, and things entering and leaving a facility. The typical *animal barrier* is a dog. *Energy barriers* include protective lighting and intrusion alarm systems.

A search of the Web shows many companies offering security products and services. Also, standards for security products can be found on the Web.

The most common type of barrier is a *chain-link fence* topped with barbed wire. It is advisable that the chain-link fence be made of at least 9-gauge or heavier wire with 2″ × 2″ diamond-shaped mesh. It should be at least 7 feet high. Its posts should be set in concrete and spaced no more than 10 feet apart. The bottom should be within 2 inches of hard ground; if the ground

Figure 4-4 A gate is often used as a controlled access point along a perimeter.

is soft, the fence can become more secure if extended a few inches below the ground. Recommended at the top is a *top guard*: supporting arms about 1 or 2 feet long containing three or four strands of taut barbed wire 6 inches apart and facing outward at 45 degrees.

Gates are necessary for traffic through fences. The fewer gates, the better because, like windows and doors, they are weak points along a perimeter.

Vehicle barriers control traffic and stop vehicles from penetrating a perimeter. The problems of drive-by shootings and vehicle bombs have resulted in greater use of vehicle barriers. These barriers are assigned government-certified ratings based on the level of protection; however, rating systems vary among government agencies. *Passive vehicle barriers* are fixed and include decorative bollards, large concrete planters, specially engineered and anchored park benches, hardened fencing, fence cabling, and trees. *Active vehicle barriers* are used at entrances and include gates, barrier arms, and pop-up type systems that are set underground and, when activated, spring up to block a vehicle. As we know, no security method is foolproof, and careful security planning is vital. In 1997, to protest government policy, the environmental group Green-peace penetrated government security in Washington, DC, and dumped four tons of coal outside the Capitol building. The driver of the truck drove the wrong way up a one-way drive leading to the building.

Walls are costly and a substitute for fences when management is against the use of a wire fence. Attractive walls can be designed to produce security equal to fences while blending into surrounding architecture. Walls are made from a variety of materials: bricks, concrete blocks, stones, cement. Depending on design, the top of walls 6 or 7 feet high may contain barbed wire, spikes, or broken glass set in cement. Offenders often avoid injury by throwing a blanket or jacket over the top of the wall (or fence) before scaling it. Many jurisdictions prohibit ominous features at the top of barriers. Check local ordinances. An advantage of a wall is that outsiders are hindered from observing inside. However, observation by public police during patrols also is hindered; this can benefit an intruder.

Hedges or shrubbery are useful as barriers. Thorny shrubs have a deterrent value. A combination of hedge and fence is useful. Hedges should be less than 3 feet high and placed on the inside to avoid injury to those passing by and to create an added obstacle for someone attempting to scale the fence. Any plants that are large and placed too close to buildings and other locations provide a climbing tool, cover for thieves, and a hiding place for stolen goods.

Municipal codes restrict the heights of fences, walls, and hedges to maintain an attractive environment devoid of threatening-looking barriers. Certain kinds of barriers may be prohibited to ensure conformity.

Access Controls

Access controls regulate people, vehicles, and items during movement into, out of, and within a building or facility. With regulation, assets are easier to protect. If a truck can enter a business facility easily, back up to the shipping dock so that the truck driver can load valuable cargo illegally, and then drive away, that business cannot last long. But if the truck has to stop at the facility's front gate, where a uniformed officer issues a pass and records the license and other information, and appropriate paperwork is exchanged at the shipping dock under the watchful eyes of another officer who restricts the driver's access into the facility, then these controls can prevent losses.

Access controls are vital for the everyday movement of employees, customers, vendors, service people, contractors, and government inspectors. Any of these people can be someone who would steal. In addition to merchandise, confidential information, such as classified industrial documents, and employee and customer information must be protected. In one company a security officer was fired because he permitted two salespeople from another company to enter a restricted area.

Access control varies from simple to complex. A prime factor influencing the kind of system employed is need. A research laboratory developing a new product requires strict access controls, whereas a retail business would require minimal controls.

Safety must be a major concern for access control systems. Unauthorized exits locked from within create a hazard in case of fire or other emergency. To ensure safety yet fewer losses, emergency exit alarms on each locked door are a worthwhile investment. These devices enable quick exit, or a short delay, when pressure is placed against a horizontal bar that is secured across the door. An alarm is sounded when these doors are activated, which discourages unauthorized use.

What If?

As a Security Officer, What Do You Do if You Catch a Person Entering a Building Through a Door That Was Propped Open?

A major strategy of security is to limit access points. When people and vehicles enter and exit through a limited number of access points, security is increased through close observation, record-keeping (i.e., people, vehicles, items) and, depending on the business, searches.

When people use alternative, unauthorized access points, security is compromised because offenders may enter and exit at these points, there is no accountability of who is entering and leaving, and contraband can be brought in or taken out. Upon discovering a door propped open, security personnel can install a covert CCTV system to learn more about who is using the unauthorized access point and why. This situation is a ripe opportunity for security to possibly catch offenders committing a crime. However, employees may only be interested in a shorter route to and from their vehicles.

When security officers catch outsiders using an unauthorized access point, the person must be escorted to a reception area if they have legitimate business on the premises. If the person appears to be a trespasser, the officer should request backup, ask for identification, escort the person off the premises or make an arrest, and complete a report of the incident, with a full description of the individual. If employees are caught using an authorized access point, inform them about policies and procedures, escort them to the authorized access point, request ID, and complete a report. Naturally, each organization will vary on how these situations are handled.

SEARCHING EMPLOYEES Management can provide, in the contract of employment, that reasonable detentions are permissible, that reasonable searches may be made to protect people and company assets, and that searches may be made at any time of desks, lockers, containers carried by employees and vehicles. Case law has permitted an employer to use a duplicate key, known to the employee, to enter a locker at will. On the other hand, an employee who uses a personal lock has a greater expectation of privacy, barring a written condition of employment to the contrary that includes forced entry. When a desk is assigned to a specific employee, an expectation of privacy exists. If employees jointly have access to a desk to obtain items, no privacy exists.

Policies and procedures on searches should consider input from management, an attorney, employees, and a union, if on the premises. Also consider business necessity, what is subject to search, signed authorization from each employee, signs at the perimeter and in the workplace, and searches of visitors and others.

VISITORS Visitors include customers, salespeople, vendors, service people, contractors, and government employees. A variety of techniques are applicable to visitor access control. An appointment system enables preparation for visitors. When visitors arrive without an appointment, the person should lead them to a waiting room. Whatever the reason for the visit, the shortest route to specific destinations, away from valuable assets and dangerous conditions, can avert theft and injuries. Lending special equipment, such as a helmet, may be necessary. A record or log of visits is wise. These records aid investigators. Whenever possible, procedures should minimize employee-visitor contact. This is especially important in the shipping and receiving department, where truck drivers may become friendly with employees and conspiracies may evolve. When telephones, restrooms, and vending machines are scattered throughout a plant, truck drivers and other visitors who are permitted easy access may actually steal the place blind. These services should be located at the shipping and receiving dock and access to outsiders should be limited.

CONTROLLING THE MOVEMENT OF PACKAGES AND PROPERTY The movement of packages and property also must be subject to access controls. Some locations require precautions against packaged bombs, letter bombs, and other hazards. Clear policies and procedures are needed for incoming and outgoing items. To counter employee theft, outgoing items require both scrutiny and accountability. Uniformed officers can check outgoing items while a property pass system service the accountability function.

EMPLOYEE IDENTIFICATION SYSTEM The use of an employee identification (card or badge) system will depend on the number of employees that must be accounted for and recognized by other employees. An ID system not only prevents unauthorized people from entering a facility but also deters unauthorized employees from entering restricted areas. For the system to operate efficiently, clear policies should state the use of ID cards, where and when the cards are to be displayed on the person, who should collect cards from employees who quit or are fired, and the penalties for noncompliance. A lost or stolen card should be reported so that the proper information reaches all interested personnel.

Simple ID cards contain employer and employee names. A more complex system would include an array of information: name, signature, address, employee number, physical characteristics (e.g., height, weight, hair and eye colors), date of birth, validation date, authorized signature, location of work assignment, thumbprint, and color photo. The card can also serve as a miniature computer to record and store information and be used as a "card key" for access.

AUTOMATIC ACCESS CONTROL Keys are difficult to control and easy to duplicate, so there are limitations to the lock-and-key method of access control. Because of these problems, the need for improved access control, and technological innovations, a huge market has been created for electronic card access control systems. These systems are flexible. Unauthorized duplication of cards can be difficult, and personnel (i.e., an officer at each entrance) costs are saved. The card contains coded information "read" by the system for access or denial.

Before an automatic access control system is implemented, several considerations are necessary. *Safety must be a prime factor to ensure quick exit in case of emergency.* What if the system breaks down? Is a backup source of power available (e.g., generators)?

Tailgating is another concern. This is when an authorized user lets in an unauthorized user. To thwart this problem, a security officer can be assigned each access point, but this approach is expensive when compared to applying CCTV, revolving doors, or turnstiles. Revolving doors can be expensive initially and they are not an approved fire exit. Optical turnstiles contain invisible infrared beams to count people entering to control tailgating.

A summary of cards used in card access systems follows:

- *Magnetic stripe cards* are plastic, laminated cards (like credit cards) that have a magnetic stripe along one edge onto which a code is printed. When the card is inserted, the magnetically encoded data is compared to data stored in a computer and access is granted on verification.

- *Magnetic dot cards* contain magnetic material, often barium ferrite, laminated between plastic layers. The dots create a magnetic pattern that activates internal sensors in a card reader.

- *Weigand cards* employ a coded pattern on a magnetized wire within the card to generate a code number. To gain access, the card is passed through a sensing reader.

- *Bar-coded cards* contain an array of tiny vertical lines that can be visible and vulnerable to photocopying or invisible and read by an infrared reader.

- *Proximity cards* need not be inserted into a reader but placed in its "proximity." A code is sent via radio frequency, magnetic field, or microchip-tuned circuit.

- *Smart cards* contain an integrated circuit chip within the plastic that serves as a miniature computer as it records and stores information and personal identification codes in its memory. Security is increased because information is held in the card, rather than the reader. These cards permit a host of activities from access control to making purchases, while almost eliminating the need for keys or cash.

Biometric security systems have been praised as a major advance in access control. These systems verify an individual's identity through fingerprint-scan, hand-scan (hand geometry), iris-scan (the iris is the colored part around the pupil of the eye), retina-scan (the retina is the sensory membrane lining the eye and receiving the image formed by the lense), voice patterns, physical action of writing, and facial-scan. The biometric leaders are fingerprint, hand, and iris which offer the best balance of accuracy, reliability, and cost. In the near term we will not see facial-scan pick a known terrorist out of a crowd, but the technology is evolving. At this time facial-scan is unreliable with crowds because digitized photos shot at angles or in poor light can be flawed in comparison to police mug shots. Basically, these systems operate by storing identifying information in a computer to be compared with information presented by a subject requesting access. Although biometric systems have been touted as being invincible, no security is foolproof, as illustrated by terrorists who cut off the thumb of a bank manager to gain entry through a fingerprint-based access control system.

Access controls often use multiple technologies. For example, magnetic stripe and smart card technologies can complement each other on a single card. One location may require a card and a personal identification number, or PIN, whereas another requires scanning a finger and a PIN (Figure 4-5).

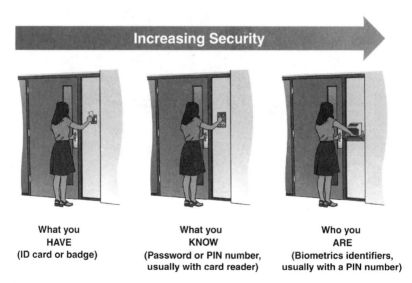

Increasing Security
What you **HAVE** (ID card or badge)	What you **KNOW** (Password or PIN number, usually with card reader)	Who you **ARE** (Biometrics identifiers, usually with a PIN number)

Figure 4-5 Three technology approaches to access control. Courtesy: National Institute of Justice, *Appropriate and Effective Use of Technologies in U.S. Schools* (Washington DC: U.S. Department of Justice, Sept. 1999).

One feature is an alarm that sounds during unauthorized attempted entry. Access systems can be programmed to allow select access according to time, day, and location. The logging capabilities are another feature.

Locks and Keys

The basic purpose of a lock-and-key system is to hinder unauthorized entry. Attempts to enter a secure location usually are made at a window or door to a building or at a door somewhere within a building. Many see a lock as only a delaying device that is valued by the amount of time needed to defeat it.

As with other types of physical security, standards exist for locks that assist consumers in purchasing decisions while improving protection. For example, the American National Standards Institute (ANSI) <www.ansi.org> offers standards for locks that are followed by manufacturers.

Almost all locking devices are operated by a key, numerical combination, card, or electricity. Most key-operated locks (except padlocks) use a bolt or latch (Figure 4-6). The *bolt* (or *deadbolt*) extends from a door lock into a bolt

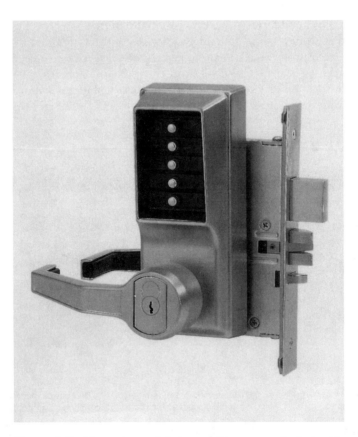

Figure 4-6   Heavy-duty, stand-alone pushbutton mortise lock with deadbolt, latch, and lever handle. Courtesy: Ilco Unican.

receptacle within the door frame. Authorized entry is made by using an appropriate key to manually move the bolt into the door lock. *Latches* are spring loaded and less secure than a bolt. They are cut on an angle to permit them to slide right into the strike when the door is closed. Unless the latch is equipped with a locking bar (deadlatch), a knife can be used to push the latch back to open the door.

The *cylinder* part of a lock contains the keyway, pins, and other mechanisms that permit the bolt or latch to be moved by a key for access (Figure 4-7). Double-cylinder locks, in which a cylinder is located on each side of a door, are a popular form of added security as compared to single-cylinder locks. *Double-cylinder locks require a key for both sides.* With a single-cylinder lock, a thief may be able to break glass or remove a wood panel and then reach inside to turn the knob to release the lock. For safety's sake, locations that use double-cylinder locks must prepare for emergency escape by having a key readily available.

Key-in-knob locks are used universally, but are being replaced by key-in-the-lever locks (see Figure 4-6) to be "ADA compliant." As the name implies, the keyway is in the knob or lever. "ADA compliant" refers to the Americans with Disabilities Act of 1990 that prohibits discrimination against individuals with disabilities and increases their access to services and jobs. Since this Act, security designers seek to remove barriers and promote access for individuals with disabilities. The door hardware industry offers several products and solutions to aid the disabled, one being the use of levers rather than knobs at doors.

KINDS OF LOCKS Volumes have been written about locks. The following briefly summarizes the common kinds of locks.

- *Warded* (or *skeleton key tumbler*) *lock.* This older kind of lock is disengaged when a skeleton key makes direct contact with a bolt and slides it back into the door. It is an easy lock to pick. A strong piece of L-shaped wire can be inserted into the keyway to move the bolt. Warded locks are still in use in many older buildings and are recognized by a keyway that permits seeing through. Locks on handcuffs are of the warded kind and can be defeated by a knowledgeable offender.

- *Disc tumbler* (or *wafer tumbler*) *lock.* Originally designed for the automobile industry, its use has expanded to desks, cabinets, files, and padlocks. The operation of this lock entails spring-loaded flat metal discs, instead of pins, that align when the proper key is used. These locks are mass produced, inexpensive, and have a short life expectancy. More security is offered than a warded lock can provide, but disc tumbler locks are subject to defeat by improper keys or being jimmied.

- *Pin tumbler lock.* Invented by Linus Yale in 1844, the pin tumbler lock is used widely in industry and residences. Its security surpasses that of the warded and disc tumbler kinds.

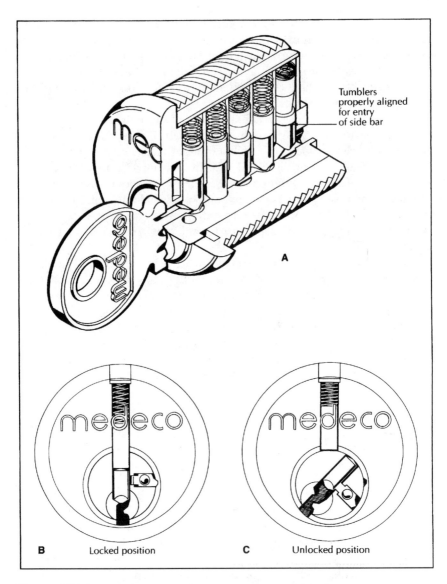

Tumblers
properly aligned
for entry
of side bar

A

B   Locked position   C   Unlocked position

Figure 4-7 Pin Tumbler Lock. (A) A cutaway of a pin tumbler lock showing the springs and tumblers. When the correct key is inserted into the lock, it will align all of the tumblers in a straight line to allow the plug to turn and operate the locking mechanism. (B) Locked position. Notice how the spring is forcing the tumbler to project partway into the inner core (plug) of the lock, making it impossible for the plug to rotate. (C) Unlock position. The tumbler is now outside the plug, thereby allowing it to be rotated. Courtesy: Medeco Security Locks, Inc.

- *Lever lock.* Lever locks vary widely. Basically, these locks disengage when tumblers are aligned by the proper key. Those found in cabinets, chests, and desks often provide minimal security, whereas those found in bank safe deposit boxes are more complex and provide greater security. The better quality lever lock offers more security than the best pin tumbler lock.

- *Combination lock.* This lock requires manipulating a numbered dial(s) to gain access. Combination locks usually have three or four dials that must be aligned in the correct order for entrance. These locks provide greater security than key locks because a limited number of people probably will know the lock combination and keys are unnecessary. They are used for safes, bank vaults, and high-security filing cabinets. A serious vulnerability results when an offender watches the opening of a combination lock either with binoculars or a telescope. Retailers sometimes place combination safes near the front door for viewing by patrolling police; however, unless the retailer uses his or her body to block the dial from viewing, losses may result. This same weakness exists where access is permitted by typing a secret code into a keyboard for access to a parking lot, doorway, or secure area.

- *Combination padlock.* This lock is similar in operation to a combination lock. It is used on employee or student lockers and in conjunction with safety hasps or chains. Some of these locks have a keyway so they can be opened with a key.

- *Padlock.* Requiring a key, this lock is used on lockers or in conjunction with hasps or chains. Numerous kinds of construction are possible, each affording differing levels of protection.

Automatic locking and unlocking devices also are a part of the broad spectrum of methods to control access. Digital locking systems open doors when a particular numbered combination is typed. If the wrong number is typed, an alarm is sounded. Combinations can be changed when necessary. *Electromagnetic locks* use magnetism, electricity, and a metal plate around doors to hold doors closed. When the electricity is turned off, the door can be opened. Remote locks enable opening a door electronically from a remote location. Before releasing the door lock, an officer seated in front of a console identifies an individual at a door by use of CCTV and a two-way intercom.

Trends taking place with locks and keys include increasing use of electronics and microchip technology. For example, hybrids have been developed whereby a key can serve as a standard hardware key in one door and as an electronic key in another door. Manufacturers also offer mechanical locks and keys with microchip technology to produce an intelligent system that can provide an audit trail. Such systems are self-contained on a door and use a common watch-type battery. A key collection device is used to retrieve data.

As electronics get smaller, we will see more of it being merged with mechanical locks.

KEY CONTROL Without adequate key control, locks are useless and crime is likely to climb. Accountability and proper records are necessary. Keys should be marked with a code to identify the corresponding lock; the code is interpreted via a record stored in a safe place. A key should never be marked, "Key for room XYZ." When not in use, keys should be positioned on hooks in a locked key cabinet or vault. The name of the employee, date, and key code are vital records to maintain when a key is issued. These records require continuous updating. Employee turnover is one reason why precise records are vital. Departing employees will return keys (and other valuables) if their final paycheck is withheld. To hinder duplication of keys, "do not duplicate" may be stamped on keys, and company policy can clearly state that key duplication will result in dismissal. Lock changes are wise every eight months and sometimes at shorter intervals on an irregular basis. Key control also is important for vehicles such as autos, trucks, and forklifts.

Doors

An all metal door offers maximum protection. However, businesses and institutions generally use aluminum doors with glass. Without adequate protection, the glass is vulnerable, and prying the weak aluminum is not difficult. As with other security hardware, the Web offers a host of vendors and standards for doors.

Hollow-core doors render complex locks useless because an offender can punch right through the door. Thin wood panels or glass on the door are additional weak points. More expensive, *solid-core doors* are stronger; they are made of solid wood (over an inch thick) without the use of weak fillers. To reinforce hollow-core or solid-core doors, one can attach 16-gauge steel sheets, via one-way screws.

Whenever possible, door hinges should be placed on the inside. Door hinges that face outside enable easy entry. By using a screwdriver and hammer, one can raise the pins out of the hinges to enable the door to be lifted away. To protect the hinge pins, it is a good idea to weld them so they cannot be removed in this manner. Another form of protections is to remove two screws on opposite sides of the hinge, insert a pin or screw on the jamb side of the hinge so that it protrudes about half an inch, and then drill a hole in the opposite hold to fit the pin when the door is closed. With this method on both top and bottom hinges, even if the hinge pins are removed, the door will not fall off the hinges.

Contact switches applied to doors offer electronic protection. Greater protection is provided when contact switches are recessed in the edges of the door and frame. Other kinds of electronic sensors applied at doors include vibration sensors, pressure mats, and various types of motion detectors aimed in the area of the door. These topics are covered in subsequent pages.

Windows

Glass can be designed to block penetration of bullets, defeat attempted forced entry, remain intact following an explosion, and protect against electronic eavesdropping. The Web shows many standards for glazing from the American Architectural Manufacturers Association, Underwriters Laboratories (UL), and other groups. UL classifies *bullet-resistant windows* into eight protection levels, with levels 1 to 3 rated against handguns and 4 to 8 rated against rifles. Level 4 or higher windows usually are applied by government agencies and the military. Protective windows are made of either glass or plastic or mixtures of each.

Burglar-resistant windows, rated UL 972, Burglary Resisting Glazing Material, protect against hammers, flame, "smash and grab," and other attacks. Combined bullet- and burglar-resistant windows are available. Although window protection is an expense that may be difficult to justify, insurers offer discounts on insurance premiums for such installations.

Following the Oklahoma City bombing, considerable interest focused on the vulnerability of flying glass due not only to explosions but also accidents or natural disasters. Vendors sell shatter resistant film to reduce this problem. However, others claim that the destroyed windows permit deadly gases to escape, enabling occupants to survive. This controversy continues.

Businesses and institutions often contain widows that do not open. For windows that do open, a latch or lock on the inside provides some protection. By covering windows with grating or security screens, additional steps have been taken to impede entrance by an intruder or items being thrown out by a dishonest employee. *When planning window protection, one must consider the need for emergency escape and ventilation.*

Categories of electronic protection for windows are vibration, glass-breakage, and contact-switch sensors. *Vibration sensors* respond to vibration or shock. They are attached right on the glass or window frame. These sensors are noted for their low false alarm rate and are applicable to fences, walls, and valuable artwork, among other things. *Glass-breakage sensors* react to glass breaking. A sensor the size of a large coin is placed directly on the glass and can detect glass breakage several feet away. Some types operate via a tuning fork, which is tuned to the frequency produced by glass breaking. Others employ a microphone and electric amplifier. *Contact switches* activate an alarm when the contact (i.e., electrical current) is interrupted by opening the window.

Intrusion Detection Systems

An *intrusion detection system* detects and reports an event within its detection area (Figure 4-8). A response to correct the reported problem is essential.

Three fundamental components of an intrusion detection system are sensor, control unit, and annunciator. *Sensors* detect intrusion by, for example, heat or movement. The *control unit* receives the alarm notification from

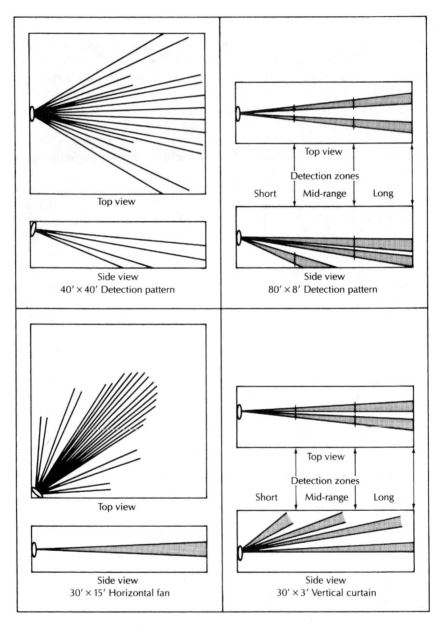

Figure 4-8   Indoor infrared motion detection patterns.

the sensor and then activates a silent alarm or *annunciator* (e.g., a bell or siren), which usually produces a human response.

Standards for intrusion alarm systems are from UL, the Institute of Electrical and Electronics Engineers (IEEE), plus other groups in the United

States and overseas. UL, for example, "lists" installation companies who are authorized to issue UL Certificates on each installation. This means that the installer conforms to maintenance and testing as required by UL, which conducts unannounced inspections.

SENSORS APPLIED INTERNALLY A *balanced magnetic switch* consists of a switch mounted to a door (or window) frame and a magnet mounted to a moveable door or window. When the door is closed, the magnet holds the switch closed to complete a circuit. An alarm is triggered when the door is opened and the circuit is interrupted. An ordinary magnetic switch is similar to the balanced type, except simpler, less expensive, and providing a lower level of security. Switches provide good protection against opening a door; however, an offender may cut through a door or glass.

Mechanical contact switches contain a push-button actuated switch that is recessed into a surface. An item is placed on it that depresses the switch, completing the alarm circuit. Lifting the item interrupts the circuit and signals an alarm.

Pressure-sensitive mats contain two layers of metal strips or screen wire separated by sections of foam rubber or other flexible material. When pressure is applied, as by a person walking on the mat, both layers meet and complete an electrical contact to signal an alarm. These mats are applied as internal traps at doors, windows, main traffic points, and near valuable assets. The cost is low and these mats are difficult to detect. If detected by the offender, he or she can walk around it.

Grid wire sensors are made of fine insulated wire attached to protected surfaces in a grid pattern consisting of two circuits, one running vertical, the other horizontal, and each overlapping the other. An interruption in either circuit signals an alarm. This type of sensor is applied to grill work, screens, walls, floors, ceilings, doors, and other locations. Although these sensors are difficult for an offender to spot, they are expensive to install and an offender can jump the circuit.

Trip wire sensors use a spring-loaded switch attached to a wire stretched across a protected area. An intruder "trips" the alarm (i.e., opens the circuit) when the wire is pulled loose from the switch. These sensors are often applied to ducts.

Vibration sensors detect low frequency energy resulting from the force applied in an attack of a structure. These sensors are applied to walls, floors, and ceilings.

Capacitance sensors create an electrical field around metallic objects that, when disturbed, signal an alarm. These sensors are applied to safes, file cabinets, grills at openings (e.g., windows), and other metal objects. One sensor can protect many objects; however, it is subject to defeat by using insulation (e.g., heavy gloves).

Infrared photoelectric beam sensors activate an alarm when an invisible infrared beam of light is interrupted. If the system is detected, an offender may jump over or crawl under the beam to defeat it.

Ultrasonic motion detectors create a pattern of inaudible sound waves that are transmitted into an area and monitored by a receiver. These detectors operate on the *Doppler effect,* which is the change in frequency that results from the motion of an intruder. These detectors are installed on walls or ceilings or used covertly (i.e., disguised within another object). They are subject to nuisance alarms from high-pitched noises or air currents and can be defeated by objects blocking the sensor or by fast or slow movement. This detector has been labeled as obsolete because of false alarms.

Microwave motion detectors operate on the Doppler frequency shift principle. An energy field is transmitted into an area and monitored for a change in the pattern and frequency, which results in an alarm. Because microwave energy penetrates a variety of construction materials, care is required for placement and aiming. However, this can be an advantage in protecting multiple rooms and large areas with one sensor. These sensors can be defeated (like ultrasonic ones) by objects blocking the sensor or by fast or slow movement.

Passive infrared intrusion sensors (PIR) are passive in that they do not transmit a signal for an intruder to disturb. Rather, moving infrared radiation (from a person) is detected against the radiation environment of a room. When an intruder enters the room, the level of infrared energy changes and an alarm is activated. Although the PIR is not subject to the many nuisance alarms as ultrasonic and microwave detectors, it should not be aimed at sources of heat or surfaces that can reflect energy. The PIR can be defeated by blocking the sensor so it cannot pick up heat.

Passive audio detectors listen for noise created by intruders. These detectors can use public address system speakers in buildings, which can act as microphones to listen to intruders. *Such audiovisual systems must be applied with extreme care to protect privacy, confidentiality, and sensitive information, and to avoid violating state and federal wiretapping laws.*

Fiber optics is growing in popularity for intrusion detection and for transmission of alarm signals. It involves the transportation of information via guided light waves in an optical fiber. This sensor can be attached to or inserted in many things requiring protection. When stress is applied to the fiber optic cable, an infrared light pulsing through the cable reacts to the stress and signals an alarm.

Two types of sensor technologies often are applied to a location to reduce false alarms, prevent defeat techniques, or fulfill unique needs. The combination of microwave and passive infrared sensors is a popular example of applying *dual technologies* (Figure 4-9). Reporting can be designed so an alarm is signaled when both sensors detect an intrusion (to reduce false alarms) or when either sensor detects an intrusion.

SENSORS APPLIED EXTERNALLY Table 4-1 describes intrusion detection systems. These systems have gone through several generations leading to improved performance. Not in the table is *magnetic field* which consists of a series of buried wire loops or coils. Metal objects moving over the sensor

Figure 4-9 Ceiling-mounted intrusion detection sensor. Dual technologies are often applied to reduce false alarms.

induce a current and signal an alarm. Research shows the vulnerability to defeat (VD) for magnetic field, infrared photo beam, and taut wire systems is high. Microwave, electric field, fence disturbance, seismic sensor cable, and video motion systems all have a medium VD. The VD for ported coaxial cable systems is low. Visible sensors are relatively easy to defeat but cost effective for low-security applications. Multiple sensors, and especially covert sensors, provide a higher level of protection.

Fiber optic perimeter protection can take the form of a fiber optic net installed on a fence. Optical fibers can be attached to or inserted

Table 4-1   Types of Intrusion Alarm Systems*

System	Graphic Idea	Concept	Advantages	Disadvantages
Motion detection				
Fence-mounted sensor		Detection depends on movement of fence	Ease of installation; early detection on interior fence; relatively inexpensive; requires little space; follows terrain easily	Frequent false alarms (weather and birds); conduit breakage; dependent on quality, rigidity of fence, and type of installation
Seismic sensor cable (buried)		Detection depends on ground movement (intruder walking over buried movement sensors, or other seismic disturbances)	Good for any site shape, uneven terrain; early warning; good in warm climate with little rain	False alarms from ground vibrations (vehicles, thunderstorms, heavy snow); not recommended for heavy snow regions; difficult installation and maintenance
Balanced capacitance		Detection depends on touching of cable, interfering with balance of cable	Few false alarms; good for selected areas of fence, rooftops, curves, corners, any terrain	Not to be used independently; for selected areas only
Taut wire		Detection depends on deflecting, stretching, or releasing the tension of wire that triggers alarming mechanism	Good for any terrain or shape; can be used as interior fence; extremely low false alarm rates	Relatively expensive; possible false alarms from snow, ice, birds, etc.; temperature changes require adjustments
Energy field				
Microwave sensor		Based on line of sight; detection depends on intrusion into volumetric area above ground between transmitter and receiver	Does not require a great deal of maintenance	Not good on hilly or heavily contoured terrain; costly installation; potential false alarms caused by weather (snow, ice, wind, and rain); vegetation must be removed

Energy Field

Type		Detection	Advantages	Disadvantages
Infrared photo beam sensor		Based on line of sight; detection depends on intrusion into beam(s) stacked vertically above ground	Good for short distances, building walls, and sally ports	Distances between transmitter and receiver must be short, requiring more intervals; potential false alarms by animals and weather conditions (fog, dust, snow); voltage surges
Ported coaxial cable		Detection depends on interruption of field in terms of mass, velocity, and length of time	Adaptable to most terrains	False alarms caused by heavy rain (pooling of water), high winds, tree roots; relatively expensive installation and maintenance
Video motion detection		Detection depends on change in video-monitor signal	Good for enhancing another system; good for covering weak spots	Lighting is a problem
Electric field sensor		Detection depends on penetration of volumetric field created by field wires and sensor wires	Good on hilly or heavily contoured terrain; can be freestanding or fence-mounted	Requires more maintenance; sensor wires must be replaced every 3 years; vegetation must be controlled

*Sources: Information from New York State Department of Corrections, Pennsylvania Department of Corrections, South Carolina Department of Corrections, and Federal Bureau of Prisons. Reproduced from U.S. Dept. of Justice, National Institute of Justice, *Stopping Escapes: Perimeter Security* (U.S. Government Printing Office, August 1987), p. 6.

within numerous items to signal an alarm, including razor ribbon, security grilles, windows, and doors, and it can protect valuable assets such as computers.

No one technology is perfect; many protection programs rely on dual technology to strengthen intrusion detection. When selecting a system, it is wise to remember that manufacturers' claims often are based on perfect weather. Security decision makers must clearly understand the advantages and disadvantages of each type of system under a variety of conditions.

ALARM SIGNALING SYSTEMS Alarm signaling systems transmit data from a protected area to an annunciation system. Local ordinances and codes may restrict certain systems, designate to whom the alarm may be transmitted, or limit the length of time the alarm is permitted to sound.

Local alarm systems notify, by sound or lights, people in the hearing or seeing range of the signal. This includes the intruder, who may flee. Typically, a bell rings outside of a building. Often, local alarms produce no response—in urban areas responsible action may not be taken, and in rural areas nobody may hear the alarm.

A *central station* alarm system receives intrusion or fire signals or both at a computer console located and monitored a distance away from the protected location. When an alarm signal is received, central station personnel contact police, firefighters, or other responders. Resources for central station design are available from UL and other organizations.

A variety of data transmission systems are utilized to signal an alarm. Telephone lines have been used for many years. Here, the earlier technology is covered first before the more modern technology.

Automatic telephone dialer systems are of two kinds: tape dialer and digital dialer. Tape dialer systems seldom are used today. They deliver a prerecorded or coded message to an interested party (e.g., central station, police department) after that party answers the telephone. Digital dialers do not use a recorded tape message; coded electronic pulses are transmitted, and an electronic terminal decodes the message onto a panel or teletype.

With *direct connect* systems the intrusion device is connected by wire directly to an alarm receiver located on the premises, at a police station, or some other location. Local ordinances may not permit direct reporting to police stations.

Radio frequency (RF) and *microwave* data transmission systems often are applied where telephone lines are not available or where hardwire lines are not practical. The components include transmitter, receiver, repeaters to extend range, battery backup, and solar power.

Fiber optic data transmission systems, as discussed earlier, transport data by way of light waves within a thin glass fiber. These cables are either underground or above ground. The components include transmitter, receiver, repeaters, battery backup, and solar power.

Signals should be backed up by multiple technologies. Options for off site transmission of activity include satellite, LAN, WAN, cellular, and the

Internet. Cellular is especially useful for backup since it is more likely to remain in operation in certain disasters.

Among the advances in alarm monitoring is remote programming. By this method, a central station can perform a variety of functions without ever visiting the site. Capabilities include system arming and disarming, unlocking doors, diagnostics and corrections, and with access systems, adding or deleting cards.·

Closed-Circuit Television

Closed-circuit television, or CCTV (see Figure 4-10) assists in deterrence, surveillance, apprehension, and prosecution. CCTV allows the viewing of multiple locations by one person. A simple *CCTV system* consists of a television camera, monitor (TV), and cable. The camera and monitor are plugged in,

Figure 4-10   Closed-circuit television camera.

and the cable is connected between them before both are turned on. Accessories include zoom lenses, remote pan (i.e., side-to-side movement), and tilt (i.e., up-and-down movement) mechanisms that enable viewing mobility and opportunities to obtain a close look at any suspicious activity. Low-light-level equipment permits viewing when limited light is present.

Several methods can be applied to transmit the camera image to the monitor: coaxial cable, fiber optics, microwave, radio frequency, telephone lines, and the Internet. Furthermore, it will be common to see video images on personal digital assistants and cell phones. What we have is the opportunity (as with other electronic security systems) for say, an executive in New York, to monitor inside a business in Hong Kong.

Changing technology has brought about the *charged coupled device* (CCD) or *"chip" camera*, a small, photosensitive, solid-state unit designed to replace the tube in the closed-circuit camera. CCD technology is found in camcorders. CCD cameras have certain advantages over tube cameras: CCD cameras are more adaptable to a variety of circumstances, they have a longer life expectancy, "ghosting" (i.e., people appearing transparent) is less of a problem, there is less intolerance to light, less power is required, and less heat is produced, thereby requiring less ventilation and permitting installation in more locations.

Cameras commonly are placed at access points, passageways, shipping and receiving docks, merchandise storage areas, cashier locations, parts departments, computer rooms, and overlooking files, safes, vaults, and production lines. Wherever cameras are located, careful planning is essential to avoid harming employee morale. Constant monitoring of a CCTV system ensures its loss prevention capabilities. Personnel that are not rotated periodically become fatigued from watching too much TV. This is a serious problem that is often overlooked. Regular employees may "test" the monitoring of the system by placing a bag or rag over a camera or even spraying the lens with paint. If employees see that there is no response, CCTV becomes a hoax. The use of dummy cameras is not recommended because, when employees discover the dummy, loss prevention appears to be a deceitful farce.

As with the newer digital systems, the older video cassette recorder (VCR) systems, combined with a CCTV system permits recording visual evidence. This is helpful in the prosecution of offenders and may be used in court.

CCTV capabilities can be enhanced by using a video motion detector. A *video motion detector* operates by sending, from a camera, a static (i.e., having no motion) picture to a memory evaluator. Any change in the picture, such as movement, activates an alarm. These systems assist security officers in reacting to threats.

Increasing "intelligence" is being built into CCTV-computer-based systems. The *digital multiplex recorder* enables users to record events directly to a hard drive, reducing storage space. This technology facilitates the move from video monitors to computer monitors, and we will see increasing use of security video at the desktop computer and remote monitoring (e.g., watching a business from many miles away).

The extent of the use of hidden surveillance cameras is difficult to measure, especially because many individuals are unaware of the existence of these cameras in workplaces. Pinhole lenses are a popular component of hidden surveillance cameras. They get their name from the outer opening of the lens, which is $1/8$ to $1/4$ inch in diameter and difficult to spot. Cameras are hidden in almost any location, such as clocks, file cabinets, computers, sprinkler heads, and mannequins.

If cameras are capable of viewing other cameras, personnel can check on viewing obstructions, sabotage, vandalism, or other problems. Tamperproof housings will impede those interested in disabling cameras. Different models are resistant to bullets, explosion, dust, and severe weather. Housings are manufactured with heaters, defrosters, windshield wipers, washers, and sun shields. Low-light-level cameras provide the means to view outside when very little light is available. When no visible light is available, an infrared illuminator creates light, invisible to the naked eye, but visible to infrared-sensitive cameras. Another option is thermal imaging cameras, which sense heat, and are especially helpful to spot intruders in darkness, fog, smoke, and foliage.

Lighting

From a business perspective, lighting can be justified because it improves sales by making a business and merchandise more attractive, promotes safety and prevents lawsuits, improves employee morale and productivity, and enhances the value of real estate. From a security perspective, two major purposes of lighting are *to create a psychological deterrent to intrusion* and *to enable detection.* Good lighting is considered such an effective crime control method that the law, in many locales, requires buildings to maintain adequate lighting.

One way to analyze lighting deficiencies is to go to the building at night and study the possible methods of entry and areas where inadequate lighting will aid a burglar. Before the visit, one should contract local police as a precaution against mistaken identity and to recruit their assistance in spotting weak points in lighting.

ILLUMINATION *Lumens* (of light output) per watt (of power input) is a measure of lamp efficiency. *Illuminance* is the intensity of light falling on a surface, measured in foot-candles (English units) or lux (metric units). The *foot-candle* (FC) is the measure of how bright the light is when it reaches one foot from the source. One lux equals 0.0929 FC. The light provided by direct sunlight on a clear day is about 10,000 FC, an overcast day would yield about 100 FC, and a full moon about 0.01 FC. A sample of outdoor lighting illuminances recommended by the Illuminating Engineering Society of North American are self-parking area, 1 FC; attendant parking area, 2 FC; covered parking area, 5 FC; active pedestrian entrance, 5 FC; building surroundings, 1 FC. It generally is recommended that gates and doors, where identification of persons and things takes place, should have at least 2 FC. An office should have a light level of about 50 FC.

LAMPS The following lamps are applied outdoors:

- *Incandescent* lamps are commonly found at residences. Light is produced by passing electrical current through a tungsten wire that becomes white hot. These lamps produce 10 to 20 lumens per watt, are the least efficient and most expensive to operate, and have a short lifetime of from 1000 to 2000 hours.

- *Halogen* and *quartz halogen* lamps are incandescent bulbs filled with halogen gas (like sealed-beam auto headlights) and provide about 25 percent better efficiency and life than ordinary incandescent bulbs.

- *Fluorescent* lamps pass electricity through a gas enclosed in a glass tube to produce light, producing 40 to 80 lumens per watt. They create twice the light and less than half the heat of an incandescent bulb of equal wattage and cost 5 to 10 times as much. Fluorescent lamps do not provide high levels of light output. The lifetime is 10,000 to 15,000 hours. They are not used extensively outdoors, except for signage.

- *Mercury vapor* lamps also pass electricity through a gas. The yield is 30 to 60 lumens per watt and the life is about 20,000 hours.

- *Metal halide* lamps are also of the gascous type. The yield is 80 to 100 lumens per watt, and the life is about 10,000 hours. They often are used at sports stadiums because they imitate daylight conditions and color appear natural. Consequently, these lamps complement CCTV systems, but they are the most expensive light to install and maintain.

- *High pressure sodium* lamps are gaseous, yield about 100 lumens per watt, have a life of about 20,000 hours, and are energy efficient. These lamps are often applied on streets and parking lots, cut through fog, and are designed to allow the eyes to see more detail at greater distances.

- *Low pressure sodium* are gaseous, produce 150 lumens per watt, have a life of about 15,000 hours, and are even more efficient than high pressure sodium. These lamps are expensive to maintain.

Each type of lamp has a different *color rendition*, which is the way a lamp's output affects human perceptions of color. Incandescent, fluorescent, and certain types of metal halide lamps provide excellent color rendition. Mercury vapor lamps provide good color rendition but are heavy on the blue. High pressure sodium lamps, which are used extensively outdoors, provide poor color rendition, making things look yellow. Low pressure sodium lamps make color unrecognizable and produce a yellow-gray color on objects. People find sodium vapor lamps, sometimes called *anticrime lights*, to be harsh because they produce a strange yellow haze. In many instances, when people park their vehicles in a parking lot during the day and return to find their vehicle at night, they are often unable to locate it due to poor color rendition from sodium lamps; some report their vehicle as being stolen. Another problem is the inability of witnesses to describe offenders accurately.

Mercury vapor, metal halide, and high pressure sodium take several minutes to produce full light output. If they are turned off, even more time is required to reach full output because they first have to cool down. This may not be acceptable for certain security applications. Incandescent, halogen, and quartz halogen have the advantage of instant light once electricity is turned on. Manufacturers can provide information on a host of lamp characteristics including the "strike" and "restrike" time.

The following three sources provide additional information on lighting:

- *National Lighting Bureau*
  www.nlb.org
  Publications.

- *Illuminating Engineering Society of North America*
  www.iesna.org
  Technical materials and services; recommended practices and standards; many members are engineers.

- *International Association of Lighting Management Companies*
  www.nalmco.org
  Seminars, training, and certification programs.

Safes, Vaults, and File Cabinets

SAFES Protective containers secure valuable items (e.g., cash, confidential information). These devices generally are designed to withstand losses from fire or burglary. Specifications vary and an assessment of need should be carefully planned. Management frequently is shocked when a fire-resistive safe in which valuable items are "secured" enables a burglar to gain entry because the safe was designed only for fire. The classic *fire-resistive* (or *record*) *safe* has a square (or rectangular) door and thin steel walls that contain insulation. During assembly, wet insulation is poured between the steel walls; when the mixture dries, moisture remains. During a fire, the insulation creates steam that cools the safe below 350° F (the flash point of paper) for a specified time. Record safes for computer tapes and discs require better protection because damage occurs at 150° F and these records are more vulnerable to humidity. Fire safes are able to withstand one fire; thereafter, the insulation is useless.

The classic *burglary-resistive* (or *money*) *safe* has a thick, round door and thick walls. Round doors were thought to enhance resistance, but today many newer burglary-resistive safes have square or rectangular doors. The burglary-resistive safe is more costly than the fire-resistive safe.

Better quality safes have the UL rating. This means that manufacturers have submitted safes for testing by UL. These tests determine the fire- or burglary-resistive properties of safes.

The following measures are recommended to fortify the security of safes and other containers:

1. Utilize alarms (e.g., capacitance and vibration), CCTV, and adequate lighting.
2. Locate the safe in a well-lighted spot near a window where police or pedestrians can see it. Hiding the safe gives the burglar better working conditions.
3. Secure the safe to the building so it is not stolen. (This also applies to cash registers that may be stolen in broad daylight.) Bolt the safe to the foundation or secure it in a cement floor. Remove any wheels or casters.
4. Do not give the burglar an opportunity to use any tools on the premises; hide or secure all potential tools. A ladder or torch on the premises can be used.
5. A time lock permits the safe to be opened only at select times. This hinders access even if the combination is known. A delayed-action lock provides an automatic waiting period (e.g., 15 minutes) from combination use to the time the lock mechanism activates. A silent signal lock triggers an alarm when a special combination is used to open a safe.
6. At the end of the day, turn the dial several times in the same direction.
7. A written combination is risky. Change the factory combination as soon as possible. When an employee leaves who knows the combination, change it.
8. Maintain limited valuables in the safe through frequent banking.
9. Select a safe with its UL rating marked on the inside. If a burglar identifies the rating on the outside, an attack is made easier.

VAULTS A walk-in vault is actually a large safe; it is subject to similar vulnerabilities from fire and attack. Because a walk-in vault is so large and expensive, typically only the door is made of steel, and the rest of the vault is composed of reinforced concrete. Vaults are heavy enough to require special support within a building. They commonly are constructed at ground level to avoid stress on a building.

FILE CABINETS File cabinets typically contain proprietary information that is vital to a business. These important records include accounts receivable, inventory lists, legal documents, contracts, research and development, and personnel data. Such records must be protected because they are the lifeblood of an organization and help to support losses during insurance claims.

File cabinets that are insulated and lockable can provide fair protection against fire and burglary. The cost is substantially lower than a safe or vault, but valuable records demanding increased safety should be placed in a safe or vault, or stored off-site. Special computer safes are designed to protect against forced entry, fire, and moisture that destroys computer media.

Combining Strategies

Fences can be overcome, alarms can malfunction, and dogs can be poisoned. That is, no security method is foolproof. As a result, a combination of strategies provides multiple defenses and protection. If one method should fail, one of the other methods will hopefully ensure protection. Figure 4-11 shows a business with multiple security strategies.

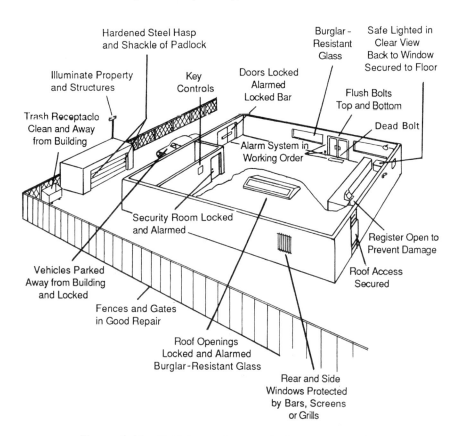

Figure 4-11 Multiple security strategies improve protection.

CHAPTER REVIEW

A. Multiple Choice

1. Crime prevention can best be described as
   a. obtaining adequate insurance to cover losses.
   b. quick police response after a crime takes place.
   c. strategies designed to keep crime from occurring.
   d. using modern equipment to fight crime after it occurs.
2. Which of the following is not a crime prevention program?
   a. target hardening
   b. operation identification
   c. neighborhood watch
   d. crime prevention anonymous
3. Perimeter security can best be defined as
   a. security along the outer boundary or property line.
   b. physical security defenses inside a building.
   c. surveillance opportunities from within a building.
   d. built-in features of a building that play a role in crime prevention.
4. Select the strategy least likely to be used to protect a solid-core wood door with no window.
   a. contact switch
   b. welded hinge pin
   c. dead bolt
   d. capacitance sensor
5. Which of the following is not one of the three basic parts of an intrusion alarm system?
   a. control unit
   b. cylinder
   c. sensor
   d. annunciator

B. True or False

1. Security officers are rarely involved in crime prevention activities.
2. Private security is usually more prevention-oriented than public police.
3. Proximity access cards need not be inserted into a reader for access.
4. Gates and doors, where identification of persons and things takes place, should have at least 2 foot-candles.

5. A central station is typically the meeting place for private as well as public police so information can be exchanged.

Applications

Application 4A

With the following security system form, answer the questions at the facility where you are being instructed or select another site. Obtain permission before performing the survey.

Security Survey Form

Location: Your Name:
Address: Date:

What type(s) of perimeter security exist at this facility?
How are doors and windows protected on the outer part of the building?
If intrusion alarms have been installed, what type of sensors are being used?
What additional security or crime prevention strategies are being used at this location?
What is the response time of local public police?
What suggestions would you recommend to improve overall security? (Make sure your ideas are worth the expense for the business.)

Application 4B

Refer to Figure 4-11, "multiple security strategies improve protection." Applying critical thinking skills, what are the positive and negative aspects of security at this business? What recommendations would you suggest to improve security?

5

Post Assignments and Security Patrols

CHAPTER OUTLINE

OBJECTIVES

After studying this chapter, you will be able to:

- List the purposes of post assignments and security patrols.
- List and describe at least five types of equipment that are helpful to security officers.
- Explain at least five guidelines for fixed-post duty.
- List at least five guidelines for foot patrol.
- Explain at least five guidelines for vehicle patrol.
- List at least five things to check when on patrol.
- Describe methods to improve observation skills.
- Explain suggestions for traffic duty, field contacts, crimes in progress, and protecting a crime scene.
- List at least ten additional guidelines for security officers.

Purposes of Post Assignments and Security Patrols

Security officers provide a basic form of protection for people and assets. They may be assigned to perimeter security, parking lots, and access points. The primary objectives for deploying security officers include:

- Maintain order.
- Prevent crime.
- Enforce company policies and criminal laws.
- Control access.
- Direct traffic.
- Observe and investigate suspicious activity.
- Apprehend offenders.
- Promote safety.
- *Observe* and *report* incidents, hazards, and emergencies.
- Assist employees and customers.
- Render basic first aid.

Christopher A. Hertig, a noted authority on the professionalization of security officers, writes the following observations on the duties of security officers following the September 11, 2001 terrorist attack:

> Private security can also be harnessed to combat major criminal activity and terrorism. Terrorist groups often rob banks, shoplift, commit credit card fraud and engage in other theft offenses as "fund raisers." Private protection officers are therefore in a position to help uncover serious terrorist threats. Protection officers are on the front lines in the fight against crime. They often feed intelligence and preliminary investigative information to public law enforcement entities. In many cases, security officers at retail stores, shopping centers, colleges, health care facilities and parks apprehend criminals and turn them over to police. This may not be fully recognized or appreciated—either by the public, facility management, or academia.

Equipment

There are various objects or pieces of equipment that security officers should carry or have access to. The following discusses the importance of some of these items. All of these elements will enable you to fulfill your important responsibility as a security officer.

Licenses

Always carry proper identification when on duty. This often includes a state-issued license/registration card. Also, if you carry a gun, the proper permit is required.

Notebook and Pens

Both of these items are essential items for you to carry. If a security officer is to properly observe and report, a record of an incident helps a security officer to remember crucial facts. Also, a notebook should contain important telephone numbers for emergencies.

Orders and Regulations Booklet

Security officers may be provided with a booklet containing guidelines for the job. These orders and regulations booklets vary among security organizations. However, common topics include:

- Preparation for duty.
- Care of uniforms and equipment.
- Dos and don'ts.
- Personal conduct (e.g., smoking).
- Emergency procedures and telephone numbers.
- What to check when on duty.
- Access controls.

- Traffic rules.
- Property receipts.
- Key control.
- Basic first aid.
- Types of fire extinguishers and usage.

Flashlight

A good flashlight is vital for duty as a security officer. In fact, the need for a backup flashlight cannot be overemphasized. If you have ever directed traffic at night and had your flashlight fail, the reason for carrying a backup or extra batteries and a bulb is easy to understand.

If you are walking into a dark area, always hold the flashlight away from your body in the hand that you would not use to fire your weapon. A criminal may think you are right behind the light and fire at it.

Weapons

The issuance of weapons to security officers is a serious decision for management. Locations with the potential for violence or a history of violence, or with high-value assets on the premises, are likely to issue weapons. However, without quality training in the care and use of weapons, serious consequences, such as injury, death, and civil and criminal liability, can result. Most security officers do not carry firearms. More on weapons in a subsequent chapter.

Data Scanner

Lower insurance premiums are possible through the use of monitored patrols. Records may be subjected to inspection by insurance personnel.

Historically, *watchclocks* were used to monitor officer patrols along preplanned routes. This older technology was carried by the officer while on patrol. The watchclock is a timepiece that contains a paper tape divided into time segments. The watchclock is operated by an officer by using keys mounted in walls at specific vulnerable locations along a patrol route. The keys are located in metal boxes and chained to walls. When inserted into the watchclock, the key makes an impression in the form of a number on the tape. Supervisor examination of the tape shows when the officer visited each key location to complete the scheduled route.

Bar-code or *touch button* technology provide modern avenues for monitoring patrols. A security officer carries a scanner or wand that makes contact with a bar code or touch button to record data that is later downloaded into a computer. Bar codes or buttons are affixed at vulnerable locations for a swipe by the scanner to record the visit by the officer, who can also swipe bar codes or buttons carried by the officer that represent various conditions (e.g., fire extinguisher needs recharging).

To improve the efficiency of security officers, a wireless tablet PC (see Figure 5-1) enables an officer to leave a monitoring post and take the work-

Figure 5-1 The tablet PC is a mobile workstation enabling a security officer to leave a post and do many things mobile that are done from a desktop PC, such as view CCTV, monitor alarms, and open doors. Courtesy: Hirsch Electronics, Santa Ana, CA.

station with him or her. If, for example, an officer must leave a control center to investigate an incident, the officer can bring the tablet PC and continue to watch CCTV, monitor alarms, and open doors for employee access.

Vehicles

Automobiles, trucks, golf carts, motor scooters, motorcycles, and bicycles offer the advantage of quick transportation. An automobile provides shelter from adverse weather and protection as a barricade. Vehicle equipment can include emergency lights and siren, two-way radio, public address system, spotlight, first-aid kit, and fire extinguisher. The selection of vehicles and equipment depend on need and budget constraints.

Other Items

Basic equipment may also include a radio, cell telephone, handcuffs, keys, a watch, and report forms. Also, for certain companies and specialized assignments, additional equipment is used, such as a hard hat, steel-toed shoes, special weapons, and monitoring devices (e.g., temperature and radiation).

Figure 5-2 Security booth at the National Aeronautics and Space Administration (NASA). Courtesy: B.I.G. Enterprises, Inc.

Fixed Posts

Another name for fixed post is stationary post. Basically, a security officer is assigned to a specific location, Figures 5-2. Common sites for a fixed post are at main entrances, gates, doors, lobbies, and control centers. Access control is a key objective of the fixed post. Security officers on such assignments control and record people, vehicles, and assets entering and leaving a facility. At the same time, violence is prevented, the theft of assets is curbed, and general protection duties are performed.

Fixed posts may require a security officer to be standing for long periods. Periodic breaks and relief from adverse weather should be provided to security officers.

Fixed-post assignments often involve considerable contact with employees and the public. Consequently, good human relations skills are needed so security officers will make favorable impressions on others and complete job duties in a professional manner.

Guidelines

Some guidelines for fixed-post duty are as follows:

1. Always report to duty on time.
2. Do not leave a post unless relieved.
3. Enforce company regulations and the law.
4. Maintain a businesslike and courteous manner. Keep conversations to a minimum.
5. Report emergencies promptly. For example, a fire should be reported immediately since a quick response can prevent disaster.
6. Contact your supervisor concerning unusual situations.
7. Always remain alert. Watch out for tricks designed to distract or divert you from your post duties.
8. When relieved, state any important information to the security officer arriving for duty.

Identification Cards

Security officers at fixed posts spend much of their time controlling access. To help maintain protection on the premises, employers often establish rules stating that anybody who enters the property must possess a company-issued identification (ID) card or badge. Such rules are specific as to the types of information required on the ID card, where it is to be worn, and penalties for infractions. Enforcement varies considerably depending on the facility and management support. Management must provide proper guidance concerning access control policies and procedures. As a professional, your responsibility is to know and understand these policies and procedures.

Employees

ID cards typically contain a host of information, such as an employee's name, a color photograph, and employee number. Usually the ID card is clipped on a person's shirt or blouse and provides easy identification for security personnel and others. Color-coded ID cards can be used to indicate what areas employees are authorized to enter. For example, a green ID card may indicate that an employee is permitted to enter all areas, including inner rooms where confidential information is stored. On the other hand, the blue card would allow an employee to enter all areas except where confidential information is located.

One problem with ID cards is the occasional situation where an employee appears at an access point without an ID card. Common excuses are that the card was stolen, lost, or at home. When this occurs, a security officer must follow company rules that may require the security officer to telephone a supervisor. If the employee becomes impatient or abusive, company rules must still be followed since the employee may have been fired and is inclined to criminal action. If you allow the employee to pass, your job may be in jeopardy. *Many security officers have lost their jobs because they did not follow company policies, yielded to a persistent individual, and allowed an unauthorized person to gain access.*

"The Irony of Security"

A sociologist named David L. Altheide used the above title in *Urban Life* to describe his research that suggests access controls in security, ironically, may provide a path to gain unofficial entry. This research is valuable to security personnel because a sharp criminal may use the same research methods, behavioral observations, or tricks to gain unauthorized access. For six years, Altheide observed, conducted interviews, and participated in access control activities. Some of Altheide's observations and viewpoints are listed.

- Rules for discerning legitimacy, normalcy, in general, whether one is above or below suspicion can be manipulated to obtain unauthorized access. For example, security personnel use appearance as a clue to criminality, so criminals can produce a false front to alter security's perception of them. A well-dressed and groomed person may appear at first sight to "fit in."
- If an offender understands security procedures and routines, and is able to produce appropriate behavior, successful penetration is possible. Criminals may use moving vans and enter through garage doors rather than windows, while other offenders may wave to store managers as bad checks are written. These crafty criminals arrive acting as friends. They may dress as security officers, police, firefighters, safety inspectors, maintenance technicians, etc. Presidential-aspirant George Wallace was shot by a man wearing a Wallace button.
- Despite access control policies and procedures, security personnel often look for actions, facial expressions, and so forth to indicate whether a person knows where he or she is going and that he or she belongs at the location.
- One trick used to gain unauthorized access is directing a question at someone who is legitimately entering an access point (to give the impression the parties are together). If people are usually harried at the location, an offender may try to walk at a brisk pace from the security officer's blind side—another method of crafty criminals.

Visitors

Company policies also require visitors to have proper identification. Examples of visitors are salespeople, repair personnel, delivery workers, and government officials. Typically, a security officer is the first person who greets visitors. Policies may require the security officer to obtain basic information from the visitors, such as name, employer, driver's license, and who on the premises is to be visited. This information can be recorded on a log and a multicopy visitor pass. The officer can telephone the employee to be visited to ensure the employee is available. Then a copy of the pass is given to visitors to display on their jacket. Also, a hard hat and safety glasses may have to be issued. When visitors depart, the pass and equipment are returned.

Package and Property Control

The movement of packages and property out of or into a facility should be subject to access controls. Security officers should remain alert to the many methods used by employees to smuggle company assets past a perimeter. A property pass system, as covered in the previous chapter, ensures accountability when company property is legitimately removed from the premises.

Depending on the location, screening for packaged bombs, letter bombs, bio-terrorism, and other hazards may also be required. Incoming mail and packages have become an increasingly serious threat over the years. Special equipment can play a role in screening and viewing the inside of mail.

Contraband Detection

Contraband is an item that is illegal to possess or prohibited from being brought into a specific area. Examples are weapons, illegal drugs, and explosives. Security officers play a crucial role in spotting contraband at airports, courthouses, schools, and many other locations. Besides performing physical searches of people and items, security officers use special devices to locate contraband and these expensive systems are as good as the personnel behind them. Here is an overview of these devices.

Metal detectors transmit a magnetic field that is disturbed by a metallic object that sets off a light or audio signal. Two types of metal detectors are handheld and walk-through. False alarms are a common problem. Figures 5-3 and 5-4 illustrate how offenders seek to circumvent access controls.

X-ray scanners use pulsed energy to penetrate objects that are shown on a color monitor. Drugs, plastic explosives, and firearms with plastic parts are difficult to identify with this method of detection.

Dual-energy systems use x-rays at different energy levels to classify objects as organic, inorganic, or mixed. Colors are assigned to each classification to help spot contraband. When color and shape are observed, these systems are good at detecting explosives since most are organic.

Figure 5-3 "Passback" of a weapon from someone outside the facility to a person who has already cleared the scanning process is a common defeat method. Courtesy: National Institute of Justice, *Appropriate and Effective Use of Security Technologies in U.S. Schools* (Washington, DC: U.S. Department of Justice, September 1999), p. 77.

Figure 5-4 Here, the scannee is attempting to influence the operator by claiming that the chain is causing the alarm, when, in actuality, there is a hidden weapon. Courtesy: National Institute of Justice, *Appropriate and Effective Use of Security Technologies in U.S. Schools* (Washington, DC: U.S. Department of Justice, September 1999), p. 91.

Computed tomography scanners are like CAT scanners used in hospitals. An x-ray source is spun around an object taking slice pictures that show on a computer. Although expensive, detection of items is good.

Searches

Fixed-post assignments, especially at access points, may require the searching of employees. Since this is a sensitive issue, security officers must follow company policies and procedures. See the previous chapter for guidance.

At a very few locations, depending on company needs and the product(s) produced, body searches may be required. As a security officer, never search a member of the opposite sex without having an additional person present. In other words, have a witness. Try to have a female search a female. Again, have a witness. Many companies require only searches of things carried by employees, such as lunch boxes, newspapers, and umbrellas. What if an employee refuses to be searched? Generally, it is best not to force a search on an employee. Record as much information as possible about the employee, such as name, ID number, and physical characteristics. Then, report the incident to your supervisor. Caution must always be exercised when an individual is confronted since they may believe their rights are being violated and a lawsuit can result.

It is important to distinguish between searches of people at access points and searches of suspected criminals following an arrest. If, for example, a security officer arrests a burglar on the premises who was caught in the act, the officer should exercise extreme caution and search for weapons and evidence. This subject is covered in a subsequent chapter on arrest procedures.

What If

As a Security Officer on Post in the Lobby of an Office Building, What Do You Do if You Spot an Employee Attempting to Leave the Building with Company Property?

Companies often have policies and procedures for employee removal of company property from the premises. A property pass is usually required and it describes the property to be removed, the person permitted to remove the property, and an authorized signature. E-mail is an alternative avenue to inform security.

Sometimes employees ignore this system of accountability and state a variety of excuses. Examples: "It is my property." "My boss is not available to sign the property pass." "I have an appointment and you are getting me angry." "My boss said it was OK, but did not issue me a property pass."

Security officers have a duty to protect company assets. First, make sure the item is indeed company property. If it is, explain company policy and request that the employee wait until you contact their supervisor or someone else who can approve the movement of the property. At the same time, record basic information such as the employee's name and a description of the item. CCTV systems often record lobby activity and the recording can serve to assist in the investigation. If the employee refuses to wait, let the employee go, then complete a report. Force must not be used to protect property. The employee could be committing a larceny by boldly and unexpectedly passing through the lobby and acting agitated to deceive the security officer. Your report will serve as a foundation for action by management.

Access Control for Vehicles

Companies vary as to the level of access control required for vehicles entering and leaving the premises. Many firms have a vehicle inspection system and provide a pass to drivers. When a truck arrives, it is stopped for inspection. Driver and truck identifying information are recorded. This information can include a driver's license number and tag number. The date and time are also recorded. A pass is issued to the driver who is to stop for inspection and return of the pass upon leaving the facility. When the vehicle is stopped on the way out, it should be checked to ensure that the contents match the shipping papers. Depending on company policy, various parts on the truck can be inspected to uncover unauthorized items. The officer can check the cab, engine, and underneath the vehicle. Before the truck departs, retrieve the vehicle pass from the driver and note the date and time of departure. Here again, the company policies and procedures will dictate the thoroughness of the search.

Certain companies conduct truck inspections at the loading dock. Two or more employees may count outgoing merchandise and then place a seal (metal clasp) on the locked truck doors. These seals are used only once and are then cut off. Each seal should have a serial number, recorded on shipping papers, to prevent another seal from being used after merchandise is stolen. As trucks are about to leave the premises, security officers should check to make sure seals are fully connected. One tactic of offenders is to not lock both ends of the seal together, though it may look like it is connected. Later, the truck is stopped, items are stolen, and then the seal is fully connected.

Security Patrols

Foot Patrol

Foot patrol by public police and private security has existed for many years. Dating before 1829 when Sir Robert Peel of London organized the first Metropolitan Police, foot patrols are still very much a part of policing and security. Foot patrol has advantages over other methods of patrol (e.g., motorized). It provides the best opportunity for observation within range of the senses and for close contact with people and things. Consequently, the officer is of maximum service as an information source and counselor. Whether a public police officer is walking through a neighborhood on an assigned beat or a private security officer is patrolling on the premises, foot patrol provides a basic crime prevention and protection function.

According to *Security Supervision*, "Patrols are necessary to insure the integrity of the overall security program. Frequent and total coverage of the protected area is needed to provide the most timely discovery and correction of security, safety and fire hazards."

Foot patrols can be assigned during the day when a facility is in full operation and after hours when no one but security personnel are present. Day assignments typically involve considerable contact with people. Thus, security officers should be especially alert to good public relations while on patrol. Foot patrols during the night often result in less interpersonal contact but more observation of a facility in an idle state. Security officers patrolling when a facility is idle must ensure that the area is secure from intrusion, that all doors and windows are locked, and that unusual conditions are reported. Businesses vary since a manufacturing plant may operate three shifts per day and rarely stop production.

As with all security assignments, foot patrol requires an officer to be alert at all times. A constant watchfulness must be maintained. Observe the "big picture" of an area before entering. Do you see anything out of the ordinary? Stop for a minute periodically to listen for unusual noises. Do you smell any toxic substances?

One major problem of foot patrol assignments is that security officers may become a *creature of habit*. If a criminal studies the daily routine of a security officer and can predict where the security officer will be at a specific time, such information helps the criminal to succeed. To counter this vulnerability, vary patrol patterns and double back periodically. Try to be inconsistent. If a criminal is watching you with binoculars, a telescope, or sophisticated night-vision equipment, an inconsistent patrol pattern will definitely frustrate his or her plans. And if you can appear where you are not expected and make a safe arrest, you have utilized your security training and crime prevention techniques successfully!

Foot patrol assignments vary. Officers patrol at such locations as industrial sites, shopping malls, office buildings, schools, hotels and motels, construction sites, parking lots, and sports events. The patrol duties, responsibilities, and techniques differ among these locations. For example, at shopping malls, officers often have to search for lost children or help with customer vehicle problems, such as keys locked in automobiles or dead batteries. Officers should be familiar with all stores and the times and locations of special activities. On the other hand, a construction site would require strict access controls and the prevention of vandalism and theft. Building materials, tools, and equipment at construction sites are popular consumer items. Once these items, especially building materials, leave the premises, it is difficult to prove ownership. When workers are leaving the construction site, and after hours, security officers should be more alert to theft. Obviously, access control at a construction site differs significantly from a shopping mall.

Vehicle Patrol

The use of a vehicle for patrol offers the advantage of being able to quickly cover a large area. However, because a security officer is traveling at a faster pace than on foot, the observation of activities may be less intense, and certain information may be harder to obtain. Also, deviations and hazards may be more difficult to spot. Vehicle patrol also has the disadvantage of engine noise and headlights that might warn criminals. However, a marked security vehicle with emergency lights and a spotlight can act to deter crime. Because of the advantages and disadvantages of foot and vehicle patrol, security officers often alternate between both.

GUIDELINES The following list provides some guidelines for vehicle patrol.

1. Before security officers accept an assignment for vehicle patrol, it is important that they possess a valid operator's license.
2. Prior to use, the patrol vehicle should be thoroughly checked for damage, missing equipment, and evidence or weapons left by an arrestee.
3. Safety must be a prime concern when operating a motor vehicle. Safe driving habits prevent accidents, injury, and liability.
4. As with foot patrols, vehicle patrols must not become routine and predictable.
5. Never keep the vehicle radio on high volume. This warns offenders.
6. Always close windows and lock doors when leaving a vehicle. Make a conscious effort to hold the keys in your hand before locking the doors.

Other Types of Patrol

Besides foot and vehicle patrol, other types of patrol are available for security personnel. A properly trained protective dog, controlled by a security officer, is an effective deterrent. This team is capable of thoroughly searching an area, and in less time compared with a group of security officers. Sensitive hearing, smell, and sight make a dog an excellent companion. Dogs can be trained to work alone in empty buildings and along perimeters. Crowd control is another use for dogs.

Horse patrols are beneficial for perimeters, parking lots, traffic control, crowds, and rough terrain. Mounted officers can be seen easily, and the size of the officer–horse team presents an awesome obstacle for an offender or a crowd. The care and cost of maintaining horses must be considered before purchase.

Additional forms of patrol include bicycle, motorcycle, boat, and air. The type of security problems and budget limitations are two primary considerations that determine patrol strategies.

Security Changes at Ace Manufacturing

For many years, the security department at Ace Manufacturing appeared to create more problems than it solved. The day shift consisted of plant employees who were too ill to work in production. These employees had developed heart problems and were assigned to the security department until retirement. The chief of security set a poor example and reinforced a lax security atmosphere. A bad image for security resulted from no training or motivation, sloppy uniforms, and antagonism between security officers and regular employees. When the plant remained idle on the second and third shifts, security officers were permitted to sleep in trucks or at the security office and not patrol the plant. Almost all second and third shift security officers had full-time day jobs separate from the plant.

Then, one day Ace Manufacturing was bought by a large corporation. The new management team immediately began questioning why so much money was spent on security. For the first few weeks after the purchase the security department operated as usual, except one new security officer was hired. By the second month, security in its present state was doomed. Only one security officer remained on the job. The chief and the other day shift security officers settled for an early retirement. All the second and third shift security officers were fired. The new security officer was actually the handpicked security manager who wanted to study security the way it was really operating. Contract security officers were brought in to fill the vacancies. The security manager emphasized the need for a quality security program that could contribute to the corporation and not waste resources.

What to Check When on Patrol

When on patrol check fences, lights, doors, windows, locks, and security equipment. It is possible to find doors unlocked that are supposed to be locked. Public police and private security, while "shaking doors," are sometimes surprised when they discover an unlocked front door to a business, such as a jewelry store. Merchants may simply forget to lockup as they leave through a rear exit.

Security officers on patrol should check for damaged or vandalized security equipment. Individuals have been known to paint the front lens of CCTV cameras and redirect or readjust motion detectors. At doors, one technique is to place a small rock at the bottom of a doorway. When the door is closed, it does not close completely, and therefore does not automatically lock.

Patrol both internal and external areas on the premises. The shipping and receiving dock and inventory storage areas are prime locations for theft. Parking lot patrols protect people and deter theft. Employees should be informed about leaving valuables in view in their vehicles and locking doors. Inspect in and near garbage dumpsters that are a favorite location where thieves hide stolen items before making a transfer to their vehicle.

Safety factors must also be checked. Are emergency exits blocked? Are fire and smoke alarms damaged? What is the condition of water sprinkler systems? Are fire extinguishers charged? What is the condition of chemical storage containers? Any unusual chemical odors? Are people smoking in areas that are designated as no smoking?

Never take anything for granted. A closed door does not mean that it is locked. Even a padlock may appear locked, but a good tug may force it open. A sprinkler system may have its water source turned off. Security officers should check for the unexpected and prove their value to the business by reporting unusual occurrences.

Improving Observation Skills

Security officers should keep a mental file of what to observe in critical situations. This is not a difficult process. For example, a crime has just occurred and you observe the offender's automobile departing. You have only a few seconds to observe the vehicle. What do you note? Most people would answer by stating the license number. This is very important. However, a crafty criminal may use a stolen car or stolen plates or apply colored tape to the plate to change numbers and letters. Other descriptive items are model, color, body style, and especially characteristics of occupants. Also note dents, customizing, and other features that make the vehicle different. This is vital for identification purposes.

To improve observation skills, first make a mental list of important items to note about vehicles. Then, while driving, practice on nearby vehicles.

The observation of people requires another mental file of characteristics to observe. The most important are gender, height, weight, age, race, and clothing. Several other characteristics helpful for positive identification are scars, teeth, hair, eyes, nose, ears, speech, manner of walking, tattoos, and personality. Because security officers encounter so many people, the skill of observing people can be practiced frequently. Magazines can also be used for practice. Look at a picture containing many items. Study it for a few minutes and then look away. Write down everything you observed. Then, look at the picture again to see what you missed.

Observation skills are useful in many situations. For example, as an officer patrols a building, numerous characteristics can be observed. This includes doors regularly kept open, number of computers in a room, timetable for janitorial duties, customary noises, and so forth. Observation of deviations from the norm must be investigated.

Make a mental or written note of unusual or suspicious situations. Examples include a person wearing excessive clothes in warm weather, someone asking about security methods, a person observing from a vehicle or circling a building, or someone on the premises or nearby with no legitimate purpose for being there.

Although report writing is covered in another chapter, an officer must remember to immediately write notes after observing an incident. Never rely on memory because too many mental distractions can cause anyone to forget important information.

What If

While on Patrol in a Company Parking Lot, What Do You Do if You Notice a Tow Truck Driver Making a Connection to an Employee Vehicle?

As you approach the tow truck you politely ask the driver if the car is having trouble. The driver's response is that an employee called his company for the car to be picked up and taken to the shop for repair. You ask for the name of the employee and the driver says, "Nancy Jackson." Your suspicion and imagination cause you to think about how you and the security department will be perceived if a car is stolen in the parking lot as you watched. Your next words to the driver are: "Please don't leave the lot with the car until I check with Ms. Jackson." You head to the security office while writing the license tag and description of the vehicle and driver. Within about two minutes you hear a loud roar from the tow truck as it departs quickly, without a car in tow. A call to Ms. Jackson supports your suspicion and imagination—she did not request the repair work and drives a car different from the one the tow truck driver was at. You contact your supervisor with the facts and complete a report.

It is the sharp security officer who knows that offenders are known to act boldly, sometimes under the watchful eyes of unsuspecting security officers and, further, with the assistance of unknowing security officers. If you become suspicious of someone, maintain a polite manner and ask questions to verify or dispel your theories. By maintaining a customer-friendly manner of questioning, you place yourself in a favorable position if you learn your suspicions are unfounded.

In this case perhaps the company and security force can pool their ideas on increasing protection in the parking lot. Should access controls be tighter? The tow truck could have been stopped at a gate to verify the repair request. Are "No Trespassing" signs posted? Do policies and procedures need refining?

Special Problems On Patrol

The activities that occur during patrol are varied. To a large extent, these activities depend on the particular situation. We will now discuss some of these situations, the activities that occur, and some suggestions to improve performance.

Traffic Duties

1. Generally, traffic on public streets is controlled by public police. On the other hand, traffic on private property is controlled by private security.

2. Before directing traffic, try to observe the flow of vehicles so the best possible plan can be implemented.

3. Always practice safe procedures. Some examples are to wear bright, reflective material; carry an extra flashlight and traffic wand (i.e., an orange plastic cone attached to the end of a flashlight); maintain a position where you can be seen by approaching vehicles; and keep alert.

4. Use a traffic whistle, if appropriate.

5. When walking into a busy area to direct traffic, stop all lanes, and then start fresh by allowing one set of opposite lanes to move.

6. Establish a timed pattern and allow all vehicles to move without excessive delay.

7. Exercise emotional control if certain drivers do not respond immediately to your commands. Stopping traffic to criticize a poor driver is not a wise decision.

Traffic Accidents

1. Traffic accidents occurring on public roadways must be investigated by public police.

2. On private property, state law and company policy dictate the action taken by security officers.

3. States require public police to be notified if a traffic accident causes death, injury, or damage beyond a certain amount.

4. After an accident on private property, a security officer should park safely, summon medical assistance and tow trucks if necessary, control traffic, interview those involved and witnesses, and complete a report.

5. If private security officers are to complete thorough traffic accident investigations on the premises, company management should support appropriate training on topics such as interviewing skills, photography, the analysis of skid marks, and report writing.

6. State law and company policy will determine if security officers will write traffic citations. Some businesses use their own citations while others may have special permission to use state-issued citations payable to the local government.

7. When issuing a citation, security officers should not block traffic; radio-in license, vehicle information, and location; maintain courtesy; and, above all, approach the vehicle cautiously. Proper training for traffic stops is essential.

Field Contacts

1. The first few seconds after a security officer approaches a person are critical in order to establish a professional and polite tone.

2. Safety should be a prime consideration. Keep at least one arm's distance from the person.

3. Always attempt the polite, reasoned approach first, before having to resort to being stern.

4. Notes should be recorded on the field contact for future reference.

5. Since all contacts are different, a good security officer will develop a range of skills to rely on for cooperative and uncooperative individuals.

Crimes in Progress

1. A crime in progress becomes a big test for a security officer. When it occurs, it is too late to go back and obtain more training or develop additional skills. At this point there may be no time to even check your equipment.

2. Caution must be a dominant thought in a security officer's mind. Strive for the safety of yourself and others.

3. Obtain as much information as possible when notified of a crime in progress. Where is the offender? Is he or she armed? Any injuries? Were public police notified?

4. Approach the scene cautiously but do not enter the scene until the situation has been carefully studied. Note people leaving and those inside.

5. If people have their hands up or they are not moving, obviously the crime may still be in progress. For safety, do not rush into the crime scene.

6. Remain at a distance in a defensive position and observe. Prepare for the suspect to depart. By waiting for the suspect to depart, victims are safer than if the security officer went into the scene and forced a shoot-out.

7. Watch for an unseen suspect or a bystander who is really a suspect.

8. Communicate with responding police officers about the crime in progress. Tell them the location of the suspect, weapons involved, and your location.

9. When security officers are not armed, let public police take action.

10. When the offender departs, armed security officers and public police, from a defensive position, should order the offender to drop his or weapon and surrender. Deadly force may be the only alternative if life is threatened.

11. If the offender takes a hostage, remain in a defensive position and keep the offender talking.

12. Do not give up your weapon or exchange yourself for the hostage. Such action adds to the problem. Keep the offender talking and stall for time. Additional responding police will help prevent escape.

Protecting a Crime Scene

1. Criminals often leave identifying items at a crime scene that tie them to the crime. Examples include fingerprints, DNA, clothes, and tools. They also take evidence with them. Examples are DNA from a victim or stolen merchandise.

2. Security officers who first arrive at a crime scene should be alert for the suspect(s), tend to the injured, and then protect the area to prevent the contamination, destruction, or theft of evidence.

3. A physical barrier or crime scene tape can be used to keep out unauthorized people.

4. People walking on the crime scene and adverse weather can destroy valuable evidence.

5. Public police should be notified as soon as possible after a crime so an investigation can be conducted and the offender can be arrested.

6. Accountability of evidence, before it reaches a court, can have a serious impact on a case. The "chain of possession" must be controlled. Investigators typically photograph, videotape, and sketch the scene and properly label, package, and store evidence. These procedures support a case when the following questions are asked in court:

   a. Precisely where was the evidence located?

   b. Who touched it first?

   c. How was it stored?

   d. Who had access to it?

Additional Guidelines for Security Officers

1. Always report to work in a clean, pressed uniform with appropriate equipment. Before you leave for work, check again in a mirror.

2. Arrive at work a few minutes early to prevent poor relations with those who are relieved. Also, this additional time allows you to collect information on earlier events and activities.

3. Avoid smoking when on patrol. There is the danger of fire or explosion from fumes. Furthermore, smoke may let a criminal know your location. A glowing cigarette at your mouth provides a target to the head in a dark area. Using after-shave lotion or perfume is another way in which your location can be exposed.

4. When entering an area where someone may be hiding, turn your portable radio off after notifying the dispatcher. Or turn it to the lowest possible volume. This will also prevent your position from being exposed to an offender.

5. Some security officers can be heard walking from a considerable distance. Each security officer can check by walking in a quiet area. Some items can possibly be removed, such as excessive keys or squeaky shoes.

6. At night, cover or remove reflective objects on your uniform that may expose your position.

7. In dangerous or hazardous situations, such as confronting a hostile person, always call for backup.

8. Always maintain a mental note of your position in case you have to call for assistance.

9. Security officers should be in good physical condition. Physical fitness is important for good health. It also makes an officer more fit for the job.

10. When confronted by an aggressive adversary, security officers should act *defensively* to protect themselves and others.

11. Security work may at times result in fear. Those who have confronted an armed criminal, or patrolled alone in a desolate building when conditions did not seem right, know of fearful times. A security officer should exercise sound judgment supported by quality training and/or self-study to deal with these events. There is nothing wrong when a security officer is fearful and admits it during and after such

occurrences. Talking with a friend after the event helps to alleviate some of the stress.

12. Always maintain a positive attitude about learning from others. Many aspects of patrol can be learned from experienced security officers.

13. Keep alert to tricks. One criminal, while working with another, may try to distract you. Smart criminals may string thread across a road or hallway to check on your patrol patterns. Invisible powder (visible with a "black light") or flour may be used for the same purpose and placed on floors or door knobs. Security officers can use these same techniques to check if an intruder is lurking about or following behind.

14. Security officers may be subject to integrity testing where an investigator, acting as an offender, asks an on-duty officer to look the other way for $100 so some merchandise can be removed.

15. Penetration attempts are another test for security officers. A company ID badge with a picture of Porky Pig may be used by an undercover investigator to see if a security officer is thorough rather than haphazard when access is attempted. In a more daring test, requiring extreme caution, an investigator penetrates a perimeter and tampers with doors, windows, and so forth to see if the security officer notices the problems.

CHAPTER REVIEW

A. Multiple Choice

1. When on patrol and walking into a dark area known to contain an intruder, you should hold your flashlight
   a. straight up to ensure dim light.
   b. away from your body.
   c. in front of your eyes for maximum sight.
   d. with your hat covering the light to prevent glare.
2. Which of the following is least likely to be a location for a fixed or stationary post?
   a. gate
   b. lobby
   c. along a perimeter
   d. at a control center
3. The best reason for color-coded ID cards is they
   a. show security personnel who is working undercover.
   b. indicate nationality.
   c. signify rank and salary in an organization.
   d. signify what areas cardholders can access.
4. When on patrol security officers should
   a. avoid smoking.
   b. lower the volume on their radio.
   c. always know their position in case of emergency.
   d. all of the above.
5. Which of the following statements is not correct.
   a. Equipment for traffic duty includes reflective clothing, flashlights, and a whistle.
   b. Security officers are responsible for investigating traffic accidents on public roads near the premises.
   c. During a hostage situation, do not give up your weapon or exchange yourself for the hostage.
   d. Upon arriving first at a crime scene, a security officer should be alert for the suspect(s), tend to the injured, and then protect the scene so evidence is not destroyed.

B. *True or False*

1. Another name for fixed post is stationary post.
2. As a security officer on duty, if an individual shows up and wants to gain access, but forgot their ID card, you should let them in after asking for their name.
3. Almost all states authorize security officers to conduct thorough searches of employees as they leave the workplace and make arrests for refusals to be searched.
4. One major problem of foot patrol assignments is that security officers may become creatures of habit.
5. A security officer should write notes after observing a critical incident, rather than relying on memory.

Applications

Application 5A

As a security officer, how would you prioritize the following items upon reaching the scene of an assault in the parking lot at the facility where you are employed?

- a witness to the assault wants to talk to you
- a person is scaling the perimeter fence to exit the parking lot
- an employee approaches you for help because he locked his keys in his car
- you receive a radio transmission from your supervisor who wants to meet with you immediately
- the victim is down and bleeding
- you must complete an incident report for this case
- a car alarm has been activated

Application 5B

List five precautions, in general, for security officers. Prioritize the list. In small groups, debate and then formulate one prioritized list. Have each group share their list with the class and then have the entire class formulate a prioritized list acceptable to everybody.

Application 5C

Role-play an incident where an employee appears at work without an ID card and argues with a security officer to permit access even though the facility has a strict policy prohibiting access without an ID.

6

Communications and Report Writing

CHAPTER OUTLINE

OBJECTIVES

After studying this chapter, you will be able to:

- List quality telephone skills.
- List quality interviewing skills.
- Explain the importance of using senses.
- Explain the importance of gathering evidence.
- List the reasons why report writing is important.
- List and explain the six questions that are the foundation of report writing.

- Describe at least ten guidelines to improve skills for taking notes.
- Describe at least eight techniques and characteristics of quality reports.
- Describe at least two types of reports.
- Complete an incident report.

Communications

Communication skills, such as speaking on the telephone, interviewing, and writing reports, are the foundation of many professional positions. A major part of a security officer's job is to *observe* and *report* (i.e., communicate) events including crimes, unsafe conditions, fire hazards, and violations of policies and procedures. *The overall purpose of such reporting is to protect people and assets.* Observation skills were covered in the previous chapter as an important part of post assignments and security patrols. Once security officers use their senses to learn of significant events, it is their duty to communicate facts to a control center or supervisor. Good communications skills are essential, not only to collect information, but also to send the information, either verbally or in the form of a written report. Collecting information can result from a telephone conversation, an interview, or through observations at the scene of a loss.

Telephone Skills

We have all had experiences of being treated rudely on the telephone by a representative of an organization. The unfortunate result is that the rude person did not serve as a positive link between the organization and a customer or potential customer. Furthermore, a customer who is treated rudely may share the negative experience with others. Positive customer interaction increases business and strengthens job security. Here are tips for improving telephone skills:

- Answer the telephone promptly as a professional: "Officer Smith, can I help you?"
- Always maintain a courteous manner, even when speaking with a rude customer.
- Never argue; remain calm. Be aware of the tone of your voice and what you are saying.
- Speak slowly and clearly. This will help the customer and provide you with extra time to think before you speak.
- Seek to *help* the caller by offering information and/or guidance.
- Show genuine concern.
- When receiving information from a caller, repeat the information back to the caller to avoid errors.

Interviewing Skills

A security officer may be assigned to gather facts and evidence for a report. Victims, witnesses, suspects, and informants are prime sources of information. They should be asked the six basic investigative questions (Who? What happened? Where? When? How? Why?) explained in subsequent pages. The following list provides guidelines to interview people when gathering information and evidence.

1. Identify yourself.
2. Maintain good public relations by being polite.
3. Maintain eye contact.
4. Try to obtain the names, addresses, and telephone numbers of all interviewees.
5. Repeat statements and numbers to a source, such as a witness, while you are recording. This strengthens the accuracy of information.
6. Avoid yes/no questions. Ask open-ended questions to elicit lengthy answers. Example: "What happened next?"
7. Keep an open mind. For instance, people reporting or involved in an accident may have ulterior motives. A worker may claim to have been injured on the job. However, the injury actually occurred at home prior to arriving at work.
8. Listen closely and maintain attention. Do not interrupt the interviewee or jump to conclusions.
9. Record slips of the tongue.
10. Watch for nervousness.
11. Maintain control of the interview.
12. Carefully study hearsay (statements by one person as to what another told him or her).
13. Remember that the interviewee may not be truthful or may exaggerate the facts.
14. Test honesty by asking questions for which you know the answers.
15. If possible, ask the same questions to several people and compare results.
16. If necessary, use silence and eye contact to possibly make the interviewee feel uncomfortable and thereby make more statements.
17. A witness may be hesitant to talk to protect himself or herself or others.
18. Never question someone of the opposite sex in privacy. Have a person of the same sex present.

19. If a witness refuses to help, ask for their assistance and appeal to their sense of duty to help. Witnesses cannot be forced to cooperate or be held until public police arrive.

Using Senses and Gathering Evidence

Using Senses

Security officers should use all five senses when collecting information for a report. These senses include sight, hearing, smell, touch, and taste. Upon arriving at a scene, a security officer may see something odd, such as damage to an alarm system. The scene of an accident can produce all sorts of unusual noises, such as the whining of a motor, the sound of escaping steam, or faint cries for help. The sense of smell is important to report a dangerous leak of toxic chemicals, or at a crime scene, the smell of alcohol or other drug. A victim initially thought to be dead would have to be touched to find a pulse. A vehicle can be touched near the engine to find out if it is warm, hot, or cold to signify when it was used. Foul substances in the air can result in an unpleasant taste. Security officers should refrain from tasting substances thought to be drugs (as seen on TV and the movies) since a minute amount of certain substances can be fatal.

Sometimes we hear about a sixth sense. According to John Coleman in his book *Practical Knowledge for a Private Security Officer,* "This sixth sense is not as obvious as the other five but the officer's perception or conclusion, based on his experience, knowledge, and the utilization of the other senses, must be given consideration as a viable information gathering source."

After several years of experience, an individual may develop a sixth sense that can help to gather evidence and solve cases. Basically, several factors concerning an incident are analyzed to produce a conclusion that causes an experienced security officer to become suspicious. For example, after interviewing several witnesses to a crime, an officer becomes suspicious when each witness produces a similar story. Usually witnesses have slightly different stories about what they observed. Another example is when a security officer enters a shipping and receiving dock and notices that the location is unusually quiet, that workers avoid eye contact with the officer, and the customary horseplay and chatter is gone. Since no criminal activity has been observed, the security officer may decide to patrol that area more frequently and contact a supervisor. Theft, illegal drug usage, and gambling are some of the possible activities occurring. However, since no illegal acts were observed, no action should be taken.

Gathering Evidence

The scene of a loss requires protection from unauthorized people who may destroy, alter, or steal evidence. The previous chapter outlines how to protect a crime scene.

This protection is especially important in serious situations where an investigator is to conduct a thorough inquiry. An investigator looks for fingerprints and other clues to solve a crime. Equipment is usually examined after an accident to determine the reason for the accident. Interviews, photographs, videotaping, and sketches are part of the inquiry as information and facts are gathered.

The information gathered for a report may become evidence in a court of law. Evidence is basically used to prove a fact. Two major types of evidence are *testimony* by a victim or witness, and *physical evidence*, such as a weapon with an offender's fingerprints on it. Physical evidence can consist of almost anything, since an offender who was at the crime scene probably left something unique. It is the job of security personnel and police personnel to find these clues. One example is when a burglar uses a screwdriver to pry a door to enter a business. Sometimes, the screwdriver breaks and the tip remains embedded in the door. If the tip is found and matched with a screwdriver found on the suspect after a lawful arrest, this links the suspect to the crime scene and assists with the prosecution of the case. Many more cases are solved when a victim or witness comes forth prepared to testify, rather than from physical evidence.

Modus operandi, or *MO*, is another avenue to solve crimes. It means method of operation, or the particular way an offender commits a crime. If a rash of auto break-ins is occurring in a company parking lot and each auto has been entered by breaking the driver's side window, then it is possible that the same offender may be involved in all the cases. Offender MOs vary in terms of victim selected, tools, and so forth. The point is that something or several characteristics are unique to the offender. Many police departments maintain MO files and use computers and special software to enhance this investigative strategy. After a crime occurs, these files are checked for suspects whose MO matches that which was evident at the crime in question.

Report Writing

Importance of Report Writing

Study the following list. An understanding of these points can have an impact on a security officer's career.

1. Report writing reflects on a security officer's communications abilities.
2. Supervisors get to know their subordinates through reports.
3. Performance evaluations are partially based on the quality of report writing by subordinates.
4. Many supervisors consider report writing a major factor in promotions.

5. Security and loss prevention managers use individual reports and summations of many reports to study loss trends and to plan and budget.

6. In many cases, a sole security officer may be the first person to respond after a serious event, such as an accident. In certain instances, the security officer may be a witness. All concerned parties will look to the security officer for facts and a report (Figure 6-1).

7. Once a report is prepared, it may serve as a reference for the security officer, supervisors, managers, public police, or those involved in criminal and civil proceedings.

8. The value of a quality report is illustrated when, at a later date, the security officer has to testify about its contents in court.

9. The value of quality reports is illustrated when an analysis of several reports produces a suspect in a series of crimes or reveals a serious safety hazard that can be corrected.

Figure 6-1 Report writing is an essential part of security officer duties. Courtesy: Wackenhut, Inc.

Where Report Writing Begins

Six basic questions are the foundation of taking notes and report writing. When security officers arrive at the scene of an incident, they should seek answers to the following questions. A standard form prepared by the company usually contains these questions.

1. *Who?*
   a. Who contacted security about the incident?
   b. Who are the individuals involved?
   c. Who are the victims?
   d. Who are the witnesses?
   e. Who are the suspects?
   f. Who will sign the complaint?
   g. Names, addresses, telephone numbers, and other identifying information are important.

2. *What happened?*
   a. What is the whole story of the incident?
   b. What happened before, during, and after the incident?
   c. What actions were taken by all those involved?
   d. What was stated by each individual?
   e. What evidence was collected?
   f. What authorities were contacted after the incident?

3. *Where?*
   a. Where did the incident occur?
   b. Where were all the individuals before, during, and after the incident?
   c. Where was evidence found?

4. *When?*
   a. When did the incident occur?
   b. When was it discovered?
   c. When was it reported?
   d. When did authorities arrive at the scene?
   e. When was an arrest made?

5. *How?*
   a. How did the loss occur?
   b. How was it discovered?
   c. How did security and loss prevention strategies function?

    d. How expensive was the loss?

    e. How can the loss be prevented in the future?

6. *Why?*

    a. Why did the loss take place?

    b. Why was the crime committed?

    c. Why did the parties involved act the way they did?

Naturally, many other questions may be asked during an inquiry. However, the above six questions are universally accepted in the private and public sectors as a beginning point to record the facts after a critical incident.

It is important to point out that not all questions asked will produce complete and accurate answers. Several reasons can be given as to why this happens. A victim or a witness may be reluctant to speak, the parties involved may hide the truth, or ulterior motives may obscure the facts.

The "why" question is particularly difficult to answer, even though it helps establish a motive. In one case, security personnel at a manufacturing plant were trying to discover why vandalism was increasing in the company cafeteria. Finally, investigators narrowed the culprit to the expensive, bland food served at the cafeteria, which seemed to be an indirect cause of the problem. Soon after, the food service contractor was changed and the vandalism stopped. In another case, security officers tried to answer why two forklifts collided, resulting in injuries and damage. Persistent questioning revealed the forklift drivers were playing "chicken" while workers bet on the contest.

Private Security Investigations

The topics of this chapter on report writing are actually at the foundation of investigations. For example, when we speak of the "six basic questions" for reports, these same questions are at the heart of all investigations. Once security officers have mastered the basics of gathering facts after an incident, they should seek out specialized information from other publications, training programs, and experienced investigators. And, as security officers gain experience and knowledge, they may have an opportunity to apply for an investigative position. Here, an overview of private security investigations is presented.

Many types of investigations are conducted in the private sector as well as the public sector. Businesses and institutions require investigations of crimes, accidents, fire/arson, job applicants, civil cases, and loss of proprietary information, among others. Public police concentrate their investigations on crimes such as murder, rape, burglary, robbery, larceny, and so forth.

continued

Each type of investigation can become very specialized. The methods used by criminals and techniques of investigation vary. These topics are learned through experience and study over time. In large organizations, individuals frequently specialize in one or two types of investigations and develop their expertise. In smaller organizations, an investigator must be a "jack-of-all-trades," in other words, knowledgeable of several types of investigations.

Private sector investigations can be divided into proprietary and contract. Proprietary investigations are in-house. For example, a corporation hires a full-time investigator to conduct investigations for itself. Contract investigative businesses supply investigative services to those companies who do not want to hire a full-time in-house investigator.

Another way in which private investigations can be divided is overt and undercover. Overt (open) investigations are characterized by an investigator responding to the scene of a loss and gathering facts. An undercover investigation is secret. The investigator, under a false background, infiltrates employee informal groups and gathers facts. In the internal theft chapter of this book we will learn that undercover investigations can play a crucial role in uncovering employee theft rings. Both overt and undercover investigations are used extensively in the private and public sectors.

Improvement of Skills to Take Notes

As a security officer, if you arrive at the scene of a loss, one of the first objectives after providing for the safety of people and assets is to begin recording facts. A pocket notebook is useful to write the basic facts. Later, at a quiet time, a company standard report can be completed with the help of the earlier notes.

The following guidelines provide useful tips to improve your skills for taking notes.

1. Always carry at least one pen and one pencil. If one is broken, the other will be available. A small pocketknife can be carried to sharpen the pencil. Extremes in temperature or unusual surfaces can affect writing implements. Notes written in pen, rather than pencil, are more acceptable in court.

2. A small, loose-leaf notebook capable of fitting into a pocket is best. This is an essential item.

3. It is not recommended that a security officer rely on memory as the major source of information to complete a subsequent report. When an emergency occurs, many activities are quickly taking place. Therefore, facts can easily be forgotten or distorted.

4. When notes are taken while an event is occurring, or soon afterwards, accuracy is enhanced.

5. Witnesses, victims, and offenders may change their story or cite inaccurate information at a later date. The security officer's notebook can play an important role in refreshing memory and/or refuting erroneous testimony.

6. Notes on a loss event should be written in chronological order. In other words, what happened before, during, and after the event.

7. Use abbreviations and symbols to note as many important details as possible, especially if time is limited. Later, when preparing the final report, avoid abbreviations and provide complete information.

8. Concentrate on the main events of an incident.

9. Diagrams, specific measurements, photographs, and videotaping may be required in certain cases.

10. Security officers should keep in mind that a notebook and its contents may be questioned in court if a case goes to trial.

11. Since court cases can take many years to resolve in our system of justice, notes and records should be saved for several years.

12. Provide proper protection for notebooks to prevent loss or alteration of information.

Quality Reports

TECHNIQUES Facts recorded in a notebook after an incident prove to be valuable during the writing of a report. A good place to begin the report is to *develop a rough outline* (list the main points) so facts can be presented in logical order. This helps to *organize* a report in a *narrative style* (the story of the events) with a *chronological sequence* (according to time) of events. For example, the suspect was first seen at 8:00 P.M. across the street from the main gate. At 8:15 P.M. the suspect was observed and apprehended while trying to cut through the perimeter fence 50 feet north of Third Street on Lake Avenue.

Ronald Woodruff, in his book *Industrial Security Techniques*, states:

> *Narrative reporting should always be written in terms of the third person, i.e., "this officer" rather than "I," or "the suspect" rather than "he." This method of writing promotes a more impersonal, business-like air.*
>
> *When referring to persons in the report, they should be identified as to their involvement with the incident, such as "subject #1" and "subject #2" or "victim was found in," and so on. Obviously, the complete names of the persons involved should appear on the report, but they should be indexed to a descriptive term.*

CHARACTERISTICS Reports must be *factual* and *accurate*, since future decisions may be based on their content. A lawsuit may follow. Since this possibility exists, personal opinions should *not* be incorporated into reports.

Reports should be *concise.* Use short sentences and common words. Get to the point with facts. Eliminate unnecessary words, phrases, and sentences.

Complete reports contain as many important details as possible. Include additional background information that may be helpful to a supervisor or investigator. A standard report form prepared by management assists security officers in remembering to ask appropriate questions. A standard form can be used as a guide while asking questions and taking notes at the scene. Later, the quickly written notes can be neatly printed on a fresh report form.

Editing of a report should be accomplished before the final draft is prepared. This involves deleting or relocating certain words or sentences, or making additions to improve the report. Look for misspelled words, awkward sentences, and unnecessary repetitions of words. As the report is proofed for errors, use a dictionary.

A *neat* report reflects on the security officer. The report should look good. Neat penmanship is important, as well as an absence of wrinkles in the paper, food or liquid stains, and dirt. If possible the report should be typed, otherwise print neatly.

A *timely* report is submitted when due. Usually, incident reports are required at the end of the shift. Reports submitted on time reflect on the security officer. Furthermore, when a report is prepared as soon as possible, the facts are fresh in your mind.

What If?

As a Security Supervisor, What Do You Do if You Supervise an Officer Who Writes Substandard Reports?

You supervise Security Officer Frank Parks who is a good officer overall, except that he writes awful reports. His reports are sloppy, difficult to read and understand, contain many misspelled words, and are often returned to him for clarification. His blunders in reports include the following: "The woman caused the loss because her newborn son was branded as illiterate." In another report: "The sick employee was honestly in bed with the doctor for two weeks even though he gave her no relief." The latter blunder was read in court by a plaintiff's attorney in a negligent security case against the company. On several occasions you explained to Officer Parks the importance of quality reports. Still, he continues his awful reports. What are your options?

Since the poor reports are a recurring problem and you have given several verbal warnings, assign a competent officer to work with Officer Parks on his reports. Require Officer Parks to go through the competent officer for a review of all reports before they reach you. Suggest to Officer Parks to take a report writing course. Place these items in writing to Officer Parks, with a copy to your supervisor. Include a warning that improvements in report writing will avert disciplinary action.

Types of Reports

The reports used by security personnel vary among organizations. Computers and special software have enhanced the capabilities and benefits of reports. Although each company has different needs, the following is a brief discussion of some typical reports.

DAILY REPORTS Many security officers complete a *daily report* to describe the activities they encountered during their shift, Figure 6-2. Although much of the information may appear minor, it can become valuable at a later date. Supervisors and managers use these reports to evaluate existing conditions (e.g., hazards) and the activities of the security officer on duty.

DAILY LOGS A *daily log* describes the activities at a particular post, Figure 6-3. The log consists of a ledger where entries are made in pen to be used as a permanent record. Examples of activities include people and vehicles entering and leaving through an access point. These records can be helpful during investigations.

INCIDENT REPORTS *Incident reports* enable security officers to record basic questions (Who? What happened? Where? When? How? Why?) concerning a crime, fire, accident, or other incident, Figure 6-4. Much information is recorded in incident reports because of the serious nature of loss events. Supervisors, managers, top executives, government personnel, and insurance representatives are some of the many people who may review incident reports. They are interested in as much information as possible to evaluate loss events.

OTHER REPORTS In addition to these three major reports, a host of other reports or papers may be used to increase the effectiveness of security. For example, a daily truck report is helpful to register trucks entering and leaving the premises. Also, visitor passes help to maintain accountability of temporary visitors. Property passes provide an authorization and description of property to be removed from the premises.

Corporate Security Department

Daily Report

Officer's Name: _____   Date : _____

Badge No.: _____   Day: _____

Post: _____   Shift: _____

Relieved By: _____

Badge No.: _____

Name the Keys and Equipment Received During Shift Change: _____

_____

_____

_____

Changes in Special Orders: _____

_____

_____

_____

Unusual Occurrences During Shift: _____

_____

_____

_____

Post Inspected By: _____ Time: _____

Time Officer Left Post: _____

Signature of Officer Completing Report: _____

Figure 6-2 Daily Report.

Corporate Security Department
Daily Log

Date	Time	Signature of Person Granted Access	Initials of Security Officer	Signature of Person Departing	Time Departing	Initials of Security Officer

Figure 6-3   Daily Log.

Corporate Security Department

Incident Report

Report #: _____

Type of Incident: _____

Date of Incident: _____ Location: _____ Time: _____

Date Reported: _____ Time: _____

Reported by Whom: _____ Telephone #: _____
Address : _____
_____

Victim's Name: _____ Telephone #: _____
Address : _____
_____

Narrative (Answer: Who? What Happened? Where? When? How? Why?): _____

_____

_____

_____

_____

_____

_____

_____

Date of Report: _____ Report Prepared by: _____
Badge #: _____

Report Reviewed by: _____

Figure 6-4 Incident Report.

CHAPTER REVIEW

1. Explain the importance of communications.
2. Explain how using senses and gathering evidence relate to report writing.
3. Explain four reasons that illustrate the importance of report writing.
4. List the six basic questions helpful when taking notes and preparing a report.
5. Explain four tips useful to improve skills for taking notes.
6. Describe four techniques for writing quality reports.
7. List and describe the three major types of security reports.

Applications

Application 6A

Study Incident Report A, Figure 6-5. Locate errors, questionable information, and areas that need to be improved. Formulate a list and explain the problem areas.

Application 6B

Use a copy of Incident Report B, Figure 6-7, to write a report based on the notes from your notebook, Figure 6-6.

Corporate Security Department

Incident Report A

Report #: _472_

Type of Incident: _domestik_

Date of Incident: _2-11-01_   Location: _Howard Ave. Parking Lot_   Time: _8 o'clock_

Date Reported: _2-10-01_   Time: _2 o'clock_

Reported by Whom: _J. West_   Telephone #: _728341_

Address : _Dept 14 Apt. 14_
         _S. 1st St._

Victim's Name: _Leslee West_   Telephone #: _342-7117_

Address : _38 Hobart St._

Narrative (Answer: Who? What Happened? Where? When? How? Why?): _This officer responded to scene at 4 o'clock to find West victim of robery. Clothes were torn. Scratches on face. West said that $20. was missing from pants pocket. West said criminal was a short white person w/a new beard long har, blue eyes, and small scar over eye from a nife. He was wearing a red T-shirt with "Nicks" on it & number 46. Also wearing wite basket shoes (size 12), wite sox and blue pants. The age is 21 1/2 years._

Date of Report: _2-10-01_   Report Prepared by: _Collins_

Badge #: _472_

Report Reviewed by: _____

Figure 6-5   Incident Report A.

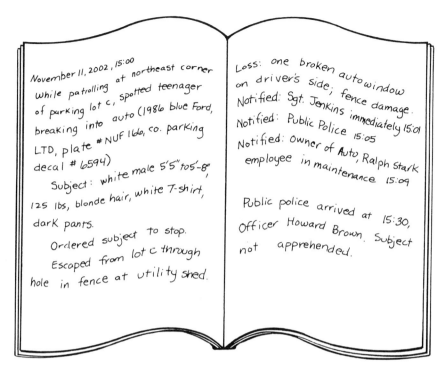

Figure 6-6 Notes.

Application 6C

Print the correct spelling to the right of each word. (Note: These words are sometimes misspelled on security and police reports. Imagine yourself a supervisor reading a report from a subordinate and trying to figure out these words.)

Misspelled Word	Correct Word
a. fellaknee	a.
b. viktim	b.
c. asalt	c.
d. robary	d.
e. guvanile dalinkwent	e.
f. sakurity	f.
g. misdameaner	g.
h. domestick	h.
i. marawanna	i.
j. krimical	j.

Corporate Security Department

Incident Report B

Report #: _____

Type of Incident: _____

Date of Incident: _____ Location: _____ Time: _____

Date Reported: _____ Time: _____

Reported by Whom: _____ Telephone #: _____
Address : _____
_____

Victim's Name: _____ Telephone #: _____
Address : _____
_____

Narrative (Answer: Who? What Happened? Where? When? How? Why?): _____

_____

_____

_____

_____

_____

_____

_____

_____

Date of Report: _____ Report Prepared by: _____
Badge #: _____
Report Reviewed by: _____

Figure 6-7   Incident Report B.

Application 6D

Role-play an incident. Have everyone in class complete an incident report. Compare reports.

7

Criminal and Civil Law

OBJECTIVES

After studying this chapter, you will be able to:

- Explain the differences between criminal law and civil law.
- List and explain the four ways criminal offenses are classified based on actions.
- Name and define at least two crimes against property and two crimes against the person.
- Describe the five groups of officials and their responsibilities in the criminal justice system.
- List and explain criminal justice system procedures.
- Name and define at least four torts.
- Explain whether a security officer who makes a mistake when taking legal action can be arrested and sued.
- Explain civil procedures before trial and during trial.
- Describe how the justice system controls private security and public police.
- List and explain at least three amendments to the Bill of Rights.

Introduction

A basic understanding of criminal and civil law is an asset to all security officers. This knowledge provides direction when deciding to take legal action, such as making an arrest. With quality training and a good knowledge of law, there is a greater chance that a security officer will make the best possible decision under the circumstances. This chapter is an introduction to criminal and civil law on which you can build to guide your actions as a professional security officer. Without this knowledge, the chances increase that a security officer will make a legal mistake and subject himself or herself to civil and criminal action. The next chapter will expand on this topic and provide information on how to make legal arrests while preventing errors.

English Heritage

The American legal system and the legal system of other English-speaking countries evolved from England. As the American colonies were being formed, the *common law* of England provided standards for such crimes as murder and larceny and for matters such as contracts, the ownership of property, and the payment of claims for personal injury.

Common law is based on community customs and is actually judge-made law or case law developed over many years. After numerous judges decided the same legal question in a similar way, the decision became law. The English common law method called *stare decisis* (i.e., let the previous decision stand) was adopted in America. It means that the court determines the law in a case by following the standard (i.e., precedent) set in previous cases that were factually similar. The states and the federal government have codified much of the old common law into statutes and penal codes.

Differences Between Criminal and Civil Law

Figure 7-1 shows many differences between criminal law and civil law. Basically, *civil law* involves disputes among persons, businesses, and government. *Criminal law* involves crimes against society.

Criminal Law

Defined by Actions

Congress and state legislatures specify what actions are to be defined in the criminal law. Federal and individual state statutes vary as to specific definitions for crimes and penalties. There are four ways that criminal offenses are often classified. These classifications are defined by actions, Table 7.1.

When going from one state to another state, criminal law is likely to differ. The crime of larceny serves as a good illustration. Basically, larceny refers to taking and carrying away the personal property of another without permission. Larceny is divided into grand larceny and petty larceny. The amount dividing the two depends on the state where the crime takes place. It may

Table. 7-1 Types of Criminal Offenses

Types of crime	Definition	Examples
capital crime	most serious crime resulting in death sentence	murder
felonies	serious crimes often punishable by one year or longer in prison	robbery, burglary, grand larceny, arson
misdemeanors	less serious crimes often punishable by less than one year	public drunkenness, disorderly conduct, trespassing, petty larceny, shoplifting
infractions (or violations)	least serious offenses, typically resulting in a fine	traffic offenses

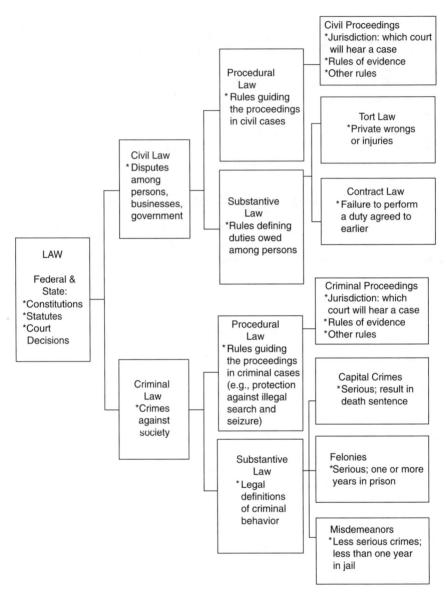

Figure 7-1 Criminal and civil law.

be $200, $250, or higher. For example, if you are a security officer in a state where the dividing amount is $200 and an item stolen is valued at $350, then the suspect you apprehend would be charged with grand larceny. If the item stolen was really valued at $50 and you overestimated the amount, then the suspect would not be charged correctly.

States also vary on the arrest powers granted to security officers. *Most states specify that private security officers will have only citizen arrest powers.* Simply, officers can arrest only for felonies. Other states may grant greater arrest powers. For instance, in South Carolina, security officers have arrest powers equal to the public police on the protected property.

For example, suppose you are a security officer in a state granting only felony arrest powers to security personnel. If you misjudge the value of a stolen item and make an arrest for grand larceny (a felony), when in fact the crime is really petty larceny (a misdemeanor), then the arrest would be in jeopardy. The preceding examples of larceny and arrest powers illustrate why a knowledge of law is vital.

Crimes Against Property and Crimes Against the Person

Another way crimes can be classified is to distinguish between "crimes against property" and "crimes against the person." We will define in general terms common crimes in these two categories. Remember that criminal law varies among the states and federal system.

CRIMES AGAINST PROPERTY *Burglary* is a break-in of a dwelling or building at night for the purpose of carrying out a felony or theft. In certain states, a "break-in" or a "night requirement" may not be part of the crime elements necessary to convict an offender of burglary.

Larceny is carrying away the property of another with intent to steal.

Embezzlement is the fraudulent taking of money or property entrusted to one's care. Employees sometimes take money and try to conceal the crime by falsifying business records.

Shoplifting is taking merchandise from a retail store with intent to steal, alter a price label, or commit an act to deprive the merchant of the retail value of the merchandise.

Arson is the malicious and unlawful act of burning a building or other property.

CRIMES AGAINST THE PERSON *Homicide* is the willful killing of another. This does not include deaths caused by negligence, suicide, accident, or justifiable homicide.

Assault and Battery. Assault is threatening to harm another. *Battery* is the actual contact (e.g., act of beating).

Robbery is taking personal property from another by using force or threat of force.

Criminal Justice System Participants

The criminal justice system responds to crime through the involvement of citizens, as well as agencies, levels, and branches of government.

Private Sector

The first response to crime may come from individuals, families, neighborhood associations, business, educational institutions, or the news media, or any other private service to the public. For example, as taxpayers and voters, citizens take part *indirectly* in the criminal justice system and its processes. Also, citizens take part *directly* in the criminal justice process through the following ways:

- By reporting crime to the police.
- By being a reliable participant, such as a witness or juror, in a criminal proceeding.
- By accepting the system as just or reasonable.

Government

The response to crime is also founded in the intergovernmental structure of the United States. In other words, state and local governments and laws define the criminal justice system and delegate authority to various jurisdictions, officials, and institutions. Also, Congress has established a criminal justice system at the federal level to respond to such crimes as bank robbery, kidnapping, and transporting stolen goods across state lines. However, the response to crime is mainly a state and local function.

Officials

Within the criminal justice system, there are professionals who guide and direct the system. They have a minimum level of training and orientation. Some common classifications of officials and their responsibilities are discussed. As you read the following common classifications of officials and their responsibilities, keep in mind that each official (with respect to each duty) must decide:

- Whether or not to take action.
- How to take action.
- Where the situation fits in the scheme of laws, rules, and precedent.
- Which official response is appropriate.

POLICE Police have the responsibility to:
1. Enforce specific laws.
2. Investigate specific crimes.
3. Search people, vicinities, and buildings.
4. Arrest or detain people.

PROSECUTORS Prosecutors have the duty to:
1. File charges or petitions for adjudication.
2. Seek indictments.

3. Drop cases.
4. Reduce charges.

JUDGES OR MAGISTRATES Judges or magistrates have the responsibility to:
1. Set bail or conditions for release.
2. Accept pleas.
3. Determine delinquency.
4. Dismiss charges.
5. Impose sentence.
6. Revoke probation.

CORRECTIONAL OFFICIALS Correctional officials have the duty to:
1. Assign to type of correctional facility.
2. Award privileges.
3. Punish for disciplinary infractions.

PAROLING AUTHORITIES Paroling authorities have the responsibility to:
1. Determine date and conditions of parole.
2. Revoke parole.

Criminal Justice System Procedures

As you might expect based on the preceding discussion, criminal cases and procedures vary within different jurisdictions. This is also a result of the intergovernmental structure of the criminal justice system. However, court decisions based on the due process guarantees of the U.S. Constitution require specific steps in the administration of criminal justice.

Entry into the System

The justice system does not respond to most crime. This is because much of crime is not discovered or reported to the police. Law enforcement agencies learn about crime from the reports of citizens, from discovery by a police officer in the field, or from investigative and intelligence work.

Once a law enforcement agency has established that a crime has been committed, a suspect must be identified and apprehended for the case to proceed through the system. Sometimes, a suspect is apprehended at the scene. However, identification of a suspect may require a thorough investigation. Sometimes, no one is identified or apprehended.

Prosecution and Pretrial Services

After an arrest, law enforcement agencies provide information about the case and the accused to the prosecutor. The prosecutor will decide if formal charges will be filed with the court. If no charges are filed, the accused must be released. The prosecutor can also drop charges after making efforts to prosecute.

A suspect charged with a crime must be taken before a judge or magistrate without unnecessary delay. At the initial appearance, the judge or magistrate informs the suspect of the charges and constitutional rights. The judge decides whether there is probable cause to detain the suspect. Sometimes, if the offense is not very serious, the determination of a guilty verdict and assessment of a penalty may also occur at this stage.

In many jurisdictions, the initial appearance may be followed by a preliminary hearing. The purpose of this hearing is to discover if there is probable cause to believe that the accused committed a known crime within the jurisdiction of the court. *Probable cause* is the amount of evidence that would cause the judge to believe that the suspect committed the crime.

Reasonable grounds to believe means the same as probable cause. If the judge does not find *probable cause*, the case is dismissed. However, if the judge or magistrate finds probable cause, or the accused waives his or her right to a preliminary hearing, the case may go to a grand jury.

Adjudication

Once an indictment (from a grand jury) or information (from a prosecutor) has been filed with the trial court, the accused is scheduled for arraignment. At the arraignment, the subject is informed of the charges, advised of the his or her rights, and asked to enter a plea to the charges. Sometimes a plea of guilty results from negotiations between the prosecutor and the defendant. This is referred to as *plea bargain*. By entering a plea of guilty, the defendant expects reduced charges or a lenient sentence.

If the accused pleads guilty or accepts penalty without admitting guilt (called *nolo contendere*) the judge may accept or reject the plea. If the plea is accepted, no trial is held. Also, the offender is sentenced at this proceeding or at a later date.

If the accused pleads not guilty or not guilty by reason of insanity, a date is set for the trial. A person accused of a serious crime is guaranteed a trial by jury. However, the accused may ask for a bench trial, rather than a jury trial. In this case, the judge serves as finder of fact. In both cases, the trial results in acquittal or conviction on the original charges or on lesser charges.

Sentencing and Sanctions

After a guilty verdict or guilty plea, sentence is given. In most cases, the judge decides on the sentence, often subject to legislative guidelines to promote uniformity and fairness. However, in some states, the sentence is decided by the jury, especially for capital offenses such as murder.

The sentencing choices that may be available to judges include one or more of the following:

- The death penalty.
- Incarceration in a prison, jail, or other confinement facility.
- Probation that means the convicted person is to remain at liberty but has certain conditions and restrictions.
- Fines that are primarily applied as penalties in minor offenses.
- Restitution that requires the offender to provide financial compensation to the victim.

Corrections

Offenders sentenced to incarceration usually serve time in a local jail or a state prison. Jails hold offenders who are serving short sentences (often less than a year) or are awaiting trial and unable to be released on bail. Prisons are for long-term incarceration.

Because of the problems of recidivism (i.e., offenders committing a crime following release from prison and returning to prison) and unsuccessful rehabilitation, correctional agencies have been subject to intense criticism. Parole, which is early release from prison, has also been criticized because critics argue that parole boards have made poor decisions on releasing inmates and public safety has been affected. Some states and the federal system have abolished parole (an executive branch function) and replaced it with legislative guidelines on early release for courts and prisons to follow. Other states have adopted enhanced parole guidelines to improve rehabilitation, justice, and public safety. A variety of innovative correctional programs have also been implemented to foster successful entry of offenders back into the community. Examples include work-release and intensive supervision of inmates in the community.

Juvenile Justice System

The processing of juvenile offenders is different than the processing of adult offenders. Many juveniles are referred to juvenile court by law enforcement officers. But many others are referred by school officials, social service agencies, neighbors, and parents for behavior or conditions that need intervention by the justice system.

When a juvenile is referred to juvenile court, a juvenile court intake department or a prosecuting attorney will determine whether sufficient grounds exist to file a petition. A petition is a document that requests a hearing or a transfer to criminal court. In some states, a prosecutor, under certain circumstances, may file criminal charges against a juvenile directly in criminal court. The court with jurisdiction over juvenile matters may reject the petition or the juvenile may be directed to other agencies or programs instead of further court processing. If a petition for a hearing is accepted, the juvenile may be brought before a court. This court is unlike the court with jurisdiction over adult offenders. In disposing of cases, juvenile courts usually have more discretion than adult courts. The sentencing choices that may be available to juvenile courts include one or more of the following:

- Probation (i.e., supervision by a court without confinement).
- Fines.
- Restitution.
- Commitment to correctional institutions.
- Removal of children from their homes to foster homes or treatment facilities.
- Participation in special programs aimed at shoplifting prevention, drug counseling, or driver education.
- Referral to criminal court for trial as adults.

Civil Law

Civil law is used to adjust conflicts among people, corporations, governments, and others. It includes a wide range of rights and duties that courts decide upon. In the civil justice system, the wrongdoer is subject to pay the injured party for losses. Or, the court may direct one party to do or refrain from doing a specific act. This contrasts with the criminal justice system where the convicted offender can receive a prison sentence and a fine. Civil action is called a "suit" initiated by a wronged party called a "plaintiff" against the alleged defendant. Recall that in criminal cases, the prosecutor, who represents the state, brings criminal charges against a defendant. Both civil and criminal cases are adversary in nature. In other words, opposing attorneys "battle" each other in court. To win a civil case, you must show a "preponderance of evidence," a lesser burden of proof than required in a criminal case that requires "proof beyond a reasonable doubt." Preponderance of evidence is defined as the greater weight of evidence or sufficient evidence to overcome speculation. In a criminal case, the defense side seeks to cast a *doubt* on the prosecutor's case by, for example, claiming that the evidence is weak or suspect. Contrary to what is seen on television and in the movies, most civil cases never make it to trial but are settled out of court after negotiation between attorneys. Likewise, most criminal cases never make it to trial. Civil violations usually fall into two categories, breaches of contract and torts.

Breaches of Contract

Breaches of contract deal with failure to perform some duty that was agreed to earlier. Most of the business activity in our country depends on contracts among people. Examples are promises to pay back loans, deliver goods, perform services, pay salaries, and pay rent or a mortgage.

Torts

Torts are particularly important for those in the security field. Torts are civil wrongs that interfere with personal rights. Some examples and their definitions are listed here.

False imprisonment is the unlawful confinement or restriction of the freedom of another.

Malicious prosecution is groundless initiation of criminal charges against another.

Assault is intentional causing of fear in another.

Battery is violent contact with another.

Trespass is unauthorized entering of another's property.

Infliction of emotional distress is intentionally causing emotional distress in another.

Defamation (libel and slander) is harming the reputation of another by making untrue statements. Libel refers to the written word, slander to the spoken word.

Invasion of privacy is disclosing private information or intruding upon another's physical solitude.

Negligence is causing injury to a person or property by failing to use reasonable care or by taking unreasonable risk.

Security Officer Liability

Probably, you are wondering about your liability in your role as a security officer. In other words, as a security officer, what happens if you make a mistake when taking legal action? Are you subject to arrest and a lawsuit? The answer is yes. The boxed case study nearby of Security Officer Dan Smith illustrates this situation.

Much can be said about the many mistakes in this case. Dan should have listened to his boss and "just observe." Security training should have taken place before Dan performed security work. Dan's actions were wrong, and management was negligent in supervision and training.

Of course, management liability with respect to security can extend to other areas. Some of these other areas include failing to take steps to prevent crimes that occur on the premises (Figure 7-2) and inadequately screening job applicants.

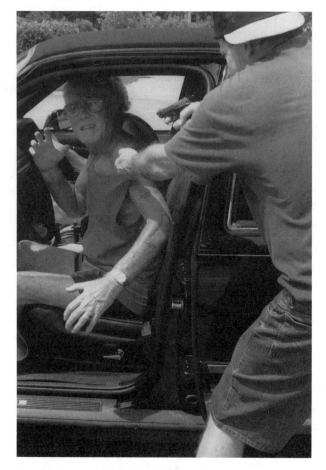

Figure 7-2 Management liability can result from failure to prevent crimes that occur on the premises.

Dan Smith, Security Officer at Midwest Department Store

Dan Smith had been a security officer for two weeks at the Midwest Department Store. Although he was scheduled for training in another week and was told by his boss to just observe, Dan felt as if he could handle anything.

One day, at about 12:30 P.M., Dan became suspicious of a female shopper. He watched the lady closely for fifteen minutes. Dan believed that since she had a large pocketbook, was dressed poorly, and was in the women's department, she was likely to be shoplifting. As the lady was about to leave the store without making a purchase, he grabbed her by the arm and shouted, "Stop lady, you shoplifted!" While he was pulling the lady, her shoe fell off. She tried to retrieve her shoe, but Dan thought she was resisting and trying to get away. Dan reacted by pushing the lady into a counter and then handcuffing her. Then he dragged her to the security office where he locked her so he could find his boss. About an hour later, his boss returned from lunch, studied the situation, and decided to call the police. After the police arrived, they asked Dan what proof he had that the lady had shoplifted and where was the stolen merchandise. Dan's story established no proof. The police called an ambulance for the lady's injuries.

Soon afterwards, Dan was arrested for assault and battery and false arrest. Dan, his boss, and the Midwest Department Store were sued for half a million dollars. Dan was stuck with a criminal record, no job, and the need for a new career. The plaintiff won a sizeable award in civil court from all the defendants.

Sexual Harassment

The problem of sexual harassment has resulted in numerous lawsuits. The Equal Employment Opportunity Commission (EEOC), a federal administrative agency with law enforcement powers, defines *sexual harassment* as unwelcome sexual conduct that has the purpose or effect of unreasonably interfering with an individual's work performance or creating an intimidating, hostile, or offensive work environment. Although the *Civil Rights Act* was passed in 1964, only during the 1970s did courts begin to recognize sexual harassment as a form of gender discrimination under Title VII of this Act. Thereafter, the EEOC issued guidelines for determining what activity is sexual harassment, and these guidelines influence courts.

The two theories upon which an action for sexual harassment may be brought are explained here. *Quid pro quo* involves an employee who is required to engage in sexual activity in exchange for a workplace benefit. For example, a male manager tells his female assistant that he will get her a promotion and raise if she engages in sex with him. A second theory of sexual harassment is *hostile working environment*, which occurs when sexually offensive behavior by one party is unwelcome by another and creates workplace difficulties. Examples include unwelcome suggestive remarks or touching or posted jokes or photos of a sexual nature.

Civil Justice System Procedures

Civil procedures vary among jurisdictions. However, civil procedures both before a trial and during a trial require much time and the process can be expensive. Since a security officer may become involved in a civil case, an understanding of these procedures provides knowledge of the path of a civil case.

Civil Procedures Before Trial

Figure 7-3 illustrates the stages of civil procedures *before* trial. The diagram provides a foundation for the following information that explains each of the stages.

1. *Plaintiff* initiates lawsuit resulting from commission of tort, breach of contract, or other event.

2. *Defendant* prepares defense after receiving summons (court order to appear in court) and complaint (a pleading of facts and claims filed in court). Failure to appear in court and defend a complaint can result in losing the lawsuit.

3. *Opposing attorneys confer* and communicate issues, evidence, and settlement options. This may take place anytime throughout the proceedings.

4. *Discovery* is where opposing attorneys obtain all factual information in possession of the other. This stage helps to narrow the issues and saves time in dispensing justice.

5. *Motions filed in court.* For example, the defendant often claims that the plaintiff's complaint is without foundation.

6. *Answer* is the response to the lawsuit. The defendant files an answer with the court and includes denials and counterclaims.

7. *Motions* are additional motions in court by opposing attorneys who claim that the allegations in the opponent's pleadings cannot be proven.

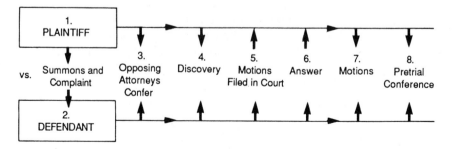

Figure 7-3 Civil procedures before trial.

Testimony

Security officers periodically testify in depositions or in court. A *deposition* is a pretrial discovery method whereby the opposing party in a case asks questions of the other party (e.g., victim, witness, expert) under oath, usually in an attorney's office, and while a word-for-word transcript is recorded. Depositions help to present the evidence of each side of a case and assist the justice system in settling cases before the expensive trial stage.

Well-prepared testimony in both criminal and civil cases can be assured most readily by the following suggestions.

1. Prepare and review notes and reports. Recheck evidence that has been properly labeled and identified. Confer with an attorney.
2. Dress in a conservative manner, if not in uniform. Appear well groomed.
3. Maintain good demeanor (conduct, behavior). Do not slouch or fidget. Do not argue with anyone. Remain calm (take some deep breaths without being obvious).
4. Pause and think before speaking. Do not volunteer information beyond what is requested. Never guess. If you do not know an answer, say so.

---

8. *Pretrial conference* is where opposing attorneys and the judge meet to work toward settlement or face trial.

Civil Procedures During Trial

Over 95 percent of civil cases are settled *before* reaching the trial stage. In other words, as was previously mentioned, civil cases are settled out of court. The following list explains each stage of civil procedures *during* trial as illustrated in Figure 7-4.

1. *Jury selection* occurs when potential jurors are questioned and selected by opposing attorneys.
2. *Opening statements* are those comments from the opposing attorneys. This includes explaining the facts to the judge and jury.
3. *Presentation of plaintiff's case* is done by the plaintiff's attorney. The plaintiff's attorney presents evidence, such as witnesses and documents, to support allegations in the complaint.
4. *Defendant's motion for dismissal* is where the defendant's attorney moves for a dismissal if the attorney believes that the plaintiff's case failed to prove allegations. If the judge denies the motion for dismissal, the trial continues.

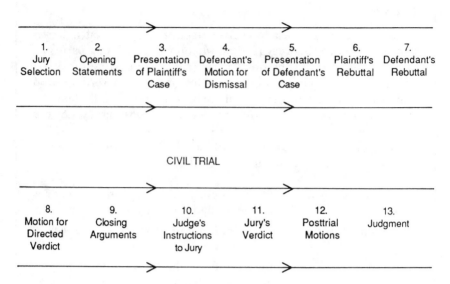

Figure 7-4   Civil procedures during trial.

5. *Presentation of defendant's case* occurs when the defendant's attorney presents evidence to disprove (rebut) the plaintiff's case.

6. *Plaintiff's rebuttal* occurs when the plaintiff's attorney attempts to disprove the presentation of the defendant's attorney (from the preceding stage).

7. *Defendant's rebuttal* occurs when the defendant's attorney attempts to disprove newer issues argued by the plaintiff's attorney (from the preceding stage).

8. *Motion for directed verdict* is where either or both parties move for a directed verdict. In other words, the judge takes the decision away from the jury and informs them of what to decide. This situation results from a failure of evidence, overwhelming evidence, or the law applied to the facts favors one of the parties. If the motion is denied, the trial continues.

9. *Closing arguments* are summaries of the evidence presented to the jury by the plaintiff's attorney and the defendant's attorney.

10. *Judge's instructions to jury.*

11. *Jury's verdict* occurs when the jury makes a decision.

12. *Posttrial motions* occur after a trial. An example is the motion for a new trial.

13. *Judgment* occurs when the judge declares which party prevailed at the trial (i.e., which party won the lawsuit) and the amount of recovery to be awarded.

Many of the strategies and procedures used in civil trials are also used in criminal trials; although the rules will vary. These procedures include discovery, motions, jury selection, questioning of witnesses in court by opposing attorneys, judge's instruction to a jury, verdict, posttrial motions, and many more.

Control of Private Security and Public Police by the Justice System

Private Security

Private security personnel are largely controlled by the threat of a lawsuit if they make a legal mistake. Furthermore, citizens' rights must be preserved. When a private security officer makes a legal blunder, an injured party may sue those allegedly responsible. If the plaintiff is successful, an award is often ordered by a court.

In addition to security officers, management should be aware of a lawsuit threat. Management is ultimately responsible for providing a safe environment for people on the premises. Also, management is responsible for properly selecting, training, supervising, and evaluating security officers, and maintaining policies and procedures and life safety and physical security programs.

Research by Liability Consultants, Inc. www.liabilityconsultants.com provides a picture of trends of premises liability cases from 1993 to 1997 and draws comparisons to the company's first report covering 1983 to 1992.

- Defendants are winning more and paying less when losing.

- Crimes in parking lots are more likely to lead to litigation against the property owner than crimes occurring elsewhere on the premises.

- Apartment and condominium complexes are sued most often. This was true in the first study. Office buildings and restaurants placed second and third in the newer study, while hotels and retail stores were second and third earlier. This change could be due to lawsuits leading to increased security at hotels and retail stores and a shift in crime to less secure locations.

- Both studies show the most litigious states as NY, TX, FL, and CA.

- Compared to the first study, most verdicts favored the defense and awards for damages have decreased.

- The new study found that the largest percentage of case verdicts and settlements were for under $250,000. For the earlier study, the figures were for between $250,000 and $500,000.

- The reasons why most verdicts favored the defense are: property owners are increasing crime prevention efforts; defense attorneys and insurers are learning how to improve their defense strategies; and the changing standards of foreseeability in certain jurisdictions (i.e., establish a connection between the crime and the alleged security deficiency).

What If?

As a Security Supervisor, What Do You Do if You Respond to a Call and Learn That One of Your Officers Has Made Serious Mistakes in an Emergency Situation?

As a security supervisor at a shopping mall, you begin your tour of duty and learn of a shooting on the premises. You arrive quickly at the scene. The victim is down and EMS and police are on the way. The security officer at the scene, Officer Remson, explains that the victim was shot in the parking lot during a robbery by three young men who fled. Two daughters of the victim complain bitterly to you that when they sought help in the nearest store, the manager refused to call EMS or police. Then they went to another store and a retail employee telephoned mall security. When Officer Remson arrived at the scene ten minutes after he got the call, he leaned over the victim and said, "you're not shot." This was stated because Officer Remson said that he did not see any blood. Initially, he refused to summon EMS and police. Following about five minutes, and pleas from the victim's daughters, Officer Remson decided to call EMS and police. Later it was learned that the victim was indeed shot. A .22 caliber bullet was lodged in his stomach. Also, you learn that Officer Remson was finishing his dinner when the call came to him and he completed it before responding quickly to the shooting.

As a supervisor, Officer Remson should be disciplined for not responding quickly to the serious call and not calling for police and EMS immediately. The mall security force requires additional training so these problems do not occur again. Training should include professional action and behavior as a first-responder. Policies and procedures must be refined and reviewed in training. All mall employees should receive information on actions and behavior in emergency situations.

As the supervisor at the scene, you will be contacted by various parties to answer questions concerning this incident. This incident may result in a lawsuit for alleged negligent security and you may have to testify at a deposition and trial. Rather than violating ethics and law, always tell the truth. Do not become part of a cover-up and subject yourself to criminal and civil action. This case illustrates the importance of screening job applicants, training, policies and procedures, supervision, and discipline.

Public Police

Public police, who have greater arrest powers than private security, are limited in their action by the Bill of Rights to the U.S. Constitution. One easy way to understand the Bill of Rights is to regard it as a list of citizen rights against government action. Certain amendments to the Bill of Rights are particularly important in guiding agencies of criminal justice. A brief summary is listed here.

Fourth Amendment

- Police are prohibited from unreasonable searches and seizures.
- Arrest warrants and search warrants must be based on probable cause (more than suspicion).
- Warrants must be specific as to the place to be searched and the persons or things to be seized.

Fifth Amendment

- No person should be compelled in any criminal case to be a witness against himself/herself.

Sixth Amendment

- Citizen has right to an attorney.
- Citizen has right to a trial by jury.

Eighth Amendment

- No excessive bail or fines, nor cruel and unusual punishment imparted on any person.

Fourteenth Amendment

- No *state* shall deprive any person of due process of law or equal protection of the laws.

Our system of justice is involved in a never-ending job of balancing citizen rights and police power. Citizens want protection against aggressive police. At the same time, police want to reduce crime through such methods as searches, seizures, and questioning.

Police are controlled internally (mechanisms within police agencies) by carefully selecting police recruits, training, supervision, policies and procedures, internal investigations, and discipline. External controls include the courts, external investigations and commissions, citizen review boards, the media, and public interest groups.

Although the previous discussions emphasize private security controlled by fear of a lawsuit and public police controlled by the Bill of Rights, these are generalizations. Public police are increasingly being sued and private security has faced constitutional limitations. For example, the West Virginia Supreme Court overturned a shoplifting case because a private security officer did not afford a defendant Fourth, Fifth, and Sixth Amendment protections. The court referred to an unreasonable search, the guarantee against self-incrimination, and the officer's refusal to allow the suspect access to an attorney. In this case, the court stressed the "increasing role in the enforcement of criminal laws played by private security forces."

CHAPTER REVIEW

A. Multiple Choice

1. Which of the following types of crimes is most serious and likely to result in a death sentence?

   a. felonies

   b. misdemeanors

   c. capital crimes

   d. infractions

2. The act of taking personal property from another by using force or threat of force is known as

   a. larceny.

   b. robbery.

   c. assault and battery.

   d. shoplifting.

3. Select the burden of proof required to convict a defendant in a criminal case.

   a. probable cause

   b. a preponderance of evidence

   c. reasonable suspicion

   d. proof beyond a reasonable doubt

4. This amendment prohibits unreasonable searches and seizures.

   a. Fourth

   b. Fifth

   c. Sixth

   d. Eighth

5. This amendment affords citizens the right to an attorney in criminal cases.

   a. Fourth

   b. Fifth

   c. Sixth

   d. Eighth

B. True Or False

1. All states have similar criminal laws.

2. Embezzlement is the fraudulent taking of money or property entrusted to one's care.

3. Defamation refers to the causing of injury to a person or property by failing to use reasonable care or by taking unreasonable risk.

4. Private security is controlled primarily by the Bill of Rights.

5. Our system of justice prohibits public police from being sued.

Applications

Application 7A

As an experienced security officer, you are assigned the task of supervising the on-the-job training of a new security officer. How would you explain to the new officer how private security legal authority is controlled? What recommendations do you make to the new officer to prevent legal mistakes?

Application 7B

As a security supervisor, one of your subordinates made an arrest after catching an intruder inside a perimeter fence loading a truck with about $10,000 worth of company equipment. After the intruder is handcuffed and public police are called, your subordinate asks you what criminal charges will be filed. What is your response?

8

Arrest Law and Procedures

CHAPTER OUTLINE

OBJECTIVES

After studying this chapter, you will be able to:

- Define and state the purpose of an arrest.
- List at least seven questions of consideration prior to making an arrest.
- Explain the arrest powers of citizens, security officers, special police officers, and public police.
- List at least ten guidelines for a safe arrest.
- List at least five guidelines for a legal arrest.
- Define reasonable force.
- Explain the legal bounds of searches by public police and private security officers
- Explain the legal guidelines for public police and private security officers when they question suspects.
- Describe three arrest situations: burglar, employee-thief, and shoplifter.
- List those things a security officer should do and should *not* do when confronting an employee-thief.
- List those things a security officer should do and should *not* do when confronting a shoplifter.
- Explain civil recovery.

Introduction

Although this chapter emphasizes arrest law and procedures, a word of caution is appropriate here. Security officers are less likely to make arrests than public police. In fact, at many locations, security officers are instructed to avoid making arrests and just **observe** *and* **report***. Factors that influence whether security officers will make arrests include the type of business, management philosophy, training, policies, and liability issues. For those security officers that are directed to make arrests, this chapter serves as a foundation for further training.*

Security officers seek to *prevent* loss events through protection methods, and they de-emphasize arrests. Public police, on the other hand, have been traditionally "reactive." In other words, they respond to calls for service, investigate and collect evidence, and make arrests. At the same time, public police have made some efforts at "proactive" policing (i.e., prevention; controlling crime before it occurs) by, for instance, identifying and tracking career criminals and by recruiting citizens to watch neighborhoods and report suspicious activity.

Citizen Rights and Arrests

Our justice system works to balance citizens' rights versus police and private security protection efforts (Figure 8-1). In countries where citizen rights are

Figure 8-1 The United States Supreme Court plays a major role in balancing citizen rights and crime control efforts.

of minimal concern, police aggressively search, arrest, and confine people based on questionable evidence. This is not the case in the United States where the Bill of Rights of the U.S. Constitution explains citizen rights against the government. For example, the Fourth Amendment prohibits unreasonable searches and seizures and requires arrest and search warrants to be based on probable cause (i.e., more than suspicion). Furthermore, a citizen's option to sue is also a deterrent to police and security personnel who abuse their authority.

An *arrest* can be defined as seizing a person and restricting his or her movements and freedom. The purpose of an arrest is to bring an individual into the criminal justice system to answer criminal charges. Because an arrestee is deprived of freedom and may be subject to the use of force, a security officer must carefully consider the decision to arrest.

When an arrest occurs, considerable responsibility has been placed on a security officer. Every arrest should be done legally because there is no second chance.

Arrest Guidelines

Before taking on the responsibility for making arrests, security officers should mentally review and consider several important questions. The following questions should be thoroughly understood by security personnel since there may be only a few seconds prior to an arrest.

1. Am I thoroughly familiar with arrest law and the arrest powers I possess?

2. What are the company policies and procedures concerning arrests?

3. Is the arrest practical?

4. Do I have the training and equipment to handle the arrest?

5. Am I protected from disease transmission during an arrest? (See Chapter 13.)

6. Am I prepared to use force, if necessary, to restrain the arrestee?

7. What type of backup, if any, can I expect from other security officers and public police? What is the response time of each?

8. What is the ratio of security personnel to offenders?

9. Can I handle the arrestee safely if assistance arrives late?

10. Should I refrain from an arrest and let the public police handle the incident?

Arrest Authority

One way to understand arrest powers is to study the legal authority of citizens, private security officers, special police officers, and public police.

Citizen Arrest Powers: Felonies

The most common type of arrest power held by security officers is that held by a citizen. Introduction to Security, 6th ed. by Robert Fischer and Gion Green, states "The exact extent of citizen's arrest power varies, depending upon the type of crime, the jurisdiction (laws), whether the crime was committed in the presence of the arrestor, or on the status of the citizen (strictly a private citizen or a commissioned officer)." Most states have passed laws to clarify the conditions under which citizens can make arrests. Therefore, since there is a lack of uniformity among states concerning citizen arrest powers, practitioners must fully understand state laws and relevant court decisions in the state in which they work.

For example, Kentucky gives citizens limited felony arrest powers. According to *Legal Aspects of Private Security*, "A private person may make an arrest when a felony has been committed in fact and he has reasonable grounds to believe that the person being arrested has committed it. If a felony has not been committed in fact, even though the arrestor has reasonable grounds to believe that it has been, there is no statutory authority to arrest." Thus, a citizen must be absolutely positive that a felony has occurred.

Kentucky law can be contrasted with Illinois law that provides more authority to citizens. "Any person may arrest another when he has reasonable grounds to believe that an offense other than an ordinance violation is being committed," as stated in *Protective Security Law*.

Many states have statutes similar to that adopted by Alaska, where: "A private person . . . may arrest a person:

1. for a crime committed or attempted in his presence;
2. when a person has committed a felony, although not in his presence;
3. when a felony has been committed and he has reasonable cause for believing the person committed it," also found in *Protective Security Law.*

In those states without statutes authorizing private citizens to arrest, this does not mean that a citizen cannot make an arrest. State court decisions may provide guidance for citizen arrests.

Practical Guidelines

On a practical note for the citizen or the security officer with citizen arrest powers, *the following guidelines are recommended to prevent making an illegal arrest. A cautious approach is emphasized.* Also, some examples are provided.

1. If a felony is not observed, or if there is uncertainty as to whether one was committed or that the suspect committed the crime, *do not make an arrest.*
2. Although many states permit a citizen to make an arrest based on "reasonable cause" to believe that a crime occurred, a case is much stronger when the arrestor witnessed the crime rather than relying on circumstances following the crime.
3. There are circumstances when a crime may appear to have taken place when in fact it has not. For example, as a security officer, you see a janitor quickly place a computer in a car near an exit. The janitor runs back into the building. You immediately make an arrest for larceny. As it turns out, the janitor was to transport the computer to a repair business and was authorized to place it in the car.
4. Basing an arrest decision on another person's word, unless a trusted individual (e.g., security officer or police officer), can be hazardous. If you are approached by an upset person who points to another claiming a serious crime has occurred, watch out! The person seeking help may be involved in a domestic dispute or an argument with a foe. For example, you see a woman sitting on the pavement screaming. She yells rape and points to a fleeing man. You catch the man who supposedly sexually assaulted the woman and hold him until police arrive. Later, you find out that the man and woman are married, were quarrelling, and no sexual assault occurred.
5. An error in judgment can result in criminal and civil action.
6. The ultimate test of an arrest may be decided by a criminal court jury and civil court jury. If an opposing attorney can cast doubt on the legality of the arrest, the case can be lost.

EXAMPLE OF CITIZEN ARREST While cashing a paycheck at a community bank, Joe Brown, a citizen, observes an armed robbery in progress at the bank. As the robber flees, he trips over carpet near the exit, and his pistol slides across the floor. Joe quickly grabs the pistol and holds the robber until the police arrive.

EXAMPLE OF SECURITY OFFICER APPLYING CITIZEN ARREST POWERS While patrolling the company parking lot, security officer Smith observes a juvenile stealing an employee's vehicle. The officer is able to block the only exit. The youth bolts from the stolen car, but is apprehended by the officer while trying to climb a fence. Police are called to the scene immediately.

Citizen Arrest Powers: Misdemeanors

State laws regarding citizen arrests for misdemeanors are even less consistent than those laws involving citizen arrests for felonies. Certain states grant considerable power to citizens to arrest for any misdemeanor. Other states prohibit citizen arrests for misdemeanors under any circumstances. Illinois provides its citizens with broad powers to arrest. *Legal Aspects of Private Security* states, "Any person may arrest another when he has *reasonable grounds to believe* that an offense other than an ordinance violation is being committed." On the other hand, Alabama law exemplifies what several other states specify in reference to citizen arrests for misdemeanors. That is, "A private person may arrest another for any public offense *committed in his presence*," according to the same source. Thus, by studying the Illinois statute, we can see that "reasonable grounds to believe" is less evidence than what is required in the Alabama statute that requires direct observation ("committed in his presence"). Also, although many states have statutes that are similar to each other, variations in applications of the laws are reflected in each state's court interpretations.

Arrest Powers of Special Police Officers

Inbau and colleagues, in *Protective Security Law*, 2nd ed., explain that special police officers are individuals who are employed by businesses and institutions to protect people and property. The term special police officers may also cover security officers contracted to businesses and institutions by security service companies. These officers are granted arrest powers similar to those of public police officers, but such powers may be restricted to the premises being protected. It is important to note that when a special police officer leaves the protected property, citizen arrest powers may prevail. However, state laws vary.

Depending on individual state law, special police officers may be referred to as being deputized, commissioned, or granted special police or constable authority. These special officers may also be provided with the right to bear arms. Training increases in importance as arrest powers increase and officers are armed.

A good example of special police officers is seen at colleges and universities. Campus police are frequently provided with full police powers on the protected property as prescribed by state law.

A word on private detectives here will help the reader understand how these individuals fit into the range of arrest powers. When compared with special officers, private detectives possess less arrest powers. Although licensed and regulated by state agencies, private detectives simply have citizen arrest powers. Depending on the state, they may even be prohibited from carrying a firearm, as is the case in South Carolina.

Arrest Powers of Public Police Officers

Public police officers possess considerable arrest powers beyond that of citizens and security officers. When compared to citizens and security officers, there are more situations where public police (and special police officers) can make arrests while being less likely to suffer from civil or criminal legal action if a mistake is made. Examples include felonies and misdemeanors where suspects were not observed by police committing the crimes. Public police officers, for instance, can make an arrest based on knowledge that an arrest warrant has been issued on a specific individual. Also, public police are afforded protection from civil liability for false arrest as long as probable cause exists that a felony has been committed. Additionally, public police officers have probable cause to stop and arrest a suspect whose description was transmitted over a radio following a crime (Figure 8-2). A victim of an

Figure 8-2 Probable cause to stop and arrest a suspect can be established from a radio transmission that describes the suspect following a crime. Courtesy: Wackenhut, Inc.

assault and battery who describes the offender for police also provides probable cause for police to make an arrest.

Probable Cause

Probable cause is necessary to make a valid arrest and to obtain an arrest warrant. Probable cause is the amount of evidence required that would cause a reasonable person to believe that an individual committed a crime. It is more than mere suspicion. The term *reasonable grounds to believe* means the same as probable cause.

Probable cause is also required for a search warrant. For example, a reliable informant tells police about the location of illegal drugs, stolen merchandise, or a wanted felon. The information from the informant is the foundation of probable cause when police seek a search warrant from a judge.

The Fourth Amendment prohibits unreasonable searches and seizures by police. This Amendment requires that both *arrest* and *search* warrants must be based on probable cause and that warrants must be specific about the place to be searched and the persons or things to be seized.

In misdemeanor cases, public police arrest powers are even more pronounced. Besides making arrests for misdemeanors committed in their presence, police officers can also make arrests for certain misdemeanors not observed. Examples include domestic violence and driving while intoxicated. Even though the actual crime was not observed, if the incident is "fresh," probable cause is established for an arrest. In other words, the circumstances reveal the misdemeanor was just committed by the suspect.

What are the arrest powers of full-time public police officers working part-time as security officers? The answer to this question is complex and varies among the states. Legal guidance is found in state statutes, court decisions, and state attorneys general legal opinions. Some courts hold the viewpoint that when police officers moonlight as private security officers, they may be generally considered a private security officer. Other courts hold an opposite opinion stating that police officers' duties are not limited by specific time or place and that it is immaterial whether moonlighting police were on or off duty at the time of the incident. Police departments often regulate moonlighting by prohibiting officers from serving in security positions or restricting the number of hours worked per week. Other departments encourage businesses to hire officers on a part-time basis.

Guidelines When Confronting a Suspect

The basic job of security personnel is to protect people and assets. This includes the investigation of crimes and other business losses. Whenever a suspect is confronted, care must be exercised to protect citizen rights. In the earlier chapter on criminal and civil law, we learned that if security officers make mistakes when taking legal action, they may be subject to arrest and a lawsuit.

Security personnel should be provided with quality training before being assigned to duties. Periodic training is vital to keep personnel up-to-date on legal changes. It is important to understand state statutes, local ordinances, and state and federal court decisions. Constitutional limitations may apply to security personnel who possess citizen arrest powers when these security officers act in cooperation with public police on criminal cases. As we learned in the preceding chapter, the primary way public police are controlled is through the Bill of Rights, whereas private security personnel are controlled by the threat of a lawsuit. However, each may be subject to both criminal and civil action.

Guidelines for a Safe Arrest

1. If time permits, notify a supervisor about an impending arrest.

2. Know your limitations and consider that you may have to disengage and/or escalate. Whenever possible, call for assistance to make an arrest. Superiority of numbers increases safety and success.

3. Try to plan an arrest. Knowledge of a building's floor plan, exits, and avenues of escape help avoid errors during arrests.

4. If the offender flees, conform to legal guidelines on the limits of a chase. The property line or nearby is often the norm. Never pursue the offender in a low- or high-speed chase. Obtain a description and call public police.

5. Security officers must use good judgment and act in a professional manner without hesitation. At the same time, it is important to maintain an even temperament and remain calm.

6. A security officer must have proper identification during an arrest. If the security officer is out of uniform, proper identification is especially important since the arrestee may think he or she is being attacked or make such a claim at a later time.

7. All arrest situations are potentially dangerous. Never become complacent and think, for example, that "this little old fellow would never do anything violent." Young, old, male, or female are all capable of inflicting harm. Also, watch for multiple assailants; criminals have backup too.

8. Because a subject's freedom is restricted during an arrest, there may be strong feelings of anxiety and hostility.

9. Since an arrest represents a strong social and legal control mechanism over an individual who supposedly did wrong, the psychological impact and shame on a person can be devastating. The reaction from the subject may be to submit peacefully, offer a bribe, escape, resist and hurt you and others, take a hostage, or try to commit suicide. Although most arrestees willingly comply, it takes only one unsuspecting person to kill you.

10. Watch for nonverbal communications that may signal a threat. Examples are anger or clenched fists. Remain alert since the subject may quickly grab your weapon or one that was hidden.

11. Maintain psychological and physical control of the arrestee from the beginning of the interaction. Use a clear audible voice when stating simple orders. Do not become distracted by answering questions or granting any "last requests" for the arrestee.

12. Use handcuffs as an extra margin of safety to control the arrestee.

13. Following the use of handcuffs, search the arrestee. The basic purpose of searching a person during an arrest is to protect the officer (i.e., search for weapons) and to look for evidence before it is destroyed. A person who is the same sex as the arrestee should conduct the search. Recruit a nonsecurity person if necessary.

14. While waiting for public police to arrive, the arrestee should be taken to an office or holding area. This prevents others from interfering, while reducing the chances of a crowd gathering. At least two security officers should be present at all times with the arrestee.

15. A request by the arrestee to use the rest room or get something left in another area should be viewed with skepticism. This could be an excuse to hide, escape, obtain a weapon, or destroy evidence. No favors should be granted. If a trip to the rest room is necessary, it is advisable, if possible, to have three security officers of the same sex present.

16. Notes and a report should be completed as soon as possible. This documentation proves its usefulness in many ways after the incident ends. Include answers to the six basic questions: who, what happened, where, when, how, and why.

17. When public police arrive to pick up the prisoner, they will focus their questions on what happened and the probable cause to support the arrest. Supply public police with all necessary information. Obtain the police officer's name and badge number for your report.

Guidelines for a Legal Arrest

1. Before an arrest is made, a security officer must be sure that a crime was committed and that probable cause exists.

2. A person being arrested should be informed that he or she is under arrest. The specific charge should also be stated. If the arrest is being made while the crime is actually occurring, such statements to the arrestee may have to wait until later, since the safety of the security officer and the apprehension of the suspect are primary concerns.

3. The statement "you are under arrest," is not mandatory to produce an arrest situation. By restricting the movement of a person and not permitting him or her to leave, a civil or criminal court jury may view such action as an arrest although the security officer may disagree. A lawsuit for *false arrest* is always a possibility whenever a security officer restricts a person's movement.

4. When time permits, notes should be taken on the time of arrest, when police were called, and when they arrived and departed with the arrestee. Such records help disprove claims that the arrestee was held for an unreasonable length of time.

5. The justice system handles juveniles (usually 16 years and younger) differently than adults. Juvenile courts treat young people less severely in anticipation of their maturing and leading a law-abiding life. Procedures are distinctly different as discussed in the previous chapter.

6. When a security officer or a citizen makes an arrest, public police should be contacted. The arrestee should be turned over to the police upon their arrival for transportation to jail.

7. After an arrest, the victim or complainant signs a complaint against the offender. An arrest warrant is subsequently prepared and signed by a judge after the judge studies the probable cause to arrest.

8. Successful prosecution of a case depends on the statements and trial testimony of the arrestor and/or victim. If the prosecutor sees that this evidence is not forthcoming, then the prosecutor will likely drop the case and the arrestee set free. At this point, civil action may result. Police and prosecutors are displeased when security officers make an arrest and do not follow up by signing a complaint and testifying.

Use of Force

Only *reasonable force* is permitted when making an arrest. This means the amount of force that a reasonable person would use under similar circumstances to arrest and control the subject. For example, it would be unreasonable to continue to use force on an aggressive arrestee who becomes calm after being wrestled to the ground for the application of handcuffs. Excessive force can easily lead to criminal and civil legal action.

Deadly force should be restricted to situations where one's life or another's life requires protection. When property is at stake, the use of deadly force is not permitted.

A Case of Excessive Force

A security officer in a retail store observes a shopper conceal store merchandise. An arrest is attempted for shoplifting, but the offender runs. The security officer catches the shoplifter and tries to apply handcuffs. But the offender punches the security officer in the face and runs again. The security officer catches the offender again. The security officer brings the offender to the ground and the offender stops resisting. The officer then kicks the offender. This is excessive force. The offender quickly gets up, punches the security officer again, and runs. The security officer shoots the offender. This also is excessive force.

Searches

As we have learned, the Fourth Amendment of the Bill of Rights restricts unreasonable searches and seizures. Security officer involvement with search warrants is likely to be with public police who will obtain a search warrant from a magistrate and execute it. The following review of searches by public police will precede guidelines for security officers.

Warrantless Searches by Public Police Officers

Although subject to constitutional limitations, there are several situations where public police have considerable power to conduct warrantless searches. Some of these opportunities include the following.

1. *During a lawful arrest,* with or without an arrest warrant (it would be obtained as soon as possible), a police officer is permitted to search an arrestee and the immediate area (i.e., arm's reach). Such action has been consistently upheld by the courts to protect the police officer and to prevent the destruction of evidence.
2. *A consent search* signifies that an individual has given permission to the police to conduct a search of his or her person, property, or home. Signed, written permission should be obtained by the police.
3. Police may *stop and frisk* (also called a "Terry stop" from the U.S. Supreme Court case, *Terry v. Ohio*) an individual appearing dangerous in order to search for illegal weapons and to establish identity. A frisk can be described as a "pat down" or crushing of the subject's clothing. The standard of proof required for a "Terry stop" is "reasonable suspicion." For example, a person who repeatedly walks slowly past a liquor store (as if casing the store) that has been robbed several times, may be subject to a "Terry stop."

4. *When a vehicle is likely to be moved* before a search warrant can be obtained, police can search without a warrant. Known as the *Carroll Doctrine*, police must have probable cause that a car or other vehicle (e.g., truck, watercraft) contains evidence of a crime, and that a warrantless search was justified.

5. A *plain view* observation may yield evidence. This means that a police officer, lawfully at a specific location, who sees contraband (illegal drugs or weapons, stolen items) in direct sight, without having to conduct a search, may seize evidence. An example would be cocaine on a table.

6. During *emergencies* (also called "exigent circumstances") when there is no time to obtain a search warrant, police can search without a warrant. Such warrantless searches usually involve a grave offense involving violence; a life in jeopardy; an armed and dangerous suspect who may escape; a police officer in "hot pursuit" of a fleeing offender who just committed a crime; or a situation where evidence may be destroyed.

7. The *open fields doctrine* allows police to search and seize contraband in an open space without a warrant. A marijuana field serves as an example. Abandoned property is also subject to search and seizure. Evidence can be collected from garbage placed on a public street or when an offender throws a package (e.g., containing illegal drugs) while being followed by police.

Searches by Private Security Officers

State statutes typically lack guidelines on searches by private citizens. However, there are federal and state cases that have upheld the right of a private citizen to search an arrestee for weapons and stolen items.

As we know, certain states grant private security officers arrest powers equal to the public police, but only on the premises. Such security personnel are likely to possess stop and frisk authority in order to protect themselves when questioning highly suspicious individuals.

Realizing that legal guidelines for private searches are not plentiful, the Private Security Advisory Council has listed the following instances as appropriate search situations by private security personnel:

- Incidental to a valid arrest.
- Actual consent by a person.
- Incidental to valid conditions.
- Implied consent as a condition of employment or part of an employment contract.

Many businesses contain merchandise that can be easily concealed on a person or taken with the aid of lunch boxes, work clothes, umbrellas, and so forth. An employer has a limited search privilege, as a condition of employment, to conduct searches as employees depart. Searches can also be extended to lockers, desks, and automobiles parked on the premises. Employers should strengthen such searches through policies and procedures and signs in the workplace. Also, employers should obtain a consent to search form, signed by each applicant or employee as a condition of employment. Refusal by the employee to be searched would be justification for dismissal. It is important to realize that these searches are of the "consent" variety. In other words, an employee gives permission for the security officer to search. Each business differs as to the need for searches.

What If?

As a Security Officer, What Do You Do if You Notice Possible Evidence in a Vehicle in the Parking Lot?

While on patrol in the parking lot at a small private college you are approached by three young male students who claim that their vehicle will not start. They suspect a dead battery so you offer help. After the owner signs a release, a "jump" does not work so the men leave the vehicle to walk home for help. After they leave you notice on the back seat of the vehicle two hammers, gloves, and paper bags. Because two nights ago the windows of several vehicles were broken in the parking lot and items were stolen, you grow suspicious. The vehicle is unlocked, you follow up on your hunch, and search it. You find a small quantity of a substance that appears like marijuana. You summon your supervisor and wonder if your actions were legal.

Whether acting as a public police officer or security officer, a greater weight of evidence is required to justify a search of this vehicle. The hammers and gloves on the back seat do not provide probable cause to search the vehicle. The illegal search taints a drug arrest.

As a security officer, if you saw in "plain view," in the vehicle, stolen items, then public police should be contacted for a possible search under the "Carroll doctrine." This doctrine is based on the U.S. Supreme Court case, *Carroll v. U.S.* (1925), that permits warrantless searches where probable cause exists to believe that a vehicle contains contraband and/or the occupants have been arrested. Illegal drugs found under a legal "Carroll" search can be the basis for drug charges.

Questioning

The Fifth Amendment protects citizens from being compelled in any criminal case to be a witness against themselves. When a suspect is in the custody of the public police, there is often subtle pressure on the suspect to assist in an investigation. Whether in the custody of public or private police, no suspect is ever under an obligation to answer questions. Any forced confessions are inadmissible in court. Consequently, the Miranda rights warn a suspect about the right to remain silent and the right to an attorney.

Miranda Rights

Public police are required to read Miranda rights to a suspect *when the suspect is in custody and when they are about to question the suspect.* The questioning may not occur at the time of arrest so the Miranda rights may not be read to the suspect until later.

Many private security personnel read the Miranda rights to suspects as an extra precaution even though it may not be required in their jurisdiction. In fact, the U.S. Supreme Court has issued no ruling stating that the Miranda rights must be read by private security personnel prior to questioning suspects. Those security people who are granted special police powers or are working closely with public police are more likely to be required by a court to read the Miranda rights. These rights are typically read as follows:

1. You have the right to remain silent and say nothing.

2. If you make a statement, it can be used against you in a court of law.

3. You have the right to an attorney, even if you have no money, and to have your attorney present while you are being questioned.

4. You have the right to stop answering questions.

After the warning, a waiver of these rights can be secured through an affirmative reply to the following questions:

1. Do you understand each of these rights I have explained to you?

2. Having these rights in mind, do you wish to talk to us now?

The standard procedure is to obtain the suspect's signature on a statement listing these rights and the waiver.

Exclusionary Rule

The exclusionary rule emphasizes that any evidence obtained by public police in violation of the Fourth Amendment is inadmissible in criminal court. It was the famous U.S. Supreme Court case of *Mapp v. Ohio* that stated that illegally seized evidence is inadmissible in any state or federal criminal court. An example would be police going into someone's home without a valid search warrant and seizing evidence.

In reference to private security officers (not acting in cooperation with public police), evidence secured from an illegal search *may be* admissible in criminal or civil court. This legal standard is supported by the U.S. Supreme Court decision in *Burdeau v. McDowell.* Although private security may not be restricted by constitutional limitations, as are public police, the threat of a lawsuit for invasion of privacy is a possibility.

Furthermore, state court decisions may impose constitutional restrictions on security personnel. In the case *People v. Zelinsky*, the court ruled that the exclusionary rule applies to security officers and that their acts are "government actions." Therefore, the full force of the Constitution governs those acts. The Zelinsky case does show discontent from the California Supreme Court concerning only limited constitutional restraints on private security.

Different Arrest Situations

As a security officer, procedures involving a confrontation with a burglar, an employee-thief, or a shoplifter all differ. The next discussion is about these three arrest situations. The differences among them and the interplay of procedures and law are presented.

Burglar

Suppose as a security officer, you notice an intruder inside a perimeter fence carrying away what looks like company equipment. As an armed security officer, you pull your pistol and order the offender to halt. You use your radio to summon assistance and then cautiously handcuff and search the arrestee. If you are unarmed, more caution is advised: Obtain a good description and summon assistance. Catching a felon in the commission of a crime entails great risk, especially when compared to confronting an employee-thief or shoplifter.

Employee-Thief

In this type of situation, the employee-offender is less likely to be armed and dangerous. Also, the subject is often easy to identify and locate, especially since a paycheck and other benefits draw the individual to the workplace. Aggressive arrest procedures are usually not necessary.

The following two sections briefly list those things that the security officer should and should *not* do when confronting an employee-suspect. These sections emphasize a cautious approach that preserves employee rights while pursuing what is a delicate inquiry.

WHAT SHOULD BE DONE

1. Contact a supervisor for assistance.
2. Be prepared to show intent. That the stolen item is company property; that it was concealed or removed from the premises; that it was concealed or removed by the subject.
3. Notify the union if necessary.
4. Maintain accurate and complete documentation.
5. If you search the subject's belongings, *request* permission first.
6. Have a witness present at all times who is the same sex as the subject.
7. If a confession is made by the subject, have him or her write it and those present sign it.
8. *Ask* the suspect to sign a statement showing that no force or threats were applied.
9. When dealing with juveniles, consult with an attorney or local criminal justice agencies.

When you are absolutely certain that a suspect is hiding stolen merchandise (because you saw the theft and never lost sight of the subject) and the police have been called, let the police conduct the search. This transfers some liability to the police. In fact, contacting the police may be the only alternative for a difficult employee-suspect who refuses to return concealed merchandise.

WHAT SHOULD NOT BE DONE

1. Never accuse unless you are absolutely certain. The best witness is a reliable eyewitness.
2. Do not threaten the suspect.
3. If the suspect wants to leave, never detain him or her.
4. If possible, do not touch the suspect.
5. Do not think that private restitution is without problems. If you accept payments for stolen items, this may be construed as a bribe, and it can interfere with a bond or insurance.
6. Do not hesitate to seek competent legal advice.
7. Do not call the public police unless you have sound evidence (an eyewitness).

Shoplifter

A confrontation with a suspected shoplifter must be carefully handled. When a cautious approach is used (e.g., *asking* the subject to walk to an office to discuss a matter), a mistake by security personnel is easier to correct, and the chances of a lawsuit are reduced. As with a suspected employee-thief, aggressive arrest procedures are typically not necessary. A key strategy is to never take your eyes off the suspect. If you saw a person lift a store item off a shelf, conceal it, and leave the store without paying, there should be no doubt that shoplifting occurred. However, mistakes do occur. For example, you see a male shopper put a bottle of aspirins in his pocket and then leave the store. Later, after arresting the shopper, you discover that the aspirins were purchased at another store. What *actually* happened was that the shopper walked past the aspirin counter and decided to take some aspirins that were removed from his pocket and then returned to the pocket. Unfortunately, you began observing the shopper when he returned the aspirins to his pocket.

Tricking the Suspect Into Uncovering Evidence

If you have a suspect under arrest who will not give up evidence hidden on his or her person, let the individual have some privacy. An employee-thief or a shoplifter who refuses a request by security personnel to hand over concealed valuables can be left alone in a room that has surveillance capabilities. The offender, upon being concerned about the arrival of public police and a subsequent search, may hide the stolen valuables in the room while alone.

A security officer can use the same technique when a suspect is left alone in the backseat of a patrol car while the officer is supposedly occupied with some task. Frequently, offenders, even when handcuffed, stuff evidence (e.g., drugs, weapons, stolen items) into the seat. The backseat of a patrol car must be thoroughly searched whenever a person is removed. This procedure helps ensure that the right person is tied to the uncovered evidence. Typically, officers search the backseat of their patrol car when their tour of duty begins and then every time a subject exits the backseat.

Many states have shoplifting statutes that permit retail employees to temporarily detain suspected shoplifters to investigate the ownership of merchandise. Probable cause is a requirement for detention. All actions by the retailer must be reasonable. Usually a suspect is held for thirty minutes to one hour. Typically, shoplifting statutes are unclear as to how merchandise is to be removed from the suspect. A retailer should request that the shoplifter return all concealed merchandise. Public police can be called for difficult subjects. However, the retailer must be absolutely certain about the case. A criminal charge for shoplifting, rather than larceny, should be maintained since a retailer is afforded some protection for the detention under certain shoplifting statutes.

A key distinction between arrest and detention is that the arrest involves public police who arrive and transport the subject to jail. The retailer then supports an arrest warrant with probable cause. A detention can lead to public police involvement, but generally police are not contacted. During detention, retail personnel will request the shoplifted items, ask the subject to sign a confession and a statement that no coercion was applied, and warn the person not to return to the store.

Legal opinions differ on detention and arrest. Many view a detention similar to an arrest because the subject's freedom is restricted. A jury often makes the final decision.

There are some important rules to observe when confronting a person suspected of shoplifting. Here is a list of things that a security officer should and should *not* do when confronting a suspected shoplifter.

WHAT SHOULD BE DONE

1. Watch suspects carefully.
2. Remember, a reliable eyewitness is good probable cause.
3. Make sure that the item is removed from the counter or rack and *concealed* on the person. Concealment must be in a place where the merchandise is usually not worn. For example, do not arrest someone who put on a hat and departed. Politely bring the action to the customer's attention.
4. When you confront the suspect, *ask* him or her to accompany you to the office.
5. Have a witness present at all times who is the same sex as the subject.
6. Ask for a sales receipt.
7. Show intent. In other words, the item is the property of the store; it was concealed on the person; it was removed from the premises by the suspect. To prove intent, some locales require that the suspect pass the cash register. Other locales require that the suspect exit the store.
8. Document everything.
9. Interview for a reasonable amount of time.
10. Use reasonable force only as a last resort for the protection of yourself and others. It is better to let the subject go if he or she flees. Call the public police (with a good description of the subject) rather than risk a violent struggle, injuries, and a subsequent lawsuit.

11. *Ask* the subject to empty his or her belongings and pockets. If he or she refuses and you have probable cause (an eyewitness), call the public police.

12. If a confession is made by the subject, have him or her write it and all those present sign it.

13. *Ask* the subject to sign a statement showing that no force or threats were applied.

14. Make sure that the witness signs the criminal complaint.

15. When dealing with juveniles, consult with an attorney or criminal justice agencies.

16. Study the laws of your state and how the courts have interpreted statutes.

17. Check your local jurisdiction.

18. Remember that a guilty conviction is a good defense to a civil suit.

19. Make sure that each confrontation is cost-effective.

WHAT SHOULD NOT BE DONE

1. Do not ever take your eyes off a suspect.

2. Never accuse unless you are absolutely certain.

3. Do not forget that the responsibility to investigate the ownership of merchandise rests with the merchant, not police. Complete this process and establish intent before deciding to file charges.

4. Never yell at the subject or make loud accusations. This can result in a slander suit.

5. Never threaten the subject.

6. If possible, do not touch the subject.

7. Never search the subject; let public police do it.

8. If your employer requires you to pursue fleeing shoplifters, do not chase suspects beyond the premises unless you know what distance is permissible. Usually, it is not beyond the parking lot.

9. Never accept money from the subject.

10. Do not forget that many consider detention the same as arrest.

11. Never arrest an accomplice unless he or she actually participated in the crime. Mere presence is not sufficient proof of the accomplice's role.

12. Do not hesitate to plan a good shoplifting program and to seek competent legal counsel.

Many retail stores and security personnel use a "release" as a form of protection against a lawsuit for false arrest following a shoplifting incident. A release is a written statement signed by the subject who agrees not to bring suit against security personnel and the retail store. The release may contain a confession and statements that no force or threats were applied, and that the subject voluntarily cooperated with the investigation. Once the release and confession are signed, many retail stores end the detention and release the subject, or an arrest is made and public police are called.

Although a release may be signed by the subject, it does not relieve the arrestor from liability. The release actually has psychological value in that the person who signs it may mistakenly believe that a suit is not possible even though a claim can be made that the release was signed under duress.

Civil Recovery

Civil recovery is a strategy used by businesses to recover losses following a theft incident. Basically, a shoplifter is held liable for such costs as attorney fees and the expense of security. Locales may permit up to triple damages. State laws and procedures vary. Such laws may extend to cases of employee-theft, besides shoplifting. Since a person is innocent until proven guilty, it is probably better to wait for a guilty verdict before attempting civil recovery.

The basic procedures for civil recovery can include a couple of steps, depending on the response of the offender. First, the retailer sends an offender a demand letter for payment. This letter also contains civil recovery law and procedures. Second, if the offender does not respond, subsequent letters are sent stating that civil court action may result. Last, if the offender continues to not respond, the retailer must then decide whether it is cost-effective to pursue the case and the likelihood of the offender being able to pay for civil damages.

The retail business may elect to contract civil recovery to an external, specialized firm. These firms charge the business a percentage of the money they collect from the offender. This saves the retailer time and administrative expenses.

CHAPTER REVIEW

A. Multiple Choice

1. The most common type of arrest power held by security officers is
   a. equal to a deputy.
   b. special police powers.
   c. citizen arrest powers.
   d. arrest powers equal to the public police.
2. The most common type of arrest power held by private detectives is
   a. equal to a deputy.
   b. special police powers.
   c. citizen arrest powers.
   d. arrest powers equal to the public police.
3. Probable cause is required to
   a. obtain a search warrant.
   b. obtain an arrest warrant.
   c. make an arrest.
   d. all of the above.
4. This kind of search means that an individual has given permission to police or security to conduct a search.
   a. plain view
   b. lawful
   c. Carroll Doctrine
   d. consent
5. A key strategy when making a shoplifting case is to
   a. request payment immediately for the stolen item.
   b. never take your eyes off the suspect.
   c. arrest the suspect only when public police arrive.
   d. always handcuff a shoplifter as soon as they conceal merchandise.

B. True or False

1. All state statutes contain similar arrest powers for citizens.
2. An employee observed in an unauthorized area holding company property provides enough probable cause for a security officer to make an arrest on the premises.
3. In all states, public police are prohibited from working as security officers.

4. The statement "you are under arrest" is not mandatory to produce an arrest situation.
5. Deadly force should be restricted to situations where one's life or another's life requires protection.

Applications

Application 8A

Research the arrest powers of security officers in your state.

Application 8B

Create a situation where sufficient evidence is lacking for a security officer to make an arrest.

Application 8C

Create a situation where sufficient evidence exists for a security officer to make an arrest.

Application 8D

Prepare a list of procedures to follow for an unarmed security officer confronting a burglar on the premises. Role-play this situation.

Application 8E

Prepare a list of procedures to follow for a security officer confronting an employee-thief. Role-play this situation.

Application 8F

Prepare a list of procedures to follow for a security officer confronting a shoplifter. Role-play this situation.

9

Self-Defense and Weapons

CHAPTER OUTLINE

OBJECTIVES

After studying this chapter, you will be able to:

- Explain why a security officer must avoid the use of force whenever possible.
- Understand how to apply defensive techniques against attackers.
- Explain the use-of-force continuum.
- Understand how to handcuff and search an arrestee.
- Describe the use of the baton.
- Describe the use of chemical sprays.
- Discuss problems and misconceptions concerning the arming of security officers.
- Explain the legal aspects of firearms.
- Discuss revolvers and automatics.
- List at least eight safety rules for firearms.

Use of Force

All security officers should be well trained and prepared to *avoid* the use of force whenever possible. Force not only includes using a firearm, but also employing nonlethal methods, such as defensive techniques, a baton, or chemical spray. In earlier years, a major qualification for police and security officers was size. The bigger the person was, the greater was the likelihood of being hired. Brute force or "street justice" were common job duties. Today, however, the slightest force—even holding someone's arm—can result in a lawsuit. An alleged victim of excessive force can sue the officer, the supervisor, the employer, and the manufacturer of the weapon used. Those who conducted the training are also subject to being sued. Consequently, a wise security officer uses psychology, human relations skills, and empathy to avoid force. *The use of force must be a last resort.*

An unfortunate result of using force is that even if an officer reacts to an aggressive subject by applying minimum force, the officer can still be sued. Furthermore, an officer may be involved in an incident where serious injury to a suspect occurs even though the officer only intended to control the individual. For example, as an officer is attempting to handcuff a shoplifter, the offender breaks free and falls into a glass cabinet. The offender sustains severe lacerations and nerve damage.

As covered in the previous chapter, when an arrest occurs, the force applied must be *reasonable*. This means the amount of force that a reasonable person would use under similar circumstances to control the subject. Force should never exceed that which is necessary to control the situation.

Self-Defense

Security officers must always be prepared for a subject who may attack. When such a confrontation occurs, an officer must control the subject for obvious safety reasons. Previous self-defense and martial arts training are a definite asset when defending oneself against attack. For those not trained in self-defense, specialized publications and training are plentiful.

Protective Stance and Basic Moves

A few basic moves can provide a security officer with improved protection against an unarmed attack by a subject. Frequently, a subject will try to punch or kick a security officer during a confrontation or arrest. Security officers must always be prepared for this aggressive action by maintaining a safe distance (three to four feet) away from a subject. Also, avoid standing in front of a subject if you believe an attack is likely, Figure 9-1. Provide the potential attacker with less of a target by standing to the side, Figure 9-2. Try not to make this defensive position appear obvious. If a punch to the head is arriving, this position provides an improved opportunity to move and step out of the way. Your left arm can also be raised, with a fist, to block an oncoming punch. If a kick to the groin is attempted by the subject, the left leg can act as a shield, refer again to Figure 9-2.

If you are grabbed from behind, thrust your elbow back to the midsection of the attacker. When close to a subject, an elbow is more powerful than a fist. If you can step to the side slightly (left side for example), cup your left hand over your right fist while your right fist and arm are being raised up to gain momentum. Then, you can swing your right elbow back into the subject's solar plexus (above stomach) or head. This can be a devastating blow. Two other moves when grabbed from behind are to swing your head back into the attacker's nose and use the heal of your shoe to kick the attacker's shin.

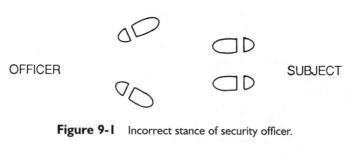

Figure 9-1   Incorrect stance of security officer.

Figure 9-2   Correct stance of security officer.

These are only some basic moves. Use them as your starting point as you begin to develop your self-defense skills.

Defense Against a Weapon

A subject may attack with a club or similar object or a sharp tool (knife or ax). This is a life-threatening situation. Only the most skilled security officer should attempt to defend against such an attack without using a weapon. However, a surprise assault may occur and the security officer must immediately raise an arm to block and/or step out of the way. The security officer should then use whatever means are available to neutralize the attack. This includes use of a baton, spray, a nearby object, a swift kick to the groin, or a firearm. In these life-threatening attacks, deadly force may be the only avenue of protection for the security officer.

Faced with a Gun

Security officers' options are obviously limited when a subject is pointing a gun at them. However, the following are some suggestions.

1. For safety, avoid quick movements and abusive comments.
2. Speak in a low, calm, reassuring voice. Try to reason with the subject.
3. Stress that you can play a role in helping the subject.
4. Keep the subject talking.
5. Never hand over your weapon. The offender's weapon may be unloaded or a toy.
6. If the subject is unwilling to hand over the weapon, suggest that it be carefully placed on the ground.

What If

As a Security Officer, What Do You Do if You Are Unarmed and Observe a Robbery-in-Progress?

As a uniformed security officer, while on patrol at a mall, you observe a robbery-in-progress at a shoe store. A robber is pointing a pistol at a cashier. You are surprised because you have never seen a robbery-in-progress before, but you know you must take quick action. You look around and notice that customers in the store are shopping as if they are unaware of what is happening. The area is busy both inside and outside of the store. What do you do?

Since the chain-of-events will change rapidly, quickly get a description of the robber, immediately remove yourself from the area, and use your radio to report the event. If the robber were to see you, the situation could become more dangerous for everyone. If

continued

possible, and without being seen, follow the robber as you maintain radio communications. You may be able to identify the exit the robber uses, a getaway vehicle, and direction of travel. This will aid in apprehension. Exercise extreme caution and maintain a wide distance between you and the robber because if the robber notices you, the robber may fire a weapon and injure or kill someone. If the firearm was discharged in the store, avoid following the robber and tend to the needs of victims; use your radio to report on the status of the situation and whether an ambulance is needed.

When a robbery is in progress, safety is the highest priority. It is always better to let the robber leave the area where innocent bystanders are located. Furthermore, a confrontation with a robber by armed officers should occur when dispatch knows of the event and a description of the robber, and adequate backup is available.

Controlled Defense

Security work requires emotional control. Security officers who lose their tempers frequently or act emotional when something goes wrong should concentrate on emotional control. This is not an easy task, but it can be mastered through hard work and effort. We previously discussed some strategies for improving human relations. Here are some additional guidelines:

1. Always avoid a physical confrontation by calming subjects. Do not provoke anger from them. It takes little skill to make nasty remarks to a person. The professional security officer is "human relations smart."
2. Self-defense skills must be used strictly for defensive purposes.
3. Once a subject is controlled, defensive action must stop.
4. Security officers must be aware of their emotions, maintain self-control, and act in a professional manner.

Use-of-Force Continuum

The use-of-force continuum has been taught for several years to police and security personnel. It consists of multiple levels of force with each level representing an escalation depending on aggressive actions of the opposing subject. *The use-of-force continuum assumes that a security officer is well-trained, conditioned, and equipped with pepper spray, baton, handcuffs, and a firearm. Usually, this is not the case. When security officers encounter an aggressive subject without such equipment, they should observe, report, and let public police handle the problem.* Company policies and procedures should be well-planned so that security officers know what to do when faced with aggressive subjects. Reporting requirements should also be included in policies and procedures, especially when force is applied. Training should include a variety of scenarios.

There are variations to the use-of-force continuum and the variations are debated. Here is a use-of-force continuum:

1. *Officer presence.* The physical presence of an officer can serve to prevent or stop aggressive behavior by a subject. However, none of the levels presented here come with guarantees. In fact, the sight of a security officer may cause greater anger by the subject. Consequently, the next level becomes especially important.

2. *Verbalization.* In combination with a physical presence, a calm, nonthreatening, but firm message can de-escalate a tense situation. Use respectful words and a mild, friendly tone. Emphasize that you want to help the person. Consider demeanor. For example, avoid threatening gestures such as pointing. Also, a protective stance will provide a physical advantage.

3. *Control holds and restraints.* Attempts at avoiding a confrontation are not always successful. This level involves bare hands to guide, hold, or restrain. Handcuffs may be used at this level if an arrest is made. When the decision is made to make physical contact, potential liability will increase.

4. *Chemical agents.* This level is activated when levels one through three have not been successful. However, sprays may be unsuccessful on the insane, drug addicts, or hysterical persons. Also, it may cause a severe reaction and even death to a suspect with medical or allergy problems. The spray may also harm officers due to wind or a misdirected spray.

5. *Temporary incapacitation.* This level is applied because of an extreme and violent situation. It stops short of deadly force. Training and conditioning are essential if an officer is to apply this level of the continuum. Techniques include evasive actions, arm and baton blocks, kicks, takedowns, restraints, ground fighting, weapon retention, and defense against knives, firearms, and other weapons. Potential liability is significant. However, violence from the offender requires self-defense. For example, an offender is physically beating an officer, and the offender continues the attack, so the officer thrusts a baton into the offender's stomach which halts the attack.

6. *Deadly force.* This level is applied when a security officer is in fear of being killed or another person's life is in danger. Deadly force can result from hands, impact tools, firearms, among other methods. The potential liability is significant. The continuum is likely to be used as a test of whether the deadly force was justified and whether other methods were attempted first.

Handcuffing

A security officer is never secure against attack once handcuffs are applied to a prisoner. Although a subject's wrists are locked, a swift kick becomes a serious threat. If the handcuffs are applied incorrectly, or if a security officer takes too much time to apply the second cuff, the subject can turn this restraining device into a lethal weapon. Some offenders after being handcuffed from behind can bring their wrists down to their feet, step back over their wrists, and attack with the cuffs in front.

Double-Locking Handcuffs

The double-locking handcuffs are widely used by police and security officers. After the handcuffs are applied, the top of the key is inserted into a small hole containing a pin on each handcuff stem, Figure 9-3. This pin is pushed in with the top of the key to double-lock. Manufacturers vary on the double-locking mechanism. Double-locking is supposed to prevent a prisoner from picking the lock. However, handcuff locks are relatively easy to pick. Sharp criminals carry a handcuff key or are able to fashion such a key from a small piece of metal or other hard object. By looking at the key, we can see that it is not difficult to make a copy. Another reason for double-locking is to outwit those prisoners who, while wearing handcuffs not yet double-locked, tighten the cuffs and then claim their wrists hurt in order to trick the arrestor into taking the cuffs off for an adjustment. When handcuffs are double-locked, it is unlikely that a prisoner will be able to tighten or loosen the cuffs.

Use of Handcuffs

When should handcuffs be used? Policy and procedure manuals often answer this question. Typically, when a felon is arrested, handcuffs are appropriate regardless of sex or age. Sometimes, an arrestee may seem calm and cooperative, so handcuffs are not applied. However, as soon as the officer is distracted, the once "harmless" arrestee attacks with a vengeance. Many public police have been killed because they thought they could predict the behavior of an arrestee and decided not to handcuff. The following list provides some general guidelines to use when handcuffing an offender.

1. If possible, have a second security officer present before handcuffing and searching.
2. When handcuffing, first face the prisoner away from you (Figure 9-4). Then, bring the prisoner's right hand and arm back with the thumb up and palm facing out. Apply the cuff with the keyway facing out. Always keep the prisoner off balance (e.g., feet widely spread apart). Bring the left hand back, thumb up and palm out. Apply the other cuff with the keyway facing out. Then double-lock the handcuff.

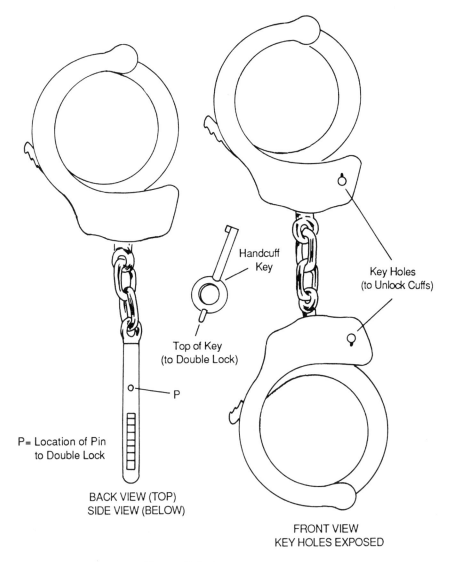

Handcuff
Key

Top of Key
(to Double Lock)

P

P= Location of Pin
to Double Lock

BACK VIEW (TOP)
SIDE VIEW (BELOW)

Key Holes
(to Unlock Cuffs)

FRONT VIEW
KEY HOLES EXPOSED

Figure 9-3 Handcuffs and key.

3. To further secure the prisoner, after applying one cuff, pass the unattached cuff under the subject's belt before applying it to the other wrist.

4. Avoid cuffing a prisoner from the front.

5. Do not "slap" the cuffs on a prisoner as seen on television. This can break the wrists.

6. Never cuff only one wrist and hold the other cuff to lead the prisoner. The subject may break away and use the loose cuff as a weapon.

7. Refrain from handcuffing yourself to the prisoner.

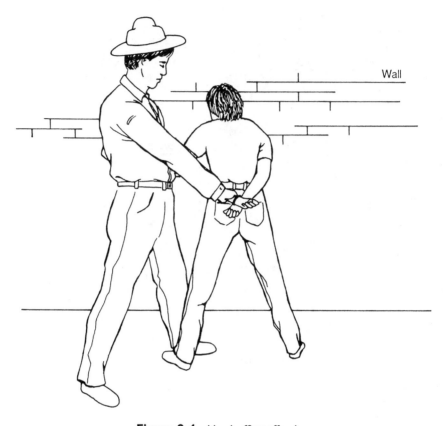

Wall

Figure 9-4 Handcuffing offender.

8. If only one pair of handcuffs is available for two prisoners, first face the prisoners away from you, side by side. Then, bring the right arm of the prisoner to the right, back for cuffing. Pass the free cuff through the same prisoner's belt, and then attach the second cuff to the right wrist of the other prisoner, Figure 9-5. Both prisoners will find any quick movements or running very uncomfortable.

9. Never handcuff a prisoner to an object that may create a dangerous situation. Examples are vehicles and street signs.

10. Remember that handcuffs are not foolproof. Offenders may attack, escape, or remove the handcuffs with the aid of a hidden tool.

11. To unlock handcuffs that have been locked, insert the key and turn. For handcuffs that have been double-locked, insert the key and then turn one way and then the other.

12. Always carry an extra handcuff key hidden somewhere on yourself in case of emergency.

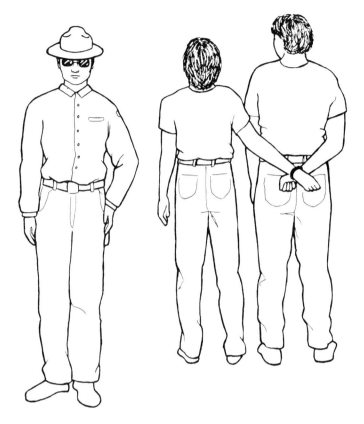

Figure 9-5 Handcuffing two prisoners with one pair of handcuffs.

What If?

As a Security Officer, What Do You Do if a Public Police Officer Asks You to Put Your Handcuffs on a Prisoner When the Police Cuffs Are Removed?

You are a hospital security officer who was just assigned to assist a public police officer who is guarding a prisoner who was brought to the hospital for stitches for an injury received during an arrest by the police officer. The local jail refused to take the prisoner until he received medical attention.

During the wait for a doctor, the police officer asks you: "How about putting your cuffs on the prisoner when I take mine off? I have to leave for a few minutes, but I'll be back soon." As the security officer, how do you respond to this request?

The prisoner is the responsibility of the police officer. The police officer could have an ulterior motive for wanting to retrieve the cuffs and have you apply your cuffs. Tell the police officer that you rather not make the switch. If the police officer insists, call your supervisor.

Searching after Handcuffing

As an added precaution, an arrestee should be handcuffed before a search. Security and police officers often conduct a "frisk" after an arrest. This entails a *pat-down* of the arrestee's clothing to retrieve weapons and evidence. A *field search* is a more thorough investigation where the officer inspects the inside of pockets. Correctional authorities sometimes conduct a *strip search* that involves removing the prisoner's clothing at the correctional facility. *Body cavity searches* are conducted at correctional facilities by medical personnel.

Viewpoints and procedures concerning the searching of an arrestee have varied over time. The *wall search* ("Up against the wall!") has been popular for many years, but what does an officer do if no wall is available? Training programs should consider various circumstances while continuously researching safer and more effective methods of conducting searches. The following list provides some suggestions for searching.

1. Maintain control over the prisoner through clear commands.
2. After an arrest, handcuff first and then search.
3. If a traditional wall search is used, order arrestees to raise their hands high, and spread them wide and flat on the wall. At the same time, prisoners' feet should be spread wide and back away from the wall. This "spread eagle" position provides a defensive advantage for officers. It enables officers to kick prisoners' legs or knock an arm, thus causing prisoners to lose their balance. As an added precaution, order prisoners to spread their feet apart and back while leaning their foreheads on the wall. This makes a quick move more difficult.
4. If a wall search is not possible, similar search techniques can be used in an open space.
5. Allow one hand to search while the other hand is prepared for defensive action (e.g., holding the prisoner or a weapon).
6. Always keep your eyes on the subject and do not become distracted.
7. If a second security officer is available, one can search while the other holds a weapon ready. Officers searching should never pass in front of officers holding the weapon.
8. If a security officer must deal with two or more subjects placed under arrest, they can be ordered into a kneeling position with ankles crossed and hands raised high and forward. Then they should be handcuffed, Figure 9-6. Order them into a line and always approach the last subject first while the front subject is looking forward.
9. Weapons and evidence are of all shapes and sizes and can be hidden anywhere on a person and nearby.

Figure 9-6 Kneeling position with ankles crossed.

10. A complete search covers hat to shoes. Search for items taped to the body, within a belt or waistband, and inside shoes, socks, cuffs, collars, hair, pens, cigarette packs, and so forth.

Nonlethal Weapons

Baton

A baton is capable of extending a security officers reach while enabling the officer to subdue an attacker without killing. It is also a good psychological tool to deter attack.

As with other weapons, employers should provide quality training before a baton is issued to security officers. Since this weapon has the capacity to cause death, security officers must exercise care in its use. A strike to the offender's head or chest should only be made in life-threatening situations. Strikes to other body locations can be used to control a subject. Examples include shins, back of leg behind knees, and elbows. A jab to the stomach can knock the wind out of an aggressive subject. A baton can be devastating if a security officer is able to block an incoming punch, kick, or other type of assault. Since use of a baton can break bones or cut, it can subject security officers to claims of brutality and a lawsuit. Thus, a baton must be used in a reasonable manner to control a subject or stop an attack.

Any weapons carried by the security officer must be approved by the employer. Large heavy flashlights and blackjacks are examples of items that must be avoided since these items can cause fatal injuries.

Chemical Sprays

Three major types of chemical nonlethal weapons are chloroacteophenone (CN), orthochlorbenzalmalononitrile (CS), and oleoresin capsicum (OC). Although these substances are called by various names, they are used to temporarily disable an attacker while preventing the need to apply deadly force. *Training is essential.*

This weapon is contained in an aerosol cannister. The dispenser can be small, such as the size of a pen, or large for crowd control. A security officer's handheld cannister is worn in a holster attached to the belt. When sprayed in the face, these substances can cause burning watery eyes, nasal and skin discomfort, coughing, restricted breathing, and nausea. Subjects may drop to the ground holding their faces. The adverse reaction is temporary, but provides the officer with enough time to apply handcuffs. Officers must watch for wind direction and exercise caution when using sprays, especially in a confined place, since these substances may land on a security officer's face or the wrong person. State laws should be checked since usage may be restricted. Depending on the state, the use of chemical weapons may also require the subject to be examined and treated by a medical doctor.

CN has been criticized for not being as effective as CS, especially when a subject is drunk or high on drugs. During the last half of the twentieth century the military and police began a switch from CN to CS because CS takes effect faster, it is more potent and less toxic, and it is effective in low concentrations. Today, OC is the most popular spray and regarded to be the most distressing to experience. It is extracted from chili peppers.

Firearms

Armed versus Unarmed

The controversy over whether to arm security officers with firearms is continuous. As with other topics subject to debate, it is important to understand both sides of the issue. If people and assets are to be protected in a high crime area, then armed officers can be a deterrent. However, other factors require consideration. What type of training is available? Would armed security officers create a safety problem? Would employees or customers find firearms offensive? What is the level of public police protection? What is their response time? The security industry trend is away from armed officers. In other words, armed officers may be more of a liability than an asset.

Management is typically concerned about a mistake, such as an officer who fires a weapon and hits an innocent bystander. Also, insurance is expensive to protect a business against a mistake in the use of deadly force. And, when a serious error does occur, a lawsuit can cost millions of dollars.

Here are Web resources on armed personnel:

National Association of Security and Investigative Regulators: www.nasir.org

International Association of Law Enforcement Firearms Instructors: www.ialefi.com

American Society for Law Enforcement Training: www.aslet.org

Misconceptions and Problems

Misconceptions exist concerning the use of firearms. Television programs distort the frequency that firearms are used by public and private police. Although the star of a police or detective show may shoot several criminals between each commercial, the reality is that most security officers or law enforcement personnel never fire their weapons when on duty during their entire career.

A major misconception and problem concerns the training of security officers. A lot of the firearms training in both the public and private sectors does not simulate actual combat conditions. Depending on training requirements, security officers may spend a few hours on a firing range every six months. Some have not practiced in years. Fifty to one hundred rounds are typically fired by each security officer when on a range. Security officers qualifying on a firing range concentrate on stance, aiming, breathing, and basically scoring as many "bull's-eyes" as possible. However, in an actual shoot-out, there is usually no time to stand correctly and aim. Within a few seconds many shoot-outs are over. Firearms training may exclude night firing and use of moving targets. When practice rounds or "wad cutters" are used for training, this low-power ammunition may not really prepare officers for the noise, kick, and trajectory of real service ammunition. One study found that police officers missed their intended target between 75 and 90 percent of the time in real combat situations. The chance of hitting a bystander is high. With all these problems in mind, firearms in-structors are working to improve training.

Legal Aspects

State laws vary concerning a security officer carrying and using a firearm. The privilege may equal that of a private citizen. A special permit is often required. Other states allow a state registered, licensed, and trained security officer to carry a firearm to and from work and on the job. A concealed weapon should never be carried without a proper permit; a violation is a felony in many states. State law should be studied.

Firearms are to be used when security officers attempt to save their life or the life of another. The burden of proof is on the security officer to justify why the weapon was fired. Did the circumstances allow the security officer to use alternative methods to control the subject?

An armed security officer can face civil and/or criminal liabilities for using excessive force, shooting an innocent bystander, or accidentally discharging a firearm. For example, a security officer catches a group of youths painting automobiles on the premises and orders them to halt. They run, of course, and throw their cans of spray paint at the security officer. The security officer shoots one of the youths. This is excessive force.

Warning shots should never be fired. A bystander can be accidentally shot and property damage may occur.

Revolver and Automatic

Organizational policy often dictates which type of weapon is carried. If a security officer does have a choice, the best approach is to first study several sources of information on each type of weapon.

REVOLVER The .38 caliber revolver with a four inch barrel (Figure 9-7) was especially popular during the twentieth century. This weapon has numerous parts. The *cylinder latch* is moved to open the cylinder to load and unload. When the *cylinder* is opened it swings to the side exposing six chambers into which cartridges are inserted to load. The *ejector rod* protrudes from the center of the cylinder, and when pushed into the cylinder, it helps to unload. When the *trigger* is pulled the *hammer* goes back before being released to strike the firing pin which strikes the cartridge and results in the weapon being fired. This is called double-action shooting. The weapon is properly aimed when the front *sight* is lined up within the *rear sight*. Eyes should focus on the front sight. This is called sight alignment, Figure 9-8. A major advan-

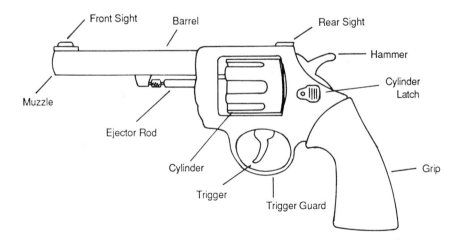

Figure 9-7   .38 Caliber Revolver.

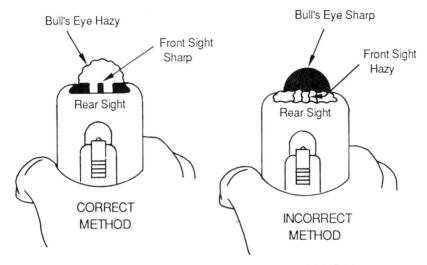

Bull's Eye Hazy

Front Sight Sharp

Rear Sight

CORRECT METHOD

Bull's Eye Sharp

Front Sight Hazy

Rear Sight

INCORRECT METHOD

FRONT SIGHT CONCENTRATION
Eye should be focused on front sight rather than target.

Figure 9-8 Sighting.

tage of a revolver is that if a round fails to fire, a security officer can pull the trigger to fire the next round.

The Technology Assessment Program of the National Institute of Justice, in conjunction with independent testing laboratories, tested twenty-two different models of revolvers (.38 and .357 caliber) against minimum performance requirements. Revolvers were required to fire 600 rounds of ammunition, and withstand drop and hammer safety tests, among other research. Half of the revolvers tested (11 of 22) were capable of firing the required 600 rounds of ammunition without failures described in the standard, according to the results of this test.

AUTOMATIC The term "automatic" (Figure 9-9) refers to a handgun that fires a cartridge in a chamber, ejects the spent cartridge case, cocks the hammer, and loads a new round from a magazine containing cartridges. Another squeeze of the trigger begins the sequence again. Essentially, gases from the fired cartridge are trapped and force the hammer back and a new round is loaded for firing. The automatic pistol has the advantage of speed when it is fired and reloaded. A preloaded clip facilitates easy, quick loading. Also, revolvers usually hold six rounds, while an automatic will contain from eight to sixteen rounds. Unlike a revolver, if an automatic does not fire, an officer must pull back the slide and clear the chamber before firing again.

The Technology Assessment Program tested twenty different models of autoloading (automatic) pistols (9 mm and .45 caliber). Testing included the requirement that each pistol fire 600 rounds and withstand a drop safety test.

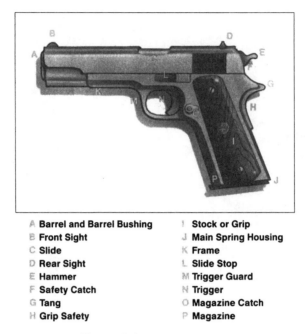

A Barrel and Barrel Bushing	I Stock or Grip
B Front Sight	J Main Spring Housing
C Slide	K Frame
D Rear Sight	L Slide Stop
E Hammer	M Trigger Guard
F Safety Catch	N Trigger
G Tang	O Magazine Catch
H Grip Safety	P Magazine

Figure 9-9   Automatic Pistol.

Just under three-quarters of the pistols tested (14 of 20) were capable of firing the required 600 rounds of ammunition without failures described in the standard, according to the results of this test.

FIREARMS AND AMMUNITION   Firearms and ammunition vary in effectiveness. For example, although a .22 caliber firearm can kill, it typically lacks the power to consistently stop a life-threatening attack. The traditional .38 caliber is more powerful than the .22. However, it may also lack the "knock down" necessary to keep an offender from killing. In contrast, the .357, .44, .45, .40, 9 mm, and 10 mm are more reliable for stopping a killer. Two major disadvantages of these larger calibers is the powerful recoil and the possibility of these rounds passing through people, walls, doors, and so forth, creating obvious safety problems. Hospitals, office buildings, and most locations avoid powerful firearms. The danger is too great.

Safety Guidelines

Safety is very important when dealing with weapons. The following lists offer safety guidelines for firearms and for the firing range.

Firearms Safety

1. Firearms should be regarded as a last resort only when other defensive techniques fail.

2. Always treat all firearms as if they are loaded.

3. Accidental discharge of firearms causes numerous deaths and injuries each year. Eugene Finneran states in his book that "These accidents are caused due to lack of knowledge, failure to properly secure, careless handling, or using the deadly weapon as if it were a toy."

4. When passing a firearm to another person, always point it down, without placing any fingers near the trigger. It should be transferred unloaded.

5. When receiving a weapon, always request that it be unloaded and pointed to the ground. Upon receiving a weapon, *always* check to see if it is unloaded. *Never* take someone's word for it.

6. Safety must extend to the home, besides work. Unload and securely lock all weapons and ammunition.

7. Never point a weapon at someone unless you intend to use it.

8. Inspect and clean weapons regularly.

9. Repairs should be done by a qualified gunsmith. Never tamper with a weapon unless you are qualified and know what you are doing.

10. When on duty in an environment prone toward violence, consider wearing a bullet-resistant vest. Modern ballistic armor can repel many types of bullets and also knives.

Guidelines for the Firing Range

1. When on a range, always pay close attention to commands from the supervisor or range master.

2. Anyone seeing a dangerous situation on the range should shout "cease fire!"

3. Proper protection for eyes and ears is important.

4. Several types of courses exist for firearms qualification on a firing range. These courses include timed or not timed, varied distances, varied amounts of ammunition fired, moving or stationary targets, and day or night firing. Positions also vary. Examples include standing, kneeling, crouching, sitting, prone, and use of a barricade. A good course for beginning security personnel would be firing twenty rounds from the seven yard line, twenty from the fifteen yard line, and ten from the twenty-five yard line.

5. Firearms should be gripped without squeezing too hard. Individual preference often dictates how a weapon is gripped.

6. Correct sight alignment is vital. The shooter's eyes should focus on the front sight.

7. An eye examination may reveal the need for corrected vision. Improved performance on the firing range can result.

8. As you breathe, your body moves. During sight alignment, take a normal breath in and hold it until firing is complete.

9. A trigger should be squeezed and not jerked.

10. Remember that everyone must fire a weapon for the first time. Nobody is born with this skill.

CHAPTER REVIEW

A. Multiple Choice

1. Which of the following defensive moves is least likely to be used by a security officer who is grabbed from behind?

   a. Swing an elbow back to the subject's solar plexus or head.

   b. Kick back to the subject's shin.

   c. Grab the subject's head for a headlock.

   d. Swing your head back into the subject's nose.

2. Oleoresin capsicum (OC) is made from

   a. tomatoes.

   b. radishes.

   c. avocadoes.

   d. chili peppers.

3. Select the incorrect statement concerning handcuffing.

   a. To further secure the prisoner, after applying one cuff, pass the unattached cuff under the subject's belt before applying it to the other wrist.

   b. Refrain from handcuffing yourself to the prisoner.

   c. Handcuff keys are difficult to duplicate.

   d. Double-locking prevents a prisoner from picking the lock.

4. Which statement is incorrect about the criticisms of firearms training?

   a. A lot of firearms training does not simulate actual combat conditions.

   b. Most firearms training occurs during the day.

   c. Practice ammunition may not prepare security officers for use of service ammunition.

   d. Most range masters emphasize that firearms will be used frequently when on duty.

5. Select the incorrect statement.

   a. A .38 is more powerful than a .22.

   b. An automatic pistol often contains more rounds than a revolver.

   c. Most hospitals favor arming security officers with .357 caliber ammunition.

   d. A .22 caliber firearm can kill.

B. True or False

1. The slightest force, even holding someone's arm, can result in a lawsuit.

2. When involved in a physical confrontation, an elbow is more powerful than a fist.

3. Once an aggressive arrestee is controlled, security officers have a duty to teach the subject a lesson through punishment.

4. When a prisoner is secured by handcuffs, security officers are safe from attack.

5. Before shooting a subject who is threatening a life, always fire a warning shot.

Applications

Application 9A

Arrange students in groups of two, one playing the role of an attacker, the other playing a security officer. Practice a security officer's defensive response to:

a. a punch to the face.

b. a kick to the groin.

c. a grab around the neck or chest from the front and then from behind.

d. an attack with a club or knife.

e. an offender pointing a gun.

Application 9B

As a security officer on patrol, you see a woman being pistol-whipped by a man. What do you do as an unarmed officer? What do you do as an armed officer?

Application 9C

Research the arming of security officers in your area. Answer the following questions.

a. What percentage of security officers are armed?

b. What types of firearms are carried?

c. What type of training is required?

Application 9D

As a security supervisor at the Mid-City Plaza you must prepare a report for management concerning the use of force by one of your subordinates. Last Friday evening, Security Officer Ellen Arnold shot a suspect. Apparently she received a radio transmission of a robbery at the Fast Food Fair. While chasing the suspect, he turned around, reached for something in his pocket, and

Officer Arnold shot him in the groin. The suspect told public police investigators that he was reaching for candy that he had shoplifted from the Fast Food Fair. He was unarmed. Officer Arnold was called to a robbery and expected a robber, not a shoplifter. A manager at the Fast Food Fair admitted that he called in a robbery to receive a faster security response.

At this point the suspect is recuperating at a local hospital and Officer Arnold has been assigned to CCTV surveillance. The police are continuing their investigation and an arrest of Officer Arnold is unlikely. The suspect has been charged with shoplifting. Management at Mid-City Plaza is concerned about possibly being sued by the suspect. They are thinking of having unarmed security officers only, even though Officer Arnold and other armed officers are screened and trained by certified firearms instructors.

What do you write in your report? Was Officer Arnold justified in her decision to shoot the suspect? Should she be disciplined or fired? Should all security officers be unarmed at the Mid-City Plaza?

SECTION
3

COUNTERING
BUSINESS LOSSES

10

Combatting Internal Losses

CHAPTER OUTLINE

OBJECTIVES

After studying this chapter, you will be able to:

- Explain internal losses and internal theft.
- State the costs of internal theft and explain whether internal or external thieves are a more serious threat to an organization.
- Describe the types of employees who steal.
- Explain the reasons for employee theft.
- List ten techniques of internal theft.
- Describe at least ten signs that may help detect internal theft.
- List and describe at least ten strategies to combat internal theft.

Internal Losses

Internal losses include many types of events that can harm people and create a financial drain on an organization. Crimes, fires, and accidents are major internal loss problems. Employees, customers, contractors, visitors, and others who have easy access to an organization may, for example, destroy property, commit violence in the workplace, or steal proprietary information. Internal losses are broad and can result from lost productivity due to substance abuse or theft of time by employees who leave work early or take extended lunch breaks.

The internal threat to information technology (IT) is another serious problem. Although the media focuses on high-profile outsider cyber-attacks, the greatest threat to corporate information systems is from within. Because information on many insider attacks is not released to the public, the frequency of the following scenario is impossible to gauge. A systems administrator in one hospital learned that she was about to be fired so she arranged for a "severance package" for herself by encrypting a critical patient database. Her supervisor feared the worse and loss of his job, so in exchange for the decryption key, the manager arranged for a termination "bonus" and an agreement that the hospital would not prosecute. The dilemma facing the hospital, as to whether to meet the offender's demands or prosecute, can produce interesting debate. How long could the hospital function without the critical patient database? How much time would be required by the criminal justice system to resolve the case? More on IT security in Chapter 14. Although there are many sources of internal losses, this chapter focuses on internal theft and countermeasures.

As we know, outsiders also pose potential threats to organizations. Access controls and physical security are important measures to prevent losses as covered in Chapter 4.

Internal Theft

Internal Theft Defined

Internal theft and *employee theft* are used interchangeably in this chapter and can be defined as stealing by employees from their employers. *Pilferage* is stealing in small quantities. For example, a worker taking home a tool. *Embezzlement* involves stealing money or property that has been entrusted to an employee. For instance, a bookkeeper writes checks to himself or herself and cashes the checks. Although pilferage may seem to be less of a cost to a business than embezzlement, this may not always be the case. For example, numerous employees can steal small amounts during one week that can have a total loss that exceeds one case of embezzlement.

Fraud is defined as a knowing misrepresentation of the truth or conceal-ment of a fact to cause another to act to their detriment. A bookkeeper in a business may, for example, alter checks for personal gain. *Insurance fraud* occurs when an insured party lies on a policy application or falsely claims a loss. *Fraud on the market* occurs when an issuer of stock provides false infor-mation that affects the market price of the stock causing people to buy or sell the stock (Figure 10-1).

Figure 10-1 Employee theft involves employees stealing from their employ-ers. Fraud refers to a misrepresentation of a fact to cause another to act to their detriment, an example being fraud on the market.

Costs of Internal Theft

Employees often fail to notice the impact internal theft has on a business. The seriousness of the problem and how it permeates a workplace are typically underestimated.

The total estimated cost of employee theft varies from one source to another, mainly because theft is defined and data is collected in so many different ways. According to the U.S. Chamber of Commerce, 30 percent of business failures result from employee theft with more than $120 billion lost annually to American companies. The Association of Certified Fraud Examiners found that 6 percent of an organization's revenues are lost to employee fraud and abuse, totaling $400 billion annually.

When internal and external thieves are compared, the greatest threat is from within. For example, when fraud and embezzlement losses in financial institutions (banks, savings and loans, and credit unions) are compared with external crime (robberies, burglaries, and larcenies), the problem is clear. FBI statistics reveal that bank employees steal fifteen times more than bank robbers. Employees have easy access to the organization and they are familiar with system weaknesses.

Pilferage at Graystone Industries

Graystone Industries had been manufacturing automobile replacement parts for over fifty years. The huge plant was the major employer in Florence City. Since the plant produced popular items such as spark plugs, fan belts, and oil and air filters, internal theft always seemed to be a major problem. The president of the company, Howard Brown, permitted employees to purchase automobile replacement parts at slightly above cost. Employees did take advantage of this offer. However, theft remained a serious problem. To reduce the continued losses, employees were no longer allowed to go to their automobiles during lunch. Also, the elimination of all but one major access point enabled security officers to observe entering and departing employees, although long lines formed as time cards were punched. Unfortunately, internal theft worsened. President Brown pleaded with workers about rising costs and the need to stay competitive. Two additional security officers were hired to observe departing workers. When the plant manager asked for more money for security, Brown put a cap on the security budget. It was not long before the first twenty-five workers were laid off.

Theft of Time at Master Foil Printing Company

Master Foil was a busy New Jersey company involved in printing whiskey labels and boxes for pharmaceutical products. The day shift ran smoothly. However, the second shift had serious production problems and inadequate supervision. Management had suspected theft of time on the second shift. Before taking corrective action, an undercover investigation was conducted. A contract investigator, with a fictitious background, was hired as a porter. It was not long before information was collected on a serious problem—theft of time.

The security officers were charging second shift employees $2 each to punch their cards so the employees could leave early. If overtime was involved, the going rate was $4 per card. The undercover investigator regularly saw an exchange of cash between employees and security officers. Security officers routinely punched ten to twenty-five cards when the second shift ended, even though the workers had left earlier.

When the theft of time was tallied by management, the seriousness of the losses became evident. For example, one night eight pressmen making $40 per hour each departed four hours early. Thus, total cost was $1280. During the same night, ten operators (those who load paper into the printing press and unload finished products) making $20 per hour each also departed four hours early. Thus, in this situation, the total cost was $800. Eight porters (those who clean the machines), not including the newly hired undercover investigator, also left four hours early. At $12 per hour, the total cost was $384. The total theft of time for one night amounted to $2464. Furthermore, the losses averaged $12,320 per week.

To make matters worse, the pressmen would increase the speed of printing presses to complete assigned jobs quicker. This caused frequent breakdowns while creating a safety hazard. Since certain parts for repairs could only be ordered from Germany, an expensive printing press often remained idle for two to three days.

The head of security at Master Foil was also the head of maintenance. This individual was observed (by the undercover investigator) ordering more parts and supplies than what was needed to make repairs and putting the excess in an automobile trunk before leaving the premises. It was learned that this person was in the contracting business. Ironically, this same individual constantly complained about everybody stealing.

After three months, the undercover investigation ended. Since business began to decrease as the investigation came to an end, the entire second shift was laid off. Management reassessed the second shift operations.

Types of Employee-Thieves

Internal theft is committed by all types and levels of employees, from the assembly line worker who pockets a tool to the corporate executive who overstates (pads) an expense account. Additional suspects include part-time or temporary employees, contractors, and consultants. Unfortunately, a small percentage of security officers also steal.

Reid Psychological Systems, a Chicago honesty testing company, conducted large-scale surveys to find what percentage of employees steal from their employers. This research found that 26.2 percent of manufacturing employees, 32.2 percent of hospital employees, and 41.8 percent of retail store employees admitted stealing.

A Department of Justice study in 1987 surveyed senior management on employee theft. The study revealed that one-third of respondents named management or senior staff when asked which employees were responsible for the most serious crime problems. Also, for major fraud, managers were viewed as the primary source of the problem by 60 percent of respondents. As might be expected, misconduct such as abuse of company services and petty theft were seen by two-thirds of the companies as coming from all employees or from a very broad employee group.

For professional security officers who have supervisors involved in internal theft, this serious problem presents difficult questions. Should the security officer contact a senior executive? This approach could prove damaging to the security officer if all senior executives in a company are stealing. Is it best to seek another job? Probably so. However, all circumstances are different. There are no easy answers. The following two guidelines should be remembered during decision making.

1. Never become involved in criminal activity.
2. Management has the responsibility to set an example for ethical behavior.

Reasons for Employee Theft

An offender often mentally reviews a series of excuses as to why a theft is appropriate. These excuses are called rationalizations. The purpose is to reduce guilt and ill feelings. Examples of rationalizations are, "everybody does it," "the company can afford it," and "I am only borrowing."

One way to understand why employees steal is to look for common factors in these cases. *Motivation* and *opportunity* are prime factors that cause internal theft.

MOTIVATION   Motivation comes from a need to have money or something of value. This need may result from the perceived pressure to have things that other people possess. Additional motivators behind stealing include the joy of getting something for nothing; a substance abuse or gambling problem;

financial difficulties; getting even with the boss; winning approval from others; and the challenge of beating the system.

OPPORTUNITY The second major factor influencing employee theft is opportunity. Security can play a role in reducing opportunities through patrols, security technology, and so forth. However, management must spearhead the opportunity-reduction effort by setting a good example, providing quality supervision, establishing controls and audits throughout an organization, and by supporting security. These strategies produce a workplace environment that minimizes opportunities for theft.

A Case of Collusion

A purchaser, a receiving clerk, and an accounts payable clerk in a company were in collusion with an employee of an outside supply company. They took advantage of weak accounting controls. Items were ordered and paid for but not delivered. The group sold the stolen merchandise and split the money. Their method was as follows. The purchaser completed a purchase order and mailed it to the supplier. An invoice was mailed to the purchaser. The purchaser then altered the invoice by increasing quantities and costs. Accounts payable then received the altered invoice and paid the supplier after the receiving clerk "verified" receiving the proper supplies. Several items were paid for but not received. When one of the group felt that their fair share was getting smaller, an argument led to the exposure of the fraud.

Techniques of Internal Theft

The techniques used by employees to steal can be simple or complex. Security personnel should always maintain an open mind to the creative ways in which valuables can be stolen. The following list describes some methods of employee theft.

- Pilfering manufactured products, raw materials, tools, office supplies, and so forth from the workplace.
- Hiding an item in clothing, a briefcase, a lunch box, and so forth, and leaving the premises.
- Throwing items over a fence or in a dumpster to be retrieved later.
- Using company tools and equipment for one's own purposes.
- Making long-distance telephone calls or using employer computer services for a part-time business.

- Purposely damaging merchandise to purchase it at a discount.
- Stealing money from a petty cash drawer.
- Overcharging customers and pocketing the difference.
- Allowing friends and relatives to purchase expensive merchandise at a low cost.
- Abusing coffee and lunch breaks.
- Abusing sick time.
- Padding expense accounts and mileage.
- Writing dummy refunds and pocketing the cash.
- Keeping people on the payroll who have left and cashing the paychecks.
- Mailroom workers who mail stolen items to themselves or an associate.
- Purchasers who receive kickbacks to favor certain suppliers.
- Purchasers who are in collusion with suppliers to pay higher than normal prices.

Many employees during their career participate in one or more of these illegal and/or unethical behaviors. The losses to businesses are substantial. However, management's reaction to each type of employee theft varies. One company may be lax when enforcing policies on coffee breaks while at the same time favoring prosecution of all employees caught stealing company property. Another company may only investigate cases involving a value over a certain amount of money. In other words, *management will dictate the meaning of employee theft on the premises.* Those in security must understand management policies and procedures in order to deal with employee theft.

Valuable Garbage

At one manufacturing plant, a janitor conspired with a trash removal driver who picked up boxes containing pilfered company equipment and merchandise. Twice each week, the janitor would place valuables in a damaged cardboard box and mark it with a green crayon. The box would be placed three large steps to the right of the dumpster and would be picked up by the truck driver. An alert security officer thought it was very strange when the driver got out of the truck to "clean up" around the dumpster. Most drivers would never leave the truck cab because the truck forks would lift the dumpster to be emptied into the truck. One day the security officer, a supervisor, and public police observed the theft process. The damaged box with green markings contained assorted hand tools and light bulbs. Both offenders were arrested.

Indicators of Possible Internal Theft

There are certain clues that *may* indicate employee theft. A security officer should look for signs of theft while on patrol or performing other duties. If theft appears to be taking place, the best approach is to collect facts and report the information to a supervisor. *Never assume anything or jump to conclusions.* Look for the following signs:

- Employees act suspicious or get upset when questioned.
- Employees are very friendly with certain customers or truck drivers.
- Employees are working unusually fast to load a truck.
- Employees are wearing heavy clothing during warm weather.
- Employees have serious personal problems, such as financial, substance abuse, or gambling.
- Employees are living beyond their income.
- Employees are constantly borrowing money, requesting advances, or writing bad checks.
- Items are at odd locations. Examples are an automobile parked at a shipping dock or merchandise found hidden near an exit.
- Merchandise is missing from cartons.
- Valuables are found in trash.
- Merchandise wrapping materials, labels, string, authorization stamps, and so forth are found in an odd location.
- Security devices are found damaged or readjusted. For example, sometimes individuals will paint camera lenses or force objects in keyways to render a lock inoperable.
- Windows and doors are found unlocked or opened.
- Signs of forced entry exist, such as scratch marks near a lock or on it.
- An unsupervised, after-hours cleaning crew have their own keys.
- Inventory records show losses.
- Increased amounts of raw material are needed for producing the same amount of finished products.
- Discrepancies in cash are present.
- An unexplained increase in refunds occurs.
- Altered documents appear.

Empty Boxes Hide Theft

At the Hometown Outlet, a sales associate devised a method to steal watches and avoid exposure after inventories. The associate knew that when an inventory was conducted, boxes of watches were counted. However, nobody inspected the contents of the boxes. The associate placed the empty boxes at the very bottom of stacks of boxes containing watches. An undercover investigator working as a sales associate in an adjoining department became suspicious when the offender was seen quickly slipping two watch boxes at the very bottom of a pile of boxes. The thief was subsequently fired.

Strategies to Combat Internal Theft

Numerous strategies can be applied to the problem of employee theft. Security officers should have a basic understanding of these strategies since security officers are part of the solution.

Prevention

Prevention is a key strategy. It establishes obstacles that cause people to refrain from committing crimes. Prevention strategies should reduce opportunities to steal.

Fear of Discovery

Fear of discovery is another method to combat internal theft. When employees believe they are likely to get caught if they steal, internal theft should decrease.

Management

The importance of security should be communicated to all employees by management. In fact, the whole security effort, whatever it may be, evolves from management. Executives decide on the seriousness of internal crime, what should be done about it, and how much will be spent on security officers and systems. Management also writes policies and procedures to prevent losses. Executives are concerned about the costs of security and whether it is worth the expense. Consequently, a security executive must plan and budget and repeatedly demonstrate that security expenditures are a worthwhile investment.

Management should carefully study security problems and consider the advantages and disadvantages of various strategies. For example, security should not hinder production. Also, employee rights must be considered. Lawsuits are to be avoided. Such factors go into the formulation of security policies and procedures that are enforced by security officers.

Management can play a crucial role in reducing employee theft through the fair and equitable treatment of employees. This entails many things beyond good wages. Examples include a good cafeteria, clean rest rooms, a safe workplace, and recognition and appreciation of employees. These efforts by management show employees that the company cares about its employees. Job satisfaction improves and management generates respect and cooperation. As a result, employees may find it more difficult to rationalize theft.

Security Surveys

Security officers are sometimes required to watch certain departments following a security survey or a critical incident. An internal security specialist or an outside consultant usually conducts a survey of a business. Basically, a checklist is used as a guide during a "walk-through" of a facility. Weaknesses are noted such as those relating to security methods, policies and procedures, and the layout of the facility. Recommendations are made to management and corrective action may follow. For example, a survey may reveal that the shipping and receiving department is an easy target for theft (this is often the case) and tighter supervision and counting procedures are required, plus the installation of a CCTV system. Or, that trash removal should be observed by at least one other employee. Additional security personnel, equipment and systems, and changes in policies and procedures are frequently recommended.

Policies and Procedures

Policies are written by management as a guide for employees as they do their jobs. Organizations and employees are controlled through policies. Procedures guide the actions of employees as policies are implemented. Memos, and policy and procedure manuals are references for employees to guide their action.

THEFT Policies and procedures are an excellent strategy to combat employee theft. Examples are numerous, but the following are some examples.

1. Theft will not be tolerated in the workplace.
2. A valid identification card is required before access.
3. A security officer must be present during trash removal.
4. Employees are restricted from using company equipment, services, and supplies for personal use or to support another vocation.
5. Punching another employee's time card is prohibited.
6. Documents and property are not to leave the premises without authorization. An illustration of procedures for this policy is that security officers are required to check property passes and retain a copy for filing.

EMBEZZLEMENT AND FRAUD The bookkeeping and financial activities of all businesses require good quality policies and procedures (often called accounting controls) to prevent embezzlement and fraud. The following list includes widely adopted policies and procedures used in the financial world.

1. Strict assignment of responsibility is given to employees. Therefore, a mistake can be traced to the person responsible.
2. Separate job functions are assigned. As a result, employees can check on each other's work. For example, one employee counts arriving supplies while another prepares a check for payment. The check is signed by a third employee who also counts arriving supplies.
3. When possible, employees are rotated. Thus, one individual never has total control over a job function without anyone else being able to do the job. Also, this forces employees to take vacations so others can do the job temporarily and check on the accuracy of work.
4. Accurate and up-to-date inventory records are maintained. Therefore, missing items can be quickly identified.
5. Audits are conducted to check on deviations from policies and procedures.

Employment Applicant Screening

The screening of employment applicants is a common method to prevent theft and other losses. Most organizations have human resources specialists who are familiar with the many laws pertaining to hiring and employer–employee relations. Such laws focus on equal employment opportunity, discrimination, testing, labor relations, and privacy, among other areas.

If applicants prone to crime are not hired, an organization can possibly prevent future problems. To prevent losses, a business can apply a series of screening methods to select the best qualified applicants. These methods include the completion of an application, an interview, a background investigation, and tests (e.g., drug screening, psychological). The polygraph is another screening technique. However, because of the Employee Polygraph Protection Act of 1988, most employers are restricted from using this device for pre-employment screening or during the course of employment. There are exemptions, especially for certain security positions.

When we look at the whole screening process, the courts have repeatedly stated that screening is discriminatory if it is not related to the job opening and differentiates on the basis of race, sex, or religion. The famous 1971 case of *Griggs v. Duke Power Co.* serves as a good illustration. Willie Griggs and other black workers sued Duke Power because they were required to take a paper-and-pencil test for a manual labor job. The U.S. Supreme Court agreed, claiming the test was discriminatory and not job related.

Training and Awareness Programs

Even before employees are hired, an organization should project an image that internal theft will not be tolerated. This can be accomplished by signs in the human resources office and by statements on employment applications. Security officers often become active in security training and awareness through a short speech or the demonstration of equipment. The number of topics is endless. Examples include basic crime prevention, access control, identification badges, parking, protecting information, and reporting losses.

Reward Programs

Reward programs are used by many companies (and police departments) to gather information on crime. Because we live in a complex world, the identification of sophisticated theft can be difficult. If it were not for reward programs, management would probably never know about many crimes. These programs offer a toll-free number, Web page/e-mail address, anonymity, and payments of thousands of dollars. Many companies have benefited from reward programs by reducing losses. In certain companies, all employees can receive a bonus if losses significantly drop.

What If?

As a Security Officer, What Do You Do if Another Employee Informs You That They Saw an Employee Place Company Property in Their Car Trunk?

While on duty at an access point, you are approached by an employee named Danny Marquez who claims to have seen an employee named Bill Thompson sneak out of the plant through an unauthorized exit and place company property in the trunk of his (Mr. Thompson's) car. What do you do?

The first step in this situation is to collect as much information as possible about what Mr. Marquez observed. But if you are at an access point, other people may hear the conversation and you are not authorized to leave your post for a private conversation. Call a supervisor, or if another security officer is available, ask them to take over your post for a few minutes.

The interviewing of Mr. Marquez will follow the universally applied six basic investigative questions: Who was involved? What happened? Where did it happen? When? How? Why? The interviewee may not know the answers to all of these questions, especially the "why" question. However, the answers serve as the foundation of the investigation. Once information is collected, contact a supervisor.

If Mr. Thompson is due to leave the workplace soon (e.g., end of his shift), the investigation must proceed quickly. Find out from Mr.

continued

Thompson's supervisor if Mr. Thompson is authorized to remove company property from the premises. Seek an explanation from the supervisor about the incident. Was a property pass issued? Is the property owned by Mr. Thompson or another employee? The supervisor may also be a suspect, but exercise extreme caution and do not accuse anyone of anything. At this point of the investigation only facts are being collected.

What is the condition of the door through which Mr. Thompson allegedly brought out company property? Did the door contain a controlled exit device (i.e., emergency exit bar)? Was it operational? Was anyone near the door during the time of the incident who could serve as another witness?

If the facts point to "probable cause" that a theft may have occurred, follow company policies and procedures on stopping and searching vehicles on the premises. Management authorization may be required.

In this case, management authorized stopping Mr. Thompson before he started his vehicle at the end of his shift. Management felt comfortable about this decision because of the legal steps it had taken in planning for such events: clear policies and procedures on searches, signs at access points stating that people and vehicles are subject to searches, and employee authorized searches, in writing, as a condition of employment. Mr. Thompson's supervisor and two security officers asked Mr. Thompson to open his trunk. His first statement was: "You Caught Me!" As it turns out, Mr. Thompson had been warned earlier about conducting transactions on the premises for his part-time job in catalogue sales. The trunk contained returned merchandise, not company property. The door that he used was not working properly and he used a small pebble to prop it open so he could return through it. Mr. Thompson was disciplined and warned again.

If Mr. Thompson had refused to open his trunk, he would have been violating policy and his written authorization for a search as a condition of employment. He would have been reminded about these facts. If he still refused to open his trunk, his job would have been in jeopardy and public police called.

In this scenario, security personnel and management were prepared for such events and acted professionally. The investigation proceeded cautiously as facts were gathered prior to taking action.

Theft Prevention and Detection

To remedy property losses within an organization, four recommendations are: (1) set up an inventory system, (2) mark property, (3) use metal detectors, and (4) install an electronic article surveillance system.

An *inventory system* maintains accountability for property such as tools. When employees borrow or use equipment a record is kept of the item, its serial number, the employee's name, and the date. On return of the item, a notation is made, including the date, by both the clerk and the user.

Marking property (e.g., tools, computers, furniture) serves several useful purposes. When property is marked with a serial number, or a firm's name is etched with an engraving tool, thieves are deterred because the property can be identified if the thief is caught with the stolen property. Publicizing the marking of property reinforces the deterrent effect. Many public police agencies are active in a similar program called *operation identification* and are willing to loan etching tools and supply standard inventory forms.

Chemical marking can be used to identify property. An ultraviolet light is necessary to view these invisible marks, which emerge as a surprise to the offender. Since people cannot see what items are marked, this strategy acts as a deterrent to theft.

Organizations sometimes experience the theft of petty cash. To expose such theft, fluorescent substances, in the form of powder, crayon, or liquid, are used to mark money. The typical scenario involves a few suspects who are the only people with access to petty cash after hours. Before these after-hour employees arrive, the investigator handling the case places bills previously dusted with invisible fluorescent powder in envelopes at petty cash locations. The bills even can be written on with the invisible fluorescent crayon. Statements such as "marked money" can be used to identify the bills under ultraviolet light. Serial numbers from the bills are recorded and retained by the investigator. Before the employees are scheduled to leave, the "planted" bills are checked. If the bills are missing, then the employees' hands are checked under an ultraviolet light. Glowing hands expose the thief, and identification of the marked money carried by the individual strengthens the case. The marked money must be placed in an envelope because the fluorescent powder may transfer to other objects and onto an honest person's hands. A wrongful arrest can lead to a false-arrest suit. A check of a suspect's bills, for the marked money, helps avoid this problem. Many cleaning fluids appear orange under an ultraviolet light. The investigator should analyze all cleaning fluids on the premises and select a fluorescent color that is different from the cleaning substances. The use of a pinhole lens camera for covert surveillance is another investigative technique covered soon.

Walk-through *metal detectors*, similar to those at airports, are useful at employee exists to deter theft of metal objects and to identify employee thieves. Such detectors also uncover weapons being brought into an area. Handheld metal detectors are also helpful.

Electronic article surveillance systems deter and detect offenders. Tags are placed on items and when an item passes a certain point, such as an exit, an alarm is sounded, plus CCTV can be automatically directed to the exit to record the offender. More on this topic in Chapter 11.

Investigations

Employee thieves often are familiar with the ins and outs of an organization's operation and can easily conceal theft. In addition, knowledge of security is common to employee thieves. Consequently, an undercover investigation is an effective method to outwit and expose crafty employee thieves and their conspirators.

If the ABC Company is experiencing inventory shortages and internal theft is suspected, ABC may contact a firm that specializes in undercover investigations. An investigator, under a false identity, applies for a job at ABC. Since at least one senior executive at ABC knows of the investigation, the investigator is hired. Working in maintenance or some other area, the undercover investigator infiltrates the employee informal groups and collects and reports on internal crime. This method is usually successful in exposing employee thieves.

As a security officer, if you suspect a worker is an undercover investigator, it is best to ignore the situation. Say nothing and treat the person like other employees.

Another popular method to investigate employee theft is by using a pinhole lens camera (Figure 10-2). These small cameras (containing a tiny lens) are hidden in areas where theft is a problem. Placed in walls, ceilings, clocks, file cabinets, equipment, and so forth, these cameras are connected to TV monitors for viewing and recording. Usually, employees are unaware of these

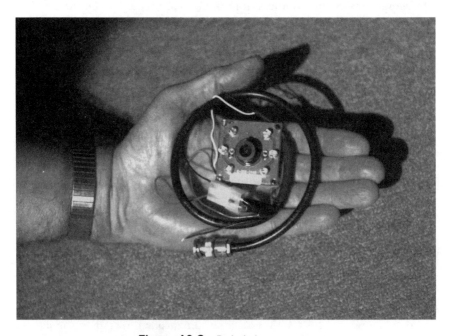

Figure 10-2   Pinhole lens camera.

cameras. When a crime does occur, security has a tremendous advantage in catching a thief who thinks he or she is not being observed. Arrest and prosecution are also greatly aided through a recording of the incident.

Prosecution

Security personnel are assigned the duty of gathering facts. The prosecution decision rests with management. A strong policy of prosecuting all employee-offenders can prevent and reduce internal crime. However, the decision to prosecute is complex. There are advantages and disadvantages to prosecution. On the positive side, prosecution sets an example. If the offender is fired, which is usually the case, the organization has rid itself of a thief and future losses. On the other hand, a disadvantage is the loss of an experienced employee in which the company has invested training dollars. Bad publicity may also surface. Further, if the case against the employee fails, a civil suit can result. Management often looks at prosecution as a business decision. Executives frequently argue that their business exists to make money, not to become involved in criminal cases. For those security personnel who are employed by executives who are hesitant to prosecute, the prevention of crime becomes all the more important.

Physical Security and Security Officers

Physical security systems and security officers play a major role in preventing crime from both insiders and outsiders. In Chapter 4 we covered a variety of physical security topics such as perimeter security, access controls, intrusion detection systems, lighting, and property and package control. Post assignments and security patrols were explained in Chapter 5. Security officers play an interdependent role in physical security. When systems malfunction or break, it is the security officers who usually fill the gap in protection.

CHAPTER REVIEW

A. Multiple Choice

1. Stealing in small quantities is known as
   a. embezzlement.
   b. pilferage.
   c. fraud.
   d. pocketing.
2. According to the U.S. Chamber of Commerce, what percent of business failures result from employee theft?
   a. 2%
   b. 10%
   c. 20%
   d. 30%
3. Motivation and _____ are prime factors behind internal theft.
   a. embezzlement
   b. crime prevention
   c. opportunity
   d. collusion
4. _____ is a key strategy to curb employee theft.
   a. Surveillance
   b. Pilferage
   c. Public police involvement
   d. Prevention
5. Which of the following strategies is least likely to be used to prevent employee theft?
   a. policies and procedures
   b. reward programs
   c. public police patrols
   d. employment applicant screening

B. True or False

1. According to the FBI, bank robbers steal more from banks than employees.
2. Executives decide on the seriousness of internal crime, what should be done about it, and how much will be spent on security officers and systems.
3. Management can play a crucial role in reducing employee theft through the fair and equitable treatment of workers.

4. Employers have considerable power to polygraph any job applicant or employee.

5. The use of pinhole lens cameras in the workplace is prohibited.

Applications

Application 10A

Locate the security hazards in the drawing below (Figure 10-3). What recommendations would you suggest to prevent internal theft?

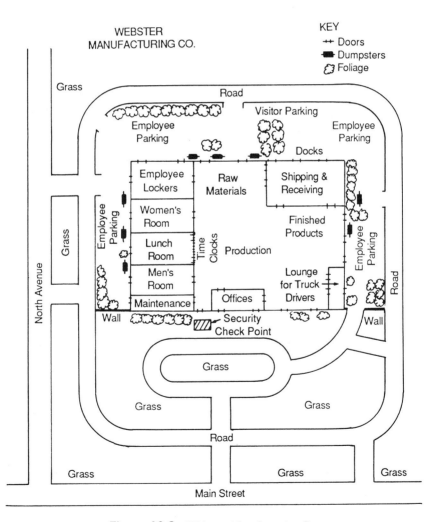

Figure 10-3 Webster Manufacturing Co.

Application 10B

Role-play a scenario of an employee-theft case. Include the theft incident, the subsequent investigation, and the disposition of the case, whether in-house or through the justice system. Establish a panel to evaluate security personnel actions and provide constructive criticism. (Refer to Chapter 8, *Arrest Law and Procedures*, for a review of legal guidelines.)

11

Retail Loss Prevention

CHAPTER OUTLINE

OBJECTIVES

After studying this chapter, you will be able to:

- List at least eight retail crime problems.
- Explain shrinkage.
- Discuss the reasons for losses in retail stores.
- List and explain at least eight retail loss prevention methods.
- List and explain at least five loss problems at the point-of-sale and countermeasures.
- Discuss at least five strategies to combat shoplifting.
- List at least five strategies to minimize the robbery threat.
- List at least five strategies to minimize the burglary threat.
- Discuss shopping mall security.

Introduction

Loss prevention is a term often used in the retail industry. As defined in Chapter 1, it takes security several steps further by applying a broader range of methods to protect people and property. Examples are safety and fire protection.

Retailers must take action to prevent losses from a variety of events. Crime is not the only threat to retail businesses. Precautions must be implemented to provide a safe and secure environment for customers, employees, and others who enter the premises. This can be accomplished through an accident prevention program and through fire prevention and fire suppression strategies. Because of the easy-access nature of retail stores, retailers must be especially alert to protecting people from crimes by third-parties; in other words, offenders who enter the premises and commit crimes (see Chapter 7). It is the wise retailer who institutes comprehensive prevention programs and utilizes insurance as a backup. In this chapter the emphasis is on retail crime.

Retail security efforts are faced with unique problems. Let us compare a high-tech manufacturing firm with a retail store. In the former, access control is tight. Only authorized people are permitted to enter. And when individuals do enter, they are restricted to specific areas. Complete records are maintained on all movements of people, vehicles, and things. In contrast, retailers want as many outsiders as possible to enter and shop. Access controls are minimized. The more people who enter the premises, the greater the potential for sales. Furthermore, merchandise is made to appear attractive and inviting so customers (and employees) will desire to purchase it. Customers are even given the opportunity to handle the store's merchandise. Sales do result from these marketing techniques. However, easy access to the premises and merchandise presents challenges for security personnel. The role of security personnel is to respond to the needs of retailers who are in business to make a profit. *Security should not hinder sales.* As this chapter will explain, much can be done to protect retail stores without interfering with business.

Retail Crime Problems

Losses from retail crime can be staggering. If management does not take positive steps to curb such losses, business failure may occur. Threats to retail stores include:

- Internal theft.
- Shoplifting.
- Bad checks.
- Credit card fraud.
- Refund fraud.
- Counterfeiting.
- E-business fraud.
- Robbery.
- Burglary.

Measuring Losses

In the retail industry, *shrinkage* is a common method of measuring losses. Shrinkage is the amount of merchandise that disappears through internal theft, shoplifting, damage, mismanagement, and paperwork errors. It is expressed in a percentage form and calculated after an inventory. A retail business, for instance, with a 6 percent shrinkage level is suffering more serious losses than a company that is able to hold down shrinkage to 3 percent. Since shrinkage is based on the results of an inventory, the inventory must be conducted accurately. The effectiveness of security and management is often evaluated through shrinkage. If it remains high, top executives may decide to replace those in charge of a store, including security personnel. The University of Florida's *National Retail Security Survey* for 2001 noted that retail shrinkage was 1.75 percent, calculated to $32 billion in losses.

Reasons for Losses

What makes retail stores particularly susceptible to theft, fraud, and other losses are the problems of employee turnover, low pay, many part-time and temporary employees, and inexperience. The Christmas season is a time when these problems peak. A constant influx of new employees frequently results in lax job applicant screening, especially during busy holidays. Low pay can cause an employee to rationalize theft and fraud to compensate for hard work and a small paycheck. Part-time, temporary employees have a more difficult time developing loyalty to a company when they know their employment will be short-term. Thus, theft is more likely. Employee inexperience presents serious weaknesses for any security program dependent on cooperation from all employees. Offenders are attracted to inexperienced, young retail workers since they are an easy mark for assorted crimes, cons, and fraud.

All of these factors contribute to retail losses. These elements are also the difficult realities of retailing. Imagine the difficulties faced by security personnel (who may be subject to similar personnel problems) trying to train salespeople on shoplifting, bad checks, refund fraud, and so forth. The best approach for security is to accept the realities and challenges of the retail business and maintain a positive attitude while working toward creative solutions. Many successful security strategies have been implemented in retail environments to curb losses. We will explain positive and results-oriented retail security.

Who Steals the Most: Employees or Shoplifters?

The true cost of internal theft and shoplifting in retail stores is difficult to gauge. Not all crimes are discovered or reported. One point is clear: each problem is costing retailers billions of dollars in losses each year.

The *National Retail Security Survey* for 2001 found that loss prevention executives attributed shrinkage to the following sources: 46 percent to employee theft, 31 percent to shoplifting, and 23 percent to vendor theft and fraud. Average costs per incident were: $1587 per employee theft and $198 per shoplifting.

Corporate Security reported that the *13th Annual Retail Theft Survey* conducted by Hayes International showed that dishonest employees steal about 6.7 times the volume of merchandise that shoplifters take. In addition, one in every 22.4 employees was apprehended for theft at work.

If retail employees argue that shoplifting is greater than internal theft the reason may be because employees are stealing and blaming it on shoplifters. Thus, shoplifters are a convenient scapegoat for employee-thieves. The same can be said about reasons for inventory shrinkage. That is, shoplifters can be conveniently blamed. Furthermore, because employees are familiar with security measures and accounting controls, theft becomes easier for these employees when compared to shoplifters.

Research by Altheide, in the book *Crime at the Top*, describes the thoughts of a retail employee-thief:

[O]ur informant at the large chain store was a bit surprised by how well things worked out in the various departments, including the ones he stole from. We never really worried about how the different departments would explain their inventory losses. Clothing wear departments usually explained their losses through shrinkage which usually meant that shoplifters had gotten their stuff. I never found out how the hardware department explained the loss of the two chain saws, which we removed. I think that most department managers tend to cover up their losses.

The most common way employees could beat security was to use the rules for their own purposes. . . . The security personnel were primarily concerned with catching shoplifting customers. Most of their time was spent behind two-way mirrors with binoculars observing shoppers . . . while the security personnel caught a customer concealing a pair of pants in her purse, an employee was smuggling four pairs of Levis out the front door.

Thus, security personnel should maintain a broad view of losses. Avoid too much emphasis on catching shoplifters, since employee theft may be the more serious problem. The previous chapter on internal theft is applicable to retail environments.

Retail Loss Prevention Methods

Employment Applicant Screening

The completion of an application by a job seeker is the standard method to screen applicants. Because of turnover and numerous part-time and temporary employees, many retailers spend little time studying and investigating each application. In today's competitive world, job seekers frequently exaggerate and falsify applications and expect haphazard screening by employers. Obviously, job applicant screening can be a primary screening tool to prevent and reduce theft. The following are a few tips that promote good hiring practices:

1. Provide applicants with an application upon their initial visit. Request that they complete it at home and mail it in. Later, when they arrive for an interview, ask them to complete a second application for comparison before the interview.

2. Look for inconsistencies in an application and what is stated in an interview.

3. Search for "red flags" that may signal deception. For example, "self-employed" may be used to hide periods of imprisonment or substance abuse.

4. Not signing an application may signal deception.
5. Social security numbers are issued by state. Obtain a list to verify where applicants say they lived.
6. An applicant will typically provide references who are likely to state positive comments about the applicant. Obtain a reference from a reference for a more thorough inquiry. Telephone at least two references.
7. To test the applicant's truthfulness, ask some questions for which you know the answers.

More thorough applicant screening methods are available to obtain the best possible employees. These methods include background investigations, in-depth interviews, credit checks, paper-and-pencil honesty tests, and drug screening. However, in reality, when retail salespeople are sought, screening is usually not thorough, especially during busy holiday seasons.

Training and Awareness Programs

In a retail environment, the problems of shoplifting, fraud, and employee theft should be broadcast through training and awareness programs. Certain retailers believe that the topic of employee theft is too sensitive to discuss in the workplace. However, losses can be reduced when everybody understands the seriousness of this problem and how it can affect the financial position of the business and job security. Crime problems, countermeasures, policies, procedures, and discipline can be communicated via initial training of new employees, periodic retraining, short seminars, posters, and other methods. Check the International Mass Retail Association at www.imra.org.

Inventory Control

A "zero shortage" environment can be promoted. This approach attempts to maintain shrinkage at its lowest possible level through a variety of measures. Examples are clear policies and procedures, good supervision, and a system for rewarding employees for good work.

Reward Programs

Reward programs have proved valuable for retailers. One retail chain, for example, promotes a "secret witness" program. A reward schedule consists of half the retail value of merchandise if the value is $100 or less. If the value is over $100, a reward of 10 percent is offered with a minimum of $50 and a maximum of $1000. During one year, this retailer paid over $35,000 in 860 different rewards and recovered over $110,000 in merchandise and money.

Package Control

Package controls are a common problem in retail stores. Since so many consumer items are sold in retail stores, employees frequently make purchases for themselves. Many companies permit employees to make purchases at a discount between 10 and 25 percent. Daily purchases by a large number of employees can present difficulties for security personnel because additional items may be smuggled out with a legitimate purchase, and coworkers may give each other unauthorized discounts. One solution is to require employees to store purchases, with an attached receipt, behind a security counter, to be retrieved at the end of the day. Before storage, a security officer can compare the receipt with the contents. Retailers may require female employees to lock their pocketbooks in a locker and use a plastic see-through purse for essential items needed on the job.

Shipping and Receiving Controls

Controls in the shipping and receiving department are particularly important in retail stores. Strict accountability should be enforced as shipments of goods enter and depart. At least two employees should count merchandise. To strengthen controls, an employee from another department can check their work. Technology such as bar-coding, CCTV, and integrated systems help to protect inventory. Testing by deliberate error serves as another measure. For example, an extra television can be added to an incoming or outgoing shipment to determine honesty. Some companies also spot-check trucks after departure to recheck shipments. This serves to deter theft, since employees never know when a truck will be stopped.

Security Personnel

When security officers are assigned to specific posts or patrol in and around a retail store, the opportunity for crime is reduced. A shoplifter may be deterred by the sight of a uniformed security officer. A security officer can be posted at a shipping and receiving dock with a view of nearby garbage dumpsters and employee vehicles in a parking lot. But if the security officer is permitted to leave the area for a lunch break without a replacement, the opportunity for crime obviously increases. Consequently, this security investment can be wasted.

Investigations

Undercover investigations provide the means to infiltrate employee groups to uncover theft. Since the investigator appears as a regular employee in informal groups, considerable information can be obtained because employees behave differently when not in the presence of a supervisor, a security officer, or a customer.

Physical Security

Physical security provides many avenues to protect retail stores at the perimeter, Figure 11-1. Examples are fences and lighting. Security officers and watchdogs are integral components of perimeter protection.

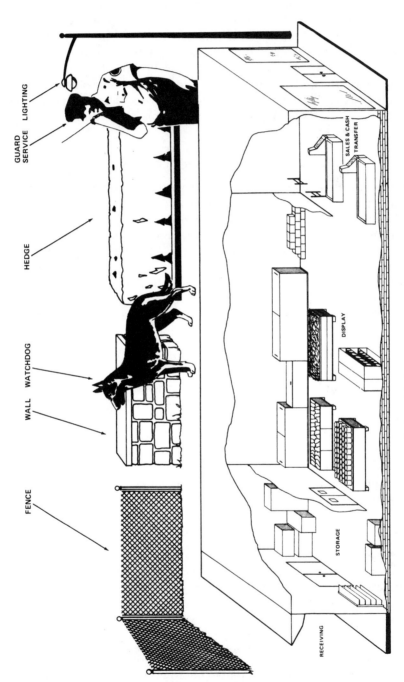

Figure 11-1   Perimeter protection.

Physical security is also applied to entry protection. Figure 11-2 shows locations at a retail store that require protection. Examples are doors, windows, and vents. Chapter 4 offers many physical security methods, such as locks and intrusion alarm systems, that apply here.

Space Protection

Space protection includes methods to monitor the interior spaces or areas of a facility, Figure 11-3. These strategies are of crucial importance in preventing and detecting crimes in a retail store. The measures include lighting (interior), key control, visibility enhancement, cameras, movement controls, shopping services, employee motivation and screening, and prosecution policy.

Point Protection

As the name implies, this strategy of security is used to prevent or detect theft at a specific point or object, Figure 11-4. In a business environment, specific items that call for extra protection include point-of-sale (POS) areas, high-value merchandise (jewelry), and safes. The selected measures include inventory control, alarm systems, electronic article surveillance, merchandise anchors, display case protection, cashier enclosures, and money handling routines.

Loss Prevention at the Point-of-Sale

Once a customer selects retail merchandise, the next step is to pay for it at the POS (or checkout). A cashier accepts cash, a check, or a bank card in exchange for merchandise. Refunds and other services may also be handled at the POS. Because of the exchange of valuables at this location, the potential for crime from both employees and outsiders is enormous.

Losses at the POS result from the following:

- Stealing money from the POS terminal, sometimes called "till tapping."

- Keeping money after payment by a customer. This is made easier for a dishonest cashier when a customer pays with exact change and does not request a receipt.

- Overcharging customers or undercharging friends and relatives.

- Giving customers the wrong change.

- Not following policies and procedures and carelessly accepting bad checks and bank cards and counterfeit money.

- Not observing merchandise that contains an altered price tag.

- Not searching large merchandise that contains stolen items.

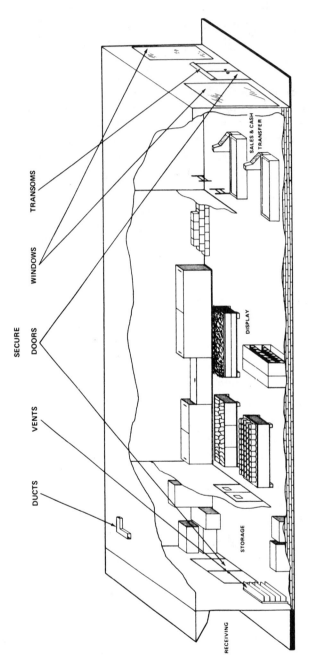

Figure 11-2   Entry protection.

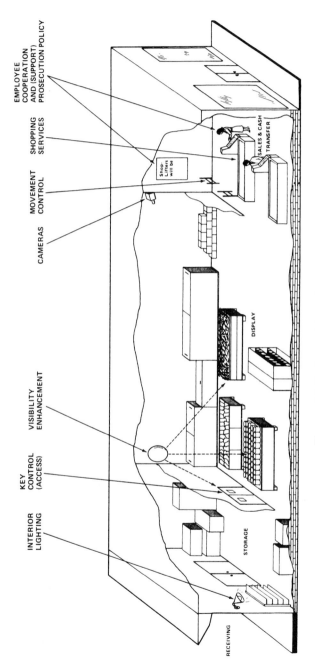

EMPLOYEE
COOPERATION
AND (SUPPORT)
PROSECUTION POLICY

SHOPPING
SERVICES

MOVEMENT
CONTROL

CAMERAS

Shop-
Lifters
will be

SALES & CASH
TRANSFER

DISPLAY

VISIBILITY
ENHANCEMENT

KEY
CONTROL
(ACCESS)

INTERIOR
LIGHTING

STORAGE

RECEIVING

Figure 11-3 Internal (space) protection.

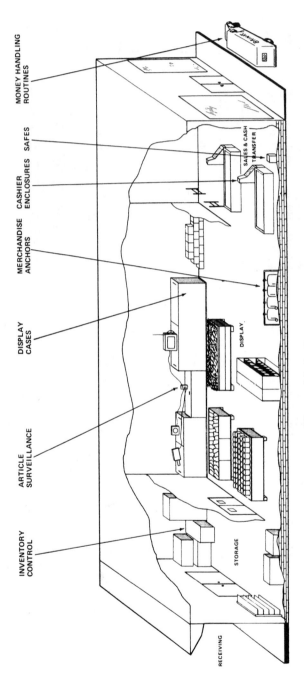

Figure 11-4 Point protection.

The following are general controls to reduce losses at the POS:

1. Provide each cashier with his or her own cash drawer.
2. Never leave a cash drawer unattended without locking it.
3. Require each cashier to call out the cash provided by each customer for payment and then count back the change.
4. Each customer must be handed a receipt or staple it to the bag.
5. Cash drawers must be closed after each transaction.
6. Provide adequate supervision, especially when cashiers make mistakes.
7. Require a supervisor to balance cash registers as cashiers end their shifts.
8. Supervisors and cashiers must remember that con artists are known to cause confusion at the POS. A quick-change artist, for example, tries to pay for an item with a high denomination bill and then requests to pay with a lower denomination. Always handle one transaction at a time.

Crime at the POS

Cashiers have been known to devise ingenious methods of stealing. One technique used with old cash registers is to remove the cash register tape and insert a new one for the last hour of business. When the register is closed out, the old tape and corresponding money are turned in. The new tape is destroyed and corresponding money is pocketed. Good supervision deters this crime. Also, with newer POS computer systems containing more sophisticated accountability, such as a recording of the time of each transaction, these losses are less likely. Another technique involves supervisors or managers setting up their own register during a busy period and keeping the proceeds.

Outsiders also devise ingenious theft techniques. Sometimes they pose as cashiers and salespeople to obtain payments from customers. In one case, a neatly dressed individual walked off the street and into a store, put on a company name tag, stood behind a counter, and then "helped" customers pay for their merchandise, which resulted in actual payment to the offender.

Reports and Records

Many retail stores maintain cashier overage and shortage reports. For instance, a limit of $5 is set and cashiers who deviate from this figure when their registers are closed out should be interviewed. Daily, weekly, and monthly reports help to pinpoint careless and dishonest cashiers. Depending on the size of the store and the volume of business, the limit will vary. With so many transactions between a cashier and customers during a day, it is unlikely for figures on a cash register tape and the money in the register to be equal—to the penny—when the register is closed out. In fact, if a cashier always seems to balance to the penny, the cashier should be interviewed and watched more closely.

Records are commonly maintained for cashier "voids" and "no sales." Voids are used to correct mistakes made by cashiers as they operate their register. Excessive voids may signal that a particular cashier makes too many mistakes. Losses can mount if a cashier devises a way to void legitimate sales and pocket the cash. Good supervision can prevent this problem. Excessive "no sales" may be the result of a register being near a pay telephone or vending machine, thus requiring frequent opening and closing of the register drawer for change. Inquiries justifying "no sales" prevent losses.

Management Information Systems

Many retailers use computers and management information systems to provide managers with data on store activities. This helps determine the business health of a store while exposing irregularities. Computer reports can be designed to expose cashiers who deviate from established standards for voids, shortages, overages, and acceptance of bad checks and bank cards. For instance, parameters can be programmed into a system so that if a cashier is ringing up, say, too many no sales or $1.00 sales, management is notified via computer. This is often termed "exception monitoring."

Use of ratios is another strategy to uncover losses. In one store a dishonest cashier was exposed when the ratio of cash sales to charge sales shifted to a decrease in cash sales because the cashier was stealing cash.

Accounting Systems and Technology

POS accounting systems and bar coding technology help retailers maintain accurate inventories while reducing losses. Merchandise displays a bar code that is read by a scanner or wand reader at the checkouts. Cash register terminals note each item read, including price and department. This system permits a perpetual (constant) inventory system. Ordering new stock is made easier, and shortages of specific items are pinpointed quicker. From a loss prevention standpoint, the POS system can be designed to supply assorted data such as shrinkage statistics, cash received, merchandise charged, and information on checks, voids, and layaways.

Modern technology permits executives to remotely monitor a store from anywhere in the world with a computer via the Internet. These capabilities include access to a variety of accounting information and CCTV surveillance of the store. For example, an executive in Chicago can check on sales data and watch the activity in a store in Paris.

Shopping Service

A shopping service is a secret operation where cashiers and salespeople are tested by investigators posing as customers. Cashier appearance, courtesy, efficiency, and honesty are noted by a shopping service. One strategy is for an investigator to pay for merchandise with exact change and then leave the store. A second investigator observes the cashier to see if the money is pocketed since the cash drawer does not have to be opened for change. Retail stores usually contract with an outside shopping service for periodic tests.

The Party Is Over!

The Bargainmart Department Store Chain was a growing retail company with stores scattered throughout four states. The most distant store was located in Bristol City, three hundred and seventy miles from company headquarters. This resulted in less frequent visits by upper management. One day the security director appeared at the Bristol store, studied the records, and was particularly concerned about losses from cashiers. The security director declared, "The party is over!" Immediately, while the store was open, the security director ordered a supervisor to balance the cash registers of two suspect cashiers. Each register was closed out and the money was counted. Both cashiers had shortages from stealing money from the register. They were fired.

To curb losses at the checkouts and throughout the store, the security director recommended more unannounced audits of cash registers, closer supervision of employees, and quicker action when store records pointed to losses from certain employees. One of the two security officers at the store was posted between the exit and the checkouts to watch for suspicious activity and customers and cashiers who could possibly be working together to steal. The security director favored the installation of a CCTV system to observe and record suspected dishonest employees as well as suspected shoplifters. Also, a POS system was being planned so all stores could be "watched" remotely from company headquarters.

Refunds

Various techniques are used by offenders to illegally obtain money from a retail refund system. Here are some examples:

- An employee may keep a customer's receipt and use it to support a fraudulent customer refund.

- Outsiders may search around a store for a receipt, look for merchandise that corresponds to the receipt and then attempt a refund.
- Merchandise shoplifted earlier is returned to the store for a refund without a receipt.
- Bold offenders may obtain an item off a rack and walk directly to the refund desk and demand cash for their "returned" item.
- An item is purchased by check and then a stop payment order is issued by the customer at his or her bank. At the same time, the item is returned for a refund at the same store or another.
- A stolen bank card may be used to purchase items and then a refund is attempted at another location.

Here are strategies to reduce fraudulent refunds.

1. Require a receipt for a refund and post signs.
2. Look for altered receipts.
3. Require the customer to complete a short form to record date, name, address, telephone number, amount, description of merchandise returned, plus employee and customer signatures.
4. If a customer is suspected of fraud, mail them a check. When a check is mailed to a fictitious address, it will likely be returned "addressee unknown."
5. Maintain accountability of refunds and corresponding returned merchandise.
6. An employee suspected of issuing fraudulent refunds can be placed under surveillance and subjected to a shopping service test.
7. Discarded receipts should be collected from floors and destroyed.

Bad Checks

Technological changes are causing retail customers to alter the methods they use to pay for merchandise. For example, *debit card* transactions are gaining momentum. This system operates with the assistance of a centralized computer, which contains individual financial records. When a customer purchases merchandise, the cost is fed into a computer (via a terminal at the store) and payment is transferred from the customer's account (savings or checking) to the store's account. *Chip cards* are also being introduced, which is a migration from magnetic stripe credit cards. Chip cards contain a tiny computer enabling several features, such as being loaded with money in advance. Because these systems will require additional years before dominating retail transactions, millions of customers will continue to make purchases with personal checks. Therefore, personal checks and a variety of other types of checks will continue to be a source of losses for retailers.

Theft by deception is a term used to describe bad checks. It is an instrument written with the intent to defraud. *A check is nothing more than a piece of paper until the money is collected.* It may be worthless. Bad checks include those written against insufficient funds or no accounts, forgeries, or stolen checks. The problem is growing worse because of computers, desktop publishing, check-writing software, newer color copier machines, scanners, and laser printers.

Characteristics of bad checks include an inappropriate date, written figures that differ from numeric figures on the same check, and smeared ink. Of about 61 billion checks written each year, about 1.3 million are fraudulent. The FBI estimates losses at $12 to $15 billion to businesses each year.

When a bad check is received, a retailer should follow the procedures and law of the locale. Many customers who realize their mistake will correct the problem. A common strategy for difficult customers is a notification by registered letter, return receipt requested. Retailers often use a standard form and enclose a copy of the check and applicable law. If too many fraudulent checks are received by a retailer, this signals that prevention methods must be intensified.

Several strategies to minimize losses are listed here:

1. Establish clear policies on checks.

    a. Do not accept checks written to receive cash.

    b. Do not accept checks from out-of-town.

    c. Only accept checks written from the customer's checking account.

    d. Require two types of identification. This includes a driver's license with a picture and a national credit card.

    e. Require supervisory authorization for checks written over a specific amount.

    f. When in doubt on a check, a cashier should contact a supervisor.

2. Concentrate on the identification presented. Does the driver's license picture match the customer? Are IDs signed? What are the expiration dates?

3. Examine the check carefully. Compare the check with identification, Figure 11-5.

4. Establish check cashing records for customers who regularly write checks. This will save time.

5. Maintain records of customers who write bad checks and employees who accept too many.

6. Retailers have the option of using cameras to photograph customers when they cash a check. Thumbprints on each check are another choice. The degree of success varies with each of these strategies.

7. Retailers should cooperate and warn each other when bad check passers arrive in their area.

Do not accept checks
with numbers 200 or less.
A large number of bad checks
are written from new accounts.

Compare name, address
and driver's license number.

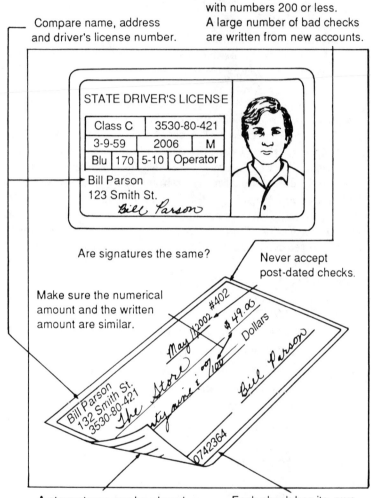

STATE DRIVER'S LICENSE

Class C	3530-80-421	
3-9-59	2006	M
Blu	170	5-10	Operator

Bill Parson
123 Smith St.

Are signatures the same?

Never accept
post-dated checks.

Make sure the numerical
amount and the written
amount are similar.

A store stamp can be placed
on the back to record vital
information not listed on the
front of the check.
The stamp containing the
retail store's name acts as
an endorsement and prevents
theft.

Each check has its own
computerized account
number. Never accept
a check without a number.

Figure 11-5   Customer check and identification.

8. A business should also protect its own check writing system. Blank checks and bank statements require security and cancelled checks should be reviewed.

9. America's Network specializes in the bad check problem: www.badcheck collector.com.

Bank Card Fraud

Bank card fraud is a widespread problem that costs billions of dollars annually. Losses are sustained by issuers (banks), acceptors (retailers), and users. Offenders obtain cards fraudulently with fictitious background information or steal them from the mail system or from individuals. Fraudulent use also involves counterfeit or altered cards. Anyone who owns a bank card should protect the card and the number since both can be used to fraudulently obtain goods and services.

Retailers who are careless when accepting bank cards can be held responsible for financial loss. Strategies to prevent fraud are listed next:

1. Examine the expiration data of the card. Is it expired or not yet valid?

2. Has the card been altered?

3. *Of particular importance for the retailer is to ensure that the card is subject to electronic authorization (swiped through the magnetic reader).* This helps to ensure that accounts are valid and purchases are within credit limits.

4. Compare the signatures on the card and charge slip.

E-Business

Mail, phone order, and e-businesses (using Internet-based technologies) are vulnerable to fraud because the customer and the bank card are not present for the transaction. Offenders obtain card numbers from many sources (e.g., discarded credit card receipts, stealing customer information in the workplace, and hacking into a business), establish a mail drop, and then place fraudulent orders.

Because e-businesses use the Internet to sell globally, this great opportunity also attracts offenders. In one case, the owner of a computer parts company in New Jersey became concerned when he received a $15,000 order from Bucharest, Romania. The owner tried to contact the credit card authorization company and the bank that works with the processing company to verify the credit cards. However, they were not able to assist, so the owner telephoned the customer and had him fax his Romanian driver's license and other documents to the owner in New Jersey. The owner then shipped the parts via UPS at about the same time the bank became suspicious and called the owner to say that all the cards used in the order were fraudulent. The owner was lucky when the shipment was intercepted in Bucharest. Other complaints abound of such fraud and the inability of card issuers to assist. E-business owners argue that "there is no financial incentives for the banks and credit card companies to do anything about the problem because it is the merchant who, in virtually all cases, ultimately bear the cost of fraudulent Internet purchases." Disinterest by law enforcement is another concern because personnel and resources are limited. In another case, an e-business owner in the United States telephoned Canadian police and told them about an individual, living a few miles from the police station, who was attempting to commit credit card fraud against the e-business owner. The police response was that nothing can be done until the e-business owner flew to Canada and posted a $10,000 bond to guarantee a court appearance to testify. Loss prevention and investigation are obviously major necessities to survive in the world of e-business. Many businesses contract fraud screening to outside firms as seen on the Internet; check "credit card fraud."

Counterfeit Money

The word counterfeit denotes an unlawful duplication of something of value. Although our discussion will concentrate on counterfeit money, retailers also encounter problems with counterfeit checks, bank cards, coupons, and merchandise. Prevention and investigation are two key strategies to combat losses.

The U.S. Secret Service, a branch within the U.S. Treasury Department, investigates cases of counterfeiting. Because citizens are not reimbursed when they receive a counterfeit bill, this often causes a citizen to continue to pass the counterfeit bill. Consequently, investigations are more difficult.

Counterfeiting is a growing problem because of the newer color copier machines, scanners, computers, and laser printers that are in widespread use. Knowing how to recognize counterfeit bills helps prevent victimization, Figure 11-6. Compare a suspect bill with a genuine bill. Look for the red and blue fibers that are scattered throughout a genuine bill. These fibers are curved, about a quarter inch, hair thin, and difficult to produce on bogus bills. Also, look for the security thread and microprinting. Another technique is to watch for $1 bills that have counterfeit higher denomination numbers glued over the lower denomination numbers. Also, compare suspect coins with genuine coins. Check: U.S. Secret Service, "Know Your Money" at www.treas.gov/usss.

Also, if a counterfeit bill or coin is received, do the following:

1. Delay the passer if possible.
2. Telephone the police or the U.S. Secret Service.
3. Obtain a description of the passer and license number of vehicle.
4. Handle the bill as little as possible.

The best method of detection is to compare the suspect counterfeit with a genuine bill.

Security thread (embedded in paper) running vertically.

Microprinting on edge of portrait.

Look for one-dollar bills having counterfeit higher denominations pasted over lower denominations.

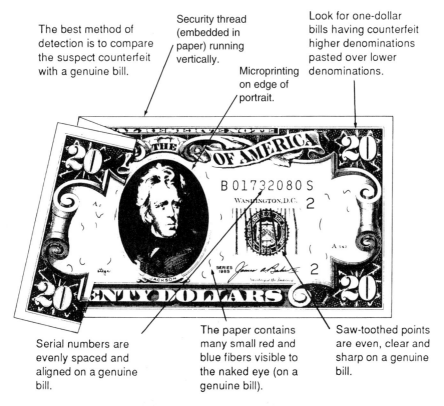

Serial numbers are evenly spaced and aligned on a genuine bill.

The paper contains many small red and blue fibers visible to the naked eye (on a genuine bill).

Saw-toothed points are even, clear and sharp on a genuine bill.

Figure 11-6 Detecting a counterfeit bill.

Shoplifting

Shoplifting is a widespread crime resulting in billions of dollars in losses per year for retailers. This crime is committed by various people from different types of backgrounds. The *amateur*, also called a "snitch," usually shoplifts for personal use and often has the money to pay for the stolen merchandise. Security personnel are most likely to encounter amateurs. The *professional*, or "booster," represents a small portion of shoplifters. These skilled professionals steal for resale purposes to obtain cash. They use booster boxes (false packages with secret openings to hide merchandise), hooks inside clothing, and deep pockets to store items while shoplifting. Juveniles, addicts, and kleptomaniacs (those with a rare impulse to steal) are among the variety of shoplifters.

Behaviors and Techniques

Awareness of how shoplifters behave and steal provides retail employees with a foundation to curb the problem. The following list provides some behaviors and techniques of shoplifters.

- Suspected shoplifters may act nervous, constantly look around, and walk past the same area several times. But this is no guarantee the suspect will shoplift.

- Watch for large handbags or anything carried (newspaper, camera case) that can be used to hide merchandise.

- Look for odd characteristics such as the wearing of too many clothes on a warm day or a baby carriage with no baby.

- Shoplifters will try any trick. For example, using a person in a wheelchair or a pregnant woman. These conditions may be staged.

- Watch for diversionary tactics, such as fainting or a fight. Groups of shoplifters often distract employees away from the one who is stealing.

- Expensive items (jewelry) may be switched with similar inexpensive items.

- Watch for the switching of price tags.

- Shoplifters sometimes ask salespeople to show more items than can be controlled.

- In fitting rooms, shoplifters put on store clothes under their own clothes and then leave the store.

- Certain business hours are attractive to shoplifters. For example, when a store opens or is about to close, meal hours, and when a store is very busy.

Countermeasures for Shoplifting

A variety of strategies are applied to the problem of shoplifting. Multiple strategies enhance protection, Figure 11-7.

RETAIL EMPLOYEES *The most important deterrent to shoplifting is well-trained employees. Good floor coverage and a simple "May I help you?" destroys the opportunity to commit the crime.* Security personnel should spend more time enlisting and training salespeople who can increase surveillance and reporting capabilities. A cooperative effort pays large dividends in preventing losses.

SECURITY PERSONNEL AND SURVEILLANCE SYSTEMS Security officers are sometimes posted at access points to remind customers of security presence. However, a shoplifter is likely to steal away from these posts. This is where a well-disguised store detective is useful. These specialists should appear like customers. For example, wearing clothes to fit the weather outside, carrying a few packages in hand, and eating a bag of popcorn while browsing through racks of merchandise. In other words, surveillance must be subtle.

Also, security personnel can remain off the sales floor and observe shoppers from various vantage points. This includes the use of binoculars from stock rooms. Observation posts can be established in stock rooms at high points near the ceiling. Sometimes ceiling tiles are raised slightly to permit a

Figure 11-7   Multiple security strategies enhance protection against shoplifting: well-trained employees, CCTV, electronic article surveillance (portals at exit), good lighting, and mirrors. Courtesy: Sensormatic, Inc.

clear and wide view of the sales floor. One-way mirrors also play a role to deter crime because the offender never knows when someone is watching. Convex mirrors are helpful when placed above a partition separating two departments. In one case, a group of retail employees on one side of a partition were able to watch a shoplifter in action who thought nobody was observing.

CCTV systems provide an opportunity to watch several locations by one person. Recording capabilities are valuable for evidence. Fatigue, boredom, and sleepiness can reduce the effectiveness of these systems. Therefore, personnel who observe monitors while sitting at a console in a control room should be rotated and assigned to other duties every few hours. Return to Chapter 4 for more extensive information on CCTV systems.

ELECTRONIC ARTICLE SURVEILLANCE Electronic article surveillance (EAS) has grown in popularity over the years as a deterrent to shoplifting. Basically, tags are attached to merchandise. If a shoplifter departs with a tagged item, a sensor at an exit will sound an alarm. The technology is improving, costs are going down, and we are seeing widespread application of these systems. Almost anything can have a tag since the tags are now being made smaller. For example, price labels on expensive meats in a grocery store sometimes contain tags. Manufactured parts are also subject to protection. One airline experiencing a problem with passengers stealing life jackets halted this theft with EAS. The technology is also being applied to people. Examples are prisoners supervised at home and mental patients who are not to leave their hospital ward.

In a retail environment, a cashier may fail to remove an EAS tag when a customer pays for an item. Consequently, an alarm is sounded. The alarm may also be activated because of a shoplifting incident. In either case, security personnel must approach the suspect with absolute courtesy because a mistake or system malfunction may have occurred and a lawsuit for false arrest must be avoided.

ALARMS Besides EAS, several other types of alarms can protect merchandise. This includes the following list:

- Loop alarms are woven through merchandise and complete an electrical circuit that, if interrupted, will sound an alarm.
- Wafer alarms, placed under items, respond when pressure is removed.
- Display cases may be alarmed with contact switches.
- Plug alarms are activated when electronic merchandise is unplugged.

SPACE PROTECTION We previously discussed space protection as a countermeasure for internal theft. However, space protection is also used to counter shoplifting. Recall that space protection includes all those methods of monitoring the interior spaces or areas of a facility.

POINT PROTECTION Point protection was previously explained as a countermeasure for internal theft. Like space protection, the point protection strategy can also be applied to shoplifting. Remember that point protection emphasizes point or object protection. This added protection is necessary in a retail store where a potential shoplifter may not be distinguished from other customers or employees in the store until he or she makes an attempt to steal merchandise.

ADDITIONAL STRATEGIES Signs are frequently found in retail stores warning offenders of the consequences of shoplifting. The effectiveness of this strategy is difficult to measure. Signs inform people that management is concerned about the shoplifting problem. Also, communication of security measures taken by the retailer may create fear in individuals with tendencies to shoplift.

Store layout is another way that theft can be reduced. Salespeople should be able to operate cash registers without having to turn away from customers. Aisles should permit easy surveillance. High merchandise can be placed along walls rather than in the middle of a sales floor. Turnstiles and corrals are useful to direct customers to the POS.

Reward programs are an option to increase employee participation in spotting shoplifters. Community involvement can involve retailers pooling information and resources.

For guidelines on confronting suspected shoplifters refer back to Chapter 8, Arrest Law and Procedures.

What If?

As a Security Officer at a Retail Store, What Do You Do if You Observe a Customer Place an Aspirin Bottle in Her Pocketbook?

While observing customers on the sales floor via CCTV, you spot a customer place an aspirin bottle in her pocketbook in front of the aspirin counter. You notify other security personnel who observe the suspect and prepare for a shoplifting apprehension. Your supervisor contacts you to verify that you observed, without a doubt, the customer place the aspirin bottle in her pocketbook. You respond, "Yes!" The suspect reaches the checkout, pays for items in the shopping cart she is using, but not aspirins, and heads toward the exit. She is stopped before the exit door and detained for shoplifting. The woman gets upset and claims she has done no wrong. She refuses to go to the security office and handcuffs are forcibly placed on the woman before she is forced to the security office. At the office she claims that she bought the aspirins at the store the week before and has a receipt at home. When public police arrive, the woman is taken to jail and booked for shoplifting.

Eventually, the shoplifting charge was dropped against the woman and the retail store found itself on the losing side of a lawsuit. The woman did indeed have a receipt for the aspirins. On the day of her arrest she was first observed by you with the aspirin bottle in her hand. She had taken the bottle out of her pocketbook, not off the store shelf.

Robbery

The FBI defines robbery as "the taking or attempting to take anything of value from the care, custody, or control of a person or persons by force or threat of force." According to the FBI, in 1998, there were 446,625 robberies. Personal robberies accounted for about two-thirds of all robberies. Gas stations lost an average of $546 and banks an average of $4516. We must remember the FBI collects data on reported crimes and not all crimes are reported.

Countermeasures

Space protection can be applied to deter robbery, especially through good lighting and surveillance cameras. Point protection can also be a strategy applied to robbery, especially by using bullet-resistant cashier enclosures and careful money handling routines.

It should be noted that certain types of both space and point protection can hinder a robber when taking items and leaving. This creates a safety problem because the robber needs to remain longer on the premises. In other words, although space and point protection can deter robbers who observe a well-protected store, employee safety is a primary concern during a robbery. Employees must do what is necessary to ensure that the violent offender leaves the premises as soon as possible. This includes giving up cash and merchandise without resisting the robber.

In addition to space and point protection strategies, the following guidelines lessen the impact of robbery to retail businesses.

1. Institute well-planned robbery prevention strategies.

2. Maintain good lighting on the premises.

3. Do not clutter windows that block the view of passing police and citizens.

4. Deposit excess cash in the bank.

5. Never openly carry a bank bag (use a bird seed bag, tool box, or something else).

6. Watch what you say to strangers.

7. Train employees for the possibility of a robbery. Emphasize safety and obtaining a description of the robber and the getaway vehicle. Include, in training, cautious opening and closing procedures and money-handling.

8. Install a silent alarm and a camera/recording system.

9. Maintain "bait" money. Record the denominations, series years, and serial letters and numbers.

10. Install a special money clip, such as a "Bill Trap," in a cash register drawer so that a silent alarm is sent to authorities when cash is removed from the clip.

11. Cooperate with public police.

The Monday Robber

Public police in an urban area had a difficult time capturing the Monday robber, as he was known. As it turns out, this robber had some clever ideas on how and when to commit business robberies. His favorite day was Monday, especially in the morning, since employees were still recovering from the weekend and dealing with the shock of a new work week. He preferred rainy Mondays since he could wear a long raincoat and carry his shotgun underneath. But what he loved the most about rainy Mondays was that after he committed a robbery he could run down the street without appearing too obvious. Also, if he needed to hide in an alley, he figured public police would not search for him in a driving rain. Eventually, his luck ran out when a slippery sidewalk caused him to fall and break an ankle. He was soon captured.

Burglary

The FBI defines burglary as "the unlawful entry of a structure to commit a felony or theft. The use of force to gain entry is not required to classify an offense as burglary." According to the FBI, in 1998, there were 2.3 million burglaries. Two-thirds of burglaries were residential; the remainder were at nonresidential locations. Nonresidential burglaries include stores, manufacturing plants, offices, schools, and so forth.

Countermeasures

Crime prevention and physical security are primary methods to protect against burglary, as covered earlier in the book. We have learned that space protection is a countermeasure for internal theft, shoplifting, and robbery. Space protection can also be a strategy used to deter burglary. This strategy should be considered only as support or back-up to perimeter and entry protection in the event of compromise or to detect the presence of a "hide-in" burglar. Point protection provides the final in a series of defenses against burglary; it protects specific assets.

Additional guidelines to protect against burglary are listed here:

1. Use physical security measures and work with public police crime prevention programs.
2. Maintain good lighting both inside and outside of the building.
3. Control cash and make daily bank deposits.
4. At the end of the business day, leave cash register drawers open with the money trays visibly turned over.

5. Do not leave any tools or equipment inside or outside that can be used to commit burglary.
6. Check for hide-ins before departing. These are people who hide inside a store before closing and then break out after stealing.
7. Before leaving, recheck windows, doors, and alarms. Retailers have been known to leave the front door unlocked after closing.

Shopping Malls

Large shopping malls contain security organizations that have more personnel than most police departments. A well-trained and competent security force is necessary to protect mall employees, assets, and the thousands of customers that shop every day. Protection is required throughout a mall, within stores, and especially in the parking lots. Crimes, accidents, medical emergencies, and fires are major incidents facing security personnel. Proper training and a prevention approach are the hallmarks of professionals.

Good public relations are necessary at malls. A sharp appearance and courtesy help to create a positive, professional image of security personnel. Retailers and customers frequently rely on security officers for assistance. Common incidents include shoplifting, theft, lost people and merchandise, and automobile problems, such as a dead battery, flat tire, and keys locked inside.

CHAPTER REVIEW

A. Multiple Choice

1. Which of the following does not describe a retail security problem that provides a challenge for security personnel?
   a. low turnover in the industry
   b. lax job applicant screening
   c. attractive and inviting merchandise
   d. many part-time and temporary employees
2. "Till tapping" means
   a. tricking a retailer into opening early so a robbery can be committed.
   b. writing bad checks.
   c. stealing money from a cash register.
   d. distracting a salesperson to shoplift.
3. A "void" is
   a. a procedure to correct a cashier mistake.
   b. another name for a bad check.
   c. a sloppy shoplifter.
   d. a useless security procedure.
4. Select the federal agency that investigates counterfeit money.
   a. Central Intelligence Agency
   b. FBI
   c. Internal Revenue Service
   d. U.S. Secret Service
5. The most important deterrent to shoplifting is (are)
   a. CCTV.
   b. well-trained employees.
   c. electronic article surveillance (EAS).
   d. security officers.

B. True Or False

1. Shrinkage is largely caused by shoplifting.
2. Access controls at retail stores should always be tight.
3. Undercover investigations are useful to uncover well-hidden employee theft.
4. A shopping service tests salespeople for courtesy, efficiency, and honesty.

5. Genuine U.S. currency contains many small red and blue fibers throughout the paper that can be seen with the naked eye.

Applications

Application 11A

Locate the security hazards in the drawing below, Figure 11-8. What recommendations would you suggest to prevent internal theft, shoplifting, and robbery?

Application 11B

Role-play a scenario of a shoplifting case. Include the theft incident, the subsequent confrontation, and the disposition of the case, whether in-house or through the justice system. Establish a panel to evaluate employee actions and provide constructive criticism. Refer to Chapter 8, Arrest Law and Procedures, for a review of legal guidelines.

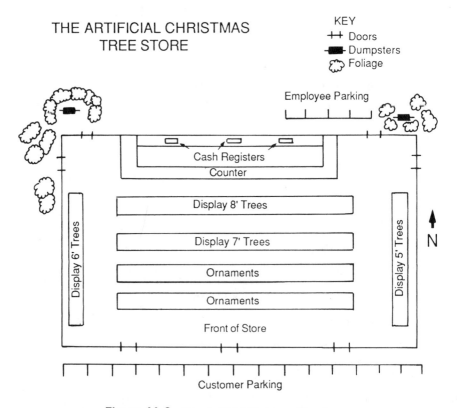

Figure 11-8   The Artificial Christmas Tree Store.

12

Safety, Fire Protection, and Emergencies

CHAPTER OUTLINE

OBJECTIVES

After studying this chapter, you will be able to:

- Define accident and safety.
- Cite workplace accident losses and costs.
- Explain the causes of accidents.
- Discuss the Occupational Safety and Health Administration.
- Briefly describe the workers' compensation system and the problem of malingering.
- Discuss the security officer's role in safety.
- Cite statistics on the seriousness of the fire problem in the United States.
- Discuss organizations involved in fire protection.
- Describe fire protection during earlier periods of history.
- Explain fire protection, fire prevention, and fire suppression strategies.
- Explain how a fire begins and what to do when it occurs.
- Discuss workplace emergencies and countermeasures.

Definitions of Accident and Safety

As with many fields of study, experts disagree on basic definitions. For our purposes, *accident* is defined as an unplanned event that may result in injury, death, or property damage. *Safety* involves positive action to prevent accidents, and the reduction of personal harm and property damage if an accident occurs.

An accident frequently results from a sequence of events. If there is an interruption in this sequence, an accident can possibly be prevented. This is where safety becomes useful. For example, a potential accident from metal filings hitting a machinist's eyes is prevented by using goggles.

Grimaldi and Simonds in their book *Safety Management* state:

The majority of cases which fill safety records could be predicted and so may not be regarded as wholly accidental. Their causes and remedies already were established by countless similar earlier occurrences. Most harmful events are the result of failures to apply known principles for their control. Persuading people to effect their application is the challenge to safety.

Accident Losses and Costs

In the past, a manual worker's welfare was of minimal concern to management; the loss of life or limb was "part of the job" and "a normal business risk." For example, in the construction of tall buildings, it was expected that one life would be lost for each floor. A 20-story building would yield 20 lost lives. Since the early 1900s great strides have been made to increase safety in the workplace. Safer machines, improved supervision, and training all have helped to prevent accidents.

Today, annual losses for American workers are: 6000 deaths from injuries, 50,000 deaths from illnesses caused by workplace exposures, and 6 million people suffer nonfatal workplace injuries. Injuries alone cost U.S. businesses over $110 billion annually.

Causes of Accidents

When a serious accident occurs, an investigation typically follows. For instance, when an airplane crashes or a train derails, an investigation occurs. Even minor accidents between two automobiles that are slightly damaged bring police to the scene for an accident investigation. But why do we require accident investigations? Besides the need for facts to determine legal liability, for insurance purposes, or government action, an investigation can pinpoint the cause of an accident that can lead to corrective action. Three major causes of accidents are human failures (80 percent), environmental hazards (15 percent), and defective agents (5 percent). We will briefly discuss each of these causes.

Human Failures

Safety specialists agree that accidents primarily result from human failure. In fact, people involved in accidents often fail to apply what they know about safety.

Human failures result from emotions and psychological conditions, bad habits, inadequate training, overconfidence, physiological factors (e.g., poor sight), use of drugs, fatigue, and other factors. Someone who has had an argument and drives in an intoxicated state, forgetting eyeglasses, is obviously facing great potential for an accident.

Environmental Hazards

Environmental factors include natural occurrences, such as rain, snow, lightning, tornadoes, and earthquakes. This category also covers environmental factors produced by humans. Examples are sloppy housekeeping and improper storage of chemicals.

Defective Agents

Defective agents point to design flaws and structural failures as the cause of accidents. For example, at the turn of the century, failure of Firestone tires were blamed for accidents involving Ford Explorers. But, each company blamed the other for the accidents.

What If?

As a Security Officer, What Do You Do if an Employee Requests Your Help in Rescuing a Coworker Who Passed-Out in a Storage Tank?

While on patrol, an employee yells to you to help rescue a co-worker who is in a storage tank, not responding, and motionless. You run to the tank and see the coworker at the bottom of the tank near the ladder. The employee who called you states that if you don't climb down the ladder to rescue the coworker, he will. You refuse and order the employee not to climb down the ladder. He disregards your order and proceeds down the ladder. As he yells to you to get a rope, he passes-out. What do you do?

This is a serious emergency. Immediately report the situation and request fire/rescue and emergency medical services.

Confined area entry can be extremely dangerous (Figure 12-1). Hazards that are not easily seen, smelled, or felt can be deadly. Some of the deadliest gases and vapors have no odor. For example, in the petroleum industry, a storage tank was rinsed and vented for several days. When checked with gas detection equipment, no flammable gases were measured. But, after workers removed loose rust, scale, and sediment, the percentage of flammable gas rose and ignited.

The cardinal rule for entry into a confined area is, "Never trust your senses." *Before entry, the following safety strategies are recommended: proper training, equipment to identify hazards, and an entry permit issued by a safety specialist.* OSHA's standard for confined spaces, Title 29 Code of Federal Regulations (CFR), Part 1910.146, contains the requirements for practices and procedures to protect employees from the hazards of entry into permit-required confined spaces.

Occupational Safety and Health Administration

Until 1970, no uniform and comprehensive provisions existed for the protection of America's workforce against accidents and health hazards. In 1970, Congress considered these annual figures:

- 14,000 worker deaths.
- 2.5 million workers disabled.
- New cases of occupational diseases estimated at 300,000.

U.S. Department of Labor
Occupational Safety
and Health Administration
No. 25

ACCIDENT SUMMARY

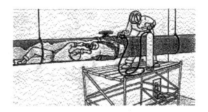

Accident Type	Fire/explosion
Weather	Fair and cold
Type of Operation	Installing water line
Crew Size	3
Collective Bargaining	Yes
Competent Safety Monitor on Site?	Yes
Safety and Health Program in Effect?	No
Was the Worksite Inspected Regularly?	Yes
Training and Education Provided?	No
Employee Job Title	Welder
Age/Sex	28/M
Experience at this Type of Work	2 years
Time on Project	2 months

BRIEF DESCRIPTION OF ACCIDENT

A welder entered a steel pipe (24 inch diameter) to grind a bad weld at a valve about 30 feet from the entry point. Before he entered, other crew members decided to add oxygen to the pipe near the bad weld. He had been grinding intermittently for about five minutes when a fire broke out enveloping his clothing. Another crew member pulled him 30 feet to the pipe entrance and extinguished the fire. However, the welder died the next day from his burns.

INSPECTION RESULTS

Following its inspection, OSHA issued three citations one willful, one serious and one repeat. Had the cited standards been followed, this fatality might have been prevented.

ACCIDENT PREVENTION RECOMMENDATIONS

1. Do not use oxygen for ventilation, cooling or cleaning in welding operations (29 CFR 1926.353(a)(b).
2. Comply with OSHA's required confined or enclosed space entry program (29 CFR 1926.21(b)(6)(i)).
3. Train employees to recognize and avoid unsafe conditions associated with their work and make sure they understand the confined space entry program and follow its procedures (29 CFR 1926.21(b)(2) and 1926.20(b)(1)).

Figure 12-1 Fatal fire in confined area.

The human and financial costs were staggering. Consequently, the Occupational Safety and Health Act (OSHAct) of 1970 was passed by Congress and signed into law by former President Richard M. Nixon. The purpose of this law is to provide a safe working environment for employees in various occupations.

OSHA rules extend to all employers and their employees in the 50 states, the District of Columbia, Puerto Rico, and other U.S. possessions. The act does not cover self-employed persons, family-owned and operated farms, and workplaces protected by other federal agencies. Although federal agencies are not covered by OSHA, agencies are required to maintain a safe working environment equal to those groups under OSHA's jurisdiction. State and local government employees are also impacted by OSHA.

OSHA Standards

OSHA is administered by the Secretary of Labor who has the authority and responsibility to establish occupational safety and health standards. Information on OSHA can be found as follows: U.S. Department of Labor, OSHA, PO Box 37535, Washington, DC 20013; Tel.: 202-219-4667; website: www.osha.gov.

Standards evolve from OSHA itself or in response to petitions from other parties such as federal agencies, state or local governments, or any interested organization or person. The National Institute for Occupational Safety and Health (NIOSH) www.cdc.gov/niosh, which is a branch of the U.S. Department of Health and Human Services, also helps develop standards while conducting research and providing information.

There are actually thousands of OSHA standards. Some pertain to specific industries and workers, whereas others are general and practiced by most industries. Examples include safety requirements for machines, equipment, and employees, such as requiring face shields or safety glasses during the use of certain machines; unobstructed aisles and exits in the workplace; prevention of electrical hazards; adequate fire protection; adequate lunchrooms, lavatories, and drinking water; and monitoring of employee exposure to chemical or toxic hazards. Employers can ask OSHA for a variance (permission to deviate) from a standard if they cannot comply because of inadequate equipment or technical personnel. The employer may try to prove their method is safe and as effective as the OSHA standard. A person adversely affected by a standard may file a petition for judicial review with the U.S. Court of Appeals. Here are examples of OSHA standards:

SUBPART I—PERSONAL PROTECTIVE EQUIPMENT

1910.132 General requirements.

(a) Application. Protective equipment, including personal protective equipment for eyes, face, head, and extremities, protective clothing, respiratory devices, and protective shields and barriers, shall be provided, used, and maintained in a sanitary and reliable condition wherever it is necessary by reason of hazards of processes or environment, chemical hazards, radiological hazards, or mechanical irritants encountered in a manner capable of causing injury or impairment in the function of any part of the body through absorption, inhalation, or physical contact.

SUBPART K—MEDICAL AND FIRST AID

1910.151 Medical services and first aid.

(a) The employer shall ensure the ready availability of medical personnel for advice and consultation of matters of plant health.

(b) In the absence of an infirmary, clinic, or hospital in near proximity to the workplace which is used for the treatment of all injured employees, a person or persons shall be adequately trained to render first aid. First aid supplies approved by the consulting physician shall be readily available.

(c) Where the eyes or body of any person may be exposed to injurious corrosive materials, suitable facilities for quick drenching or flushing of the eyes and body shall be provided within the work area for immediate emergency use.

OSHA HAZARD COMMUNICATION STANDARD This standard (1910.1200) was established because more than 32 million workers could be exposed to one or more chemical hazards; and over 650,000 hazardous chemical products exist, with hundreds of new ones being introduced annually. Also known as a *right-to-know law*, this standard requires all employers who have employees that may be exposed to hazardous substances on the job to inform them about such substances and how to deal with them. Employers are required to write and implement a hazard communication program, conduct a chemical inventory, ensure that a *Material Safety Data Sheet* (MSDS) is available for each chemical, label chemical containers, and train employees on the safe use of chemicals (e.g., protective equipment, procedures).

OSHA BLOODBORNE PATHOGENS STANDARD This standard (1910.1030) limits exposure to blood and other potentially infectious materials, which could lead to disease or death. The standard covers all employees facing potential exposure. Employers are required to establish an exposure control plan covering safety procedures, protective equipment, and the control of waste. The Hepatitis B vaccination is to be made available to all employees who have occupational exposure to blood. Post-exposure evaluation and follow-up is to be made available to all employees who have had an exposure incident, including laboratory tests at no cost to the employee. Exposure records must be confidential and kept for the duration of employment plus 30 years. Training is required on all aspects of this standard and the training records must be maintained for three years.

CONTROL OF HAZARDOUS ENERGY SOURCES OSHA standard 1910.147 is designed to control hazardous energy. Better known as lockout/tagout, the aim is to prevent the accidental start-up of machines or other equipment during maintenance and servicing. The rule requires that hazardous energy sources must be isolated and rendered inoperative before work can begin. Elements of a lockout/tagout program are written procedures, training, and audits. Examples of OSHA citations involving this standard include Lifetime Doors, for 37 alleged violations after employees suffered finger amputations at the door manufacturing plant. OSHA proposed penalties of $1.1 million. In another case, an employee of Hanna Paper Recycling entered a baler to dislodge a jammed cardboard bale and was crushed to death between the bale and the gathering ram. OSHA cited Hanna for 19 alleged violations and proposed penalties for $59,200.

Recordkeeping

To gauge the seriousness of illnesses and injuries in the workplace so corrective action can follow, OSHA requires recordkeeping and reporting by employers. All occupational illnesses must be recorded. All injuries must be recorded if they result in death, one or more lost workdays, restriction of work, loss of consciousness, transfer to another job, or medical treatment (other than first aid). In reality, not all employers report all illnesses and injuries.

Employers are required to keep employees informed about OSHA and safety and health matters. This includes basic information on OSHA, variances, citations for violations of standards, and logs and summaries of injuries and illnesses.

OSHA Inspections

OSHA has the authority to conduct workplace inspections. In *Marshall v. Barlow, Inc.*, the Supreme Court ruled that OSHA may not conduct warrantless inspections without an employer's consent. However, inspection can follow the obtaining of a judicially authorized search warrant based upon administrative probable cause or upon evidence of a violation. An appeals process is offered to employees and employers.

Assistance for Workplace Safety

Many groups offer expertise to improve safety and health in the workplace. Examples are insurance companies and trade associations. Also, the National Safety Council has an extensive information service (Address: 1121 Spring Lake Dr., Itasca, IL 60143; Tel.: 1-800-621-7615; website: www.nsc.org). The Red Cross is a source of first-aid training. An employer who is not able to locate a local chapter should contact the American National Red Cross, National Headquarters, Safety Programs, 8111 Gatehouse Rd., Falls Church, VA 22042; Tel.: 703-206-7090; website: www.redcross.org. The Web and libraries contain a wealth of information on safety and health matters.

Workers' Compensation

Although workers of today may complain about employers who "just don't care," in earlier years the situation was much worse. When employees were injured on the job and not able to work, financial support for employees and their families was nonexistent. Increasing concern for this problem led to workers' compensation laws being passed in Germany in 1885, in Great Britain in 1897, and in the United States in 1902. All states now have workers' compensation laws so employees can be compensated by their employer following injury on the job. Workers' compensation provides for the costs of medical care and rehabilitation, lost wages for injured workers, and death benefits for dependents of persons killed on the job. When these laws were first proposed and passed, intense controversy developed between business people and groups concerned about the welfare of workers.

Insurance companies have benefited from workers' compensation laws by offering policies to insure businesses fearful of financial costs in the event of worker injury. Reduced premiums are offered to businesses that implement accident prevention programs. Insurance companies provide loss prevention specialists who survey businesses and recommend measures to reduce accidents, such as safety guards on machines. Today, more companies are realizing the benefits of safety programs. In fact, effective safety programs can result in an insurer returning insurance premium dollars to the insured company at the end of each year.

Malingering

When workers' compensation laws were first passed, many workers had high hopes of being fairly compensated if an injury occurred, without having to go through a lengthy process. Today, the system has its problems. Many injured workers argue that the only way to deal with the system is to obtain an attorney. From the insurance industry's perspective, the interest of the insurer must be protected, and fraudulent claimants are a very serious problem. The wish of some workers unhappy with their jobs is to sustain a minor injury on the job, claim an inability to work, and obtain a check each month. This act of pretending incapacity or injury to avoid work is called *malingering*. In both the private and public sectors, malingering has overburdened the system. It has become difficult for employers and insurers to distinguish between those who are really unable to work and those who are pretending. This is why private sector investigations of workers' compensation claims have increased. An exposed case of malingering can save an employer and an insurer a considerable amount of money over several years.

Fraudulent Workers' Compensation Claims

Fraudulent claims take many different forms. A manufacturing employee or a public servant may falsely claim that an injury on the job caused severe back pain and an inability to work. Sometimes an injury occurs off the premises, but the employee claims that it happened on the job. Surveillance of one who is suspected of malingering may show the individual putting an extension on his or her home or playing golf. In one case, a fraudulent claimant who was a part-time actress was tricked into auditioning for a part in a phony play that required assorted acrobatic feats. The audition was set up by a creative investigator who recorded the woman's physical abilities. When investigators showed her the recording, she dropped her claim. Because of the problem of fraudulent workers' compensation claims, security officers must look for signs of faked accidents and injuries and write comprehensive and factual reports.

Security Officer's Role in Safety

By studying OSHA guidelines and insurance carrier requirements, a business can develop and refine safety policies and procedures. Depending on the industry, various safety measures can be established. Examples include wearing protective eyeglasses and shoes with steel toes, conforming to specific procedures for the safe operation of machinery, and maintaining good housekeeping practices.

Security often plays a crucial role in reporting violations or hazards to supervisors and managers who take corrective action, such as closer supervision, retraining, enforcement, and discipline. The primary role of security is to *observe* and *report*. Organizations rely on security personnel because they usually provide coverage twenty-four hours a day, seven days a week. If one accident or fire is prevented because of diligent observation and reporting by a security officer, this sends a message to management and all employees that security is worth the expense. Hazards should be promptly reported since quick action can prevent disaster.

Depending on the company and industry, security officers may be required to complete detailed safety checklists each day. Other businesses may favor only the reporting of unsafe conditions when the need arises.

Safety is everyone's business. Through training and continuous reinforcement, management, supervisors, and security personnel can create an atmosphere where safety is on the minds of all employees. Management can promote safety through carefully designed signs and posters (Figure 12-2). Some businesses reward employees when a specific number of hours are

Figure 12-2   Safety sign; supervision.

reached without a lost-time accident. Rewards may include cash, food, and leisure equipment. These incentives promote safety.

Workplace Hazards

The following list describes some hazards in the workplace that security officers should look for and report.

1. Improperly stored flammable substances.
2. Unusual odors or noises.
3. Frayed electrical wires.
4. Blocked or inoperable emergency exits.
5. Burned out lights.
6. Slippery substances on floors that can cause a person to fall.
7. Damaged floors or pavement that can cause an accident.
8. Damaged security or fire protection equipment.
9. Workers not using protective equipment or clothing.
10. Workers who circumvent safety measures when performing their job or operate machinery in a dangerous manner (Figure 12-3).
11. Horseplay by workers operating cars, trucks, forklifts, and equipment.
12. Workers who are under the influence of drugs.

The Fire Problem in the United States

The United States has one of the highest fire death rates in the industrialized world. Data from the Web in 2001, from the National Fire Data Center, showed that in 1999: 3570 Americans lost their lives and another 21,875 were injured as a result of fire; more Americans were killed by fire than all natural disasters combined; and about 1.8 million fires were reported, causing direct property loss of $10 billion.

The National Fire Protection Association reported that most structural fires in the United States were residential and that most civilian fire deaths and injuries occurred in residential blazes. The primary cause of fire deaths is smoke—not fire. Smoke contains carbon monoxide that can be lethal. Furthermore, with newer chemicals and synthetic substances being created daily, the fires of today can be very toxic. Defects in heating equipment or mishandling of it are responsible for more residential fires than any other single cause. For nonresidential fires, the two major causes are incendiary/ suspicious and electrical.

Most people do not realize how dangerous and damaging a fire is until it occurs. Besides the potential for loss of life, injury, and property damage, fire often causes a business to temporarily or permanently close. This puts employees out of work—another unfortunate result of fire. As a security officer, much can be done to save a business from the devastating effects of fire.

U.S. Department of Labor
Occupational Safety
and Health Administration
No. 2

ACCIDENT SUMMARY

Accident Type:	Struck by Nail
Weather Conditions:	N/A
Type of Company:	General Contractors
Size of Work Crew:	17
Union or Non-union:	Union
Worksite Inspection?:	No
Designated Competent Person on Site?:	No
Employer Safety and Health Program?:	No
Training and Education for Employees?:	No
Craft of Deceased Employee:	Carpenter
Age/Sex	22; Male
Time of the Job:	3:00 p.m.
Time at the Task	unknown

BRIEF DESCRIPTION OF ACCIDENT

A carpenter apprentice was killed when he was struck in the head by a nail that was fired from a powder actuated tool. The tool operator, while attempting to anchor a plywood form in preparation for pouring a concrete wall, fired the gun causing the nail to pass through the hollow wall. The nail travelled some twenty-seven feet before striking the victim. The tool operator had never received training in the proper use of the tool, and none of the employees in the area were wearing personal protective equipment.

ACCIDENT PREVENTION RECOMMENDATIONS

1. Institute a program for frequent and regular inspections of the job site, materials, and equipment by a competent person(s) (1926.20(b)(2)).
2. Require employees exposed to the potential hazards associated with flying nails to use appropriate personal protective equipment. (1926.100(a) and 1926.102(a)(1)).
3. Train employees using powder actuated tools in the safe operation of the particular tool (1926.302(e)(2)).
4. Train employees operating power actuated tools to avoid firing into easily penetrated materials (1926.302(e)(8)).

Figure 12-3   Operating a tool in a dangerous manner.

Large Loss Fires

Examples of large loss fires as reported in *Fire Journal* illustrate the seriousness of the fire problem.

A chemical plant disaster near Pampa, Texas resulted in three worker deaths, thirty-seven injuries, and a $154 million loss. It occurred after two explosions. The first explosion took place near a gas boiler. Twenty seconds later, a second explosion occurred at a reactor in which butane combined with steam was used to make acid. The explosion was so strong that windows were broken six miles away. Flames were allowed to burn to consume dangerous chemicals that could have formed an explosive toxic cloud. Butane feeding the fire was cut off. Residential areas within four miles of the plant were evacuated.

In Garland, Texas, a retail warehouse was overstocked for the Christmas season. Merchandise was stored on racks over twenty feet high. At 9:00 P.M. an employee smelled smoke. When a security officer located the fire, it was five feet in one of the racks. Fire fighters responded immediately. However they were forced to retreat when the roof began to collapse. Investigators found the fire was set deliberately in an area remote from the sprinkler system that was defeated because of the high storage of merchandise.

Another large-loss fire in a storage facility involved an automotive paint distribution warehouse in Dayton, Ohio. The 9:00 P.M. blaze began when several drums of paint fell from or were punctured by a forklift truck. The fire erupted when the flammable liquid came into contact with the hot engine of the forklift. Over one million gallons of paint and chemicals fueled the intense fire that overpowered the automatic sprinkler system and caused the concrete and metal building to fall apart in less than three hours. On the sixth day, the fire was officially declared under control.

Organizations Involved in Fire Protection

Several organizations work to reduce the problem of fire. The National Fire Protection Association (NFPA), established in 1896, is a potent voice in fire prevention and suppression. The NFPA publishes fire standards and codes that often are incorporated into state and local fire laws (NFPA; www.nfpa.com; 1 Batterymarch Park, Quincy, MA 02269-9101; Tel.: 617-770-3000).

Underwriters Laboratories, Inc., is a nonprofit corporation interested in public safety through the investigation and testing of materials and products. It is supported by fees from manufacturers who request that their products be tested for safety. Some specific departments of UL show its relationship to loss prevention: fire protection department; burglary protection and signaling department; and casualty and chemical hazards department (UL; www.ul.com; 1285 Walt Whitman Rd., Melville, NY 11747-3081; Tel.: 631-271-6200).

The Factory Mutual System works on improving the effectiveness of fire protection systems, new fire suppression chemicals, and cost evaluation of fire protection systems. The Approval Group tests materials and equipment, submitted by manufacturers, to see if they can withstand fire tests. An approval guide is published each year (www.factorymutual.com; 1151 Boston-Providence Turnpike, Norwood, MA 02062; Tel.: 781-762-4300).

The American Insurance Association (AIA) studied contributing causes of major fires in the United States during the late 1800s and early 1900s. With this information as a foundation and with NFPA standards, AIA developed codes for fire prevention in urban areas. The National Building Code evolved, which has been adopted by many local governments. A Fire Prevention Code for cities also was published by the AIA. The AIA provides safety services, publications, and database services covering hundreds of topics (www.aiadc.org; 1130 Connecticut Ave., Suite 1000, Washington, DC 20036; Tel.: 202-828-7100).

Early Fire Protection

Ancient myths depicted fire as a "two-sided god," one side having beneficial qualities and the other side having destructive qualities. We can see the benefits of fire to provide heat and light to billions of people over thousands of years. However, fire kills or destroys anything in its path. Most of the fires encountered early in history were caused by lightning. Early civilizations saw great forest fires that were not fought like today's fires. As crude shelters were built and people began to live in cities, fire became an increasingly serious threat. About 300 B.C. in Rome, fire fighting duties were delegated to slaves. In later years, Rome became more organized in fighting fires by establishing divisions made up of hundreds of people assigned particular tasks, such as carrying water to fires in jars or bringing large pillows to the scene so fire victims trapped in taller buildings could jump onto them. When the aqueducts were completed, water was more plentiful around Rome to fight fires. Hand pumps and leather hoses also came into use during this early period.

As urbanization intensified so did the fire problem. Great fires wiped out cities. During the 1100s, England began to pass ordinances requiring buildings to have stone walls. By the 1600s, building codes were greatly expanded and prohibited, for example, wooden chimneys.

In colonial America, night watchmen sounded an alarm when a fire occurred. These volunteers were called the "rattle watch" because of the large rattles they carried to sound a fire alarm. In these early towns, each home was required to maintain two fire buckets. And to enforce a unified effort to fight fires, a fine was imposed on those who failed to respond to a fire with their buckets. A large fire in Boston in 1679 led to the first paid fire department in North America.

Fire Protection Today

Fire protection can be divided into two activities—prevention and suppression. We will briefly list some general suggestions for fire protection before discussing specific prevention and suppression strategies.

Fire Protection Strategies

1. Check fire protection systems and equipment for readiness, Figure 12-4.
2. Periodically conduct fire drills.
3. Cooperate with local public fire departments.

Figure 12-4 A security officer checks a fire protection system for readiness.

4. Report those employees who violate fire safety policies. How would you react, as a security officer, if you saw an employee smoking a cigarette while pumping gasoline into a vehicle?

5. Fire exits must be clearly identified and unobstructed.

6. Elevators (inside and on each floor) should have signs warning people to avoid use during a fire. Arrows must point to the nearest stairway.

7. Emergency lighting and evacuation instructions will assist those escaping from fire.

8. Fire escapes and fire doors (specially constructed doors to prevent the spread of fire) should be periodically checked to ensure reliability.

FIRE-RESISTIVE BUILDINGS Tons of combustible materials are brought into buildings during construction and while it is operational. Furniture, carpets, papers, and so forth are examples. These items serve as fuel for a fire. Concrete, steel, and fire-resistive construction materials and furnishings impede the spread of fire.

FIRE WALLS AND DOORS The purpose of a fire wall is to prevent the spread of fire. These masonry walls are built through a building and protrude above the roof. If a blaze begins on one end of a building, the fire wall can hinder the fire at the wall and prevent the destruction of the entire building. Doorways within a building at the fire wall are weak points. Consequently, fire doors are used. These doors are made of fire-resistive materials and are designed to withstand fire for a certain period of time (e.g., one hour), when closed. Thus, fire fighters can bring a fire under control before it spreads. Fire doors can be installed that automatically close when a fire occurs. Security officers should check these doors to make sure they are closed if policy requires such a precaution. Also, obstructions should be noted that would hinder an automatic fire door from closing.

FIRE BRIGADES Many facilities maintain an on-premises fire fighting unit similar to a public fire department, called a fire brigade. Fire brigades are actually composed of employees who are trained and equipped to fight the types of fires likely to occur on the premises. Fire brigades may be required because local fire fighting capabilities and response time do not meet the needs of the particular industry and its insurer.

TECHNOLOGY The wonders of technology and computers can play a significant role in fire protection. Integrated systems can be employed to detect and pinpoint the location of smoke and fire; automatically notify emergency services; shut down electrical equipment; close doors; return elevators to the first floor; provide directions to occupants for a safe escape; and extinguish the fire automatically by water from sprinklers. Many structures, called "smart buildings," integrate environmental controls, safety, fire protection, and security.

ACCESS CONTROL During an emergency, electronically controlled doors should be connected to the life and safety system to permit escape. From the security perspective, this presents a problem because an alarm condition may provide an opportunity for an offender to enter or exit with ease. To deal with this problem, CCTV and security officers can be applied to select locations.

Building codes mandate the use of exit devices that enable quick escape during emergencies. A door locked from the outside may be easily unlocked from the inside to allow theft or unauthorized passage. Therefore, the door needs to be secured from both sides while permitting quick escape in case of an emergency. Often, the solution is a controlled exit device. These are seen as a horizontal bar on the inside of a door that reads: "EMERGENCY EXIT-PUSH. ALARM WILL SOUND." One type of controlled exit device stays locked for a fixed time, usually 15 seconds, after being pushed, while sounding an alarm. The delay, requiring signage and Braille to alert people of the delay, provides time for security to respond. In a true emergency, such a device is unlocked immediately through a tie-in with the building's fire protection system as specified in the Life Safety Code NFPA 101.11

Fire Prevention Strategies

Those who deal with the fire problem know the importance of preventing a fire to avoid its occurrence. Several steps can be taken to reduce the possibility of fire. For example, security officers should look for and report the following hazards to prevent fires:

- Poor housekeeping, such as accumulations of combustible materials and flammable liquids.
- Improperly stored substances.
- Leaks.
- Improper transportation of hazardous substances.
- Accumulated trash.
- Overheated machinery.
- Frayed wires.
- Appliances left plugged in when policy forbids it.
- Cigarette butts in no smoking areas.
- Space heaters too close to combustible items.

Security officers should use all their senses to locate hazards. In other words, look for dangers, listen for things burning, smell for smoke, and feel walls near suspicious electrical outlets to locate dangerous warm spots.

Fire Suppression Strategies

Once a fire begins, quick suppression is critical. If a small fire is extinguished at its early stage, a huge potential loss can be avoided. Suppression includes a response from properly equipped firefighters or from an employee who is able to use a fire extinguisher to douse a fire.

A major factor supporting fire suppression is preparation. Once a blaze begins, the earlier efforts in anticipation of fire prove their value. Sprinklers, hose systems, and portable extinguishers are illustrations of fire suppression methods that will now be discussed.

AUTOMATIC SPRINKLERS As business and industry expanded in the United States through the nineteenth century, a need for increased fire suppression for buildings also increased. Water pails and hose equipment proved inadequate to fight fires in large and tall structures. Thus, the advent of automatic sprinkler systems paved the way for improved fire suppression for buildings, enabled businesses to expand, and allowed insurance companies to assume larger risks.

Automatic sprinkler systems consist of piping suspended from the ceiling with sprinkler heads spaced along the pipes and fed by a water supply. When a blaze develops, heat causes each sprinkler head to open and discharge water. The National Fire Protection Association (NFPA) has developed standards for the installation of these systems that are followed by manufacturers, insurance companies, and by federal, state, and local code enforcement agencies. Today, many buildings are required to contain automatic sprinkler systems. This investment has repeatedly proven its value by saving lives and greatly reducing property damage. Insurance companies provide substantial premium reductions that can pay for a sprinkler system within a few years. The failure of these systems is primarily from human error. For instance, the water source was turned off.

Two major types of sprinkler systems are wet pipe and dry pipe. The first one always has water in the pipes. The second has air pressure in the pipes because in cold climates water in the pipes would freeze. When a fire takes place near a dry pipe system, the sprinkler heads rupture and air escapes followed by water. These systems are supplied by water through a large pipe called a riser often located in a stairway of a building. At this location, a valve can be closed to stop the water flow. Security officers should know the basics of the sprinkler systems on the premises.

A sprinkler system is useless if it has been turned off. Another problem occurs when items are stacked too close to the sprinkler heads and interfere with water flow. A space of at least eighteen inches is necessary.

STANDPIPES AND HOSES Standpipes are similar to sprinkler systems in that a pipe system within a building provides water for fire suppression. A sprinkler system is automatic while a standpipe and hose system allows people to fight a fire manually and direct water onto the blaze. Horizontal standpipes are often in manufacturing plants, warehouses, and shopping malls. Vertical standpipes are found in most buildings more than four stories high. These systems enable quicker and more convenient fire fighting in upper floors of buildings where aerial ladder equipment and fire department hoses will not reach. Combined sprinkler and standpipe systems have increased the flexibility of fire fighting, although an adequate supply of water is vital.

Vertical standpipes usually run up the wall of a building at fire escape stairwells. The hose connections are on each floor near the stairs to permit ease of escape. A wall cabinet with a glass door contains a folded $2\frac{1}{2}$-inch hose (Figure 12-5). These hoses should be carefully handled by two people. The hose should be stretched completely and the nozzle held tightly before turning on the water. This prevents injury by any whipping action of the hose and nozzle.

CLASSES OF FIRES AND EXTINGUISHERS Fires are classified into four groups. When a fire occurs, it is important to know its classification so the most appropriate suppression strategies, equipment, and chemicals can be used to fight the fire.

Class A Ordinary combustible materials such as wood, coal, plastics, paper, and cloth. They are best extinguished by cooling with water or by blanketing with certain dry chemicals.

Class B Combustible liquids such as gasoline, diesel fuel, kerosene, and grease. They are best extinguished by excluding air or by special chemicals that affect the burning reactions.

Figure 12-5 Wall cabinet containing fire hose and fire extinguisher.

Class C Combustible materials in electrical equipment. These fires are extinguished by nonconducting extinguishing agents such as carbon dioxide and certain dry chemicals.

Class D Combustible metals such as magnesium, titanium, zirconium, sodium, and potassium. They are extinguished by special extinguishing agents designed for such applications.

Extinguishers are labeled with special color-coded symbols to indicate the class or classes of fires on which they can be used. The letter corresponding to each class is often placed in a field of a specified color and shape:

Class A—green triangle

Class B—red square

Class C—blue circle

Class D—green star

Multipurpose extinguishers carry the label of each class of fire on which they can be used (e.g., AB, ABC).

For most fires an extinguisher should be aimed at the base of the fire. Before fighting the fire ensure that an available exit is at your back; in other words, plan an escape in case the fire grows. Hands-on training is the best method of training for fire suppression.

The Beginning of a Fire

The often cited fire triangle, Figure 12-6, serves as a good foundation to understand how a fire begins. Three elements are necessary for fire—heat, fuel, oxygen, and then a chemical chain reaction. A smoldering cigarette, an overheated machine, or sparks from a welder's torch can each supply enough heat to start a blaze. Fuel is everywhere. Paper, wood, and furniture exist throughout most buildings. Oxygen is also in plentiful supply. A fire can be destroyed by removing oxygen by smothering, by cutting off a fuel supply, or by removing heat by cooling. Fire suppression is, in fact, aimed at these objectives.

Security Officer's Response to Fire

As soon as a serious fire is spotted and simple extinguishment is impossible, *contact the fire department immediately*. Every second is important since a small

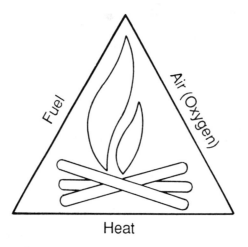

Heat

Figure 12-6 Heat, fuel, oxygen, and then a chemical chain reaction are necessary for fire.

fire can quickly spread and become a major disaster. Contacting the fire department should never be taken lightly because there have been instances when all concerned parties—security, supervisors, and management— thought the other had called in the emergency. Some people become so excited when a blaze erupts that they call the fire department but hang up before stating the location and other helpful information. Enhanced "911" emergency telephone systems help to deal with this problem because a display screen in front of the dispatcher automatically shows the address from where the call was placed. Cell telephones present a newer problem of determining from where an emergency call was placed. Security officers should verify the following two important questions when a fire takes place:

1. Who called in the emergency?
2. Was the proper address stated?

A follow-up call can serve as a double check. The following guidelines are additional suggestions to help security officers when responding to a fire:

1. When a fire is small enough to be put out with a portable extinguisher, a more serious emergency is avoided. However, as soon as a fire becomes too big to handle, the fire department must be contacted immediately!
2. The primary concern is to protect lives. An orderly evacuation must be conducted quickly. Avoid elevators, use stairs.
3. Contact occupants of nearby structures who may be in danger.
4. Ensure injured people are transported to a hospital. If necessary, render first aid.
5. The closing of windows and doors can play a role in hindering the spread of a fire.
6. Shut off all devices (e.g., fans) that are circulating the fire. Later, the same fans can be used to clear smoke.
7. Sources of fuel for the fire should be isolated, if possible.
8. Electrical circuits may have to be turned off.
9. Security officers should work with incoming firefighters by keeping crowds back, clearing traffic, and pointing out hazardous substances and other dangers.
10. Professional fire fighters have considerable training and experience in battling fires. Security officers should cooperate with these specialists.
11. Security officers must never forget that a fire could have been set to divert attention so a crime can be committed and/or covered up.
12. Clearly understand the dangers of not only fire, but smoke, gas, and the possibility of explosion. Heat from a fire can expand air and shatter doors and windows.
13. Never open a door during a fire unless you feel it for heat. The opposite side may contain fire and expanding gases that are ready to rush out and kill you when you open the door.

14. Since smoke rises, you may have to crawl on your hands and knees to breathe less toxic air.

15. After a fire is controlled, danger still remains. The building, including walls, floors, and the roof, can collapse. Toxic gases are another threat. Also, the fire, thought to be extinguished, may begin again.

16. Maintain security during and following a fire because offenders may commit a variety of crimes (e.g., theft of assets or information, destroy evidence).

Detectors and Alarms

Various types of detectors and alarms serve as an early warning system to protect lives and property. *Ionization detectors* react to invisible products of combustion during the early stages of a fire. *Photoelectric detectors* sound an alarm in response to smoke. *Infrared detectors* react to flame. *Thermal detectors* respond to heat beyond a certain temperature or when the temperature rises too quickly. *Carbon monoxide detectors* protect against what is often called the *silent killer*, because carbon monoxide is difficult to detect. In fact, victims, in their drowsy state, may be wrongly diagnosed as being substance abusers. *Gas detectors* monitor flammable gases or vapors. These devices are especially valuable in petroleum, chemical, and other industries where dangerous gases or vapors are generated. *Combination detectors* respond to more than one fire-producing cause or employ multiple operating principles. Examples include smoke/heat detector or rate-of-rise/fixed temperature heat detector.

Fire alarms vary. *Local alarms* signal people in the area. Once the fire is located, a decision must be made to call the fire department. Automatic systems notify people on the premises and firefighters, and activate sprinkler systems. *Fire alarm boxes* are another avenue to summon assistance. Security officers should know the location of all alarm boxes.

What If?

As a Security Officer, What Do You Do if You Respond to an Elevator Alarm and Several People Are Trapped Between Floors?

Communications is essential in this case. An elevator technician must be summoned immediately and, if necessary, public safety agencies. The security officer must communicate with the stranded people through intercom, a cell phone, or by shouting, if necessary. The people need to know that assistance is on the way and that they should remain calm. They should be told to stay put and not try to open either the door or escape hatch. If one of the stranded people becomes upset, speak directly to that person and reassure them that help is on the way. Avoid stating that they will be free in a set amount of time. Keep communications open and be honest to maintain your credibility.

Emergencies

OSHA defines a workplace emergency as an unforeseen situation that threatens employees, customers, or the public and disrupts operations or causes physical or environmental damage. Workplace emergencies include windstorms, floods, earthquakes, accidents, strikes, and civil disturbances. Emergencies also include bomb threats and explosions, terrorism, and violence in the workplace.

Specific, key strategies apply to workplace emergencies. Planning and training are two key strategies to reduce losses. Employees need to know what to do to protect lives and assets. Professional loss prevention managers should prepare contingency plans for all possible emergencies. These plans would cover who to contact for decision-making and emergency assistance, evacuation procedures, where to establish a command post, communications, sources of equipment and mutual aid, first aid, and salvage, among other topics. If a disaster should strike and as employees look to security for safety and direction, hopefully the best possible protection can be provided. This is the essence of a quality security program. Security officers should study emergency plans and clearly understand what to do. Training, practice, and drills increase the effectiveness of plans.

Windstorms

Tornadoes (called *cyclones* in some regions) are extremely violent and destructive, often occurring without warning. Hurricanes (called *typhoons* in the eastern Pacific Ocean) usually afford more warning time than tornadoes. The Atlantic and Gulf coasts are more susceptible to hurricanes, whereas tornadoes occur in many parts of the United States. Besides early planning, quality building design, and cooperation with emergency officials, countermeasures include the following: closely follow weather reports; establish a safe, low-level area for employees; instruct employees to stay away from windows; open doors and windows on the side of the building away from the storm to equalize pressure and prevent building collapse; establish a communications system; anchor company property; and take steps to hinder looting.

Floods

Flooding can occur in many locales from excessive rain or from nearby bodies of water. Countermeasures include the following: work with local officials for employee safety and to hinder looting; provide a safe place for valuable assets; exit from the flood area in time to avoid being marooned; if a team remains at the site, ensure adequate supplies; store valuable records, equipment, tools, and chemicals above the expected flood level; and shut off utilities.

Earthquakes

Stringent building codes and adequate building design in suspect areas (e.g., California) are vital for reduced losses. Building collapse, damage to bridges, and falling debris are major causes of injuries and deaths. If indoors, one should take cover in a basement or under reinforced floors or doorways. If outdoors, one should watch out for falling objects and electrical wires.

Hazardous Materials

Emergencies can result from accidents involving hazardous substances and materials, also referred to as HAZMAT. Such materials are used in every community and transported by trucks, railcars, ships, barges, and planes. Examples of hazardous substances and materials are plastics, fuels, corrosive chemicals (e.g., acids), and radioactive materials. A tremendous amount of information exists concerning their physical and chemical properties, methods for storage and transportation, and the most appropriate strategies in the event of fire or accident (Figure 12-7). Weapons of mass destruction (e.g., nuclear, chemical, biological) present additional problems requiring planning and preparation.

Federal legislation known as the Superfund Amendments and Reauthorization Act (SARA) of 1986 directs employers and employees to

Figure 12-7   Both public and private sectors have prepared for HAZMAT emergencies. Courtesy: Charleston, SC, Police Department.

follow OSHA 29 CFR Part 1910.20 that requires training for HAZMAT incidents. Security officers and other employees must be extremely cautious with HAZMAT incidents since death can occur. Avoid the urge to rush in because you may become part of the problem. Contact the fire department. Approaches, with proper protective clothing, should be made from upwind, uphill, and upstream, and vehicles should be parked facing out for quick escape. Initially, objectives are to isolate the area, identify the substance for subsequent action, and deny entry to reduce exposure.

Strikes

Strikes are very expensive to both businesses and workers. The losses include productivity, profits, employees and customers who never return, vandalism, security services, and legal fees. As with other emergencies, the best defense is early preparation. If labor trouble is expected, security is likely to focus more intensely on perimeter protection for the facility, the protection of key executives and their families, the protection of assets, and evidence gathering. Both private security and police will be working together in most instances.

Both striking workers and a company have certain legal rights. The *National Labor Relations Board* (NLRB) controls relations between management and labor.

It is essential that management and security personnel be familiar with labor laws to avert charges of unfair labor practices. Surveillance and investigation of union activities is a violation of the National Labor Relations Act, which makes it an unfair labor practice to interfere with, restrain, or coerce employees in the exercise of the rights to self-organization, assist labor organizations, and to bargain collectively through representatives. One type of surveillance, photographing activities of striking workers, is unlawful, unless there is a legitimate purpose, such as gathering evidence for the prosecution of criminal acts (e.g., assault or destruction of property). Care must be exercised when applying security strategies during management–labor tension. Precautions (e.g., additional officers, CCTV) to protect company property may be construed as interference with union activities. For example, courts have declared illegal the observance by officers of who is going in and out of union meetings. Also, it has been held that even "creating the impression" of surveillance (e.g., management implying that surveillance is taking place) is illegal. The NLRB found that aiming CCTV on a company building in which a union meeting was held created the impression of surveillance. Undercover investigations that conduct labor surveillance are illegal. More on labor disputes in Chapter 14.

Civil Disturbances

Citizens have a First Amendment right to peaceably express their views. However, periodically, demonstrations evolve into riots. Sometimes a precipitating incident, such as a public police arrest of a minority group member for a minor charge, sparks a riot. Or, a crowd may go into a contagious frenzy if a rock is thrown into the crowd. Whatever the cause of civil disturbances, deaths, injuries, and extensive property damage can result. The public police may not be able to contain rioters, and the private sector must be prepared for the worst. Summer months and high temperatures, when people gather out of doors, may precede a civil disturbance. Rumors also are dangerous. Early preparation and contingency plans can reduce losses.

Security officers should exercise caution when dealing with a crowd. These recommendations are offered: watch people rather than the event; avoid unnecessary conversation; watch for the ulterior motives of others and ignore those who try to manipulate you; keep calm; and use "common sense."

CHAPTER REVIEW

A. Multiple Choice

1. About how many accidental deaths occur each year in the workplace?
   a. 55,000
   b. 6000
   c. 45,000
   d. 800

2. Human failures cause _____ percent of accidents.
   a. 99
   b. 5
   c. 15
   d. 80

3. The primary cause of fire deaths is (are)
   a. heat.
   b. stroke.
   c. smoke.
   d. burns.

4. Which of the following is not a major part of the fire triangle?
   a. heat
   b. smoke
   c. oxygen
   d. fuel

5. A Class C fire involves
   a. electrical equipment.
   b. metal.
   c. gasoline.
   d. wood.

B. True or False

1. The Occupational Safety and Health Act was passed by Congress in 1970 to promote a safe working environment for employees in various occupations.

2. The Supreme Court decision in *Marshall v. Barlow* gave OSHA inspectors the power to conduct warrantless inspections of businesses.

3. Workers' compensation laws have existed since ancient times.

4. Standpipes and hoses are automatic fire suppression systems.

5. Private security surveillance and investigation of union activities is a violation of the National Labor Relations Act.

Applications

Application 12A

Arrange a tour of the building you are in or another to pinpoint safety measures that have been implemented. Look for safety hazards and discuss solutions.

Application 12B

Arrange a tour of the building you are in or another to locate fire protection measures. Look for fire hazards and discuss solutions.

Application 12C

Prepare a report on how security officers can foster safety and fire protection.

Application 12D

Prepare your own safety and fire protection survey form containing at least twenty questions.

13

Medical Emergencies

CHAPTER OUTLINE

OBJECTIVES

After studying this chapter, you will be able to:

- List guidelines for medical emergencies.
- List methods of personal protection from transmitted diseases. Explain the problem of mistaken diagnosis.
- List the emergency first-aid procedures that can be taken to respond to the following:

    a.   traumatic shock

    b.   wounds

    c.   respiratory failure

    d.   choking

    e.   cardiac arrest

    f.   drowning

    g.   seizures

    h.   broken bones

    i.   emergency childbirth

    j.   burns

    k.   chemical burns

    l.   electrical injury

    m.   heat exposure

    n.   poisoning

    o.   drug overdose

    p.   mentally disturbed person

    q.   suicide

- Explain how to manage stress.

Introduction

A security officer on duty is likely to be called during the initial stages of a medical emergency. Although many large facilities have an in-house nurse and a first-aid station, the mobility and protection function of security personnel make them appropriate individuals to render emergency first aid. The basic objective of a security officer during medical emergencies is to provide vital lifesaving assistance until medical specialists arrive. An officer should render first aid to keep the victim alive or an injury from becoming worse.

It is important to emphasize that security officers must be knowledgeable of in-house policies and procedures on medical emergencies. For example, at one organization, security officers may be well-trained and responsible for rendering emergency first aid prior to the arrival of medical specialists.

On the other hand, at another organization security officers may be responsible for reporting medical emergencies but not rendering first aid.

This chapter is only an introduction and *will not* enable security personnel to properly respond and handle medical emergencies. Security officers, security supervisors, and managers are urged to support the implementation of first aid training programs for security personnel and all company employees. Community colleges, the Red Cross, and hospitals provide quality training and refresher courses. Helpful websites include the following: www.redcross.org and www.healthy.net/clinic/firstaid/.

Medical Emergencies

The following guidelines will assist security officers in responding to a medical emergency.

Guidelines

1. To avoid liability, find out exactly what a security officer must do during a medical emergency. What exactly must an officer *not* do? Who is to be summoned immediately? What telephone numbers should be contained in each officer's notebook? All security officers should have these written guidelines in their possession. *An emphasis should be placed on calling for emergency medical assistance.*

2. During an emergency, a security officer should remain calm while quickly deciding on the most appropriate actions.

3. Think safety. Protect yourself from transmitted diseases. Also, danger may still exist when you are on the scene of a medical emergency. Is gasoline leaking from a damaged vehicle? Is a crowd gathering that is creating traffic congestion and the potential for another accident?

4. As in other types of crises, it is important that someone notify emergency medical responders. Sometimes everyone gets involved in an incident and no one summons assistance.

5. Priorities must be established. After emergency medical personnel have been contacted, a security officer should provide assistance to the most severe cases. Time should not be spent with those who have died. Attention should be given to those who are battling for their lives. A small cut is not as important as a deep wound that is causing rapid loss of blood.

6. If a nearby person appears to be a competent medical specialist and they are willing to assist, yield to their goodwill.

7. Loosen or cut victims' clothing where necessary to improve comfort.

8. Do not give fluids to an unconscious person, because the windpipe can become blocked and cause strangulation.

9. Avoid moving victims unless they are faced with danger.

10. Avoid transporting victims in your personal automobile (for liability reasons).

11. Try to keep victims from getting up. The less movement the better.

12. Do not make guesses as to the medical condition of victims.

13. Look for identification or a bracelet that indicates a preexisting medical condition.

14. Never supply victims with any medication.

15. Talk to victims in a calm voice and ask about symptoms. Reassure victims.

16. Exercise care when speaking to victims or to those nearby. Do *not* state that there is no hope for survival. Let trained medical personnel evaluate the condition of victims.

17. Collect important information and record it in your notebook. Remember the six questions: Who, what, where, when, how, and why. Also, what did the victims say.

18. Keep crowds back. This provides comfort to victims and prevents them from overhearing insensitive statements.

19. Watch out for victims' belongings. Sometimes an offender will take advantage of a crisis situation.

Personal Protection from Transmitted Diseases

Pathogens are organisms that cause infection. Examples are viruses and bacteria. Diseases may spread by contact with blood or other body fluids or through the air. *Bloodborne pathogens* can enter a security officer's body through, for examples, an open wound, dry and cracked skin, or a break in the skin around a fingernail. Other avenues include mucous membranes, such as those in the nose, mouth, or eyes. The importance of keeping one's hands away from one's face cannot be overstated. *Airborne pathogens* can enter the body by inhaling or absorbed through the eyes.

Three serious diseases are acquired immune deficiency syndrome (AIDS), hepatitis B (HBV), and tuberculosis (TB). AIDS results in a breakdown of the body's immune system making an individual vulnerable to serious illnesses; there is no cure at this time. HBV can result in cirrhosis of the liver, and/or liver cancer; there is no cure, but a vaccine is available. There are several forms of hepatitis. TB can result in respiratory failure. It was almost eradicated, but made a comeback in the late 1980s. TB is treated with antibiotics.

Both AIDS and HBV are transmitted by sexual activity, the exchange of body fluids, the use of infected needles, the transfusion of infected blood products, or accidental infections. TB is spread by airborne transmissions of saliva. When a person coughs or sneezes, tiny droplets containing the bacteria remain suspended in the air and those who breathe the contaminated air can become infected.

Depending on the work environment and duties of the security officer, OSHA standards may be required. Officers who are trained to respond to medical emergencies and/or possibly encounter suspects who may have a disease are more likely to be involved with OSHA standards. OSHA has issued guidelines for protection against pathogens, and employers and employees share responsibility for precautions. Employers develop a plan and provide training, immunizations, and personal protective equipment to employees. See the previous chapter on the OSHA Bloodborne Pathogens Standard.

Here is a list of common personal protective equipment:

- *Protective gloves* made of latex, vinyl, or other synthetic material should be used prior to making contact with a patient requiring emergency treatment. The gloves must be carefully taken off by pulling away from the hand. Hands must be washed thereafter. Note that if items (e.g., equipment, door handles) were touched while wearing gloves, contamination may occur.

- *Masks* cover the responder's mouth and nose and protect against fluid spatter and TB. Seek approved masks from the National Institute for Occupational Safety and Health, the research arm of OSHA. Later in the chapter the pocket face mask is covered for respiratory failure or CPR.

- *Eye protection* includes eyewear that resemble eyeglasses and protect, not only the front, but also the sides of the face near the eyes. This equipment protects the mucous membranes around the eyes from a fluid spatter or from absorbing pathogens in the air. Goggles are an alternative, but can fog. For those who wear eyeglasses, clip-on side protectors are available.

Mistaken Diagnosis

Only trained medical specialists are to make diagnoses. An individual's medical condition requires a careful evaluation of several factors that can easily be misinterpreted by an untrained observer. For example, diabetes is a medical condition that may cause an observer to think the patient is intoxicated. Unsteady balance, slurred speech, and a sweet odor on a person's breath (similar to an alcoholic beverage) may indicate that an individual is suffering from diabetes rather than drunkenness. And if a person lending assistance realizes that a victim is a diabetic, confusion can develop over two critical conditions: diabetic coma and insulin shock. During a diabetic coma, a diabetic's sugar level is too high in relation to the insulin level. Insulin shock is the result of a rapid drop in the diabetic's blood sugar level; treatment can consist of a drink containing sugar. If a security officer or any other helper mistakenly believes a person is suffering from insulin shock when the real problem is diabetic coma and supplies the person with sugar, the medical condition may worsen. The seriousness of misdiagnosis should not be taken lightly.

There are several other illnesses that appear as drunkenness or a drug overdose. Those with epilepsy, like people with diabetes, may wander in a dazed state or become violent. Meningitis (an inflammation of the covering of the brain), severe infections, pneumonia, brain tumors, and flu can cause a person to behave as if intoxicated and dazed.

Never Take Anything for Granted

Often, emergency calls for assistance turn out to be different from what was described by the caller. For example, in one case a young worker arrived on the job, punched his time card, and sat down on the floor at his workstation instead of working. A supervisor immediately reacted by calling security, claiming the worker was on drugs. Security officers responded and noticed the worker was in a stupefied state. The worker was helped up and escorted to the plant's first aid station. Everyone who saw the youth believed he had consumed illegal drugs, even though the youth denied such usage. Because of the young worker's continued state of drowsiness, an ambulance was summoned and he was transported to a local hospital. Later it was learned through a professional medical diagnosis the worker was suffering from carbon monoxide poisoning. The muffler in his old truck contained a huge hole, and his sickest moments were when he arrived at work after a one-hour drive and when he returned home.

In another case, two shopping mall security officers responded to a call from merchants who complained about a drunk who was harassing customers. When the security officers arrived on the scene, they saw a man staggering through a restaurant. The security officers waited and watched as the subject departed from the restaurant. Before they approached the subject, they hesitated and watched his gait. It appeared the subject was limping because of a medical problem with his left leg. The security officers finally approached the subject and asked if any assistance could be rendered. This gave them a chance to smell the subject's breath and begin a friendly conversation. The smell of alcohol was not apparent and the subject stated that he could make it to the bus stop. He also showed the officers a leg brace he was wearing. The conversation ended. The security officers went to the merchants and informed them about the subject's medical problem.

WHAT IF?

As a Security Officer, What Do You Do if You Are Approached in the Company Parking Lot By a Woman Who Is Injured and Speaks a Different Language?

Security officers are first responders—meaning that they may be the first to arrive at the scene of a critical incident. At the same time, people look to first responders for emergency assistance. Quality training is essential, as are good policies and procedures. The way in which a critical incident is handled will impact issues of alleged negligence.

When approached by the injured woman, first find out the extent of the injuries. Since she speaks a different language, your observations may be the only way you can assess the injuries. Inform dispatch to call an ambulance, that the woman speaks a different language, and that you do not yet know the cause or extent of the injuries. If you think you know the language the woman is speaking, inform dispatch.

Put on your gloves. Using hand motions, get the woman to sit or lie down. Render emergency first-aid only if properly trained. Stay close to the woman. If possible, seek witnesses and obtain basic information about them. Using hand motions, ask the woman for identification. If a crowd gathers, keep it back. Since the incident may be a crime, protect the scene and look for evidence.

Types of Medical Emergencies

Traumatic Shock

Traumatic shock is a depression of vital body functions. It may accompany injuries or severe mental reactions and can be a greater danger (death) than the original injury. Shock can result from loss of blood, burns, bone injury, and severe electrical shock, among other causes.

Signs of traumatic shock include paleness, dilated pupils, moist and clammy skin, irregular breathing, weariness, nausea, and vomiting. The circulation of blood is slowed during shock, resulting in insufficient blood reaching vital organs. First aid measures are to use personal protective equipment, have the victim remain still on his or her back, and elevate the legs so blood flows back to the torso. If nausea and vomiting are apparent, turn the person on his or her side. Do not provide drink or food. Keep the victim warm by using a blanket.

Wounds

Wounds can be labeled as open or closed. Examples of open wounds are lacerations, punctures, and abrasions. In a closed wound, called a bruise or contusion, the tissues under the skin are injured but the skin is not open.

An average adult has about five or six quarts of blood. If there is a loss of more than two or three pints, the situation becomes very serious.

A rapid loss of blood from an open wound at an artery or vein can cause death within a few minutes. Immediate first aid is necessary. Use personal protective equipment. Obtain a clean piece of cloth, such as a handkerchief, to press against the open wound. Elevate the injured area above the person's heart. The cloth or pad can be secured by a bandage with a knot placed directly over the pad. This is called a pressure bandage. If the wound is still bleeding after direct pressure, apply pressure over the artery supplying blood to the injured area. Figure 13-1 shows two pressure points.

Tourniquets should not be used except for extreme cases where an arm or leg has been amputated or mangled and other methods to control blood loss have failed. The application of a tourniquet can cause tissue injury because it shuts off the blood supply to that part of the body where injury has occurred. The American National Red Cross states, "The decision to apply a tourniquet is in reality a decision to risk sacrifice of a limb in order to save life."

A tourniquet is applied by wrapping a strong, long cloth between the wound and the heart. Tie a half-knot and place a stick on it before tying the full-knot. When the stick is twisted the tourniquet should reduce the bleeding. The stick can be secured by using another piece of cloth. Once a tourniquet is applied, it should be left in place to be removed by a medical specialist. Note the time it was applied.

The signs and symptoms of internal bleeding are similar to traumatic shock. Also, the victim may cough or vomit blood or release blood in urine or feces. The injured area is likely to result in pain, swelling, and discoloration.

First aid for internal bleeding would focus on keeping the victim on his or her back. If vomiting or coughing occurs, turn the person to the side to promote drainage and maintain an open airway. Summon emergency medical aid at once. Internal bleeding is often controlled in the operating room.

A serious accident can result in the severing of a finger, toe, arm, or leg. Multiple medical conditions will likely result in reactions such as blood loss and traumatic shock. Respiratory or cardiac failure may also occur. Use pressure points to control bleeding. A tourniquet is a last resort to stop bleeding. The severed body part should be safeguarded and packed in a moist cloth. Modern medical science is capable of reattachment through microsurgery.

Respiratory Failure

A victim of respiratory failure has only a few minutes before the brain begins to deteriorate. Death soon follows. Since time is crucial in these incidents, breathing must be restored immediately.

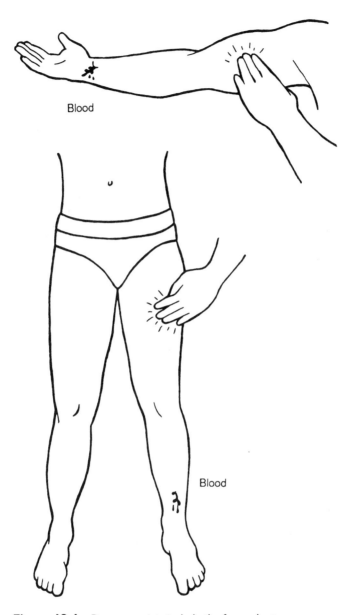

Blood

Blood

Figure 13-1 Pressure points include the femoral artery (bottom) and brachial artery (top).

Artificial ventilation is the term used to describe the forcing of air or oxygen into the lungs when a patient is suffering from respiratory failure. There are various techniques of artificial ventilation. Here the emphasis is on mouth-to-mask ventilation through the use of a pocket face mask (Figure

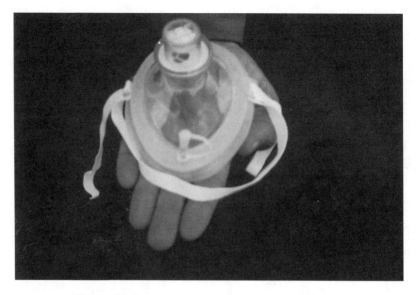

Figure 13-2   Pocket face mask for artificial ventilation.

13-2) that is collapsible and can be carried in a purse or pocket. This device prevents disease transmission and contact between the mouth of the responder and the mouth of the patient. Also, it contains a one-way valve that permits the responder to force air into the patient, but prevents the patient from exhaling air into the responder.

Here are some guidelines, however, quality training is of the utmost importance:

1. Make sure the person is on his or her back.
2. Use personal protective equipment.
3. Remove any obstructions from the victim's mouth, such as dentures that are not remaining in place.
4. Carefully apply the mask to the patient.
5. Carefully lift the chin, if possible, to provide for maximum opening of the airway, but avoid moving the victim's neck if an injury occurred to the head, neck, or spine.
6. Take a deep breath and then exhale into the mask port for about two seconds.
7. At this point, it is possible that the victim is breathing. Does the chest rise and fall? Do you hear the sound of breathing?
8. Check the pulse at the carotid artery in the neck. Continue the above process until assistance arrives.

Choking

Respiratory emergencies may result from an obstruction of the windpipe from food or other object. If the victim is coughing, it is possible the foreign object can be expelled. However, if the victim is having difficulty breathing or is turning blue, the *Heimlich Maneuver*, also called abdominal thrust, is an effective emergency procedure for choking. Since only a few minutes without oxygen can lead to death, a responder must act quickly. Follow these procedures:

1. Summon emergency medical personnel immediately and use personal protective equipment.
2. If the patient can speak or cough, let the patient try to cough the obstruction out without assistance.
3. If assistance is needed, stand behind the victim and place both hands at the waist.
4. Form a fist with one hand and place the thumb side at the abdomen above the navel and below the rib cage.
5. Grab the fist with your other hand and press it sharply into the abdomen with a quick upward thrust. This procedure should be repeated, Figure 13-3.
6. Do not squeeze the victim since ribs can be damaged. Bend your arms at the elbow to prevent injury to the victim's ribs.

The principle of the Heimlich Maneuver is that residual air trapped in the subject's lungs can be compressed by pressure. When this air is forced upward, it can dislodge an item caught in the windpipe.

When alone and choking, a similar procedure can be used. Press oneself into the edge of a table or the back of a chair.

If the victim should become unconscious, position the person on their back. See if an obstruction (e.g., food) can be removed from the mouth. Perform artificial ventilation with a mask. Try the Heimlich Maneuver again.

When an infant is choking, do not perform any procedures if the young person is able to breathe and cough. Let the natural process to expel the object take its course. If the child is unable to breathe, position the child over your forearm, with the head lower than the torso. Apply four moderately forceful blows with the heel of your hand to the back between the shoulder blades. If this method fails, turn the baby over on the back and using the index and middle fingers of one hand, press on the chest moderately four times at the level of the nipples similar to CPR. If the baby is still not breathing, perform artificial respiration and repeat the back blows and chest thrusts.

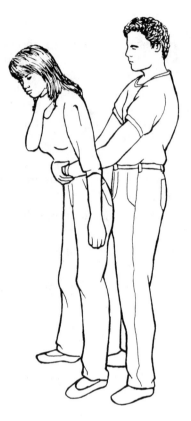

Figure 13-3   Heimlich maneuver.

Note: Each chocking incident is different and procedures successful in one case may not be successful in all cases. It is strongly advised that the reader enroll in a first aid course and participate in hands-on training.

Cardiac Arrest

If a person has no pulse, the heart has stopped. There are only a few minutes to save a person's life. The American Heart Association has designed a *chain of survival concept* for cardiac arrest patients. The chain has four elements:

1. *Early access* means that when a person sees someone collapse, emergency medical services (EMS) must be called immediately.

2. *Early cardiopulmonary resuscitation (CPR)* means that a person is available to provide CPR immediately to the patient.

3. *Early defibrillation* entails using an automated external defibrillator to deliver a controlled electrical shock to the heart in order to return it to normal rhythm.

4. *Early advance care,* also called advanced cardiac life support, includes administering medications, starting an intravenous line, and putting a breathing tube into the throat. Such procedures increase survival rates.

During cardiac arrest and as emergency medical personnel are enroute, CPR must be started immediately. Naturally, prior training of security officers and other employees can save lives.

CPR is actually a combination of artificial respiration and artificial circulation (external heart compression). It is an emergency procedure designed to restore breathing and/or heartbeat. Here are guidelines, although hands-on training is best.

1. Use personal protective equipment.

2. To prevent injury to a person who may be sleeping or intoxicated, gently shake the person and see if he or she responds. Check for signs of breathing and a pulse.

3. Call for EMS.

4. Position the victim on the floor on his or her back. Blood flow to the brain will be hindered if the head is higher than the feet.

5. Kneel beside the victim.

6. Check the airway. Carefully lift the chin, if possible, to provide for maximum opening of the airway, but avoid moving the victim's neck if an injury occurred to the head, neck, or spine.

7. Carefully apply the face mask to the patient.

8. Take a deep breath and then exhale into the mask port.

9. Check for breathing by watching the chest rise and fall.

10. Check the pulse by placing your fingertips on the Adam's apple and then slide the fingers to either side about one inch. If a pulse is felt but no breathing, provide one breath every five seconds. If no pulse or breathing is evident, begin chest compression.

11. To perform chest compression, position yourself kneeling on the side of the victim. Find the lower tip of the victim's breastbone, the edge of the rib cage above the abdomen. Place a middle finger at this point. Put the heel of the other hand on the breastbone right above the finger. Remove the finger and place this hand on top of the hand on the breastbone. Then push down on the lower one-third of the breastbone about $1\frac{1}{2}$ to 2 inches, letting your back and body do the work. Relax pressure. Begin a rhythmic compression, press, release, eighty times a minute to a count of one and, two and, three and, and so forth. You are actually squeezing the victim's heart and forcing blood out to the

body. After each fifteen compressions, provide two quick breaths. Continue the fifteen-to-two procedure until help arrives.

For younger people, CPR procedures must be modified:

1. Carefully lift the chin, if possible, to provide for maximum opening of the airway.
2. Locate the pulse over the left nipple. If a pulse is found, provide two gentle puffs every two seconds for an infant and a full breath every four seconds for a child.
3. If no pulse is found, perform compression of the infant's heart. *Use only the tips of the index and middle fingers on one hand.* For those under one year the compression rate is 100 times per minute. Press the middle of the breastbone only $\frac{1}{2}$ to 1 inch. Provide one small breath following five compressions. For children between one and eight years old, the compression rate is eighty per minute. Use the heel of one hand and compress 1 to $1\frac{1}{2}$ inches. Give one small breath after five compressions.

Automated external defibrillators (AED), Figure 13-4, are coming into greater use to increase the survival chances of heart attack victims. CPR can keep a

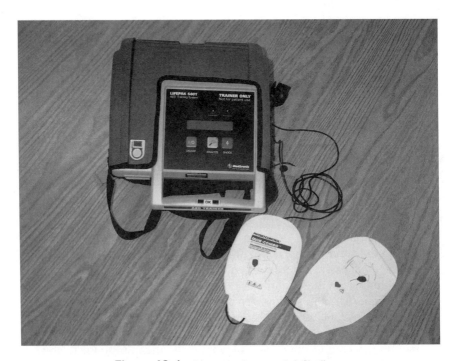

Figure 13-4   Automated external defibrillator.

victim alive, but it is unlikely CPR will restart the heart. However, an AED can deliver an electrical shock through the chest to the heart to interrupt random electrical pulses and give the heart a chance to start beating in a normal rhythm. AEDs contain a computer that analyzes the victim's heart rhythm to determine if it requires a shock. Voice and screen commands guide the responder. AEDs are compact and lightweight. The American Red Cross has developed a nationally recognized AED certification course.

No one should be touching the patient when an AED is analyzing the patient's heart rhythm or when a shock is being delivered. In the former, the responder's heart may fool the AED computer. In the latter, the responder can be shocked and injured.

Since an AED is more effective than CPR in restoring a pulse, CPR should be stopped to permit an AED to analyze rhythm and possibly give a shock. Following three shocks, CPR can be resumed if needed.

> Note: The reader is cautioned about performing CPR without proper training. Even experienced medical specialists can accidentally crack a rib. In serious cases, a damaged rib can puncture a vital organ such as a lung. Enroll in CPR and first aid courses and obtain hands-on training.

Drowning

A key strategy for water rescue is to never touch a victim who is struggling in the water. Well-meaning people themselves have become drowning victims when they allowed a frantic, panic-stricken person to grab them and pull them down under water. Always throw a rope, life preserver, or anything that will float to the victim. Or locate something long so it can be extended across the water.

If a subject is rescued and coughing water, place the person on his or her side so as much water as possible can be expelled. When breathing has stopped, use personal protective equipment and administer artificial ventilation. If the heart has stopped, CPR is advised.

Seizures

A seizure often results from epilepsy, stroke, and other causes. Persons subject to a seizure are not able to control themselves. Among the dangers are falling and biting the tongue. During a seizure the security officer can follow these guidelines:

1. Use protective equipment and summon medical assistance.
2. Avoid placing something in the patient's mouth because it may be broken and obstruct the airway.

3. Do not restrict movement; allow the convulsions to run their course.

4. Prevent injury by moving furniture and guiding the victim.

5. If the victim is choking on vomit, roll him or her to one side.

6. Calm the person when the seizure is over. The victim will often be disoriented but then will gain composure.

Broken Bones

For broken bones, a security officer can apply the following guidelines:

1. Use protective equipment and summon medical assistance.

2. The victim, especially the area of the broken bone, should not be moved. This is very important for neck or back injuries.

3. Stop any bleeding and do not try to push a protruding bone back in place.

4. Treat for shock, if necessary.

5. Do not assume a break did not occur because the subject can move an injured limb.

6. Avoid applying a splint to immobilize the limb since emergency specialists will probably arrive soon.

7. Never try to set or reposition a broken bone.

Emergency Childbirth

When a security officer responds to an emergency call involving childbirth, one important point should be remembered: let nature take its course. The labor process is usually gradual, providing time for an ambulance to arrive. However, miscalculation and other problems may require prompt emergency care. Here are guidelines:

1. Use personal protective equipment and summon medical assistance.

2. Position the woman on her back with knees up, feet flat, and thighs widely separated.

3. Place a clean sheet or cloth under the woman's buttocks.

4. Guide the baby's head as it emerges.

5. Do not touch the birth canal or pull on the baby.

6. If the umbilical cord is wrapped around the baby's neck, gently slip it over the head. If this is not possible, cut the cord to prevent strangulation. Apply sanitary ties to both ends. Ties can consist of strips of cloth boiled in water. In an extreme emergency, shoelaces can be used.

7. When the baby is out, check breathing. If the baby does not cry and breathe, rub the back or flick the bottoms of the feet. Clean debris

from the mouth. If the baby is still not breathing, provide artificial respiration with protective equipment.

8. Cover the baby and keep it warm.
9. Place the baby on the mother's abdomen.
10. The afterbirth will follow the baby. If the mother will soon be taken to a hospital, the infant can remain attached to the afterbirth by the umbilical cord.

Burns

Serious burns can result in severe pain and subsequent shock. First-degree burns cause minor skin damage. The skin turns red but does not burn through. A sunburn is an example of a first-degree burn. Second-degree burns are characterized by redness, swelling, and blisters. Third-degree burns are the most serious threat to life. The burned area will appear white or charred, and the skin, nerve endings, and blood vessels will sustain severe damage.

To treat *minor* burns, use personal protective equipment and submerge the patient's burned part in cold water (not ice). If this is not possible, immerse clean towels in cold water, wring out the water and apply to the burned area. Then apply sterile gauze or clean cloth to protect the burn. Do not break blisters or apply any substances. Guidelines for serious burns (second- and third-degree) are the following:

1. Use personal protective equipment, summon medical assistance, and, depending on the situation, call the fire department.
2. If the victim's clothes are on fire, immediately stop the burning by using water, rolling the person on the ground, or smothering the flames with a jacket or blanket.
3. Do not immerse the burn area in cold water.
4. Do not remove clothing that is attached to the burn.
5. Do not apply any substance to the burn.
6. Use a clean sheet to cover the burn.
7. Keep the victim lying down.
8. Watch for shock.
9. Do what you can to keep the person alive while you are waiting for emergency medical specialists to arrive.

Chemical Burns

Toxic substances, such as strong acids, that contact the skin can cause chemical burns. Also, fumes from chemicals can cause burns, especially to the respiratory tract. The eyes are often subject to injury from toxic chemicals.

A primary treatment for chemical burns is to immediately flood the injured area with water. Protect yourself with appropriate equipment. Industrial plants often have special showers and hoses. Avoid concern over wetting a victim's hair or clothing because injury must be held to a minimum by quick flooding. The flooding of the skin or eyes should continue for at least twenty minutes after the pain has stopped since certain chemicals have a delayed reaction. If a dry chemical caused the burn, carefully brush it away. As with a thermal burn, a chemical burn should be covered with a dry, sterile dressing. The victim should then be transported to a hospital. For serious cases of chemical burns, the fire department and rescue squad may be required. Refer to HAZMAT in the previous chapter.

Electrical Injury

The longer a victim maintains contact with a source of electricity, the greater the chance of death. To turn off the current, pull the plug, flip the main switch at the fuse box, or use a *wooden* pole or branch to separate the victim from the source of the current. Never contact water during the rescue. Never touch the victim until he or she is separated from the current. Use personal protective equipment. Check the person's vital signs. CPR and automated defibrillation may be necessary. Call for an ambulance and summon the fire department and rescue squad.

Lightning injuries are a form of electrical burn. Although lightning strikes with a force of many thousands of volts, not everyone who is hit is killed. Unconsciousness and a disrupted heart rhythm are common results of being struck by lightning. No danger of electrocution exists from touching the victim. Check the person's vital signs and administer CPR and automated defibrillation if necessary. Call for an ambulance.

Heat Exposure

A security officer may encounter an individual suffering from either heat cramps, heat exhaustion, or heat stroke. Heat cramps are muscular pains or spasms that can take place with heat exhaustion. Heat exhaustion is accompanied by weakness, headache, and nausea. In both conditions the victim is able to sweat. Heat stroke is the more life-threatening condition because the victim is not able to sweat to cool the body. The skin is hot and dry. Other symptoms are nausea, weakness, and the possible loss of consciousness. For all three conditions the victim must be cooled. Remove the person to a cooler location. Keep the skin wet by using a sponge, a hose, or buckets of water. Provide cool drinks. Call for an ambulance.

WHAT IF?

While on Patrol, What Do You Do if You Learn of a Child Locked in a Vehicle in 95-Degree Weather and Your Supervisor Orders You to Ignore the Problem?

While on patrol at the perimeter of the parking lot of your employer a lady approaches you from an adjacent shopping mall parking lot and tells you that a child has been left alone in a child seat in a locked vehicle. The temperature outside is about 95 degrees. You radio this information to your supervisor who asks if the problem in on "our" property. You radio your supervisor and state "negative." The supervisor's reply is that it is not our problem and he directs you to the other side of the company parking lot to assist an employee with a dead battery. What do you do?

The supervisor is not considering the seriousness of this situation and the danger to the child. This is a life-threatening event. Ask the lady to call 911 to report the emergency, or use your cell phone or get to a telephone to do the same. Find out the estimated time of arrival. Hopefully, a quick response will save the child. A window may have to be broken to free the child. Whoever left the child in the vehicle may face arrest.

Poisoning

Poisons enter the body through the mouth, by inhalation, by absorption through the skin, and by injection. Sources of poison are numerous. Examples are chemicals, drugs, radiation, food, plants, insects, and snakes. Symptoms vary and are characterized by nausea, cramps in the abdomen, coughing, skin discoloration, and altered vital signs. Also, treatment varies depending on the poison. However, some general guidelines to treat poisoning are:

1. Calm the victim.
2. Find out the source of the poison, and the size, weight, and age of the victim (for treatment).
3. Summon an ambulance and provide necessary information.
4. Watch vital signs and treat for shock, if necessary.

Hundreds of poison control centers exist throughout the country that are staffed twenty-four hours a day. Many are located in the emergency departments of large hospitals. Telephone numbers are readily available. Specialists at these centers have access to helpful information on antidotes (substances to counteract poisons) and treatment. Security officers should be familiar with the location and telephone number of the nearest poison control center. The security officer should let medical specialists administer the antidote and treat the victim.

Drug Overdose

Many people in our society consume illegal substances. Therefore, a security officer may encounter a person who has taken a drug overdose. Symptoms will vary and include dilated pupils, wild activity, violence, and unconsciousness. An alcoholic may be experiencing withdrawal and delirium tremens (DTs) or alcoholic hallucinations. The DTs, also called the "shakes," are the body's physical reactions after an abuser has ceased to use the abused substance upon which he or she is dependent. Such reactions can occur with abusers of other drugs besides alcohol. In the case of alcohol and heroin, for example, the subject may vomit, shake, perspire excessively, and hallucinate. Death may follow.

Caution is advised since what is thought to be a drug overdose may really be another type of serious medical condition. A security officer should use personal protective equipment, summon medical assistance and police, and let the medical specialists diagnose and treat the subject.

Mentally Disturbed Person

Because security officers encounter many people in their work, some of these people may be mentally disturbed. However, the security officer may not know a person is mentally disturbed. Drug abusers, offenders, and those who appear normal may be mentally disturbed. Because a person is an offender or drug abuser does not imply he or she is mentally disturbed. Usually, bizarre behavior provides a security officer with an indication of possible mental illness. Such an individual may appear harmless, but at the same time this person may be dangerous to everyone. Mentally disturbed individuals should be treated by mental health specialists. Here are guidelines when encountering a mentally disturbed individual:

1. Before approaching a mentally disturbed person, call for emergency medical specialists and public police.

2. Remember that the supposedly mentally disturbed person may really be a diabetic, epileptic, drug abuser, or may have recently suffered a head injury.

3. Mentally disturbed people are often confused, frightened, and distrustful. Violence may occur.

4. Approach the person in a calm and reassuring manner. Be aware of your verbal and nonverbal behavior and how each can be interpreted.

5. Do not lecture the person on right and wrong.

6. Do not label the person as "faking" or "psycho."

7. Never threaten or intimidate because a surprise attack may follow.

8. Never turn your back on the subject.

9. Never try to physically control the person by yourself. A disturbed person can exhibit what appears to be super-human strength.

Suicide

All suicide attempts must be taken seriously. A suicide attempt is often a cry for help. Most patients who attempt suicide are suffering from depression, have a substance abuse problem, or a psychiatric illness.

Upon discovering a person threatening suicide or one who has attempted or completed the act, summon emergency assistance immediately. If the subject has attempted suicide, use personal protective equipment, check vital signs. Depending on the method used by the victim, first aid may be useless. But this is a tricky decision. To illustrate, those who cut their wrists rarely bleed to death because the vessels involved are not large. A self-inflicted gunshot wound to the head does not always result in serious brain injury. Facial bleeding and airway obstruction are common. Thus, a security officer may encounter a victim who appears to have lost much blood. Such a person may survive. The security officer should stop the bleeding.

If the subject is threatening suicide, this person has reached the point where death is their best way of dealing with an unpleasant situation. Follow these guidelines:

1. Summon police and medical assistance immediately.

2. Think safety. The suicidal person may be armed and/or harm you and others. "Suicide-by-cop" is a possibility; this means that the subject behaves in a way to cause you to defend your life or another person's life by taking the subject's life.

3. Use a confident, assured voice to get the person to express his or her thoughts.

4. Ask open-ended questions so the subject will talk. Lead the person to change his or her mind about suicide.

5. Ensure the person that you care about him or her and want to help.

Stress Management

Stress can result from both unfortunate and fortunate life events. Physical activity and mental/emotional activity are two sources of stress. Stress caused by the latter is more likely to cause disease. On the other hand, physical activity can relax a person and help in coping with stress. Stress-related disorders have been recognized as a major health problem. Excessive stress costs dearly in death, ill health, increased personal problems, medical expenses, and lost productivity.

Each individual decides how to act during a particular event. Will the reaction be emotional or calm and professional? A calm and professional reaction, and perceiving an incident as a challenge, causes the mobilization of creative abilities and more effective use of skills and resources. Simply put, if you can "get a grip on yourself" in a crisis situation and think positively, rather than forecasting doom, you become a better, more professional security officer producing more positive outcomes.

Here are suggestions for managing stress:

- *Physical relaxation* involves learning relaxing techniques and practicing them on a daily basis. One method is tensing and relaxing muscles. Another method is to concentrate on relaxing before, during, and following a serious incident to prevent yourself from "losing it." Off-duty, deep relaxation and meditation can be practiced since each may result in sleep.

- *Self-management* seeks to monitor one's internal arousal level in order to strive for a controlled reaction to potentially stressful events. Each person studies his or her own stress signals and seeks to maintain control over emotions and act professionally.

- *Eat a balanced diet* including fruits and vegetables. Limit fatty foods, salt, sugar, caffeine, and alcohol. The latter two can hinder sleep.

- *Avoid nicotine.* It is a stimulant that triggers the same chemical and physiologic reaction as stress.

- *Exercise* to increase physical and mental health and to reduce stress.

- *Adequate sleep* helps to meet the physical and mental demands of job duties and other aspects of life.

- *Balance your life* through recreation/hobbies when off-duty and spend time with family and friends.

CHAPTER REVIEW

A. Multiple Choice

1. Select the guideline that would not be appropriate when a security officer responds to a medical emergency.

    a. Notify emergency medical responders.

    b. Avoid moving the victim.

    c. Administer first-aid medications.

    d. Provide assistance to those with the most serious injuries first.

2. Which of the following should be done first during CPR?

    a. Push down on the lower one-third of the breastbone.

    b. Perform chest compression.

    c. Check the airway.

    d. Provide four quick breaths.

3. Select the incorrect statement.

    a. A seizure victim going through convulsions should be controlled in a soft chair to prevent serious high blood pressure.

    b. During the childbirth process, let nature take its course.

    c. First-degree burns are the least serious.

    d. A primary treatment for chemical burns is to flood the injured area with water.

4. Select the incorrect statement.

    a. TB is spread through airborne transmissions.

    b. After an emergency childbirth, if an ambulance is due to arrive, the infant can remain attached to the afterbirth by the umbilical cord.

    c. Third-degree burns are the most serious threat to life.

    d. Heat stroke is a minor medical condition involving muscular spasms.

5. Select the incorrect statement.

    a. There is no danger when touching a victim of lightning.

    b. Poisons enter the body only through the mouth.

    c. Because a person is a drug abuser does not imply the person is mentally disturbed.

    d. A suicide attempt is often a cry for help.

B. True or False

1. For security officers, most medical emergencies are easy to diagnose and treat.

2. The Heimlich Maneuver is a universal procedure for choking.

3. A wound involving loss of blood usually requires a tourniquet.

4. If a person has no pulse the heart has stopped and only a few minutes remain to save the person's life.

5. A key strategy for water rescue is to never touch a victim who is struggling in the water.

Applications

Application 13A

When possible, enroll in a first-aid and a CPR course. (This training makes a security officer more marketable for employment.) If you completed such a course or courses, prepare a short information session for others in class.

Application 13B

While on patrol as a security officer, you encounter an employee who is sprawled on the ground and not moving. What do you do?

Application 13C

While on assignment as a security officer at the main gate of a facility, a drunk walks on the premises, up to your post, and requests help for chest pains. Before you have a chance to respond to this person's request, the individual collapses. What do you do?

14

Special Problems

CHAPTER OUTLINE

OBJECTIVES

After studying this chapter, you will be able to:

- Discuss the problems of third wave crime and countermeasures.
- Explain why proprietary information is important and how to protect it.
- Describe the terrorist threat and broad strategies to counter it.
- Discuss the problems of violence in the workplace and protection measures.
- Explain the problems of substance abuse and what can be done about it in the workplace.
- Discuss legal guidelines for labor disputes and security strategies.

Introduction

Businesses and institutions face a variety of threats that can result in personnel and property losses. In previous chapters, we covered crimes, fires, and accidents as major causes of loss. An emphasis was placed on a description of these problems and countermeasures, and the role of security officers as participants in protection efforts.

This chapter focuses on five threats to the life-blood of organizations: third wave crime and the protection of information technology (IT) and proprietary information, terrorism, violence in the workplace, substance abuse, and labor disputes. During their career, security officers are likely to be involved in one or more of these problem areas. Through an understanding of these problems and countermeasures, a security officer will be better prepared to deal with such incidents and perform in a competent, professional manner.

Third Wave Crime

Our society is in an era that has been termed the "third wave" that is based on information and technology. The "first wave," which dominated civilization for thousands of years, had agriculture at its foundation, with energy supplied by human and animal power. First wave criminals concentrated on stealing cattle, gold, jewelry, and coins. The Industrial Revolution created the "second wave" that drew energy from irreplaceable resources, such as coal, oil, and wood. Criminals focused on money and took advantage of economic and social changes, such as an increase in the number of banks to assist commerce and industry.

As world resources are being depleted, our society is becoming more dependent on technology and information. Unfortunately, there are criminals who exploit technological innovations. Although Jesse James' idea of wrecking a train before robbing it was a novel idea in 1873, he would be amazed at the techniques used by the criminals of today. An offender, in the comfort of his or her own home, with the use of a computer, can steal assets and information from a remote location without entering the premises. The criminal no longer has to break and enter and face physical security and a confrontation with security personnel or police.

When computers first began to appear in organizations, security personnel focused on access controls along the perimeter of the computer center. Today, however, the computer room and mainframe are no longer isolated, but connected via a network to computers located throughout an organization and the world. Thus, security specialists must not only protect the mainframe computer, but also prevent unauthorized access from remote locations.

Cybercrime

Cybercrime is another name for computer crime or "third wave" crime. Cybercrime can be grouped into two categories: crimes in which computers are used as *instruments* of the offense and crimes in which computers are the *object* of the offense. The former includes embezzlement, fraud, and larceny. The problem of credit card fraud via the Internet serves as another example of computers used as instruments of crimes. Computers can be the object of a crime when an offender intends to cause damage to hardware or software (programs). Examples are data destruction or alteration and vandalism of a computer system.

The greatest threat to an organization's information systems is from within (i.e., an employee). The news media seems to paint a different picture because of hackers, sensational computer crimes, and viruses originating from outside of organizations. However, information on many insider attacks is not released to the public or police agencies because organizations are concerned about adverse publicity and/or harm to investments. Also, the time and expense of a criminal case, the possibility of a lawsuit, and the risk of having to reveal proprietary information during litigation cause many organizations to seek an internal resolution to a computer crime involving an employee. Computer industry research shows the average internal attack costs a company $2.7 million, compared with $57,000 for an external attack.

Research by the Computer Security Institute (CSI) in cooperation with the FBI found that computer crime is on the rise. Eighty-five percent of 538 computer security practitioners in U.S. businesses and institutions surveyed detected computer security breaches causing losses of nearly $378 million for 2000. In 1999, 249 respondents reported losses of $266 million. Both years showed the most serious financial losses from theft of proprietary information and financial fraud. Forty percent reported outside penetration in 2000 compared to 25 percent in 1999. Thirty eight percent reported denial-of-service attacks in 2000 with 27 percent reporting such attacks in 1999. Only 36 percent reported intrusions to police, up from 16 percent five years early.

Because hacker attacks can be so devastating to businesses and organizations, the FBI and its National Infrastructure Protection Center (NIPC; www.nipc.gov) have formed an alliance with businesses and educational entities to share information anonymously. A goal is to have one chapter in each state focusing on information about attacks and security. The FBI is seeking to alert businesses under attack to avoid taking their networks offline because evidence is destroyed and the opportunity to track a hacker is reduced. Also, the Economic Espionage Act of 1996 allows the FBI to investigate cyber-attacks anonymously; this reduces the problem of unwanted publicity. Despite FBI efforts, the NIPC has been criticized for being inadequately staffed and slow to respond to "911" calls. Another source of assistance is the Computer Emergency Response Team (CERT; www.cert.org) at Carnegie Mellon University. It is a clearinghouse of computer security information and technical advisor on incident response for businesses and government agencies.

Techniques of Cybercriminals

Cybercriminals use a variety of techniques. Internal cybercriminals are often familiar with the weaknesses of an organization's IT system and they exploit these weaknesses for gain. Conversely, external cybercriminals often seek proprietary information (e.g., passwords) to gain access to IT systems prior to committing further crimes. Here is a sample list of techniques used by cybercriminals. Such lists are constantly being updated and expanded. As new defenses block cybercriminals, they seek new techniques to access and harm systems.

Distributed denial of service (DDoS). This networking prank, also called a "flood attack," initiates many requests for information to clog the system, slow performance, and crash the site. It may be used to cover up another cybercrime.

Scans. Probes of the Internet to determine types of computers, services, and connections to take advantage of weaknesses in a particular make of computer or software.

Sniffer. Software that covertly searches individual packets of data as they pass through the Internet, capturing items such as passwords.

War dialing. Programs that automatically dial thousands of telephone numbers in search of an access through a modem.

Password crackers. Software that can guess passwords. This technique can possibly be blocked by a blacklisting feature that locks out an account if too many invalid passwords are entered.

Spoofing. Faking an e-mail address or Web page to dupe users into divulging critical information like passwords or credit card numbers.

Trojan horse. A program, unknown to the user, that contains instructions that exploit a known vulnerability in software.

Viruses and worms. The purpose is to cause damage to an application or network and delete files. A worm is similar to a virus except it can self-replicate (i.e., spread itself across networks and the Internet). Defenses include behavior blockers that stop suspicious code based on behavior patterns, not signatures, and applications that quarantine viruses in shielded areas. The LoveLetter virus, which infected millions of computers within hours of its release in 2000, showed the speed that new scripts could spread as well as the limitations of conventional anti-virus defenses.

Time bomb. Also called logic bomb, it contains instructions in a program that creates a malicious act at a predetermined time. Programs are available that monitor applications seeking to change other applications or files when a time bomb goes off.

Social engineering. Tricking an employee into revealing information helpful to gain unauthorized access to a computer system. This could occur through a telephone call from an "employee" or the offender may send an e-mail posing as a network administrator who requests a password for a system upgrade.

Dumpster diving. Searching garbage for information, sometimes used to support social engineering.

IT Security

The list that follows provides some general IT security strategies for an organization.

a. Establish an IT security committee to plan and lead.

b. Because IT security changes rapidly, invest in quality training.

c. Monitor and track alert bulletins and best practices.

d. Consider efforts to establish generally accepted benchmarks for securing computer networks. Such standards define levels of security that an organization can measure itself against.

e. Use a layered approach to security. This creates multiple "roadblocks" for offenders.

f. Provide physical security for computer facilities and include desktops, laptops, and servers.

g. When designing a computer facility avoid glass walls or doors, single paths for power to communications lines, uncontrolled parking, underground locations (because of flooding), multi-tenant buildings, signs describing the facility, information about the facility on the Web or a video, and off-site tape storage that does not meet high security criteria.

h. Automatic access control systems for a computer facility are popular in combination with limited entrances, the double-door entry concept, visual verification, badge identification systems, and access control according to time, place, and specific personnel. Access controls are required not only for the computer facility but also for the computer itself. This includes protection against unauthorized remote access. Biometric access control systems enable identification by fingerprints and so forth.

i. *Passwords* or *codes* are identification procedures that permit access only after the proper code is entered into the computer. The code should be changed periodically. Alarms to signal attempts at unauthorized access should be incorporated into computer software.

j. *Firewalls* are software and hardware controls that permit system access only to users who are registered with a computer. Attempts to gain access are challenged by the use of passwords. These challenges are "layers" that data must go through before reaching its destination. A firewall sits between a company's internal computer network and outside communications. Firewall products offer a range of features such as file or virus checking, log and activity reports, encryption, security and authentication schemes, and monitoring and alarm mechanisms for suspicious events or network intruders. Putting up a firewall is similar in certain respects to implementing physical security—assess the vulnerability, determine need, and after understanding the technology, decide on a proper level of protection.

k. Use intrusion detection software which is like an intrusion detection system, but for the network.

l. Be proactive and conduct searches for hacker programs that may be used in an attack. Hackers tend to brag about their successes to the hacker community so checkout sites that attract hackers.

m. Carefully evaluate new techniques, such as those that purport to filter and trace malicious software sent over the Web.

n. Disable unused services. Most software programs include services that are installed by default. These unused services can be a path for hackers.

o. Update software for improved security. Quickly install security patches. Software firms develop "patches" for protection when hackers attack their programs. Thus, when a patch is offered to a client it should be installed as quickly as possible.

p. Use decoy programs that trick hackers into attacking certain sites where they can be observed and tracked while the important sites remain secure.

q. Audit IT security through frequent, rigorous vulnerability testing. Such tools are available from many commercial sources.

To deal with the internal threat to IT systems and the possibility of fraud and embezzlement by employees, several strategies are helpful. Also, many of the controls applicable to manual accounting systems are applicable to computerized accounting systems. Examples are: establishing clear policies and procedures, permitting no major changes in procedures without authorization, requiring that accountability be maintained when changes are allowed, making sure no one person is responsible for the complete processing of any transaction (separation of duties), rotation of personnel, and periodic audits.

Encryption

Many practitioners in the computer field consider encryption the best protection measure for data within a computer or while it is being transmitted. Once the domain of government, encryption has traditionally been used to protect military or diplomatic secrets. During the 1970s the private sector began marketing encryption products, and with the growth of computers and the Internet, encryption likewise grew. *Encryption* consists of hardware or software that scrambles (encrypts) data, rendering it unintelligible to an unauthorized person intercepting it. The coding procedure involves rules or mathematical steps, called an *algorithm*, that converts plain data into coded data. This transformation of data is accomplished through what is called a *key*, which is a sequence of numbers or characters or both. The key is used in both transmitting and receiving equipment. Key security is vital because it is loaded into both ends of the data link. Furthermore, encryption tools should be changed periodically because breaches have become something of a game. Developers of encryption systems are finding that their estimates of how long it would take to crack the codes are too long. Rapidly evolving technology has shortened the life of promising encryption systems.

Controversy has developed over whether the U.S. government should have the power to tap into every telephone, fax, and computer transmission by controlling keys. From the law enforcement perspective, such control is necessary to investigate criminals and spies. Opponents claim violations of privacy and damage to the ability of American businesses to compete internationally. Without tight controls over encryption systems, the U.S. government also fears that criminals will use such systems to send and receive secret communications, making investigations very difficult. Although the issues remain, organizations need encryption systems for sensitive information and the growing use of electronic mail, which, without encryption, is like sending a postcard.

The explosive growth of the Internet and business on the Internet has created the need for strong algorithms and their all-important key lengths to secure electronic interactions. Internet users are seeking privacy, confidentiality, and verification of individuals and businesses they are dealing with.

One major answer to the challenges cited above is the public key infrastructure (PKI) and its authentication and encryption capabilities. Whereas the handshake or handwritten agreement have been tradition for centuries, a modern trend is the digital handshake and signature through the PKI. The PKI addresses three primary security needs: authentication, nonrepudiation, and encryption. The first need verifies an individual's identity. The second need means that an individual cannot deny they have provided a digital signature for a document or transaction. The workhorse behind PKI is cryptography which encrypts and decrypts information.

Research on Computer Security

The 2000 *Information Security* reader survey, resulting in 1897 respondents, showed that destructive viruses are the number one concern of security professionals, insiders pose a more serious threat than outsiders, and layered security increases protection and increases the chances of detecting breaches.

A *Security Management* reader survey of nearly 200 respondents published in May of 2000 found that the following security strategies were in use (with percentage): virus detection systems (71), firewalls (59), encryption (34), intrusion detection systems (32), physical security for hardware (30), content monitoring or filtering software (21), penetration testing (12), tracing services for laptops (5), network/hacking insurance (5), and biometrics for computer access (2).

Research by the CSI/FBI (cited earlier) offers compelling evidence that neither technologies nor policies alone offer effective defense. Intrusions take place despite firewalls. Trade secrets are stolen despite encryption. Net abuse flourishes despite management edicts against it. Survival depends on a comprehensive approach to IT security, embracing both human and technical measurers. Also, there is the need to properly fund, train, and staff IT security.

Misuse and Errors

Crime is not the only way in which organizations sustain losses from computer operations. Losses are sustained when employees misuse computer resources. This includes viewing inappropriate websites, sending inappropriate e-mails, excessive personal use of the organization's computer, operating another business using an internal computer, and hacking.

Personnel errors involving computer operations are another cause of losses. One common error is to feed incorrect data into a computer. Other examples are seen when inexperienced employees accidentally delete files, update the wrong records, or unknowingly supply outsiders with sensitive information.

Methods to hinder errors and other losses include recruiting and employing appropriately qualified individuals, good training, establishing and communicating policies that are enforced, requiring accountability of those active with computer operations, and designing computer programs that cross-check and notify management of errors and irregularities.

Fire and Disaster Protection

Fires at computer facilities usually are caused by fires in adjacent facilities and electrical problems. Numerous wires and electrical components and accumulations of paper provide combustibles for fire. Because important records are maintained at computer centers, one fire can create financial ruin for a business. Off-site storage of backup copies of records is very important for business survival in case of fire or disaster. With adequate fire prevention and fire suppression measures, losses can be minimized.

Fire prevention entails the enforcement of no smoking rules, the proper disposal of trash, preventive maintenance, training, and audits of prevention measures. Fire suppression is aided by smoke sensors. Ionization detectors are most efficient because they detect the earliest stages of smoke or flame. Carbon monoxide (CO) gas detectors can also save lives. Detectors normally are placed on ceilings, under raised floors, in air ducts, and within equipment. The detectors should be connected to separate power supplies since electricity and air-conditioning units are often turned off during a fire. This will prevent electrocution of an employee if water is sprayed on burning equipment, reduce damage to the computer, and avoid an air-conditioning unit blowing fire and smoke to other parts of a building. Emergency lighting is important in conjunction with these strategies.

A primary method of fire suppression for computer facilities is a sprinkler system, which may be required by local codes. However, sprinklers are controversial because of the potential danger to people due to electrocution and likely equipment damage. Such systems may be activated by accident or by a small fire that could have been extinguished with a portable extinguisher. To reduce the impact of a sprinkler system, consider a dry pipe system with a shutoff valve nearby, noncombustible construction materials, a one-hour fire resistance rating surrounding the computer room, and noncombustible water-resistant covers for computer equipment.

Halon 1301 (Freon) was popular as an extinguishing agent for computer rooms; however, it is no longer being manufactured because it harms the ozone layer. Existing halon systems are not required to be removed. Carbon dioxide extinguishing systems were another earlier alternative to water, but these systems should be avoided because they smother a fire by cutting off oxygen, an obvious danger to humans.

Portable fire extinguishers are helpful to suppress small fires. If portable carbon dioxide extinguishers are used, careful planning (e.g., evacuation) and caution are important because of the danger to humans.

Human-made or natural disasters have the potential for producing considerable disruption and damage to computer centers. Through careful site location, construction, and design, the impact of disasters can be reduced. An auxiliary power supply (i.e., a generator) will provide power in case the main source of electricity fails. A backup air-conditioning/heating unit will ensure that the proper temperature is maintained so that valuable equipment is not harmed. Backup computers and the protection of records are essential considerations for the continuation of both computer operations and the organization. Special computer safes protect computer media from fire, theft, and adverse environmental conditions.

Business on the Internet has added new risks that have the potential for disaster. The primary concern should be to minimize losses and ensure business continuity.

Protection of Proprietary Information

The protection of proprietary information is a serious concern in our world of information and technology. Businesses spend millions of dollars on research to develop new products and services. If a competitor or a foreign government is able to steal a company's secrets, financial losses occur. Since the United States is a leader in the development of new technology, foreign governments and companies save themselves enormous sums on research by stealing secrets. Consequently, information is an asset requiring protection like other valuables.

The loss of important information can occur in the following ways:

1. Garbage discarded by businesses is a popular target of spies. Manuals and customer lists are some of the many items that can be found in dumpsters.
2. A new employee may actually be a spy.
3. Key employees may be influenced by competitors in various ways, such as money, sex, drugs, and blackmail to supply information.
4. Salespeople, while trying to impress customers, may unknowingly divulge proprietary information.
5. An unethical business may advertise a high-paying job that does not exist in order to interview an applicant who works for a competitor.
6. Employees are notorious for unknowingly releasing proprietary information over the telephone, on the Web, at conferences, in restaurants, and so forth.
7. Spies may claim they are conducting a survey, as a "pretext" to acquire information.
8. A spy might frequent a tavern or conference populated by engineers to listen to conversations.

9. "Reverse engineering" is a legal avenue to obtain a look at a competitor's product. The competitor simply purchases the product and dismantles it to understand the components.

The Business Espionage Controls and Countermeasures Association (BECCA; www.espionbusiness.com) is a professional society whose aim is "to make life as difficult and dangerous as possible for the espionage practitioner." In their *Business Espionage Report*, which highlights methods used by spies, the association noted the interception of digital telephones, pagers, teleconferencing systems, and wireless telephone headsets.

A business's IT system is subject to unauthorized access and hacking. For those communicating with others on the Internet and sharing ideas, this creates a database from which a "profile" can be established. Search programs are available that quickly sift through data to produce the profile, and because the writings were posted for thousands of people to read, it would be difficult to convince a court that it was private.

A good spy does not get caught, and quite often the victimized firm does not discover that it has been subjected to espionage. If the discovery is made, the company typically keeps it secret to avoid adverse publicity.

The techniques used by adversaries to acquire sensitive information are so varied that defenders must not fall into the trap of emphasizing certain countermeasures while leaving the "backdoor open." For example, a company may spend hundreds of thousands of dollars defending against electronic surveillance and wiretapping while not realizing that most of the loss of sensitive information results from a few employees who are really spies for competitors.

Putting Corporate Intelligence Gathering in Perspective

Corporate intelligence involves gathering information about competitors. This activity is not necessarily unethical or illegal. It ranges from the illegal activity of industrial espionage to the acceptable, universally applied, practice of utilizing salespeople to monitor public business practices of other companies. Corporate intelligence gathering makes good business sense, and this is why major companies have established formal intelligence programs. Because of unethical and illegal behavior by certain people and firms when gathering intelligence, the whole specialization has earned a bad reputation. But, many avenues for gathering intelligence are legal. Executives should take advantage of information that is publicly available to fulfill their duty to shareholders.

continued

The *Society of Competitive Intelligence Professionals* (scip.org) views its vocation as an honorable profession with a code of ethics. A large part of the work focuses on research of public information and interviews with experts. The information explosion—computers, networks, data banks, and specialized publications—has enabled these professionals to find out almost anything they want about competitors.

Protection Measures

Protection against information thieves, wiretapping, and electronic surveillance must be broad. Both simple and complex methods are useful to protect information.

1. Identify valuable information, classify it, and protect it, Figure 14-1.
2. Carefully screen job applicants.
3. Establish strong policies and procedures, and training. Inform employees about crafty methods used by spies.
4. Periodically conduct retraining to remind everyone in the organization about information as an asset.
5. Consider simple countermeasures. For instance, exercise care when talking on the telephone and in a public place and when using the Internet; hold meetings at unusual locations; and turn up the volume on a radio to "mask" conversations.
6. Protect company trash by shredding it, Figure 14-2. This includes papers, manuals, and computer disks and tapes.
7. Use highly trained security personnel and sophisticated equipment to conduct electronic "sweeps."
8. Consider "shielding," that is, electronic soundproofing where copper is applied throughout a room to stop radio waves from leaving.
9. Use employee nondisclosure agreements and employee noncompete agreements.
10. Implement physical security and access controls for people and property entering, leaving, and circulating within a facility.
11. Maintain state-of-the-art IT security.
12. Protect all forms of electronic communication—e-mail, network, faxes, telephone, etc.

Because intellectual property assets are often more valuable to businesses than tangible assets, Congress passed the Economic Espionage Act of 1996. This act makes it a federal crime for any person to convert a trade

Figure 14-1 Electronic lock and file cabinet; among the many methods to protect proprietary information. Courtesy: Sargent and Greenleaf, Inc.

secret to his or her own benefit or the benefit of others with the intent or knowledge that the conversion will injure the owner of the trade secret. The penalties for any person are up to ten years of imprisonment and a fine to $250,000. Corporations can be fined up to $5 million. If a foreign government benefits from such a crime, the penalties are even greater. The act defines *trade secret* broadly as information that the owner has taken "reasonable measures" to keep secret because of the economic value from it. This means that protection methods are essential.

Electronic Surveillance and Wiretapping

Electronic surveillance utilizes electronic devices to covertly listen to conversations, whereas *wiretapping* pertains to the interception of telephone commu-

Figure 14-2   Even following shredding, a determined adversary may seek proprietary information.

nications. The prevalence of these often illegal activities probably is greater than one would expect. (The legality of such acts by public police is supported by court orders.) Because detection is so difficult, the exact extent of electronic surveillance and wiretapping and what this theft of information costs businesses is impossible to gauge.

Electronic eavesdropping technology is highly developed to the point where countermeasures (debugging) have not kept up with the art of bugging. Consequently, only the most expertly trained and experienced specialist can counter this threat.

Surveillance equipment is easy to obtain. An electronically inclined person can simply enter a local electronics store and buy all the materials necessary to make a sophisticated bug. Retail electronics stores sell FM transmitters or microphones that transmit sound without wires to an ordinary FM radio. Sound is broadcast over a radio several feet away after tuning to the right frequency. These FM transmitters are advertised to be used by public speakers who walk around as they talk and favor wireless microphones; the voice is transmitted and then broadcast over large speakers. They are also advertised to listen in on a baby from another room.

Miniaturization has greatly aided spying. With the advance of the microchip, transmitters are apt to be so small that these devices can be enmeshed in thick paper, as in a calendar, under a stamp, or within a nail in a wall. Bugs may be planted as a building is under construction, or a person may receive one hidden in a present or other item. Transmitters are capable of being operated by solar power (i.e., daylight) or local radio broadcast.

Bugging techniques are varied. Information from a microphone can be transmitted via a "wire run" or a radio transmitter. Bugs are concealed in a variety of objects or carried on a person. Transmitting devices can be remotely controlled with a radio signal for turning them on and off. This makes detection difficult. A device known as a carrier current transmitter is placed in wall plugs, light switches, or other electrically operated components. It obtains its power from the AC wire to which it is attached.

Many spies use a dual system. One bug is placed so that it will be found, which in many instances satisfies security and management. A second bug is more cleverly concealed.

Telephones are especially vulnerable. A "tap" occurs when a telephone conversation is intercepted. Telephone lines are available in so many places that taps are difficult to detect.

Because telephone traffic travels over space radio in several modes—for example, cellular, microwave, and satellite—the spy's job is made much easier and safer since no on-premises tap is required. What is required is the proper equipment for each mode.

When guarding against losses of sensitive information, consideration must be given to a host of methods that may be used by a spy. These include infrared transmitters that use light frequencies below the visible frequency spectrum to transmit information. This can be defeated through physical shielding (close the drapes). Another method, laser listening devices, "bounce" laser off of a window to receive audio from the room. Inexpensive noise masking systems can defeat this technique. A spy may conceal a tape recorder or pinhole lense camera on the premises, or wear a camera concealed in a jacket or tie.

If drawings or designs are on walls or in sight through windows, a spy, for example, stationed in another skyscraper a few blocks away might use a telescope to obtain secret data. Furthermore, computers, e-mail, facsimile, and other transmissions are subject to access by spies. All of these methods by no means exhaust the skills of spies as covered earlier under "espionage techniques."

Comprehensive security methods will hinder spies and the placement of information-gathering devices. The in-house security team can begin countermeasures by conducting a physical search for planted devices. If a decision is made to contact a specialist, *only the most expertly trained and experienced consultant should be recruited.*

Terrorism

Terrorism has existed since the ancient Greek and Roman civilizations. There is little agreement on the definition of terrorism. Here we will define terrorism as the use of various methods to produce fear, coercion, or vio-

lence for political, religious, or criminal ends. Most people think of terrorism as being politically motivated. However, it can also be a violent, personal
crime, or a crime to seek money.

Political terrorists have several objectives. These include to:

a. Instill fear.

b. Create shocking violence.

c. Destroy the confidence people have in their government.

d. Capture international media attention for their cause.

Terrorists are greatly aided by international travel and mass communication. Television has brought acts of terrorism to everyone's living room.

Victims are not important during terrorist acts. One major objective is to
kill, creating shock and obtaining worldwide attention. Another objective is
to establish a bargaining position by killing a hostage and holding others to
be traded for media attention, policy changes, escape, and so forth.

Terrorists have tremendous advantages over defenses because they can
strike almost anywhere with surprise. They are often creative people. A target hardened following an attack may be avoided in the next attack to favor
an unprotected "new" target. A cycle of hardening targets emerges as terrorists seek softer targets. The expense for protection is enormous. If, for
example, airport security is improved, many other targets are available, such
as ships, schools, concerts, sports events, office buildings, and so forth.
Improved airport security can be thwarted by the use of handheld surface-
to-air missiles against airborne passenger jets. Product tampering is another
potential target for terrorists. Although certain companies have improved
packaging of their products, many items in stores are still vulnerable. IT and
communication systems of governments and corporations are additional targets. Other targets include nuclear plants, water supplies of communities,
HAZMAT shipments, chemical plants, government buildings, financial
institutions, and military installations.

Atomic terrorism is another serious threat. By placing a small amount of
plutonium dust in the air-conditioning system of a building, many people could suffer radiation poisoning. The detonation of an atomic weapon
would be a horror. Terrorists might obtain or build a nuclear device or simply decide to wrap radioactive material around a conventional bomb, called
a "dirty bomb." The explosion of such a device could close down a city-
center for decades.

And for those terrorists who cannot afford atomic weaponry, there is the
"poor person's atomic bomb"—nerve gas.

Biological and chemical weapons are a serious threat.

September 11, 2001 Terrorist Attack

The date of September 11, 2001 marked a turning point in the history of
security. In a devastating terrorist onslaught, knife-wielding hijackers crashed

two airliners into the World Trade Center in New York City, creating an inferno that caused the 110-story twin skyscrapers to collapse, Figure 14-3. Almost 3000 people were killed, including responding firefighters and police. During the same morning another hijacked airliner crashed into the Pentagon causing additional deaths and destruction. A fourth hijacked airliner failed to reach its target and crashed when heroic passengers learned of the other attacks and struggled with hijackers to control the airliner.

Because of these devastating attacks, not only have homeland defense, security, safety, and military strategies changed, but also our way of thinking has changed. We cannot afford to have failures in our planning and imagination of what criminals can do.

In past decades, international terrorists targeted U.S. citizens and interests overseas. The most memorable attacks include the 1988 bombing of Pan American Flight 103 over Lockerbie, Scotland, which killed 189 Americans; the 1996 bombing of Al-Khobar Towers in Dhahran, Saudi Arabia, resulting in the deaths of 19 U.S. military personnel; and the 1998 bombing of the U.S. embassies in Kenya and Tanzania, which killed 12 Americans and many others.

The year 1993 brought with it the beginning of serious domestic terrorism. During that year change occurred with the first bombing of the World Trade Center in New York City in which six people died and nearly 1000 were injured. In 1995, the bombing of the Murrah federal building

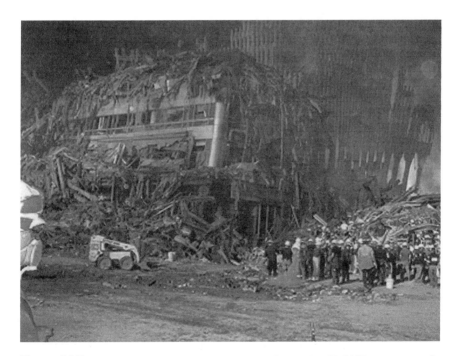

Figure 14-3   World Trade Center collapse following September 11, 2001 terrorist attack.

in Oklahoma City resulted in 168 deaths. A trend emerged whereby such crimes were occurring on American soil and becoming increasingly deadly.

The U.S. Commission on National Security completed a study in 1999 and concluded that America will become increasingly vulnerable to attack on our homeland. The Commission also predicted that foreign states and terrorists will acquire weapons of mass destruction and mass disruption, and some will use them resulting in American deaths.

Although terrorism has been intense in the Mideast, it exists throughout the world. The tension in the Mideast and the differences between Israel and its Arab neighbors has resulted in wars, besides terrorism. Because the United States has a history of being pro-Israel and has led wars in Iraq and Afghanistan, the United States has been perceived as "the great satan" and an enemy of the religion of Islam. This tension has led a minority of Middle Eastern groups to call for a "holy war." Extremists have perverted the Islamic faith in the call from God to kill Americans. This minority is violently opposed to the American way of life (e.g., equality for women, TV and films, our material possessions) because they believe it corrupts their idea of Muslim culture. Few Muslims hold these extremist and violent views. To reduce the violence, nations and groups must negotiate and reach a settlement on the issues. This is a difficult challenge, but the avenue toward peace.

Security professionals do not get involved in political disputes, nor correct deviant behavior. Rather, they deal with the symptoms of problems—crime, terrorism, and so forth. Our government is charged with the duties of diplomacy and, when necessary, military action.

Countermeasures Against Terrorism

Here is a summary or "big picture" of seven fronts to confront terrorism developed following the September 11, 2001 attack on the United States.

Diplomacy. The United States has secured a coalition of support from many nations that have deployed or pledged troops, permitted use of airspace, and shared intelligence.

Intelligence. The collection of quality information that is accurate provides the foundation for action against terrorists. Many nations have provided increased intelligence support to the United States. Intelligence is gathered from many sources such as informants, spies, electronic surveillance, satellites, and drones.

Military. A variety of armed services of the United States and other countries are coordinating their efforts to fight terrorists. To win support in hostile countries, U.S. psychological operations drop leaflets and radios and humanitarian aid is distributed.

Financial. This front aims to coordinate several federal agencies and gain support from other countries in tracking and freezing terrorist assets to starve them of funding.

Law Enforcement. The activity of law enforcement has been to investigate threats; conduct interviews, searches, and electronic surveillance; issue subpoenas; and detain and arrest. Many countries have supported criminal investigations of terrorists. The aims of law enforcement agencies are to identify, arrest, and convict offenders.

Homeland Defense. The federal government and states have established homeland defense directors to coordinate resources for protection against terrorism, Figure 14-4. The resources are broad and include coordination among public safety and emergency management agencies, medical facilities, transportation systems, utilities, infrastructure, and agencies that control access at our borders.

Business and Organizational Security. This front covers security, fire protection, and life safety at businesses, schools, hospitals, sports arenas, utilities, and many other locations.

When considering countermeasures against terrorism, first consider the methods used by terrorists, which go beyond bombings. The raw materials for both chemical and biological weapons can be purchased on the open or black markets. In 1998, a New Jersey physicist named Lawrence A. Maltz threatened to use biological and chemical devices before his arrest by the FBI. During the same year, three members of a Texas secessionist group planned to infect government officials with toxins prior to their arrest by the FBI. A disturbing trend is the increase in threats of use of weapons of mass destruction. The FBI noted that anthrax, a bacterial pathogen that can spread through contact with a powered form or by breathing an aerosol discharge, has emerged as the agent of choice among terrorists. The use of Anthrax as a terrorist tool became a reality in 2001 when it was mailed to politicians, the media, and others. It disrupted the postal system and caused deaths.

The Internet is a source of information to build assorted weapons. Various groups publish manuals on tactics to be used to advance their cause. For example, some antiabortion activists have written a manual to close abortion clinics by squirting Superglue into the locks so the clinic cannot open, drilling holes in the low points of flat roofs, and placing a garden hose in mail slots at front doors.

Critically think about the following. Government buildings in Washington, DC and the financial district of New York City are excellent terrorist targets that this author viewed as at the top of the list prior to the September 11, 2001 attacks. These targets are still at the top of the list. Think about where terrorist strikes can harm the United States the most. We continue to concentrate so much of our nation's government and wealth in

Figure 14-4   Homeland defense includes the protection of key government buildings.

"neatly packaged targets." The plans for Washington, DC, the financial district of New York City, and many other important and visible locations were designed many years ago in an age when planners had no idea about the threats of the twenty-first century. Although we must not be held like hostages because of the risk of terrorist attacks, we must think like terrorists to anticipate attacks and take precautions. This may mean moving operations and people to spread the risk. The destruction of the capitol dome where Congress meets and the killing of politicians would be a bold attack that would shock the world. Imagine the economic impact of a chemical, biological, or radioactive attack on Wall Street. If terrorists can level the World Trade Center towers with planes hijacked with box cutters, many scenarios are possible. An epidemic could be launched by infecting twenty or thirty suicidal terrorists who would wait until they became highly infectious before walking into government buildings, airports, schools, shopping malls, and sports arenas. Or, a bomb could contain not only an explosive, but also a chemical or biological agent, or all three. And, spreading the risk may not reduce losses from a well coordinated, widely dispersed attack. Since there is an endless number of possible terrorist targets and scenarios, and financial considerations prevent protecting all locations, governments, businesses, and organizations must prioritize protection.

Let us hope that nations and groups can settle their differences. However, history tells us that this is a difficult objective to reach. If terrorism intensifies, hopefully the combined efforts of the seven fronts cited earlier will prevent it. Also, consider the following suggestions for individual businesses and organizations.

a. Terrorists have tremendous advantages over defenses because they search for vulnerabilities and strike almost anywhere with surprise. A British terrorism expert, Paul Wilkinson, stated, "Fighting terrorism is like a goalkeeper. You can make a hundred brilliant saves, but the only shot people remember is the one that gets past you." Creative and security planning is essential.

b. Maintain awareness of controversies that may increase exposure to terrorism.

c. Reevaluate security, safety, and emergency plans. Seek cooperation with public safety agencies.

d. Educate people about problems and countermeasures. Include basic, simple precautions. Examples: use a bomb threat form, Figure 14-5; in a chemical attack, evacuate, cover your mouth with a cloth, and help victims only when you are wearing protective gear.

e. Increase employee awareness of terrorism and terrorist methods and tricks. Stifle and trick potential terrorists through creativity (e.g., avoid signs on the premises that identify departments, people, and job duties; periodically alter security methods).

f. Ensure building evacuation plans provide for rapid and safe escape to areas not near the building.

g. Know the business of tenants and whether they would be possible targets for violence.

XYZ Company

Bomb Threat Call

Time of Call: _____   Date of Call: _____

Number of Minutes on Telephone: _____   Location: _____

Exact Words of Caller: _____

_____

_____

_____

Questions to Ask:

When will bomb explode? _____

Where is it? _____

Why type of bomb is it? _____

What does it look like? _____

Why did you place this call? _____

Where are you calling from? _____

Description of caller's voice:

Male/ Female? _____ Old/Young? _____ Accent? (y/n) _____

What type of Accent? _____

Background noise? _____ Tone of voice? _____

Name, address, telephone, e-mail of recipient?

_____

_____

_____

Figure 14-5 Bomb threat form.

h. Consider the security and safety of childcare facilities used by employees.

i. Intensify access controls (Figure 14-6) by using a comprehensive approach covering people, vehicles, mail, deliveries, services, and any person or thing seeking access. And, test security systems and security personnel to ensure the integrity of protection.

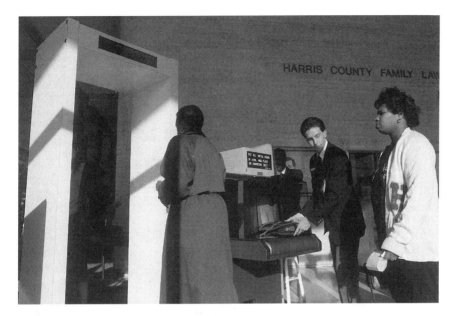

Figure 14-6 Courthouse screening; walk-through metal detector, left; x-ray scanner, right. Courtesy: Wackenhut, Inc.

j. Carefully screen employment applicants, vendors, and others seeking to work on the premises.

k. Secure and place under surveillance HVAC systems (e.g., air intake systems) and utilities.

l. Once the best possible security and safety plans are implemented, remember that an offender (internal or external or both) may be studying your defenses to look for weaknesses to exploit.

Precautions for mail include:

a. Prepare emergency plans, policies, and procedures for suspect mail.

b. Isolate the mail area and limit access. Consider handling mail at a separate, isolated building.

c. Use gloves and protective masks.

d. Do not touch or smell anything suspicious.

e. Be suspicious of mail, Figures 14-7 and 14-8.

f. Consider technology: x-ray for bombs, letter and package tracking systems, automatic letter openers, and scanning letters and sending them electronically.

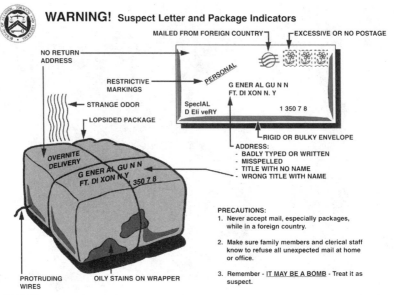

Figure 14-7 Suspect letter and package indicators.

Figure 14-8 Exercise care with suspect mail.

What If?

As a Security Officer on Patrol at an Office Building Complex, What Do You Do if You See a HVAC Crew Behaving Oddly?

While on patrol as a security officer you observe a HVAC crew at the building ventilation system. The situation appears odd. The HVAC service company truck is different than the one under contract, twice as many "technicians" as usual are servicing the unit, and the crew is standing in strategic positions, rather than hovering over the HVAC system as you have observed in the past. What do you do?

A new HVAC service company could have been hired, the increased number of technicians could be responding to a complex problem, and the crew could be just "standing around." At the same time, HVAC systems are vulnerable to terrorist attack through the introduction of chemical, biological, or radioactive substances for dispersion throughout a building. This could result in a huge loss of life, illness and injuries, and financial ruin. Contact your supervisor and the head of facilities or maintenance with as much information as possible about what you observed. If the crew does not check out, call police and the fire department.

As a security officer, consider that one or more persons under the cover of "maintenance" of anything on the premises could be an offender planting a bomb or other destructive device, or committing sabotage, theft, etc. Access controls and thorough verification improve protection. To offer an extra measure of protection to people and assets, think critically about your surroundings and the behavior of people and groups. Also, think creatively as an offender. What crafty disguises and methods could they use to deceive security and other employees? What tricks would offenders use to accomplish their objectives? They may dress and possess identification of repair personnel, safety inspectors, or police. Be inquisitive without being offensive. Exercise caution and think about your safety and the safety of others. Your hunch may be wrong, but you are doing your job!

Official Centers for Disease Control (CDC) Health Advisory Distributed via Health Alert Network October 12, 2001

HOW TO HANDLE ANTHRAX AND OTHER BIOLOGICAL AGENT THREATS

Many facilities in communities around the country have received anthrax threat letters. Most were empty envelopes; some have

continued

contained powdery substances. The purpose of these guidelines is to recommend procedures for handling such incidents.

DO NOT PANIC

1. Anthrax organisms can cause infection in the skin, gastrointestinal system, or the lungs. To do so the organism must be rubbed into abraded skin, swallowed, or inhaled as a fine, aerosolized mist. Disease can be prevented after exposure to the anthrax spores by early treatment with the appropriate antibiotics. Anthrax is not spread from one person to another person.

2. For anthrax to be effective as a covert agent, it must be aerosolized into very small particles. This is difficult to do, and requires a great deal of technical skill and special equipment. If these small particles are inhaled, life-threatening lung infection can occur, but prompt recognition and treatment are effective.

Suspicious Unopened letter or PACKAGE MARKED WITH THREATENING MESSAGE SUCH AS "ANTHRAX":

1. Do not shake or empty the contents of any suspicious envelope or package.

2. PLACE the envelope or package in a plastic bag or some other type of container to prevent leakage of contents.

3. If you do not have any container, then COVER the envelope or package with anything (e.g., clothing, paper, trash can, etc.) and do not remove this cover.

4. Then LEAVE the room and CLOSE the door, or section off the area to prevent others from entering (i.e., keep others away).

5. WASH your hands with soap and water to prevent spreading any powder to your face.

6. What to do next . . .

   a. If you are at HOME, then report the incident to local police.

   b. If you are at WORK, then report the incident to local police, and notify your building security official or an available supervisor.

7. LIST all people who were in the room or area when this suspicious letter or package was recognized. Give this list to both the local public health authorities and law enforcement officials for follow-up investigations and advice.

Envelope with powder and powder spills out onto surface:

1. DO NOT try to CLEAN UP the powder. COVER the spilled contents immediately with anything (e.g., clothing, paper, trash can, etc.) and do not remove this cover!

2. Then LEAVE the room and CLOSE the door, or section off the area to prevent others from entering (i.e., keep others away).

3. WASH your hands with soap and water to prevent spreading any powder to your face.

4. What to do next . . .

 a. If you are at HOME, then report the incident to local police.

 b. If you are at WORK, then report the incident to local police, and notify your building security official or an available supervisor.

5. REMOVE heavily contaminated clothing as soon as possible and place in a plastic bag, or some other container that can be sealed. This clothing bag should be given to the emergency responders for proper handling.

6. SHOWER with soap and water as soon as possible. Do Not Use Bleach or Other Disinfectant on Your Skin.

7. If possible, list all people who were in the room or area, especially those who had actual contact with the powder. Give this list to both the local public health authorities so that proper instructions can be given for medical follow-up, and to law enforcement officials for further investigation.

QUESTION OF ROOM CONTAMINATION BY AEROSOLIZATION:

For example: small device triggered, warning that air handling system is contaminated, or warning that a biological agent released in a public space.

1. Turn off local fans or ventilation units in the area.

2. LEAVE area immediately.

3. CLOSE the door, or section off the area to prevent others from entering (i.e., keep others away).

4. What to do next . . .

 a. If you are at HOME, then dial "911" to report the incident to local police and the local FBI field office.

 b. If you are at WORK, then dial "911" to report the incident to local police and the local FBI field office, and notify your building security official or an available supervisor.

5. SHUT down air handling system in the building, if possible.

6. If possible, list all people who were in the room or area. Give this list to both the local public health authorities so that proper instructions can be given for medical follow-up, and to law enforcement officials for further investigation.

Workplace Violence

The definition of workplace violence has expanded over the years from "violence among employees" to "any violence that occurs on the job." This includes employees, customers, vendors, and anyone on the premises. The University of Iowa, in a report entitled "Workplace Violence: A Report to the Nation," found that 2 million Americans are victims of workplace violence each year. The research divided workplace violence into four categories: criminal intent (e.g., robbery), customer/client (e.g., health care environment), worker-on-worker, and personal relationship (e.g., domestic violence). About 85 percent of all workplace homicides occur under the criminal intent category and 7 percent under the worker-on-worker category. Retailers had the largest number of nonfatal violent incidents.

Domestic violence in the workplace has become an increasingly serious issue. Domestic problems at home can spill into the workplace. Both male and female employees having domestic problems may incur lower productivity and excessive absenteeism. And, a distraught partner may access the premises with anger.

Workplace violence is costly to businesses. Losses reach into the billions of dollars each year and include medical and psychological care, lost wages, property damage, lost company goodwill, and impact on employee turnover and hiring.

There is no national law addressing violence in the workplace. OSHA has published voluntary guidelines for workers in late night retail, health care, and taxicab businesses, but these guidelines are not legal requirements. Various states have enacted laws to curb the problem.

Employers who do not take measures to prevent violence in the workplace face exposure to lawsuits. Workers' compensation may cover injured employees but the exposure of employers is much greater. Examples include premises liability and negligent hiring, training, supervision, and retention.

Protection Methods

What follows is a list of strategies for dealing with violence in the workplace.

1. Establish a committee to plan violence prevention and to respond to such incidents.

2. Consider OSHA guidelines to curb workplace violence.

3. Establish policies and procedures and communicate the problems of threats and violence to all employees.

4. Although human behavior cannot be accurately predicted, screen employment applicants.

5. Consider substance abuse testing as a strategy to prevent workplace violence.

6. Train all employees to recognize others with problems and report them to the human resources department. Use a "hot-line" service

to permit anonymity in reporting to protect employees who would otherwise not report potential violence. Include training in conflict resolution and nonviolent response.

7. A history of violent behavior can help to predict its reoccurrence. The worker who becomes violent is usually male, between 25 and 45 years old, and has a history of interpersonal conflict. He tends to be a loner and may have a mental health history of paranoia or depression. He also may have a fascination with weapons.

8. Managers and supervisors should be sensitive to disruptions in the workplace, such as firings.

9. If a person becomes angry in the workplace, listen and show that you are interested in helping to resolve the problem. Do not get pulled into a verbal confrontation; do not argue. Acknowledge and validate the anger by showing empathy, not sympathy. Speak softly and slowly. Ensure that a witness is present. Maintain a safe distance, without being obvious, to provide an extra margin of safety. If a threat is made or if a weapon is shown, call the police.

10. Remember that outsiders (e.g., visitor, estranged spouse, robber) may be a source of violence and protection programs must be comprehensive.

11. If a violent incident occurs, a previously prepared crisis management plan becomes invaluable. Otherwise, a committee should be formed immediately after emergency first responders (i.e., police, EMS) complete their duties on the premises and affected employees and their families are assisted. At one major corporation, management was unprepared when the corporate security manager was shot. A committee was quickly formed to improve security and survey corporate plants. In addition to expenditures for physical security and training, an emphasis was placed on awareness, access controls, and alerts.

What If?

As a Security Officer, What Do You Do if an Employee Who Was Just Terminated and Escorted Outside By You Wants to Re-Enter the Building?

Organizations usually have policies and procedures in place to handle terminations as safely and quickly as possible. For example, the former employee should be escorted to retrieve personal belongings and to exit the building. Terminations are often tense and unpleasant for all parties and violence is a possibility. If the former employee seeks to re-enter the building, this request should be refused, no matter what the excuse (e.g., I forgot something. I want to say good-bye to someone. I have to use the restroom.). Contact your supervisor about the request to re-enter. Sometimes a terminated employee is told that they will be considered a trespasser if they enter the premises.

Substance Abuse

Substance abuse can be defined as the misuse of any chemical substance that can be taken into the body to alter the mind and/or the body. To fully understand the monumental substance abuse threat facing our society, we should maintain a broad perspective on this problem. We must understand that many types of illegal and legal substances are abused. Commonly abused substances heard in the media include alcohol, tobacco, marijuana, cocaine, and crack. However, many other substances are abused, such as aspirin, laxatives, and glue (an inhalant).

Ivancevich, in *Human Resource Management*, writes that substance abuse affects 12 percent of the workforce, costing organizations about $150 billion annually in lost productivity and related expenses. Studies have indicated that substance abuse is one of the leading causes of increases in workplace violence. Compared to those who do not abuse alcohol, problem drinkers take two and one half times more absences of eight days or more and receive three times as much sick leave and accident benefits. Drug abusers are one-third less productive, have three and a half times more workplace accidents and make five times as many workers' compensation claims as nondrug abusers.

History

The history of substance abuse offers interesting insights into changing social and legal responses to various drugs. For example, during the 1600s, the use of tobacco in certain countries (e.g., Turkey) was punishable by death. The "stinking weed" was declared to have a very bad effect on the health and mind of many people. Later, these same countries officially accepted tobacco.

Cocaine also has an interesting history. During the late 1800s and early 1900s, coca wine was the rage. Cocaine was an ingredient in Coca-Cola until 1903 when public pressure forced the company to delete it. As public fear mounted over violent tendencies of cocaine abusers, laws were passed declaring it illegal. Today it is a widely used illegal drug.

Unfortunately, we live in a drug-oriented world. Billions of dollars are being spent by a drug consuming population who are producing increasing numbers of drug dealing millionaires. The corrupting influence of the illegal drug trade has resulted in law breaking by politicians and law enforcement officers, among others.

As a security officer, your primary job is to protect people and assets. In the workplace, the abuse of drugs cannot be tolerated. Security officers should observe and report such incidents to a supervisor. If employees drink alcohol, smoke crack or marijuana, or use other substances prior to or while at work, the following adverse consequences can occur:

- The operation of machinery or a vehicle can result in an accident, injury, or death to the abuser and others.

• Mistakes can slow production and waste company resources.

• Excessive absenteeism and increased medical expenses drain resources.

• Substance abuse can cause an employee to steal to support a habit.

• Outsiders may try to blackmail an abuser for proprietary information.

Types of Drugs

Five types of drugs commonly abused are depressants, stimulants, marijuana, narcotics, and hallucinogens. Before discussing each of these types, some definitions are presented.

Addiction is a condition involving a desire for a certain drug. There is physical and/or psychological dependence. The individual and society suffer from an addiction problem.

Tolerance is the continued use of a drug that reduces the drug's impact; thus, increased dosages are required to maintain its effect.

Withdrawal is the ill-effects of not receiving a substance to which the body is addicted. The addictive drug is sought by whatever means (e.g., crime) to avoid discomfort and pain.

DEPRESSANTS Depressants, also known as sedatives, slow the central nervous system and decrease anxiety. Here are a few types of depressants:

Alcohol is the most widely used depressant and the most abused drug in the United States. Over 10 million people have a serious alcohol problem and 200,000 die annually. Half of all traffic fatalities involve alcohol. It is devastating to society and it is a legal drug. Like other drugs, alcohol produces a tolerance. Addicted individuals require increasing amounts to maintain earlier effects. These drinkers are drug users. However, our society views alcohol differently than marijuana. Long-term abuse of alcohol can result in liver disease, memory loss, and apathy, among other problems. Withdrawal may produce hallucinations and delirium tremens (DTs). Clearly, the abuse of alcohol is harmful. A distinction must be maintained between "abuse" and "use." In fact, moderation is not harmful and even recommended by the medical community.

Barbiturates are a widely used depressant. Barbiturates are used in the medical treatment of high blood pressure, epilepsy, insomnia, and to relax patients before and during surgery. The individual who abuses barbiturates will appear drowsy or peaceful. Barbiturates are addictive and tolerance builds. Withdrawal can lead to death.

Tranquilizers relieve anxiety and relax muscles. Brand names include valium and librium. Methaqualone, another depressant, is sold under various brand names including quaalude. The dependence and tolerance properties of depressants make their abuse very hazardous. When used in combination with alcohol, these substances are extremely dangerous.

STIMULANTS Stimulants speed up the nervous system and suppress fatigue. *Amphetamines* are a widely used stimulant. For medical purposes, this drug is used to treat depression, obesity, and other problems. Street names include "speed," and "pep pills." Some brand names are dexedrine and benzedrine. The hazards of abuse are many—tolerance, addiction, withdrawal, and heart problems.

Cocaine is a widely used stimulant. It is more powerful than amphetamines. A feeling of well-being and confidence, and increased energy, make this drug very attractive. Cocaine does not produce a tolerance, nor does it result in a *physical* addiction or *physical* withdrawal. However, the *psychological consequences* of discontinuing use are devastating and include depression, irritability, and fatigue. The abuser can develop a strong craving for the drug and thus become behaviorally dependent (psychologically addicted).

Crack is a form of cocaine that is smoked, Figure 14-9. It is made by soaking cocaine hydrochloride and baking soda in water, then applying heat. The crystals that form from this solution are called crack. When smoked, the baking soda causes a cracking sound, hence the name crack. Within ten seconds of smoking, crack produces an intense rush that lasts for a few minutes. This feeling is so attractive that many users desire the drug over and over again. Its abuse has become explosive. Many lives have been destroyed as abusers give up money, relationships, and careers to pursue the rush. The hazards of abuse include damage to the respiratory system and death.

Two common stimulants whose use are not controlled by law are *nicotine* and *caffeine.* Nicotine causes increased heart rate and blood pressure and shortness of breath. Long-term dependence can result in emphysema,

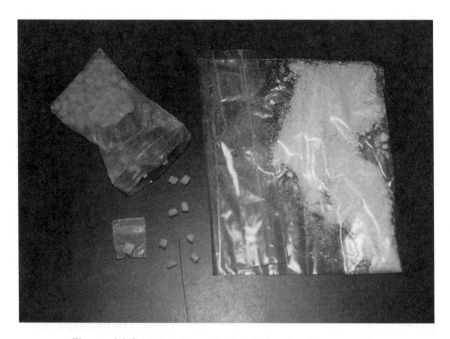

Figure 14-9   Illegal drugs. Crack, left. Powdered cocaine, right.

lung cancer, heart disease, and death. Caffeine also raises blood pressure. A tolerance and feeling of energy develops, but too much of this drug causes nervousness and an aggravation of ulcer conditions.

MARIJUANA The use of marijuana is widespread, more so than cocaine. It is obtained from the leaves and flowers of the Indian hemp plant. Hashish, also from this plant, is more concentrated. These substances produce euphoria, relaxation, and drowsiness. The effects include increased heart rate and appetite, and loss of coordination. Long-term use can result in psychological dependence, hallucinations, paranoia, and lung disease.

NARCOTICS Narcotics are painkillers obtained from the opium poppy or produced synthetically. Examples include *heroin, morphine,* and *codeine.* Of these substances, heroin is illegal in the United States. Effects are respiratory depression, euphoria, and lethargy. The hazards of abuse are very serious and include tolerance, physical and psychological dependence, painful withdrawal, overdose, and death.

HALLUCINOGENS These substances cause changes in perception and consciousness. Examples are *LSD, PCP, mescaline,* and *psilocybin.* The effects and hazards are numerous and include a tolerance (but no dependency), increased heartbeat and blood pressure, euphoria, hallucinations, paranoia, flashbacks, attempts at suicide, and birth defects.

INHALANTS Outside the realm of traditional drug use is the inhalation of agents that produce an intoxicating effect. *Glues, gasoline,* and *aerosol sprays* are examples. These substances act like depressants. The abuser may appear to be drunk. Long-term effects are damage to the liver and central nervous system.

Countermeasures

Many strategies have been implemented to counter the worldwide drug problem. Laws have been passed. Law enforcement efforts, treatment, and education programs have expanded. However, a serious drug problem remains and there are no easy solutions. For assistance check the Web at www.drugfreeworkplace.com.

As a security officer, it is important to understand the following basic strategies used by employers to deal with drugs in the workplace.

1. Managers in many organizations are realizing the serious nature of drug abuse. Consequently, strong policies and procedures have been formulated. Education and prevention programs can assist employees in understanding substance abuse, policies, and making informed decisions on life choices, health, and happiness.
2. Training of managers and supervisors has increased so abusers can be recognized and properly handled. Court cases have held employers responsible for the harm caused by intoxicated employees.

3. Employers are increasingly testing job applicants and employees for substance abuse.

4. Security officers are playing a role in countermeasures by their observation and reporting.

5. Undercover investigations are being implemented to pinpoint those employees who are using and selling illegal drugs in the workplace.

Many employers have employee assistance programs (EAPs) that incorporate a broad-based approach to such problems as substance abuse, depression, and marital and financial problems. These programs are characterized by voluntary participation by employees, referrals for serious cases, and confidentiality. The goal is to help the employee so he or she can be retained, saving hiring and training costs. The philosophy is that a company has no right to interfere in private matters, but it does have a right to impose rules of behavior and performance at work.

The Anti-Drug Abuse Act of 1988, effective March 1989, is a federal law aimed at promoting a drug-free workplace. This law impacts those businesses that have $25,000 or more in federal contracts or those who receive any federal grant. Employers are required to establish policies on prohibitions and disciplinary action, awareness programs, and counseling and rehabilitation. The penalty for violating the law includes the loss of federal contracts or grants.

Another form of regulation includes industries regulated by the Department of Transportation, such as airline, motor carrier, and rail, which are required to institute substance abuse programs, including drug testing. Although OSHA has issued no standards for substance abuse programs, it does provide information and assistance to employers and employees.

Labor Disputes

Legislation and Law

The history of labor relations contains many confrontations between workers and management. Before the earlier part of the twentieth century, organized workers were prohibited from picketing and striking. *Picketing* refers to employees who congregate near an employer's property to advertise a labor disagreement. A *strike* is a work stoppage to press for higher wages and benefits.

The Clayton Act of 1914 was the first major federal legislation helpful to the cause of organized labor. It restricted the federal courts from prohibiting picketing, strikes, and other labor strategies. The Norris-LaGuardia Act of 1932 added strength to the labor movement by further restricting federal courts from issuing injunctions initiated by employers to halt labor activities. The federal legislation with the most influence on the growth of unions was the National Labor Relations Act of 1935. This act stated the rights and obligations of unions and employers. It created the National Labor Relations Board (NLRB) to settle charges of unfair labor practices from either a union or an employer.

Examples of unfair labor practices of employers are listed here. Employers are prohibited from:

- Meddling with workers' efforts to organize and bargain.
- Discriminating against workers who participate in union activity.
- Refusing to bargain collectively with employee representatives.

Examples of unfair labor practices of unions are listed here. Unions are prohibited from:

- Coercing employees.
- Refusing to bargain collectively with an employer.
- Charging new members excessive initiation fees.

A basic purpose of labor law is to establish a fair bargaining opportunity for both workers and employers. Many legal guidelines evolve from the legislative, judicial, and executive branches of government on both the federal and state levels. Decisions of the NLRB, for example, have a major impact on labor-management relations.

Legal Guidelines

The following list provides a sampling of legal guidelines for security personnel.

1. Labor law prohibits an employer, including security personnel, from conducting surveillance and investigations of workers engaged in union activities.
2. Security personnel must avoid references to union activities in their reports.
3. Photographing strikers is unlawful, unless they commit illegal acts, such as vandalism or assault.
4. Workers have the right to picket on public property next to the employer's property. However, demonstrators cannot block entrances or disrupt business.
5. The First Amendment provides citizens with the opportunity for freedom of speech and assembly.
6. Unions have advised workers under investigation to remain silent (Fifth Amendment), not to sign anything when being questioned, and to seek the advice of a shop steward (union worker representative). Workers are entitled to union representation during questioning.

Security Strategies

The following guidelines will help security officers involved in labor disputes.

1. Security officers must understand the stress on all company employees during a labor dispute. Costs are a prime area of concern to all parties. How long can the business survive during a strike? Can production be maintained? What are the financial limits of workers and the union?

2. The best defenses for labor problems are early preparation and training.

3. If labor trouble is anticipated, security should be increased. Perimeter security is especially important at gates, public streets, and sidewalks. Cooperate with local public police.

4. Be especially alert to protecting company property from vandalism, sabotage, and theft, before, during, and after labor disputes.

5. Consider changing certain locks and recovering keys from employees due to strike. Issue special access ID cards.

6. Thoroughly check all security, safety, and fire protection equipment and systems before, during, and after labor disputes.

7. Employees who plan to work during labor unrest should carpool. Vehicles and occupants must be protected when they enter, park, and leave the premises.

8. Since security controls (e.g., searches) may be at odds with union workers prior to a strike, it is likely these issues will surface with greater intensity during labor disputes. This can put security personnel in a difficult position while trying to protect people and assets.

9. Security officers must exercise caution with words and actions during a labor dispute. An inappropriate response to a sensitive situation can trigger violence, vandalism, and other avoidable losses.

10. Security officers must not respond to insults from demonstrators or become hostile. Act as a professional.

11. A major point of crowd psychology is that collectively people will do things they would not do individually.

12. Officers must be sensitive to crowds and allow them to lawfully exercise their rights. However, crowds that become aggressive should be handled with the assistance of public police.

13. If approached by union officials or news reporters, security officers should state a designated spokesperson for the company will answer all questions. Summon a supervisor.

14. During a labor dispute, communicate with workers as little as possible. Do not ask questions (e.g., "How will you vote in the union election?"). Unfair labor practice charges can result.

CHAPTER REVIEW

A. Multiple Choice

1. This cybercrime method involves faking an e-mail address or Web page so the user will divulge critical information such as passwords or credit card numbers.
   a. war dialing
   b. spoofing
   c. cracking
   d. sniffing

2. This communication protection method consists of hardware or software that scrambles data, rendering it unintelligible to an unauthorized person intercepting it.
   a. social engineering
   b. spooking
   c. electronic surveillance
   d. encryption

3. Which of the following is not true concerning terrorism?
   a. Terrorism has existed since the ancient Greek and Roman civilizations.
   b. One major objective is to kill, creating shock and obtaining world-wide attention.
   c. Terrorists have tremendous advantages over defenses because they can strike almost anywhere with surprise.
   d. A fault of terrorists is that they are often not creative in their plans and acts.

4. When confronted with substance abuse in the workplace, security officers should
   a. observe and report to a supervisor.
   b. immediately notify public police.
   c. try to setup a buy.
   d. ignore the problem.

5. Select the statement below that is incorrect concerning labor law.
   a. Workers have the right to picket on public property next to the employer's property.
   b. Security investigations of union activity are legally permissible.
   c. Unions are prohibited from refusing to collectively bargain with an employer.
   d. Employers are prohibited from meddling with workers' efforts to organize and bargain.

B. True or False

1. Equipment for wiretapping and electronic surveillance is easy to obtain.
2. Workplace violence is primarily an employee versus employee problem.
3. The year 1993 brought with it the beginning of serious domestic terrorism.
4. Alcohol is the most widely used depressant and the most abused drug in the United States.
5. A basic purpose of labor law is to establish a fair bargaining opportunity for both workers and employers.

Applications

Application 14A

Go to the Web and use your favorite search engines to learn more about cybercrime and IT security.

Application 14B

Learn what is being done in your state to protect against terrorism. What do you think will be the next terrorist targets? What methods will they use and what can we do to thwart the plan?

Application 14C

Research the problem of domestic violence. Do you think this problem can spill into the workplace? If so, what can be done about it?

Application 14D

Why would an employer use an undercover investigator to investigate a drug abuse problem in the workplace?

Application 14E

Role-play a scenario whereby security officers are protecting company property while strikers are heckling them. How do you feel about being heckled? Can you control your emotions? Switch roles so everyone can be the recipient of heckling.

SECTION 4

YOUR FUTURE IN SECURITY

15

Career Planning

CHAPTER OUTLINE

OBJECTIVES

After studying this chapter, you will be able to:

- List the careers available to those with a security background.
- Discuss three areas of self-analysis concerning job hunting.
- List at least ten questions helpful for making career decisions.
- Explain the five factors that can assist a person to advance within the security field.
- List at least ten sources of employment information.
- Prepare at least ten guidelines for completing an employment application form.
- Prepare a cover letter.
- Prepare a resume.
- List at least twenty tips for a successful employment interview.

Introduction

The purpose of this chapter is to help you obtain a security position and advance within the profession. Job hunting is a learned skill. Many people graduate from training programs and colleges without knowing how or where to begin their employment search. After a position is obtained, it is important to understand what factors increase the chances for promotion.

Security Careers

Opportunities in the security and loss prevention field are varied and numerous. In fact, the U.S. Department of Labor has identified security as one of the fastest growing occupations, as shown in Figure 15-1. Almost all types of businesses and institutions require protection. For example, manufacturers, retailers, airlines, hotels, banks, hospitals (Figure 15-2), and schools all need and employ security personnel. Many people who presently hold a security position in these various industries began as an entry-level security officer and advanced to store detective, investigator, supervisor, or manager, among other positions.

Specializations

Once a person completes an education or training program and gains experience, there are many areas of specialization available. Examples include contract security, physical security, retail security, hospital security, nuclear security, computer security, information protection, white-collar crime investigations, background investigations, undercover investigations, executive protection, anti-terrorism security, fire protection, life safety, disaster planning, and training.

Figure 15-1 The U.S. Department of Labor has identified security as one of the fastest growing occupations. Courtesy: Pinkerton's, Inc.

Figure 15-2 Many types of organizations need and employ security personnel. Courtesy: Wackenhut, Inc.

Sales

Another option is sales. For those who are good salespeople, a variety of security services, devices, and systems are available with new ones appearing each year. As covered in Chapter 2, the security industry is a multibillion dollar industry.

Security service companies provide businesses and institutions with security officers, investigators, central station monitoring, armored truck, guard dog, and consulting, among other services. The private security industry employs between 1.2 to 1.4 million people.

Security devices and systems include locks, access control systems, intrusion detection systems, CCTV, fences, doors, glazing, lighting, and safes. Salespeople are also needed for life safety and fire protection systems.

Government

Jobs are also available through government service. Federal, state, and local law enforcement agencies, as well as the military, utilize security and crime prevention personnel.

Self-Employment

Once a person has developed an expertise in security, self-employment is another avenue for one's career. Security practitioners have gone into business for themselves as private investigators, consultants, and as owners of security companies.

Self-Analysis

Before we discuss the mechanics of job-hunting skills, it is important to present the realities of job hunting.

Attitude

First of all, we must never forget that we live in a competitive world. A positive attitude toward job hunting is indispensable. This is one of the greatest assets of a job seeker. It will make or break an employment search and a career. Disappointments can be expected. A positive attitude will provide the fuel to reach career goals. Do you have a positive attitude?

Expectations

A second important point pertains to the high expectations students often establish as they complete a training program or college degree. Students are frequently idealistic. In other words, they may dream about how they will solve the world's problems with their ideas and initiative. Illustrations include, "When I get my high-paying security job, I'm really going to reduce the crime problem in this town," and "The older security people of today really don't know what they are doing. I have ideas that can reduce losses."

Fresh ideas and new strategies are good. However, when the reality of the world of work is confronted by a recent graduate, the situation can be shocking. Organizations have strict policies and procedures that must be followed. Prepared by management, these guides are formulated after considering many factors such as an experienced executive's views on the best way to operate the organization, laws (e.g., OSHA, Equal Employment Opportunity) and litigation, past mistakes made by employees, insurance requirements, and customer needs. Hopefully, the new employee can conform. You should not set your expectations too high in terms of employment position, salary, and freedom to apply ideas. A primary objective is to "get your foot in the door." You must begin your career somewhere and a low salary in an entry-level job may be the only choice at this time. However, this step could be the beginning of a rewarding career. Can you work *with* an organization and its people? Will you try to understand internal problems and exercise patience in applying your ideas?

Persistence

A third point is to never quit a job unless you find another. Stay with the job to learn about people and positive and negative aspects of organizations. Each job can be a great learning experience that will never be forgotten. Even unpleasant jobs are beneficial because they serve as a frame of reference for comparison to subsequent jobs. Cultivate good references, continue to apply job-hunting skills, and remain positive.

Career Questions

Questions concerning personal and professional goals can be difficult to answer. An individual should formulate a list of questions for self-analysis. The following guidelines are a beginning point:

1. Would I be wise to complete my education before assuming a full-time job?
2. Can I find a part-time job while attending school to build on my employment experience and ease my transition from full-time student to full-time employee?
3. Am I patient enough to stay with a job that has limitations in order to build a resume of solid experience rather than job-hopping, which can hurt my career?
4. Do I prefer working inside or outside?
5. What are my views on traveling?
6. What are my views on working second or third shift and on weekends?

7. Would being on my feet or seated for a long period of time present a problem?
8. Do I prefer to work with people or systems?
9. Do I have skills (e.g., computer, first aid, self-defense) that would make me more valuable to an employer?
10. What did previous supervisors claim to be my greatest assets?
11. What did previous supervisors claim to be my greatest weakness?

Employer Questions

Questions concerning a prospective employer should also be created. The Web, employees of the firm, and a public library are good sources of information. Here are some employer questions:

1. What is the company's (or institution's) history? How long has it existed?
2. What are the company's plans for growth?
3. What is the company's reputation?
4. Does the company furnish uniforms and equipment?
5. Who pays for any government license or registration fees?
6. What are the training opportunities? Who pays for training?
7. What are the chances for advancement?
8. What are the pay and benefits?
9. What are the advantages and disadvantages of working for the company?

Advancing within the Field

What factors can assist a person striving to advance within a chosen field? We will discuss education, training, experience, personality, and professional development, and certification. By working on each of these areas, you increase your chances for a successful career. In fact, all of these factors can be worked on at the same time. For example, a security officer working the day shift can be enrolled in an evening college course and, on a day off during the week, attend a specialized one-day training seminar on HAZMAT. The same security officer can also be using free time to study for a certification examination for security officers. Because this officer's previous performance evaluation showed one deficiency in dealing with people, the security officer is concentrating on improving human relations skills.

Education

For those who have yet to obtain a high school diploma, this should be a major goal in life. Without this basic level of education, career opportunities may be blocked in the future. Many jobs, security being one, require good basic communication skills (i.e., speaking and writing reports) learned in high school.

Beyond a high school diploma, a college degree may be the next educational step. This can be a decision filled with fear because many people believe they cannot do the academic work when in fact they can. We are often our own stumbling blocks. Besides the knowledge and skills acquired as a student, the completion of an educational program shows employers that the job applicant has the perseverance to complete a lengthy, structured program of study.

Many colleges offer one or two security courses or a one-year certificate program. For further study in security, various colleges offer a two-year associate degree or a four-year bachelor's degree. A few universities offer a master's degree in security. A closely related field of study is criminal justice.

For motivated security officers who are unable to attend college classes because of their work schedule, on-line courses are an option. However, such courses do not provide close guidance as found in traditional classroom settings. Also, students in on-line courses miss certain verbal and nonverbal information that is shared by the instructor and students in class that would not be forthcoming in an on-line course. On-line courses are challenging and for the motivated student. The student should check to ensure that the college of interest is accredited.

Students often do not realize that when they enroll in college they are *learning how to learn*. This includes skills such as how to get the most out of publications they read, how to research a topic, where to search for information, how to write a report and present it to others, and how to think critically. As a professional, these skills are essential and used as tools to "work smarter." For example, a security officer may have an assignment to train new security officers on specific topics to be covered by using a specific instructional strategy. To learn more about the assigned task, the security officer is likely to do research. Investigators often conduct research and investigate people, businesses, organizations, and assets. Supervisors, and especially managers, use critical thinking skills to improve decision making; this is especially important today with so many threats facing organizations as well as the need for superior security planning. In our information and technology age, we are in a constant state of learning new things; our learning ability and skills in this area can make or break our career.

College study also helps us to answer many "why" questions: Why do employees steal? Why are certain security strategies successful while others are not? Scientific research helps to answer the "why" questions. Training, on the other hand, emphasizes "how." How is a quality arrest conducted? How is a fire extinguisher used? Security training is conducted in-house at companies and institutions, at school district vocational schools, proprietary schools, and through college continuing education programs. A balanced education should include college courses and training.

Once a security education program is completed, the graduate does not become a security expert, nor is guaranteed a job or success in a job. These accomplishments must be earned. In fact, interpersonal friction in the workplace sometimes develops when a recent graduate begins a job working with those possessing considerable experience but limited education. Each individual should maintain a positive attitude and learn from each other. Theories and skills learned in an education program and practical experience complement each other. Both are important to develop an improved understanding of the world and to function in the world.

Training

Training programs vary considerably. Many organizations utilize short programs of a few hours or days whereby a person can learn or refine a particular skill. Training topics include interviewing, report writing, patrol techniques, law of arrest, fire protection, and so forth.

A variety of instructional strategies are available, such as lecture, discussion, demonstration, case method, and role-playing. Technology has improved the convenience and capabilities of training programs. Various computer-assisted learning mediums are available, each characterized with certain advantages and disadvantages. Whereas the traditional classroom offers an instructor who can provide guidance and feedback to students in person, computer-assisted, self-paced, and distance learning via the Internet offer a mixture of approaches in providing guidance and feedback to students. How "hands-on" and scenario training are incorporated into the choice of learning medium, plus how simulation relates to the actual job duties, should be considered.

Employers of security personnel usually conduct in-house training, especially for new officers. Also, depending on the amount of money budgeted for training, certain security officers may be selected to attend specialized seminars or training programs conducted by various security organizations and associations. Information on these programs can be obtained from the Web or security periodicals. A professional security officer should continuously seek training opportunities to improve job performance.

Experience

When an employee has successfully fulfilled the duties of a particular job, specific competencies have been added to that person's background. The person has become familiar with the job and relevant problems and solutions. At the same time, successes and mistakes produce learning experiences. Each year of experience builds upon an increasing knowledge base of the job and how to handle many different situations in the most appropriate manner, (Figure 15-3). Newer employees are likely to look to experienced personnel for guidance.

An employee's track record in a job is one of the top factors considered by supervisors during promotional decision making. Those employees who

Figure 15-3 Security officers learn from experiences on the job how to handle many different situations in the most appropriate manner. An employee's job performance impacts promotional decisions. Courtesy: Burns Security.

are rated above average in their performance evaluations are likely to be candidates for promotion.

Personality

For our purposes, personality is described as the consistent way an individual acts. For example, some people are quiet, others are talkative and outgoing, while others are abrasive and impatient. Security officers, especially, should have a pleasing personality, since the job entails considerable contact with people. Officers should be courteous, patient, friendly, helpful, and trustworthy. Those who are ill-tempered, rude, impatient, and so forth will find that the job of security will become very difficult because such a personality destroys a cooperative atmosphere. In fact, managers and supervisors have the responsibility of eliminating job applicants and employees who do not have an appropriate personality for the job or who have violent tendencies.

Personality has a great impact on a person's opportunities in life. Attitude is an integral part of one's personality. A security officer with a positive attitude is likely to put forth considerable effort to do a good job. This can become contagious in the workplace. Others enjoy working with people who are positive. Such a trait is a definite plus for promotion.

The motivation exhibited by an individual is another aspect of one's personality. A motivated person has enthusiasm to do a good job, reach goals, cooperate with coworkers, and learn as much as possible.

Security officers who possess a good attitude and are motivated are likely to perform well in their job. Areas of interest to supervisors include maintaining a clean sharp uniform, reporting to duty on time, following orders, and performing as a professional. In other words, a good personality—and all that it entails—plays a major role in opportunities for advancement.

Professional Development and Certification

To advance within the profession, security officers should seek out professional development and certification opportunities from security organizations. Such groups provide information to members, advance the goals of members, upgrade the status of security officers, enhance the public image of security, improve liaison with police, and offer training programs. Certification is an accomplishment that supports the competence of the security officer. Typically, it requires a certain amount of experience, endorsement by one who is certified, and the passing of a written examination. Professional development and certification will enhance your career opportunities.

A major force in professionalizing security officers is the International Foundation for Protection Officers (IFPO; www.ifpo.org). The IFPO offers the certified protection officer (CPO) and certified security supervisor (CSS) programs. It publishes *Protection News*, a newsletter containing current trends of the security industry, and it covers topics on life-safety and the protection of property. The IFPO website has an excellent "security surfer" with links to numerous security associations and organizations and related periodicals.

Many security supervisors and managers join the American Society for Industrial Security (ASIS; www.asisonline.org). This group does much to advance the security and loss prevention field. It offers a variety of training programs and seminars. The ASIS created the designation Certified Protection Professional (CPP) to certify security managers. Candidates must meet college and experience requirements, be endorsed by a CPP, and pass a written examination. Each month the ASIS publishes *Security Management* magazine, an excellent source of information.

For specialized security officers, specific groups are available. For instance, the International Association for Hospital Security (IAHS; www.iahss.org), is involved in the development of standards for health care security practices and training certification.

An alternative to the above IFPO "security surfer" is a good search engine. By typing school security, health care security, bank security, computer security, or whatever type of security, you will be introduced to the many specializations in this discipline. Each specialization is likely to have an association, an agenda of objectives to advance the profession, training, certification, and a periodical updating professionals on training seminars and events.

Sources of Employment Information

- *On-line services.* The Internet is expanding into the largest database of employment listings in the world. There are several advantages: a wide variety of offerings, saved time by reviewing opportunities open worldwide, more up-to-date than most publications, and the opportunity to respond electronically. Be aware that confidentiality is limited. Look for services that are free.

- *Periodicals.* Within these sources, trends in employment and employment opportunities are common topics.

- *Professional associations.* Professional organizations serve members through educational programs, publications, and a variety of strategies aimed at increasing professionalism.

- *Trade conferences.* Trade conferences, which are advertised in trade publications, are attended by people with a common interest. By attending these conferences, a security officer or student can learn about a variety of topics. Trade conferences provide an opportunity to meet practitioners who may be knowledgeable about employment opportunities or are actively seeking qualified people.

- *Educational institutions.* Security and loss prevention and criminal justice degree programs are another source of employment information. Usually these programs have bulletin boards that contain career opportunities. College or university placement services or faculty members are other valuable sources.

- *Libraries.* A wealth of information for a career search is available at libraries. Examples include periodicals, newspapers, telephone books, directories, books on career strategies, reference works on specific corporations, and on-line services.

- *Government buildings.* Public buildings often contain bulletin boards that specify employment news, especially near the human resources office. Government agencies employ security officers to maintain security and safety at government buildings and installations.

- *Newspapers.* By looking under "security" in classified sections, listings for many entry-level positions can be found. In large urban newspapers, more specialized positions are listed.

- *Public employment agencies.* These agency offices operate in conjunction with the U.S. Employment Service of the Department of Labor. Personnel will provide employment information without cost and actually contact recruiters or employers.

- *Networking.* An informal network consists of people the applicant knows from past educational or employment experiences. It is a good idea for any professional to maintain contact, however slight, with peers. When employment-related problems develop and solutions are difficult to obtain, networking may be an avenue for answers. Likewise, this mutual assistance is applicable to employment searches.

- *Telephone books.* Both private and public entities, their addresses and telephone numbers, are abundant in telephone books. By looking up "security," "guards," "investigators," and "government offices," one can develop a list of possible employment opportunities.

- *Private employment agencies.* Almost all urban areas have private employment agencies that charge a fee. This source probably will be a last resort, and one should carefully study financial stipulations. At times, these agencies have fee-paid jobs, which means that the employer pays the fee.

Application Form

A job seeker should look at an application form as one of several screening tools used by an employer. Completing an application form is a serious matter. Several obvious and subtle questions are answered by the job seeker when completing an application. Besides the standard questions, such as name, address, and telephone number, found in application forms, several other questions may not be obvious. Some subtle questions include:

- Can the applicant follow directions?
- Can the applicant organize thoughts?
- Can the applicant print, spell, and prepare a sentence?
- Is the applicant neat?
- Is the applicant consistent with written and verbal answers to questions?

Since the completion of an application form is a primary screening tool used by employers, it must be properly completed. Consider the following recommendations:

1. Try to obtain an extra copy of the application form or make a photocopy. This is helpful to prepare a rough draft and to prevent mistakes

or changes. Some employers may require you to complete an application at home and bring it to the interview. Prior to the interview, the application is collected and another identical application is required to be completed. The second one is then compared with the first one for signs of deception.

2. Read the entire application before printing or typing.

3. Follow directions very carefully and be neat.

4. Use a dictionary for correct spelling and usage of words.

5. Complete all questions on the form. If a question does not pertain to you, print "NA" (not applicable) in the blank.

6. Be honest. A background investigation may reveal incorrect information later and dismissal may result.

7. Research may be required to answer all the questions. If you have to contact previous employers, maintain proper records for future applications.

8. If you must complete the application form on the premises, make sure you bring all necessary information with you. This includes employment and educational records, social security number, driver's license, birth certificate, and so forth.

9. Remember that when you are on the premises to request an application form, you will be observed in your manner of speaking, dress, and other clues to your personality and the behavior you would exhibit on the job.

10. On the application, note any volunteer work or other activities that relate, even indirectly, to the job for which you are applying.

11. Include a copy of your resume, educational accomplishments, letters of recommendation, awards, and so forth.

12. Ask a friend to proofread your application before mailing it.

13. Make a photocopy for reference.

14. Do not procrastinate or send the application in late.

15. Contact the employer to make sure your application arrived and is in the hands of the correct person.

16. Make follow-up contacts with the employer to reinforce your continued interest in the job.

Cover Letter

A cover letter is sent with a resume to a prospective employer. The purpose of a cover letter is to introduce the employer to the resume. It should spark the interest of the reader while highlighting the background of the applicant.

The cover letter (Figure 15-4) begins with the *heading* that is composed of the return address and the date. Both are typed in the top right corner of

---

1122 Clinton Street
New York, NY 10021
June 11, 2002

Mr. Frank Gibson
Personnel Specialist
Midtown Medical Center
New York, NY 10022

Dear Mr. Gibson,

This letter is in response to your June 11 ad in the *New York Observer* for security officers.

On June 2, I completed an Associates Degree in Security at Brooklyn Community College. During the past two years, I have worked part-time as a security officer for Eastside Medical Center. The enclosed resume provides a complete description of my background.

I am willing to provide additional information, and I am available for an interview at your convenience.

Thank you for your consideration.

Sincerely yours,

Anthony M. Rivera

AR
Enclosure

Figure 15-4   Sample cover letter.

the page. The *inside address* is typed next about five lines below the heading and to the extreme left. It includes the name, title, and business address of the person to whom you are writing. The *salutation* (or *greeting*) is typed two lines below the inside address and is typically stated as "Dear Mr. (or Ms.) Smith," for example. The *body* of the letter is next and discusses the purpose of the letter in paragraph form. The first paragraph states what motivated you to write the letter and the position of interest. The second paragraph includes a general summary of your education and experience. The last paragraph requests an interview. Finally, the *signature*, in line with the heading, provides your typed name above which your handwritten signature is located.

The following list provides additional guidelines to prepare a cover letter.

1. Type the cover letter, unless the employer requests a handwritten letter.
2. Double-check the letter for neatness and errors. The letter is a reflection of your work. It should not contain any errors. Ask a friend or educator to evaluate and provide feedback on your letter.
3. Avoid using a printer that produces a sloppy letter.
4. Use plain English and avoid jargon.
5. Always type each letter individually if you are contacting several employers.
6. Never send a photocopy of a cover letter. Keep a copy of each letter sent for your records.
7. Limit the cover letter to one page.
8. Do not repeat the resume contents in the cover letter. In other words, state the most important educational and employment accomplishments.

Resume

Resume means summary of your life, specifically your work history and professional record. It is a tool for marketing yourself to a prospective employer through a description of your experience, education, and skills (Figure 15-5). A job seeker should carefully prepare a resume since it is a major factor in reaching the interview stage.

The following list provides guidelines to prepare a resume.

1. Use standard $8\frac{1}{2}'' \times 11''$ white paper. Do *not* type on the back of the page.
2. A resume should be one or two pages. Be concise.
3. List your most recent education and experience first, then go backwards.
4. Examples of headings for resumes are education, experience, military or volunteer experience, awards and honors, community service, and personal data.
5. Never use a relative as a reference. When references are used, they must have a title and place of employment. Obtain permission from each reference.

RESUME

Anthony Michael Rivera
(212) 555-1599   1122 Clinton Street
AMRivera@scootmail.com   New York, NY 10021

EDUCATION

2000 – 2002   Brooklyn Community College, 9582 Henry Street, Brooklyn, NY 10025

Associate Degree

Major: Security. Courses included: Criminal Law, Search and Seizure, Firearms,

Crime Prevention, Safety, Fire Protection, Public Relations, and Report Writing.

1996-2000   Brooklyn South High School, 1466 New York Avenue, Brooklyn, NY 11785.

General Diploma

EXPERIENCE

2000 –   Eastside Medical Center, 212 Remsen Avenue, Queens, NY 11612

Present   *Security Officer:* Work part-time during evenings and on weekends

in emergency room. Perform patrol and stationary post duties.

Help to mediate disputes and assist with arrests.

1998 – 2000   Harvey's Thriftway, 972 Green Street, Brooklyn, NY 11519

Stock Worker: Worked part-time after school and on weekends.

Unloaded trucks and stocked shelves.

EXTRACURRICULAR ACTIVITIES

Served as tutor for high school social studies students (1997 – 1999)

Business Club (1999 – 2000)

HOBBIES

Sports, Reading, Music

REFERENCES

Available on Request

Figure 15-5   Sample resume.

6. Do not state a salary in your resume.
7. Design your resume so it is appealing to the reader. Use margins and headings.
8. Use action verbs to describe your experience. Some examples of action verbs are assisted, served, and performed.
9. Do not use abbreviations.

10. Always be honest and do not exaggerate. Most employers are aware of the serious problems of falsified resumes and applications. Background investigations are often conducted by employers to verify applicant background information.

11. A resume should contain absolutely no errors. Proofread it thoroughly at least twice and ask another person to check it.

12. Save a copy of the resume in your computer so it can be easily updated.

13. Copies should be of good quality.

14. Always send a cover letter with each resume.

Interview

A job interview is a formal meeting where the employer and the applicant learn more about each other. Such an opportunity shows the employer's interest in the applicant. An applicant should do everything within reason to convince the employer that he or she is the best choice for the job. This entails many factors such as a good appearance, being able to communicate well, and good human relations skills.

By following the guidelines presented here, you will increase the chances for a successful interview and the possibility of an employment opportunity.

1. Before the interview, obtain information about the organization. The Web and libraries are a good source for the history of companies, products or services, number of employees, income, and so forth. Such information can impress the interviewer.

2. Conduct a mock interview at home. If possible, use an audiovisual system to record and play back.

3. Try to estimate the salary range before the interview. Speak to some employees. When you are asked about salary during the interview, politely turn the question back to the interviewer and ask, "What do you usually pay for someone with my education and experience?" If the interviewer requests an answer to the original question, state a salary slightly above what you understand to be the range.

4. Prepare positive answers to these questions that are often asked:

    a. What are your strengths?

    b. What are your weaknesses? Always keep this answer positive. Examples: "I have been accused of being a workaholic." "Once I begin a project I have a difficult time taking a break until the project is completed."

    c. Why do you want to work for our company?

    d. How can you contribute to our company?

    e. Where do you want to be five years from now?

   f. How would you describe yourself?

   g. How did previous employers treat you? (Remain positive.)

   h. Name a problem you have encountered and how you dealt with it? ("On the job, when working on difficult assignments, I seek guidance from more experienced coworkers." "On difficult academic assignments, I force myself to take a break for a few minutes each hour to refresh my mind.")

   i. What causes you to lose your temper? ("This is something not part of my general personality. Such behavior is inappropriate for security work. I act as a professional.")

5. As an interviewee, you may want to ask these questions:

   a. If I obtain the job, what would my responsibilities and duties be?

   b. What are the hours and location?

   c. Is there a training program? Do I get paid during training?

   d. Are there opportunities for advancement?

   e. Does the company supply uniforms and equipment at no charge?

   f. Does the company pay for license and registration fees?

   g. Will I be required to join a union?

   h. Are there any costs that I would have to incur as an employee?

6. Dress conservatively since you are going to an important business meeting. Jacket and tie for males and pants-suit or skirt for females.

7. Proper grooming and hygiene are vital. Examples are neat hair and clothes and clean fingernails.

8. Do not smoke or chew gum. Some employers do not hire those who smoke.

9. Avoid strong after-shave lotion or perfume. Do not obtain self-service gasoline before the interview. Scents can transfer to the interviewer, for example, during a handshake.

10. Go to the interview alone.

11. Bring extra copies of your resume, diplomas, and transcripts. Do not forget information on references and your social security card.

12. Bring two pens and a piece of paper. You may have to complete forms and take notes.

13. Double check the time of the interview, directions, and schedules of public transportation. If you are driving, check the condition of your vehicle.

14. Leave early to allow time for delay. *Never* arrive late.

15. Arrive at least ten minutes early.

16. Remain calm while waiting and during the interview. Nervousness is normal. Take a few deep breaths (without being obvious) to reduce nervousness, and concentrate on relaxing your body. Dry a damp hand prior to shaking hands.

17. Always look at the interviewer in the eye but do not stare.

18. Do not slouch.

19. Maintain a positive attitude.

20. Think carefully before speaking.

21. Speak clearly and slowly.

22. Do not place too much emphasis on salary. Ask about it toward the end of the interview.

23. Avoid being overbearing and aggressive.

24. Do not condemn past employers or teachers.

25. Avoid using slang language.

26. The interviewer may make you wait several minutes for the interview to test your patience.

27. Silence may be used by the interviewer after you answer a question to make you feel uncomfortable so you will state additional information. Wait for the next question.

28. Express appreciation for the interview.

29. Before departing, ask when you can expect to hear about the job opening.

30. Follow up the interview with a thank you letter to restate your interest in the job. This reminds the interviewer about you.

31. Remain positive. Do not become discouraged if you are not selected. Several interviews are often required before obtaining a job. All people who have worked hard and advanced have faced rejection. This whole process is a learning experience.

Selection Process

Although the application, resume, and interview are major screening tools used by employers, there are several other methods that help employers make the best choice among applicants. Paper-and-pencil tests can prove knowledge and intelligence, mental health, and honesty. Drug tests will expose the use of illegal substances. A background investigation and credit check will help verify information provided by the applicant. A physical examination can support fitness for the job. The extent of the screening process will depend on the organization and the type of position.

The best approach for a job hunter is to apply to many locations. Comply with the screening methods required by each employer. Maintain a positive attitude even after numerous rejections. Make the job hunt a full-time job and do not give up. Most job seekers face numerous rejections in their life, knowing that they will eventually find a job. And after a job is obtained, never quit until another job is found. While waiting, cultivate experience and references. Good luck on your career!

CHAPTER REVIEW

A. Multiple Choice

1. The number of people employed in private security is
   a. about 500,000.
   b. over 1,000,000.
   c. under 100,000.
   d. about 60,000.
2. Select the source of employment information that should be used as a last resort.
   a. private employment agencies
   b. professional associations
   c. government offices
   d. on-line associations
3. The purpose of a cover letter is to
   a. praise the employer.
   b. praise the job applicant.
   c. provide a complete description of one's education and experience.
   d. introduce the employer to the resume.
4. Which of the following is least likely to be included in a cover letter?
   a. what motivated you to write the letter
   b. the position of interest
   c. a request for an interview
   d. salary
5. When asked about your weaknesses during a job interview, always
   a. state that you have none.
   b. turn the question back to the interviewer.
   c. keep the answer positive.
   d. be honest by discussing personal life experiences.

B. True or False

1. Older security personnel usually have limited practical knowledge of security when compared to recent college graduates.
2. Never work part-time when pursuing an education.
3. The Web contains a wealth of information for the job seeker.
4. When completing an application, a job seeker is actually answering several obvious and hidden questions.
5. One or two mistakes on a cover letter or resume are permissible.

Applications

Application 15A

Prepare a cover letter and a resume by following the guidelines presented in this chapter.

Application 15B

Conduct a mock employment interview.

Application 15C

Conduct research in the community on contract security companies, proprietary security organizations, and criminal justice agencies. Interview personnel to find out about job requirements and job openings. Each student should collect information on at least five organizations and prepare a report to the class.

Glossary: Legal Terms

Accessory: A person who in some way helps in the commission of a crime without being present.

Accomplice: A person involved with another in the commission of a crime.

Accusation: A formal charge made to a court stating that a person is guilty of a crime, subject to later adjudication.

Acquittal: A decision by a judge or jury that the accused is innocent.

Adjudication: A judgment or decision usually made by a court.

Administrative law: Rules, regulations, and decisions made by administrative agencies who are delegated power by legislative acts. The Occupational Safety and Health Administration is an example of an administrative agency.

Admission: A self-incriminating statement that falls short of an acknowledgement of guilt.

Affidavit: A written statement of fact, signed and sworn to before a person permitted by law to administer an oath.

Aid and abet: To knowingly assist or encourage someone to commit a crime.

Appeal: To petition a higher court to review the judgment of a lower court to correct an injustice.

Arraignment: An initial court hearing where a defendant is informed of the charge, of his or her rights, and required to enter a plea.

Arrest: The apprehension of a subject to answer criminal charges before a magistrate.

Bail: Money or property put up to allow the release of a person from jail until trial.

Bench warrant: A judicial order issued for the arrest of a subject usually for not appearing in court.

Best evidence: The highest level of evidence available for a case; original evidence rather than a copy.

Booking: Official administrative recording of an arrest that includes the arrestee's name and address and the crime charged. Photographing and fingerprinting are also part of this process.

Bribery: The giving or receiving of anything of value in order to influence a public official.

Burden of proof: The duty to prove the charge or facts.

Common law: Judge-made or case law developed over many years in English and American courts.

Complaint: A formal charge that an offense has been committed by the person named. Under civil procedure, a pleading (i.e., facts and claims) must be filed in court to commence civil action.

Compounding a felony: Accepting money or other gain in exchange for not prosecuting a felon.

Confession: A voluntary statement of guilt to a crime.

Contraband: Things that are illegal to possess, import, or export.

Conviction: The judgment of a criminal trial in which a defendant is found guilty. A conviction can result from a jury verdict, a judge, or a guilty plea offered by a defendant.

Damages: Money ordered by a court to be paid to a person who sustained a loss caused by another person.

Deposition: Sworn testimony reduced to writing.

Discovery: A method by which opposing parties to a criminal or civil legal action may obtain all factual information in possession of opposing parties.

Double jeopardy: A second prosecution after a first trial for the same offense. The Fifth Amendment of the Bill of Rights prohibits double jeopardy.

Due process of law: Rights guaranteed by the Bill of Rights; rules for the protection of individual rights and liberties and for fair legal proceedings.

Duress: Unlawful pressure on a person to do what would not have been done otherwise.

Dying declaration: Words of a person aware of imminent death; admissible as hearsay evidence in certain courts.

Entrapment: Government officials inducing a person to commit a crime not contemplated by him or her so criminal charges can be filed against the person. Entrapment is illegal in most cases and is a legal defense.

Exclusionary rule: The prohibition of the use of illegally seized evidence in criminal proceedings.

Fresh (or hot) pursuit: In police terminology, the close pursuit of a fleeing suspect.

Grand jury: A body of persons selected and sworn to investigate criminal activity and the conduct of public officials and to hear evidence to decide whether sufficient evidence exists to bring a person to trial.

Hearsay evidence: Testimony by a witness based upon information from another, rather than from personal knowledge or observation. Usually inadmissible in court with some exceptions (dying declaration).

Inadmissible: Evidence that cannot be admitted in court.

Incriminate: Exposing oneself or another to prosecution for a crime usually through incriminating statements.

Indictment: A formal accusation of a crime made by a grand jury upon the request of a prosecutor.

Information: A formal accusation of a crime made by a prosecutor.

Injunction: A judge's order to a person to do or to refrain from doing an act that would injure another.

Inquest: A coroner's hearing concerning the cause of death.

Intent: A person's resolve to do some act and reach a particular result.

Jurisdiction: The geographic area, the types of cases, or the particular persons over which legal action may be exercised.

Magistrate: Federal or state judicial officer; a judge.

Mens rea: Guilty mind; criminal intent.

Modus operandi: Method of operation; the way in which a criminal committed a crime.

Motive: The reason for committing a crime.

Negligence: Failure to exercise reasonable care in a situation that causes harm to someone or something.

No bill: A refusal by a grand jury to issue an indictment.

Nolo contendere: A defendant's plea of "no contest" in a criminal case where the defendant does not directly admit guilt but accepts sentencing. This plea has the same effect as a guilty plea, however such a plea may not be used against the defendant in a subsequent civil suit resulting from the same criminal act.

Nol pros: A prosecutor decides not to prosecute a case further.

Parens patriae: The legal doctrine that gives the government the power to serve as guardian over people with legal disabilities such as children and those who are incompetent or insane.

Parole: Release from prison prior to completing a sentence but subject to supervised conditions. Probation permits a convicted person to avoid confinement, subject to supervised conditions.

Perjury: A false statement under oath or affirmation, willfully made in regard to a material fact.

Petition: A written request to a court to take specific action; used in some states in place of "complaint" as the first pleading in a lawsuit; in juvenile court, the document that serves to accuse a child with having committed an offense.

Plaintiff: A person who initiates a lawsuit.

Plea: A defendant's formal response to a criminal charge (i.e., guilty, not guilty, or no contest); also a defendant's response to a lawsuit.

Plea bargain: An agreement between the prosecutor and the defense attorney, subject to court approval, usually involving a reduction in the charge against the defendant in exchange for a guilty plea to the lesser charge.

Pleadings: The opposing written statements of each party to a lawsuit.

Precedent: A court decision that sets a standard to follow when a subsequent case arises with a similar question of law and similar facts.

Preliminary hearing: A hearing to determine whether there is sufficient probable cause to bring the accused to trial.

Preponderance of evidence: Greater weight of evidence and believability of facts. This is the standard of proof required in civil cases that is less than required in criminal cases.

Probable cause: The amount of evidence required that would cause a reasonable person to believe that an individual probably committed a crime; more than a mere suspicion.

Proof beyond a reasonable doubt: The standard of proof required in criminal cases: the prosecutor must prove beyond a reasonable doubt that the accused committed the crime; the highest level of proof required in any type of trial.

Proximate cause: The real cause of an injury, accident, or loss.

Recidivism: Repeated criminal behavior especially following imprisonment.

Restitution: Court requirement that an offender pay money or perform services to compensate a victim.

Status offense: Conduct declared by statute to be an offense only when committed by a juvenile (e.g., truancy).

Statute of limitations: Time limit in which civil or criminal action can be brought against a person.

Subpoena: A court order to a person commanding attendance in court to testify or to produce certain documents.

Summons: A court order commanding a party to appear in court to defend a complaint in an action against him. Failure to appear can result in losing the suit.

Venue: The area where a case can be tried. A judge may decide on a "change of venue" when it is argued that an impartial trial is impossible.

Verdict: The decision of the jury in a jury trial or of the judge in a nonjury trial.

Vicarious liability: Indirect legal responsibility such as the liability of an employer for the acts of an employee.

Glossary: Intrusion Alarm Systems

Access control: The control of pedestrian and vehicular traffic through entrances and exits of a protected area or premises.

Access mode: The operation of an alarm system such that no alarm signal is given when the protected area is entered; however, a signal may be given if the sensor, annunciator, or control unit is tampered with or opened.

Accumulator: A circuit that accumulates a sum. For example, in an audio alarm control unit, the accumulator sums the amplitudes of a series of pulses, which are larger than some threshold level, subtracts from the sum at a predetermined rate to account for random background pulses, and initiates an alarm signal when the sum exceeds some predetermined level. This circuit is also called an integrator; in digital circuits it may be called a counter.

Active intrusion sensor: An active sensor that detects the presence of an intruder within the range of the sensor. Examples are an ultrasonic motion detector, a radio frequency motion detector, and a photoelectric alarm system. *See also* Passive intrusion sensor.

Active sensor: A sensor that detects the disturbance of a radiation field generated by the sensor. *See also* Passive sensor.

Actuator: A manual or automatic switch or sensor such as holdup button, magnetic switch, or thermostat that causes a system to transmit an alarm signal when manually activated or when the device automatically senses an intruder or other unwanted condition.

Air gap: The distance between two magnetic elements in a magnetic or electromagnetic circuit, such as between the core and the armature of a relay.

Alarm: An alarm device or an alarm signal.

Alarm circuit: An electrical circuit of an alarm system that produces or transmits an alarm signal.

Alarm condition: A threatening condition, such as an intrusion, fire, or holdup, sensed by a detector.

Alarm device: A device that signals a warning in response to an alarm condition, such as a bell, siren, or annunciator.

Alarm discrimination: The ability of an alarm system to distinguish between those stimuli caused by an intrusion and those that are a part of the environment.

Alarm line: A wired electrical circuit used for the transmission of alarm signals from the protected premises to a monitoring station.

Alarm signal: A signal produced by a control unit indicating the existence of an alarm condition.

Alarm state: The condition of a detector that causes a control unit in the secure mode to transmit an alarm signal.

Alarm station: (1) A manually actuated device installed at a fixed location to transmit an alarm signal in response to an alarm condition, such as a concealed holdup button in a bank teller's cage. (2) A well-marked emergency control unit, installed in fixed locations usually accessible to the public, used to summon help in response to an alarm condition. The control unit contains either a manually actuated switch or telephone connected to fire or police headquarters, or a telephone answering service. *See also* Remote station alarm system.

Alarm system: An assembly of equipment and devices designated and arranged to signal the presence of an alarm condition requiring urgent attention such as unauthorized entry, fire, temperature rise, and so forth. The system may be local, police connection, central station, or proprietary.

Annunciator: An alarm monitoring device that consists of a number of visible signals such as "flags" or lamps indicating the status of the detectors in an alarm system or systems. Each circuit in the device is usually labeled to identify the location and condition being monitored. In addition to the visible signal, an audible signal is usually associated with the device. When an alarm condition is reported, a signal is indicated visibly, audibly, or both. The visible signal is generally maintained until reset either manually or automatically.

Answering service: A business that contracts with subscribers to answer incoming telephone calls after a specified delay or when scheduled to do so. It may also provide other services such as relaying fire or intrusion alarm signals to proper authorities.

Area protection: Protection of the inner space or volume of a secured area by means of a volumetric sensor.

Area sensor: A sensor with a detection zone that approximates an area, such as a wall surface or the exterior of a safe.

Audible alarm device: (1) A noisemaking device such as a siren, bell, or horn used as part of a local alarm system to indicate an alarm condition. (2) A bell, buzzer, horn or other noisemaking device used as a part of an annunciator to indicate a change in the status or operating mode of an alarm system.

Audio frequency (sonic): Sound frequencies within the range of human hearing, approximately 15 to 20,000 Hz.

Audio monitor: An arrangement of amplifiers and speakers designed to monitor the sounds transmitted by microphones located in the protected area. Similar to an annunciator, except that supervisory personnel can monitor the protected area to interpret the sounds.

Authorized access switch: A device used to make an alarm system or some portion or zone of a system inoperative in order to permit authorized access through a protected port. A shunt is an example of such a device.

B. A.: The abbreviation for burglar alarm.

Beam divergence: In a photoelectric alarm system, the angular spread of the light beam.

Break alarm: (1) An alarm condition signaled by the opening or breaking of an electrical circuit. (2) The signal produced by a break alarm condition (sometimes referred to as an open circuit alarm or trouble signal, designed to indicate possible system failure).

Bug: (1) To plant a microphone or other sound sensor or to tap a communication line for the purpose of concealed listening or audio monitoring; loosely, to install a sensor in a specified location. (2) The microphone or other sensor used for the purpose of concealed listening.

Building security alarm system: The system of protective signaling devices installed at a premise.

Burglar alarm (B. A.) pad: A supporting frame laced with fine wire or a fragile panel located with foil or fine wire and installed so as to cover an exterior opening in a building, such as a door, or skylight. Entrance through the opening breaks the wire or foil and initiates an alarm signal. *See also* Grid.

Burglary: The unlawful entering of a structure with the intent to commit a felony or theft.

Cabinet-for-safe: A wooden enclosure having closely spaced electrical grids on all inner surfaces and contacts on the doors. It surrounds a safe and initiates an alarm signal if an attempt is made to open or penetrate the cabinet.

Capacitance: The property of two or more objects that enables them to store electrical energy in an electric field between them.

Capacitance alarm system: An alarm system in which a protected object is electrically connected as a capacitance sensor. The approach of an intruder causes sufficient change in capacitance to upset the balance of the system and initiate an alarm signal. Also called proximity alarm system.

Capacitance sensor: A sensor that responds to a change in capacitance in a field containing a protected object or in a field within a protected area.

Carrier current transmitter: A device that transmits alarm signals from a sensor to a control unit via the standard AC power lines.

Central station: A control center to which alarm systems in a subscriber's premises are connected, where circuits are supervised, and where personnel are maintained continuously to record and investigate alarm or trouble signals. Facilities are provided for reporting alarms to police and fire departments or to other outside agencies.

Central station alarm system: An alarm system, or group of systems, the activities of which are transmitted to, recorded in, maintained by, and supervised from a central station. This differs from proprietary alarm systems in that the central station is owned and operated independently of the subscriber.

Circumvention: The defeat of an alarm system by the avoidance of its detection devices, such as by jumping over a pressure sensitive mat, by entering through a hole cut in an unprotected wall rather than through a protected door, or by keeping outside the range of an ultrasonic motion detector. Circumvention contrasts with spoofing.

Closed circuit system: A system in which the sensors of each zone are connected in series so the same current exists in each sensor. When an activated sensor breaks the circuit or the connecting wire is cut, an alarm is transmitted for that zone.

Clutch head screw: A mounting screw with a uniquely designed head for which the installation and removal tool is not commonly available. They are used to install alarm system components so that removal is inhibited.

Coded-alarm system: An alarm system in which the source of each signal is identifiable. This is usually accomplished by means of a series of current pulses which operate audible or visible annunciators or recorders or both, to yield a recognizable signal. This is usually used to allow the transmission of multiple signals on a common circuit.

Coded cable: A multiconductor cable in which the insulation on each conductor is distinguishable from all others by color or design. This assists in identification of the point of origin or final destination of a wire.

Coded transmitter: A device for transmitting a coded signal when manually or automatically operated by an actuator. The actuator may be housed with the transmitter or a number of actuators may operate a common transmitter.

Coding siren: A siren with an auxiliary mechanism to interrupt the flow of air through its principal mechanism, enabling it to produce a controllable series of sharp blasts.

Combination sensor alarm system: An alarm system that requires the simultaneous activation of two or more sensors to initiate an alarm signal.

Constant ringing drop (CRD): A relay that when activated even momentarily will remain in an alarm condition until reset. A key is often required to reset the relay and turn off the alarm.

Contact: (1) Each of the pair of metallic parts of a switch or relay that by touching or separating make or break the electrical current path. (2) A switch-type sensor.

Contact device: A device that when actuated opens or closes a set of electrical contacts; a switch or relay.

Contact microphone: A microphone designed for attachment directly to a surface of a protected area or object; usually used to detect surface vibrations.

Contactless vibrating bell: A vibrating bell whose continuous operation depends upon application of an alternating current, without circuit-interrupting contacts such as those used in vibrating bells operated by direct current.

Control unit: A device, usually electronic, that provides the interface between that alarm system and the human operator and produces an alarm signal when its programmed response indicates an alarm condition. Some or all of the following may be provided for: power for sensors, sensitivity adjustments, means to select and indicate access mode or secure mode, monitoring for line supervision and tamper devices, timing circuits, for entrance and exit delays, transmission of an alarm signal, and so forth.

Covert: Hidden and protected.

Cross alarm: (1) An alarm condition signaled by crossing or shorting an electrical circuit. (2) The signal produced due to a cross alarm condition.

Crossover: An insulated electrical path used to connect foil across window dividers, such as those found on multiple pane windows, to prevent grounding and to make a more durable connection.

Dark current: The current output of a photoelectric sensor when no light is entering the sensor.

Defeat: The frustration, counteraction, or thwarting of an alarm device so it fails to signal an alarm when a protected area is entered. Defeat includes both circumvention and spoofing.

Detection range: The greatest distance at which a sensor will consistently detect an intruder under a standard set of conditions.

Detector: (1) A sensor such as those used to detect intrusion, equipment malfunctions or failure, rate of temperature rise, smoke or fire. (2) A demodulator, a device to recover the modulating function or signal from a modulated wave, such as that used in a modulated photoelectric alarm system. *See also* Photoelectric alarm system, modulated.

Differential pressure sensor: A sensor used for perimeter protection that responds to the difference between the hydraulic pressures in two liquid-filled tubes buried just below the surface of the earth around the exterior perimeter of the protected area. The pressure difference can indicate an intruder walking or driving over the buried tubes.

Door cord: A short, insulated cable with an attaching block and terminals at each end used to conduct current to a device, such as foil, mounted on the movable portion of a door or window.

Door trip switch: A mechanical switch mounted so movement of the door will operate the switch.

Doppler effect (shift): The apparent change in frequency of sound or radio waves when reflected from or originating from a moving object. Utilized in some types of motion sensors.

Double-circuit system: An alarm circuit in which two wires enter and two wires leave each sensor.

Double drop: An alarm signaling method often used in central station alarm systems in which the line is first opened to produce a break alarm and then shorted to produce a cross alarm.

Drop: (1) *See* Annunciator. (2) A light indicator on an annunciator.

Duress alarm device: A device that produces either a silent alarm or local alarm under a condition of personnel stress such as holdup, fire, illness, or other panic or emergency. The device is normally manually operated and may be fixed or portable.

Duress alarm system: An alarm system that employs a duress alarm device.

DWBA: The abbreviation for direct wire burglar alarm. *See* Alarm line.

E-field sensor: A passive sensor that detects changes in the earth's ambient electric field caused by the movement of an intruder. *See also* H-field sensor.

Electrical: Related to, pertaining to, or associated with electricity.

Electromagnetic: Pertaining to the relationship between current flow and magnetic field.

Electromagnetic interference (EMI): Impairment of the reception of a wanted electromagnetic signal by an electromagnetic disturbance. This can be caused by lightning, radio transmitters, power line noise, and other electrical devices.

Electromechanical bell: A bell with a prewound spring-driven striking mechanism; the operation is initiated by the activation of an electric tripping mechanism.

Electronic: Related to, or pertaining to, devices that utilize electrons moving through a vacuum, gas, or semiconductor, and to circuits or systems containing such devices.

Entrance delay: The time between actuating a sensor on an entrance door or gate and the sounding of a local alarm or transmission of an alarm signal by the control unit. This delay is used if the authorized access switch is located within the protected area and permits a person with the control key to enter without causing an alarm. The delay is provided by a timer within the control unit.

E.O.L.: The abbreviation for end of line.

Exit delay: The time between turning on a control unit and the sounding of a local alarm or transmission of an alarm signal upon actuation of a sensor on an exit door. This delay is used if the authorized access switch is located within the protected area and permits a person with the control key to turn on the alarm system and to leave through a protected door or gate without causing an alarm. The delay is provided by a timer within the control unit.

Fail safe: A feature of a system or device that initiates an alarm or trouble signal when the system or device either malfunctions or loses power.

False alarm: An alarm signal transmitted in the absence of an alarm condition. These may be classified according to causes: environmental, e.g., rain, fog, wind, hail, lightning, temperature; animals, e.g., rats, dogs, cats, insects; equipment malfunction, e.g., transmission errors, component failure; operator error; and unknown.

False alarm rate, monthly: The number of false alarms per installation per month.

False alarm ratio: The ratio of false alarms to total alarms; may be expressed as a percentage or as a simple ratio.

Fence alarm: Any of several types of sensors used to detect the presence of an intruder near a fence or any attempt by the intruder to climb over, go under, or cut through the fence.

Field: The space or area in which there exists a force produced by an electrically charged object, a current, or a magnet.

Floor trap: A trap installed that detects the movement of a person across a floor space, such as a trip wire switch or mat switch.

Foil: Thin metallic strips that are cemented to a protected surface (usually glass in a window or door), and connected to a closed electrical circuit. If the protected material is broken so as to break the foil, the circuit opens, initiating an alarm signal. Also called tape. A window, door, or other surface to which foil has been applied is said to be taped or foiled.

Foil connector: An electrical terminal block used on the edge of a window to join interconnecting wire to window foil.

Foot rail: A holdup alarm device, often used at cashiers' windows, in which a foot is placed under the rail, lifting it, to initiate an alarm signal.

Glassbreak vibration detector: A vibration detection system that employs a contact microphone attached to a glass window to detect cutting or breakage of the glass.

Grid: (1) An arrangement of electrically conducting wire, screen, or tubing placed in front of doors or windows or both that is used as a part of a capacitance sensor. (2) A lattice of wooden dowels or slats concealing fine wires in a closed circuit that initiates an alarm signal when forcing or cutting the lattice breaks the wires. Used over accessible openings. Sometimes called a protective screen. *See also* Burglar alarm pad. (3) A screen or metal plate, connected to earth ground, sometimes used to provide a stable ground reference for objects protected by a capacitance sensor. If placed against the walls near the protected object, it prevents the sensor sensitivity from extending through the walls into areas of activity.

H-field sensor: A passive sensor that detects changes in the earth's ambient magnetic field caused by the movement of an intruder. *See also* E-field sensor.

Heat sensor: (1) A sensor that responds to either a local temperature above a selected value, a local temperature increase that is at a rate of increase greater than a preselected rate (rate of rise), or both. (2) A sensor that responds to infrared radiation from a remote source such as a person.

Holdup: A robbery involving the threat to use a weapon.

Holdup alarm device: A device that signals a holdup. The device is usually hidden and may be manually or automatically actuated, fixed, or portable. *See also* Duress alarm device.

Holdup alarm system, automatic: An alarm system that employs a holdup alarm device, in which the signal transmission is initiated solely by the action of the intruder, such as a money clip in a cash drawer.

Holdup alarm system, manual: A holdup alarm system in which the signal transmission is initiated by the direct action of the person attacked or of an observer of the attack.

Holdup button: A manually actuated mechanical switch used to initiate a duress alarm signal; usually constructed to minimize accidental activation.

Hood contact: A switch used for the supervision of a closed safe or vault door. Usually installed on the outside surface of the protected door.

Impedance: The opposition to the flow of alternating current in a circuit.

Impedance matching: Making the impedance of a terminating device equal to the impedance of the circuit to which it is connected in order to achieve optimum signal transfer.

Infrared (IR) motion detector: A sensor that detects changes in the infrared light radiation from parts of the protected area. Presence of an intruder in the area changes the infrared light intensity from his direction.

Interior perimeter protection: A line of protection along the interior boundary of a protected area including all points through which entry can be effected.

Intrusion: Unauthorized entry into the property of another.

Intrusion alarm system: An alarm system to signal the entry or attempted entry of a person or an object into the area or volume protected by the system.

Ionization smoke detector: A smoke detector in which a small amount of radioactive material ionizes the air in the sensing chamber, thus rendering it conductive and permitting a current to flow through the air between two charged electrodes. This effectively gives the sensing chamber an electrical conductance. When smoke particles enter the ionization area, they decrease the conductance of the air by attaching themselves to the ions causing a reduction in mobility. When the conductance is less than a predetermined level, the detector circuit responds.

IR: The abbreviation for infrared.

Jack: An electrical connector used for frequent connect and disconnect operations; for example, to connect an alarm circuit at an overhang door.

Lacing: A network of fine wire surrounding or covering an area to be protected, such as a safe, vault, or glass panel, and connected into a closed circuit system. The network of wire is concealed by a shield such as concrete or paneling so that an attempt to break through the shield breaks the wire and initiates an alarm.

Light intensity cutoff: In a photoelectric alarm system, the percent reduction of light that initiates an alarm signal at the photoelectric receiver unit.

Line amplifier: An audio amplifier used to provide preamplification of an audio alarm signal before transmission of the signal over an alarm line. Use of an amplifier extends the range of signal transmission.

Line sensor (detector): A sensor with a detection zone that approximates a line or series of lines, such as a photoelectric sensor that senses a direct or reflected light beam.

Line supervision: Electronic protection of an alarm line accomplished by sending a continuous or coded signal through the circuit. A change in the circuit characteristics, such as a change in impedance due to the circuit having been tampered with, will be detected by a monitor. The monitor initiates an alarm if the change exceeds a predetermined amount.

Local alarm: An alarm that when activated makes a loud noise (*see* Audible alarm device) at or near the protected area or floods the site with light or both.

Local alarm system: An alarm system that when activated produces an audible or visible signal in the immediate vicinity of the protected premises or object. This term usually applies to systems designed to provide only a local warning of intrusion and not to transmit to a remote monitoring station. However, local alarm systems are sometimes used with a remote alarm.

Loop: An electric circuit consisting of several elements, usually switches, connected in series.

Magnetic alarm system: An alarm system that will initiate an alarm when it detects changes in the local magnetic field. The changes could be caused by motion of ferrous objects such as guns or tools near the magnetic sensor.

Magnetic sensor: A sensor that responds to changes in magnetic field. *See also* Magnetic alarm system.

Magnetic switch: A switch that consists of two separate units: a magnetically actuated switch, and a magnet. The switch is usually mounted in a fixed position (door jamb or window frame) opposing the magnet, which is fastened to a hinged or sliding door, window, etc. When the movable section is opened, the magnet moves with it, actuating the switch.

Magnetic switch, balanced: A magnetic switch that operates using a balanced magnetic field in such a manner as to resist defeat with an external magnet. It signals an alarm when it detects either an increase or decrease in magnetic field strength.

Matching network: A circuit used to achieve impedance matching. It may also allow audio signals to be transmitted to an alarm line while blocking direct current used locally for line supervision.

Mat switch: A flat area switch used on open floors or under capering. It may be sensitive over an area of a few square feet or several square yards.

McCulloh circuit (loop): A supervised single wire loop connecting a number of coded transmitters located in different protected areas to a central station receiver.

Mechanical switch: A switch in which the contacts are opened and closed by means of a depressible plunger or button.

Mercury fence alarm: A type of mercury that is sensitive to the vibration caused by an intruder climbing on a fence.

Mercury switch: A switch operated by tilting or vibrating that causes an enclosed pool of mercury to move, making or breaking physical and electrical contact with conductors. These are used on tilting doors and windows, and on fences.

Microwave alarm system: An alarm system that employs radio frequency motion detectors operating in the microwave frequency region of the electromagnetic spectrum.

Microwave frequency: Radio frequencies in the range of approximately 1.0 to 300 GHz.

Monitor cabinet: An enclosure that houses the annunciator and associated equipment.

Monitoring station: The central station or other area at which guards, police, or commercial service personnel observe annunciators and registers reporting on the condition of alarm systems.

Motion sensor: A sensor that responds to the motion of an intruder. *See also* Infrared motion detector; Radio frequency motion detector; Sonic motion detector; Ultrasonic motion detector.

Multiplexing: A technique for the concurrent transmission of two or more signals in either or both directions, over the same wire, carrier, or other communication channel. The two basic multiplexing techniques are time division multiplexing and frequency division multiplexing.

Multiplexing, frequency division (FDM): The multiplexing technique that assigns to each signal a specific set of frequencies (called a channel) within the larger block of frequencies available on the main transmission path in much the same way that many radio stations broadcast at the same time but can be separately received.

Multiplexing, time division (TDM): The multiplexing technique that provides for the independent transmission of several pieces of information on a time-sharing basis by sampling, at frequent intervals, the data to be transmitted.

NICAD: (Contraction of "nickel cadmium.") A high performance, long-lasting rechargeable battery, with electrodes made of nickel and cadmium, which may be used as an emergency power supply for an alarm system.

Nonretractable (one-way) screw: A screw with a head designed to permit installation with an ordinary flat bit screwdriver but which resists removal. They are used to install alarm system components so that removal is inhibited.

Normally closed (NC) switch: A switch in which the contacts are closed when no external forces act upon the switch.

Normally open (NO) switch: A switch in which the contacts are open (separated) when no external forces act upon the switch.

Open-circuit system: A system in which the sensors are connected in parallel. When a sensor is activated, the circuit is closed, permitting a current that activates an alarm signal.

Passive intrusion sensor: A passive sensor in an intrusion alarm system that detects an intruder within the range of the sensor. Examples are a sound sensing detection system, a vibration detection system, an infrared motion detector, and an E-field sensor.

Passive sensor: A sensor that detects natural radiation or radiation disturbances, but does not itself emit the radiation on which its operation depends.

Passive ultrasonic alarm system: An alarm system that detects the sounds in the ultrasonic frequency range caused by an attempted forcible entry into a protected structure. The system consists of microphones, a control unit containing an amplifier, filters, an accumulator, and a power supply. The unit's sensitivity is adjustable so that ambient noises or normal sounds will not initiate an alarm signal; however, noise above the preset level or a sufficient accumulation of impulses will initiate an alarm.

Percentage supervision: A method of line supervision in which the current in or resistance of a supervised line is monitored for changes. When the change exceeds a selected percentage of the normal operating current or resistance in the line, an alarm signal is produced.

Perimeter alarm system: An alarm system that provides perimeter protection.

Perimeter protection: Protection of access to the outer limits of a protected area, by means of physical barriers, sensors on physical barriers, or exterior sensors not associated with a physical barrier.

Permanent circuit: An alarm circuit capable of transmitting an alarm signal whether the alarm control is in access mode or secure mode. Used, for example, on foiled fixed windows, tamper switches, and supervisory lines. *See also* Permanent protection; Supervisory alarm system; Supervisory circuit.

Permanent protection: A system of alarm devices such as foil, burglar alarm pads, or lacings connected in a permanent circuit to provide protection whether the control unit is in the access mode or secure mode.

Photoelectric alarm system: An alarm that employs a light beam and photoelectric sensor to provide a line of protection. Any interruption of the beam by an intruder is sensed by the sensor. Mirrors may be used to change the direction of the beam. The maximum beam length is limited by many factors, some of which are the light source intensity, number of mirror reflections, detector sensitivity, beam divergence, fog, and haze.

Photoelectric alarm system, modulated: A photoelectric alarm system in which the transmitted light beam is modulate in a predetermined manner and in which the receiving equipment will signal an alarm unless it receives the properly modulated light.

Photoelectric beam type smoke detector: A smoke detector with a light source that projects a light beam across the area to be protected onto a photoelectric cell. Smoke between the light source and the receiving cell reduces the light reaching the cell, causing actuation.

Photoelectric sensor: A device that detects a visible or invisible beam of light and responds to its compete or nearly complete interruption. *See also* Photoelectric alarm system and Photoelectric alarm system, modulated.

Photoelectric spot type smoke detector: A smoke detector that contains a chamber with covers that prevent the entrance of light but allow the entrance of smoke. The chamber contains a light source and a photosensitive cell placed so light is blocked from it. When smoke enters, the smoke particles scatter and reflect the light into the photosensitive cell, causing an alarm.

Police connection: The direct link by which an alarm system is connected to an annunciator installed in a police station. Examples of a police connection are an alarm line or a radio communications channel.

Police station unit: An annunciator that can be placed in operation in a police station.

Portable duress sensor: A device carried on a person that may be activated in an emergency to send an alarm signal to a monitoring station.

Portable intrusion sensor: A sensor that can be installed quickly and that does not require the installation of dedicated wiring for the transmission of its alarm signal.

Positive noninterfering (PNI) and successive alarm system: An alarm system that employs multiple alarm transmitters on each alarm line (like McCulloh loop) such that in the event of simultaneous operation of several transmitters, one of them takes control of the alarm line, transmits its full signal, then releases the alarm line for successive transmission by other transmitters that are held inoperative until they gain control.

Pressure alarm system: An alarm system that protects a vault or other enclosed space by maintaining and monitoring a predetermined air pressure differential between the inside and outside of the space. Equalization of pressure resulting from opening the vault or cutting through the enclosure will be sensed and will initiate an alarm signal.

Printing recorder: An electromechanical device used at a monitoring station that accepts coded signals from alarm lines and converts them to an alphanumeric printed record of the signal received.

Proprietary alarm system: An alarm system similar to a central station alarm system, except that the annunciator is located in a constantly guarded room maintained by the owner for internal security operations. The guards monitor the system and respond to all alarm signals or alert local law enforcement agencies or both.

Protected area: An area monitored by an alarm system or guards, or enclosed by a suitable barrier.

Protected port: A point of entry such as a door, window, or corridor monitored by sensors connected to an alarm system.

Protection device: (1) A sensor such as a grid, foil, contact, or photoelectric sensor connected into an intrusion alarm system. (2) A barrier that inhibits intrusion, such as a grille, lock, fence, or wall.

Protection, exterior perimeter: A line of protection surrounding but somewhat removed from a facility. Examples are fences, barrier walls, or patrolled points of a perimeter.

Protective signaling: The initiation, transmission, and reception of signals involved in the detection and prevention of property loss due to fire, burglary, or other destructive conditions. Also, the electronic supervision of persons and equipment concerned with this detection and prevention. *See also* Line supervision; Supervisory alarm system.

Radar alarm system: An alarm system that employs radio frequency motion detectors.

Radio frequency interference (RFI): Electromagnetic interference in the radio frequency range.

Radio frequency motion detector: A sensor that detects the motion of an intruder by using a radiated radio frequency electromagnetic field. The device operates by sensing a disturbance in the generated RF field caused by intruder motion, typically a modulation of the field referred to as a Doppler effect, which is used to initiate an alarm signal. Most radio frequency motion detectors are certified by the FCC for operation as "field disturbance sensors" at one of the following frequencies: 0.915 GHz (L-Band), 2.45 GHz (S-Band), 5.8 GHz (X-Band), 10.525 GHz (X-Band), and 22.125 GHz (K-Band). Units operating in the microwave frequency range are usually called microwave motion detectors.

Reed switch: A type of magnetic switch consisting of contacts formed by two thin movable magnetically actuated metal vanes or reeds, held in a normally open position within a sealed glass envelope.

Register: An electromechanical device that marks a paper tape in response to signal impulses received from transmitting circuits. A register may be driven by a prewound spring mechanism, an electric motor, or a combination of these.

Register, inking: A register that marks the tape with ink.

Register, punch: A register that marks the tape by cutting holes in it.

Register, slashing: A register that marks the tape by cutting V-shaped slashes in it.

Remote alarm: An alarm signal that is transmitted to a remote monitoring station. *See also* Local alarm.

Remote station alarm system: An alarm system that employs remote alarm stations usually located in building hallways or on city streets.

Reset: To restore a device to its original (normal) condition after an alarm or trouble signal.

Resistance bridge smoke detector: A smoke detector that responds to the particles and moisture present in smoke. These substances reduce the resistance of an electrical bridge grid and cause the detector to respond.

Retard transmitter: A coded transmitter in which a delay period is introduced between the time of actuation and the time of signal transmission.

RFI: The abbreviation for radio frequency interference.

Robbery: The felonious or forcible taking of property by violence, threat, or other overt felonious act in the presence of the victim.

Secure mode: The condition of an alarm system in which all sensors and control units are ready to respond to an intrusion.

Seismic sensor: A sensor, generally buried under the surface of the ground for perimeter protection, that responds to minute vibrations of the earth generated as an intruder walks or drives within its detection range.

Sensor: A device designed to produce a signal or offer indication in response to an event or stimulus within its detection zone.

Shunt: (1) A deliberate shorting-out of a portion of an electric circuit. (2) A key operated switch that removes some portion of an alarm system for operation, allowing entry into a protected area without initiating an alarm signal. A type of authorized access switch.

Silent alarm: A remote alarm without an obvious local indication that an alarm has been transmitted.

Silent alarm system: An alarm system that signals a remote station by means of a silent alarm.

Single circuit system: An alarm circuit that routes only one side of the circuit through each sensor. The return may be through either ground or a separate wire.

Single-stroke bell: A bell that is struck once each time its mechanism is activated.

Smoke detector: A device that detects visible or invisible products of combustion. *See also* Ionization smoke detector; Photoelectric beam type smoke detector; Photoelectric spot type smoke detector; Resistance bridge smoke detector.

Solid state: (1) An adjective used to describe a device such as a semiconductor transistor or diode. (2) A circuit or system that does not rely on vacuum or gas filled tubes to control or modify voltages and currents.

Sonic motion detector: A sensor that detects the motion of an intruder by the disturbance of an audible sound pattern generated within the protected area.

Sound sensing detection system: An alarm system that detects the audible sound caused by an attempted forcible entry into a protected structure. The system consists of microphones and a control unit containing an amplifier, accumulator, and a power supply. The unit's sensitivity is adjustable so that ambient noises or normal sounds will not initiate an alarm signal. However, noises above this preset level or a sufficient accumulation of impulses will initiate an alarm.

Sound sensor: A sensor that responds to sound; a microphone.

Spoofing: The defeat or compromise of an alarm by "tricking" or "fooling" its detection devices such as by short-circuiting part or all of a series circuit, cutting wires in a parallel circuit, reducing the sensitivity of a sensor, or entering false signals into the system. Spoofing contrasts with circumvention.

Spot protection: Protection of objects such as safes, art objects, or anything of value that could be damaged or removed from the premises.

Spring contact: A device employing a current-carrying cantilever spring that monitors the position of a door or window.

Standby power supply: Equipment that supplies power to a system in the event the primary power is lost. It may consist of batteries, charging circuits, auxiliary motor generators, or a combination of these devices.

Strain gauge alarm system: An alarm system that detects the stress caused by the weight of an intruder as the intruder moves about a building. Typical uses include placement of the strain gauge sensor under a floor joist or under a stairway tread.

Strain gauge sensor: A sensor that, when attached to an object, will provide an electrical response to an applied stress upon the object, such as a bending, stretching, or compressive force.

Strain sensitive cable: An electrical cable designed to produce a signal whenever the cable is strained by a change in applied force. Typical uses include mounting it in a wall to detect an attempted forced entry through the wall, or fastening it to a fence to detect climbing on the fence, or burying it around a perimeter to detect walking or driving across the perimeter.

Subscriber's equipment: That portion of a central station alarm system installed on the protected premises.

Subscriber's unit: A control unit of a central station alarm system.

Supervised lines: Interconnecting lines in an alarm system that are electrically supervised against tampering. *See also* Line supervision.

Supervisory alarm system: An alarm that monitors conditions or persons or both and signals any deviation from an established norm or schedule. Examples are the monitoring of signals from guard patrol stations for irregularities in the progression along a prescribed patrol route, and the monitoring of production or safety conditions such as sprinkler water pressure, temperature, or liquid level.

Supervisory circuit: An electrical circuit or radio path that sends information on the status of a sensor or guard patrol to an annunciator. For intrusion alarm systems, this circuit provides line supervision and monitors tamper devices. *See also* Supervisory alarm system.

Surveillance: (1) Control of premises for security purposes through alarm systems, closed circuit television (CCTV), or other monitoring methods. (2) Supervision or inspection of industrial processes by monitoring those conditions that could cause damage if not corrected. *See also* Supervisory alarm system.

Tamper device: (1) Any device, usually a switch, used to detect an attempt to gain access to intrusion alarm circuitry, such as by removing a switch cover. (2) A monitor circuit to detect any attempt to modify the alarm circuitry, such as by cutting a wire.

Tamper switch: A switch installed to detect attempts to remove the enclosure of some alarm system components such as control box doors, switch covers, junction box covers, or bell housings. The alarm component is then often described as being "tampered."

Tapper bell: A single-stroke bell designed to produce a sound of low intensity and relatively high pitch.

Telephone dialer, automatic: A device that, when activated, automatically dials one or more preprogrammed telephone numbers (e.g., police, fire department) and relays a recorded voice or coded message giving the location and nature of the alarm.

Telephone dialer, digital: An automatic telephone dialer that sends its message as a digital code.

Terminal resistor: A resistor used as a terminating device.

Terminating capacitor: A capacitor sometimes used as a terminating device for a capacitance sensor antenna. The capacitor allows the supervision of the sensor antenna, especially if a long wire is used as the sensor.

Terminating device: A device that is used to terminate an electrically supervised circuit. It makes the electrical circuit continuous and provides a fixed impedance reference (end of line resistor) against which changes are measured to detect an alarm condition. The impedance changes may be caused by a sensor, tampering, or circuit trouble.

Timing table: That portion of central station equipment that provides a means for checking incoming signals from McCulloh circuits.

Touch sensitivity: The sensitivity of a capacitance sensor at which the alarm device will be activated only if an intruder touches or comes in very close proximity (about 1 cm or $\frac{1}{2}$ in.) to the protected object.

Trap: (1) A device, usually a switch, installed within a protected area, that serves as secondary protection in the event a perimeter alarm system is successfully penetrated. Examples are a trip wire switch placed across a likely path for an intruder, a mat switch hidden under a rug, or a magnetic switch mounted on an inner door. (2) A volumetric sensor installed to detect an intruder in a likely traveled corridor or pathway within a security area.

Trickle charge: A continuous direct current, usually very low, applied to a battery to maintain it at peak charge or to recharge it after it has been partially or completely discharged. Usually applied to nickel cadmium (NICAD) or wet cell batteries.

Trip wire switch: A switch that is actuated by breaking or moving a wire or cord installed across a floor space.

UL Certificated: For certain types of products that have met UL requirements, for which it is impractical to apply the UL Listing Mark or Classification Marking to the individual product, a certificate is provided that the manufacturer may use to identify quantities of material for specific job sites or to identify field installed systems.

UL Listed: Signifies that production samples of the product have been found to comply with established Underwriters Laboratories requirements and that the manufacturer is authorized to use the Laboratories' Listing Marks on the listed products that comply with the requirement, contingent upon the follow-up services as a check of compliance.

Ultrasonic: Pertaining to a sound wave having a frequency above that of audible sound (approximately 20,000 Hz). Ultrasonic sound is used in ultrasonic detection systems.

Ultrasonic frequency: Sound frequencies that are above the range of human hearing; approximately 20,000 Hz and higher.

Ultrasonic motion detector: A sensor that detects the motion of an intruder through the use of ultrasonic generating and receiving equipment. The device operates by filling a space with a pattern of ultrasonic waves; the modulation of these waves by a moving object is detected and initiates an alarm signal.

Underdome bell: A bell in which most of its mechanism is concealed by its gong.

Underwriter Laboratories, Inc. (UL): A private independent research and testing laboratory that tests and lists various items meeting good practice and safety standards.

Vibrating bell: A bell whose mechanism is designed to strike repeatedly and for as long as it is activated.

Vibration detection system: An alarm system that employs one or more contact microphones or vibration sensors that are fastened to the surfaces of the area or object being protected to detect excessive levels of vibration. The contact microphone system consists of microphones, a control unit containing an amplifier and an accumulator, and a power supply. The unit's sensitivity is adjustable so that ambient noises or normal vibrations will not initiate an alarm signal. In the vibration sensor system, the sensor responds to excessive vibration by opening a switch in a closed circuit system.

Vibration sensor: A sensor that responds to vibrations of the surface on which it is mounted. It has a normally closed switch that will momentarily open when it is subjected to a vibration with sufficiently large amplitude. Its sensitivity is adjustable to allow for the different levels of normal vibration, to which the sensor should not respond, at different locations. *See also* Vibration detection system.

Visual signal device: A pilot light, annunciator or other device that provides a visual indication of the condition of the circuit or system being supervised.

Volumetric sensor: A sensor with a detection zone that extends over a volume such as an entire room, part of a room, or a passageway. Ultrasonic motion detectors and sonic motion detectors are example of volumetric sensors.

Walk test light: A light on motion detectors that comes on when the detector senses motion in the area. It is used while setting the sensitivity of the detector and during routine checking and maintenance.

Watchman's reporting system: A supervisory alarm system arranged for the transmission of a patrolling watchman's regularly recurrent report signals from stations along the patrol route to a central supervisory agency.

Zoned circuit: A circuit that provides continual protection for parts or zones of the protected area while normally used doors and windows or zones may be released for access.

Zones: Smaller subdivisions into which large areas are divided to permit selective access to some zones while maintaining other zones secure and to permit pinpointing the specific location from which an alarm signal is transmitted.

Glossary: Locks

Ace lock: A type of pin tumbler lock in which the pins are installed in a circle around the axis of the cylinder and move perpendicularly to the face of the cylinder. The shear line of the driver and bottom tumblers is a plane parallel to the face of the cylinder. This type of lock is operated with a push key.

Active door (or leaf): The leaf of a double door that must be opened first and that is used in normal pedestrian traffic. This leaf is usually the one in which a lock is installed.

Anchor: A device used to secure a building part or component to adjoining construction or to a supporting member. May be a floor anchor, jamb anchor, or stud anchor.

Antifriction latch: A latch bolt that incorporates any device that reduces the closing friction between the latch and the strike.

Armored front: A plate or plates that is secured to the lock front of a mortised lock by machine screws to provide protection against tampering with the cylinder set screws; also called armored face plate.

Auxiliary lock: A lock installed on a door or window to supplement a previously installed primary lock; also called a secondary lock. It can be a mortised, bored, or rim lock.

Back plate: A metal plate on the inside of a door that is used to clamp a pin or disc tumbler rim lock cylinder to the door by means of retaining screws. The tail piece of the cylinder extends through a hole in the back plate.

Barrel key: A key with a bit projecting from a round, hollow key shank that fits on a post in the lock.

Barricade bolt: A massive metal bar that engages large strikes on both sides of a door. Barricade bolts are available with locking devices and are completely removed from the door when not in use.

Bevel (of a latch bolt): A term used to indicate the direction in which a latch bolt is inclined: regular bevel for doors opening in, reverse bevel for doors opening out.

Bevel (of a lock front): The angle of a lock front when not at a right angle to the lock case, allowing the front to be applied flush with the edge of a beveled door.

Bicentric pin tumbler cylinder: A cylinder having two cores and two sets of pins, each having different combinations. This cylinder requires two separate keys, used simultaneously, to operate it. The cam or tail piece is gear operated.

Bit: A blade projecting from a key shank that engages with and actuates the bolt or level tumblers of a lock.

405

Bit key: A key with a bit projecting from a round shank. Similar to the barrel key but with a solid rather than hollow shank.

Bolt: The part of a lock that, when actuated, is projected (or "thrown") from the lock into a retaining member, such as a strike plate, to prevent a door or window from moving or opening. *See also* Dead bolt; Flush bolt; Latch.

Bolt projection (bolt throw): The distance from the edge of the door, at the bolt centerline, to the furthest point on the bolt in the projected position.

Bored lock (or latch): A lock or latch whose parts are intended for installation in holes bored in a door. *See also* Key-in-knob lock.

Bottom pin: One of the pin tumblers that determines the combination of a pin tumbler cylinder and is directly contacted by the key. They are varied in length and usually tapered at one end, enabling them to fit into the "V" cuts made in a key. When the proper key is inserted, the bottom pins level off at the cylinder core shearline, allowing the core to turn and actuate the lock.

Box strike: A strike plate that has a metal box or housing to fully enclose the projected bolt and/or latch.

Bumping: A method to open a pin tumbler lock by vibrations produced by a wooden or rubber mallet.

Buttress lock: A lock that secures a door by wedging a bar between the door and the floor. Some incorporate a movable steel rod that fits into metal receiving slots on the door and in the floor. Also called police bolt/brace.

Cam: The part of a lock or cylinder that rotates to actuate the bolt or latch as the key is turned. The cam may also act as the bolt.

Cam, lazy: A cam that moves less than the rotation of the cylinder core.

Cane bolt: A heavy cane-shaped bolt with the top bent at right angles; used on the bottom of doors.

Case: The housing in which a lock mechanism is mounted and enclosed.

Chain bolt: A vertical spring-loaded bolt mounted at the top of a door. It is manually actuated by a chain.

Chain door interviewer: An auxiliary locking device that allows a door to be opened slightly, but restrains it from being fully opened. It consists of a chain with one end attached to the door jamb and the other attached to a keyed metal piece which slides in a slotted metal plate attached to the door. Some chain door interviewers incorporate a keyed lock operated from the inside.

Change key: A key that operates only one lock or a group of keyed-alike locks, as distinguished from a master key. *See also* Keyed-alike cylinders; Master key system.

Combination: (1) The sequence and depth of cuts on a key. (2) The sequence of numbers to which a combination lock is set.

Connecting bar: A flat metal bar attached to the core of a cylinder lock to operate the bolt mechanism.

Construction master keying: A keying system used to allow the use of a single key for all locks during the construction of large housing project. In one such system, the cylinder cores of all locks contain an insert that permits the use of a special master key. When the dwelling unit is completed, the insert is removed and the lock then accepts its own change key and no longer accepts the construction master key.

Crash bar: The cross bar or level of a panic exit device that serves as a push bar to actuate the lock. *See also* Panic hardware.

Cremone bolt: A surface-mounted device that locks a door or sash into the frame at both the top and bottom when a knob or lever is turned.

Cut: An indention made in a key to make it fit a pin tumbler of a lock. Any notch made in a key is known as a cut, whether it is square, round, or V-shaped; also called bitting.

Cylinder: The cylindrical subassembly of a lock, including the cylinder housing, the cylinder core, the tumbler mechanism, and the keyway.

Cylinder core (or plug): The central part of a cylinder, containing the keyway, that is rotated to operate the lock bolt.

Cylinder guard ring: A hardened metal ring, surrounding the exposed portion of a lock cylinder, that protects the cylinder from being wrenched, turned, pried, cut, or pulled with attack tools.

Cylinder housing: The external case of a lock cylinder; also called the cylinder shell.

Cylinder lock: A lock in which the locking mechanism is controlled by a cylinder. A double cylinder lock has a cylinder on both the interior and exterior of the door.

Cylinder, mortise type: A lock cylinder that has a threaded housing which screws directly into the lock case, with a cam or other mechanism engaging the locking mechanism.

Cylinder, removable core: A cylinder whose core may be removed by the use of a special key.

Cylinder, rim type: A lock cylinder that is held in place by tension against its rim, applied by screws from the interior face of the door.

Cylinder screw: A set screw that holds a mortise cylinder in place and prevents it from being turned after installation.

Dead bolt: A lock bolt that does not have an automatic spring action and a bevelled end as opposed to a latch bolt, which does. The bolt must be actuated to a projected position by a key or thumb turn and when projected is locked against return by end pressure.

Dead latch: A spring-actuated latch bolt having a bevelled end and incorporating a feature that automatically locks the projected latch bolt against return by end pressure.

Dead lock: A lock equipped with a dead bolt.

Disk tumbler: A spring-loaded flat plate that slides in a slot which runs through the diameter of the cylinder. Inserting the proper key lines up the disk tumblers with the lock's shear line and enables the core to be turned.

Dogging device: A mechanism that fastens the cross bar of a panic exit device in the fully depressed position, and retains the latch bolt or bolts in the retracted position to permit free operation of the door from either side.

Dogging key: A key-type wrench used to lock down, in the open position, the cross bar of a panic exit device.

Double-bitted key: A key having cuts on two sides.

Double-throw bolt: A bolt that can be projected beyond its first position, into a second, or fully extended one.

Double-throw lock: A lock incorporating a double-throw bolt.

Driver pin: One of the pin tumblers in a pin tumbler cylinder lock, usually flat on both ends, that is in line with and pushes against the flat ends of the bottom pins. They are projected by individual coil springs into the cylinder core until they are forced from the core by the bottom pins when the proper key is inserted into the keyway.

Drop ring: A ring handle attached to the spindle that operates a lock or latch. The ring is pivoted to remain in a dropped position when not in use.

Electric strike: An electrically operated device that replaces a conventional strike plate and allows a door to be opened by using electric switches at remote locations.

Escutcheon plate: A surface-mounted cover plate, either protective or ornamental, containing openings for any or all of the controlling members of a lock such as the knob, handle, cylinder, or keyhole.

Face plate: The part of a mortise lock through which the bolt protrudes and by which the lock is fastened to the door.

Fence: A metal pin that extends from the bolt of a lever lock and prevents retraction of the bolt unless it is aligned with the gates of the lever tumblers.

Filler plate: A metal plate used to fill unwanted mortise cutouts in door or frame.

Flush bolt: A door bolt so designed that, when installed, the operating handle is flush with the face or edge of the door. Usually installed at the top and bottom of the inactive door of a double door.

Foot bolt: A type of bolt applied at the bottom of a door and arranged for foot operation. Generally, the bolt head is held up by a spring when the door is unbolted.

Grand master key: A key designed to operate all locks under several master keys in a system.

Hold-back feature: A mechanism on a latch that serves to hold the latch bolt in the retracted position.

Jamb: The exposed vertical member on either side of a door or window opening.

Jamb peeling: A technique used in forced entry to deform or remove portions of the jamb to disengage the bolt from the strike. *See also* Jimmying.

Jamb/strike: That component of a door assembly that receives and holds the extended lock bolt. The strike and jamb are considered a unit.

Jamb/wall: That component of a door assembly to which a door is attached and secured by means of the hinges. The wall and jamb are considered a unit.

Jimmying: A technique used in forced entry to pry the jamb away from the lock edge of the door a sufficient distance to disengage the bolt from the strike.

Jimmy-pin: A sturdy projecting screw, which is installed in the hinge edge of a door near a hinge, fits into a hole in the door jamb, and prevents removal of the door if the hinge pins are removed.

Key: An implement used to actuate a lock bolt or latch into the locked or unlocked position.

Key changes: The different combinations that are available or that can be used in a specific cylinder.

Keyed-alike cylinders: Cylinders that are designed to be operated by the same key. (Not to be confused with master-keyed cylinders.)

Keyed-different cylinders: Cylinders requiring different keys for their operation.

Keyhole: The opening in a lock designed to receive the key.

Key-in knob lock: A lock having the key cylinder and the other lock mechanism, such as a push or turn button, contained in the knobs.

Key plate: A plate or escutcheon having only a keyhole.

Keyway: The longitudinal cut in the cylinder core, being an opening or space with millings in the sides identical to those on the proper key, thus allowing the key to enter the full distance of the blade. *See also* Warded lock.

Knob latch: A securing device having a spring bolt operated by a knob only.

Latch (or latch bolt): A beveled, spring-actuated bolt that may or may not include a dead-locking feature.

Lever lock: A key-operated lock that incorporates one or more lever tumblers, which must be raised to a specific level so that the fence of the bolt is aligned with the gate of the tumbler in order to withdraw the bolt. Lever locks are commonly used in storage lockers and safety deposit boxes.

Lever tumbler: A flat metal arm, pivoted on one end with a gate in the opposite end. The top edge is spring-loaded. The bitting of the key rotates against the bottom edge, raising the lever tumbler to align the gate with the bolt fence. Both the position of the gate and the curvature of the bottom edge of the lever tumbler can be varied to establish the key code.

Lip (of a strike): The curved projecting part of a strike plate that guides the spring bolt to the latch point.

Lock: A fastener that secures a door or window assembly against unauthorized entry. A door lock is usually key-operated and includes the keyed device (cylinder or combination), bolt, strike plate, knobs or levers, trip items, and so forth.

Lock clip: A flexible metal part attached to the inside of a door face to position a mortise lock.

Lock edge: The vertical edge or stile of a door in which a lock may be installed; also called the leading edge, the lock stile, and the strike edge.

Lock edge door (or lock seam door): A door that has its face sheets secured in place by an exposed mechanical interlock seam on each of its two vertical edges.

Lock pick: A tool or instrument, other than the specifically designed key, made for the purpose of manipulating a lock into a locked or unlocked condition.

Lock rail: The horizontal member of a door intended to receive the lock case.

Lock reinforcement: A reinforcing plate attached inside of the lock stile of a door to receive a lock.

Loiding: A burglary attack method in which a thin, flat, flexible object such as a stiff piece of plastic is inserted between the strike and the latch bolt to depress the latch bolt and release it from the strike. Derived from the world "celluloid"; also called knifing and slip-knifing.

Maison keying: A specialized keying system, used in apartment houses and other large complexes, that enables all individual unit keys to operate common-use locks such as main entry, laundry room, and so forth.

Master disk tumbler: A disk tumbler that will operate with a master key in addition to its own change key.

Master key system: A method of keying locks that allows a single key to operate multiple locks, each of which will also operate with an individual change key. Several levels of master keying are possible: a single master key operates all locks of a group of locks with individual change keys; a grand master key operates all locks of two or more master key systems; a great grand master key operates all locks of two or more grand master key systems. Master key systems are used primarily with pin and disk tumbler locks, and to a limited extent with level or warded locks.

Master pin: A segmented pin used to enable a pin tumbler to be operated by more than one key cut.

Mortise: A rectangular cavity made to receive a lock or other hardware: also, the act of making such a cavity.

Mortise bolt: A bolt designed to be installed in a mortise rather than on the surface. The bolt is operated by a knob, a lever, or their equivalent.

Mortise lock: A lock designed for installation in a mortise, as distinguished from a bored lock and a rim lock.

Mushroom tumbler: A type of tumbler used in pin tumbler locks to add security against picking. The diameter of the driving pin behind the end in contact with the bottom pin is reduced so that the mushroom head will catch the edge of the cylinder body at the shear line when it is at a slight angle to its cavity. *See also* Spool tumbler.

Night latch: An auxiliary lock having a spring-latch bolt and functioning independently of the regular lock of the door.

One-way screw: A screw specifically designed to resist being removed, once installed.

Panic hardware: An exterior door locking mechanism that is always operable from inside the building by pressing on a crash bar or lever.

Pin tumbler: One of the essential, distinguishing components of a pin tumbler lock cylinder, more precisely called a bottom pin, master pin, or driver pin. The pin tumblers, used in varying lengths and arrangements, determine the combination of the cylinder. *See also* Bottom pin; Driver pin; Master pin.

Pin tumbler lock cylinder: A lock cylinder employing metal pins (tumblers) to prevent the rotation of the core until the correct key is inserted into the keyway. Small coil compression springs hold the pins in the locked position until the key is inserted.

Plug retainer: The part often fixed to the rear of the core in a lock cylinder to retain or hold the core firmly in the cylinder.

Preassembled lock: A lock that has all the parts assembled into a unit at the factory and, when installed in a rectangular section cut out of the door at the lock edge, requires little or no assembly; also called integral lock, mono lock, and unit lock.

Pressed padlock: A padlock whose outer case is pressed into shape from sheet metal and then riveted together.

Privacy lock: A lock, usually for an interior door, secured by a button, thumbturn, and so forth, and not designed for key operation.

Push key: A key that operates the Ace type of lock.

Restricted keyway: A special keyway and key blank for high security locks, with a configuration that is not freely available and that must be specifically requested from the manufacturer.

Reversible lock: A lock that may be used for either hand of a door.

Rim cylinder: A pin or disk tumbler cylinder used with a rim lock.

Rim latch: A latch installed on the surface of a door.

Rim lock: A lock designed to be mounted on the surface of a door.

Rotary interlocking dead bolt lock: A type of rim lock in which the extended dead bolt is rotated to engage with the strike.

Shear line: The joint between the shell and the core of a lock cylinder; the line at which the pins or discs of a lock cylinder must be aligned in order to permit rotation of the core.

Shell: A lock cylinder, exclusive of the core; also called housing.

Slide bolt: A simple lock that is operated directly by hand without using a key, a turnpiece, or other actuating mechanism. Slide bolts can normally only be operated from the inside.

Spool tumbler: A type of tumbler used in pin tumbler locks to add security against picking. Operates on the same principles as the mushroom tumbler.

Stop (of a lock): A button or other device that serves to lock and unlock a latch bolt against actuation by the outside knob or thumb piece. Another type holds the bolt retracted.

Strike: A metal plate attached to or mortised into a door jamb to receive and hold a projected latch bolt and/or dead bolt to secure the door to the jamb.

Strike, dustproof: A strike that is placed in the threshold or sill of an opening or in the floor to receive a flush bolt and is equipped with a spring-loaded follower to cover the recess and keep out dirt.

Strike, interlocking: A strike that receives and holds a vertical, rotary, or hook dead bolt.

Strike reinforcement: A metal plate attached to a door or frame to receive a strike.

Strike roller: A strike for latch bolts, having a roller mounted on the lip to reduce friction.

Stud: A slender wood or metal post used as a supporting element in a wall or partition.

Swinging bolt: A bolt that is hinged to a lock front and is projected and retracted with a swinging rather than a sliding action; also called hinged or pivot bolt.

Tail piece: The unit on the core of a cylinder lock that actuates the bolt or latch.

Tension wrench: An instrument used in picking a lock. It is used to apply torsion to the cylinder core.

Three-point lock: A locking device required on "A-label" fire double doors to lock the active door at three points—the normal position plus top and bottom.

Transom catch: A latch bolt fastener on a transom, having a ring by which the latch bolt is retracted.

Tryout keys: A set of keys that includes many commonly used bittings. They are used one at a time in an attempt to unlock a door.

Tumbler: A movable obstruction in a lock that must be adjusted to a particular position, as by a key, before the bolt can be thrown.

Vertical bolt lock: A lock having two dead bolts that move vertically into two circular receivers in the strike portion of the lock attached to the door jamb.

Ward: An obstruction that prevents the wrong key from entering or turning in a lock.

Warded lock: A lock containing internal obstacles that block the entrance or rotation of all but the correct key.

(Source: Law Enforcement Standards Laboratory, National Institute of Law Enforcement and Criminal Justice, U.S. Department of Justice.)

References

Chapter 1: Historical Development of Security

Brinton, Crane, et al. 1973. *Civilization in the West.* Englewood Cliffs, NJ: Prentice-Hall, p. 167.

Cunningham, William C., and Todd H. Taylor. 1985. *Private Security and Police in America: The Hallcrest Report.* Portland, OR: Chancellor Press. (Study completed by Hallcrest Systems, Inc., and funded by the U.S. Department of Justice; commonly called *The Hallcrest Report.*)

Germann, A.C., et al. 1974. *Introduction to Law Enforcement and Criminal Justice.* Springfield, IL: Charles C Thomas, p. 56.

Greer, William. 1979. *A History of Alarm Security.* Washington, DC: National Burglar & Fire Alarm Association, pp. 25–28.

Post, Richard S., and Arthur A. Kingsbury. 1977. *Security Administration.* Springfield, IL: Charles C Thomas, p. 31.

Purpura, Philip. 2002. *Security & Loss Prevention: An Introduction,* 4th ed. Boston, MA: Butterworth-Heinemann.

Purpura, Philip. 2001. *Police & Community: Concepts & Cases.* Boston, MA: Allyn & Bacon, pp. 1–24.

Shelden, Randall. 2001. *Controlling the Dangerous Classes.* Boston, MA: Allyn & Bacon, p. 84.

Stead, P. 1983. *The Police of France.* New York: Macmillan, pp. 14–15.

Ursic, Henry S., and Leroy E. Pagano. 1974. *Security Management Systems.* Springfield, IL: Charles C Thomas, p. 7.

Chapter 2: Security: Business, Functions, and Professionalism

Bilek, Arthur J. 1976. *Report of the Task Force on Private Security.* Washington, DC: U.S. Government Printing Office, pp. 123–124, 245–246, 282–306. (Study supported by the U.S. Department of Justice.)

Bureau of Justice Statistics. 1999. www.ojp.usdoj.gov/bjs. February 20, 2001.

Cressey, Donald. 1971. *Other People's Money: A Study in the Social Psychology of Embezzlement.* Belmont, CA: Wadsworth.

Cunningham, William C., and Todd H. Taylor. 1985. *Private Security and Police in America: The Hallcrest Report.* Portland, OR: Chancellor Press.

Cunningham, William, et al. August 1991. *Private Security: Patterns and Trends.* Washington, DC: National Institute of Justice.

Cunningham, William, et al. 1990. *Private Security Trends: 1970–2000, The Hallcrest Report II.* Boston, MA: Butterworth-Heinemann.

Felson, Marcus. 1998. *Crime and Everyday Life: Insights and Implications for Society.* Thousand Oaks, CA: Pine Forge Press.

Newman, Oscar. 1972. *Defensible Space.* New York: Macmillan.

Purpura, Philip. 2002. *Security & Loss Prevention: An Introduction,* 4th ed. Boston, MA: Butterworth-Heinemann.

Schnabolk, Charles. 1983. *Physical Security: Practices and Technology.* Stoneham, MA: Butterworth, p. 22.

Security 37. January 2000. "Law Enforcement Count Dwarfed by Private Security," p. 7.

Security. 1989. "Exploring Security Trends." (Unpublished report by *Security* magazine.)

Security Letter XIX. September 1, 1989. No. 16, Part II.

Security Letter XXXI. February 2001. "Global Security Market Growth Continues, Finds Research."

Southerland, Randy. February 2000. *Access Control & Security Systems Integration.* "Dispatch to Nowhere," p. 1.

U.S. Department of Justice. 1988. *Report to the Nation on Crime and Justice,* 2nd ed. Washington, DC: U.S. Government Printing Office.

U.S. Department of Justice. 1985. *Crime and Protection in America: A Study of Private Security and Law Enforcement Resources and Relationships.* Washington, DC: U.S. Government Printing Office, pp. 23, 24. (Executive Summary from *The Hallcrest Report* completed by Cunningham and Taylor of Hallcrest Systems, Inc., and funded by the U.S. Department of Justice.)

U.S. Department of Justice. 1972. *Private Police in the United States: Findings and Recommendations.* Washington, DC: U.S. Government Printing Office. (Study completed by Rand Corporation and U.S. Department of Justice; commonly called *Rand Report 1972.*)

U.S. News & World Report. July 11, 1988, p. 37.

Whitehurst, Susan. February 2000. *Security* 37. "1980–2000: What a Ride!," p. 14. And, telephone call to Security Industry Association, 703-683-2075. February 22, 2001.

Chapter 3: Customer Service and Public Relations

Chapman, Elwood N. 1972. *Your Attitude Is Showing.* Chicago, IL: Science Research Associates, pp. 2–3.

Corporate Security. October 1988. New York: Business Research Publications, p. 5.

Cunningham, William C., and Todd H. Taylor. 1985. *Private Security and Police in America: The Hallcrest Report.* Portland, OR: Chancellor

Press. (Study completed by Hallcrest Systems, Inc., and funded by the U.S. Department of Justice; commonly called *The Hallcrest Report.*)

Dalton, Dennis. 1995. *Security Management: Business Strategies for Success.* Stoneham, MA: Butterworth.

Gallati, Robert. 1983. *Introduction to Private Security.* Englewood Cliffs, NJ: Prentice-Hall, p. 26.

Gilmer, B. von Haller. 1971. *Industrial and Organizational Psychology.* New York: McGraw-Hill, p. 169.

Hamit, Francis. October 2000. *Security Technology & Design* 10. "ASIS Confronts a Changing Demographic," pp. 60–62.

Hess, Karen, and Henry Wrobleski. 1988. *Introduction to Private Security.* St. Paul, MN: West Publishing Co., pp. 218–220.

Kane, Patrick. August 2000. *Security Management* 44. "People Skills Are Paramount," pp. 31–33.

Laird, Donald, and Eleanor Laird. 1975. *Psychology: Human Relations and Motivation,* 5th ed. New York: McGraw-Hill, pp. 344–345.

Manning, Gerald, and Barry Reece. 2001. *Selling Today,* 8th ed. Upper Saddle River, NJ: Prentice-Hall, p. 305.

Okun, Barbara. 1976. *Effective Helping: Interviewing & Counseling Techniques.* North Scituate, MA: Duxbury Press, p. 48.

Pierce, Jon, and John Newstrom. 2000. *The Manager's Bookshelf: A Mosaic of Contemporary Views,* 5th ed. Upper Saddle River, NJ: Prentice-Hall, p. 48.

Purpura, Philip. 2001. *Police & Community: Concepts & Cases.* Boston, MA: Allyn & Bacon.

Purpura, Philip. 1989. *Modern Security & Loss Prevention Management.* Stoneham, MA: Butterworth, p. 17.

Purpura, Philip. 1984. *Security & Loss Prevention.* Stoneham, MA: Butterworth, p. 85.

Russell, Thomas J., and Ronald Lane W. 2002. *Kleppner's Advertising Procedure,* 15th ed. Upper Saddle River, NJ: Prentice-Hall, p. 681.

Stiel, Holly. September 2001. *Security Management* 45. "Smile When You Say That," pp. 25–30.

U.S. Department of Justice. 1985. *Crime and Protection in America: A Study of Private Security and Law Enforcement Resources and Relationships.* Washington, DC: U.S. Government Printing Office.

Walton, Branch J. March 2001. *Security Technology & Design* 12. "Security and Angry Customer Confrontations: Who is Going to Win?," pp. 84–86.

Chapter 4: Crime Prevention and Physical Security

Cantrell, Betsy. October 1988. *FBI Law Enforcement Bulletin.* "A Commitment to Crime Prevention," p. 3.

Cunningham, William C., and Todd H. Taylor. 1985. *Private Security and Police in America: The Hallcrest Report.* Portland, OR: Chancellor Press. (Study completed by Hallcrest Systems, Inc., and funded by the U.S. Department of Justice; commonly called *The Hallcrest Report.*)

Ellis, David. 1991. *Becoming A Master Student,* 6th ed. Rapid City, SD: College Survival, Inc., pp. 184–185.

Goldstein, Herman. 1977. *Policing a Free Society.* Cambridge, MA: Ballinger Publishing, pp. 64–65.

Inbau, Fred, et al. 1996. *Protective Security Law,* 2nd. Boston, MA: Butterworth-Heinemann, p. 68.

Keller, Steve. January 2000. *Security Management* 44. "Framing an Alarm Design," p. 133.

Levine, James P., et al. 1986. *Criminal Justice in America: Law in Action.* New York: John Wiley & Sons, p. 198.

Murphy, Patrick M. October 2000. *Security Management* 44. "Grounds for Protection," pp. 84–88.

"National Neighborhood Watch." National Sheriff's Association, p. 12. (A program manual.)

Newman, Oscar. 1972. *Defensible Space.* New York: Macmillan.

O'Block, Robert.1981. *Security and Crime Prevention.* Stoneham, MA: Butterworth, pp. 270, 309.

O'Leary, Tim. January 2000. *Security Technology & Design* 10. "The Real Deal in Perimeter Security," p. 75.

Security Management: Protecting Property, People, and Assets. September 10, 1988. "Parking Lot Security as Customer Service," pp. 1–7.

Purpura, Philip. 2002. *Security & Loss Prevention: An Introduction,* 4th ed. Boston, MA: Butterworth-Heinemann.

Strauchs, John. January 2001. *Security Management* 45. "Which Way to Better Controls?," p. 97.

Trouten, Paul. June 2000. *Security Technology & Design* 10. "Improving Perimeter Security with Digital Signal Processing," pp. 68–72. Also, www.senstarstellar.com.

"Understanding Crime Prevention," *The Practice of Crime Prevention.* 1978. Louisville, KY: National Crime Prevention Institute Press. Vol. 1, pp. 1–2.

U.S. Department of Commerce, National Bureau of Standards. 1979. *Commercial Intrusion Alarm Systems.* Washington, DC: U.S. Government Printing Office, pp. 15, 20.

U.S. Department of Housing & Urban Development. 1975. *Improving Residential Security.* Washington, DC: U.S. Government Printing Office.

U.S. Department of Justice. 1985. *Crime and Protection in America: A Study of Private Security and Law Enforcement Resources and Relationships.* Washington, DC: U.S. Government Printing Office, p. 32.

U.S. Department of Justice. 1982. *How to Crimeproof Your Business.* Washington, DC: U.S. Government Printing Office, p. 5.

U.S. Department of Justice. 1979. *Security and the Small Business Retailer.* Washington, DC: U.S. Government Printing Office, pp. 51, 53, 124.

Van Lock Co. April 1, 2001. "Door Hardware/Electronic Audit Trail." www.vanlock.com.

Chapter 5: Post Assignments and Security Patrols

Altheide, David L. July 1975. *Urban Life* 4. "The Irony of Security."

Arnheim, Louise. November 1999. *Security Management.* "A Tour of Guard Patrol Systems," pp. 48–58.

Finneran, Eugene D. 1981. *Security Supervision.* Stoneham, MA: Butterworth, p. 199.

Fisher, Robert, and Richard Janoski. 2000. *Loss Prevention and Security Procedures: Practical Applications for Contemporary Problems.* Stoneham, MA: Butterworth.

Gourley, Douglas G., and Allen P. Bristow. 1967. *Patrol Administration.* Springfield, IL: Charles C Thomas, p. 3.

Hardison, Mark. January 2000. *Security Technology & Design* 10. "Entry Screening Station Training," pp. 93–95.

Hertig, Christopher. November 2001. *Access Control & Security Systems* 44. "The Evolving Role of Protection Officers," pp. 28–29.

Security Watch 2908. April 15, 2000. "Scanning for Trouble," pp. 1–3.

Security Watch 2917. September 1, 2000. "Teach Officers to Patrol Effectively," p. 7.

Wilson O.W., and Roy Clinton McLaren. 1977. *Police Administration,* 4th ed. New York: McGraw-Hill, p. 332.

Woodruff, Ronald S. 1974. *Industrial Security Techniques.* Columbus, OH: Charles E. Merrill, p. 16.

Chapter 6: Communications and Report Writing

Bilek, Arthur J. 1976. *Report of the Task Force on Private Security.* Washington, DC: U.S. Government Printing Office. (Study supported by the U.S. Department of Justice.)

Coleman, John L. 1986. *Practical Knowledge for a Private Security Officer.* Springfield, IL: Charles C Thomas, p. 103.

International Foundation for Protection Officers. 1998. *Protection Officer Training Manual,* 6th ed. Boston: Butterworth-Heinemann.

Minion, Ron. May 2000. *Security Management* 44. "Performance That Pays," pp. 59–62.

Security Watch 3002. January 15, 2001. "Improve Your Observation Skills," p. 1.

Watkins, Floyd C., et al. 1974. *Practical English Handbook.* Boston, MA: Houghton Mifflin, pp. 168–175.

Woodruff, Ronald S. 1974. *Industrial Security Techniques.* Columbus, OH: Charles E. Merrill, p. 108.

Chapter 7: Criminal and Civil Law

Albanese, Jay S. 2002. *Criminal Justice,* 2nd ed. Boston, MA: Allyn & Bacon.

Associated Press Release. January 1, 1985.

Bates, Norman, and Jon Groussman. February 2000. *Security Management* 44. "More Wins for Defendants in Premises Liability Cases," p. 94.

Bennett-Alexander, Dawn D., and Laura B. Pincus. 1995. *Employment Law for Business.* Chicago: Irwin, pp. 193–194.

Corporate Security. April 1988. New York: Business Research Publications.

Gardner, Thomas J. 1988. *Criminal Evidence,* 2nd ed. St. Paul, MN: West Publishing, p. 64.

Gilmer B., von Haller. 1971. *Industrial and Organizational Psychology.* New York: McGraw-Hill, p. 235.

Hames, Joanne B., and Yvonne Ekern. 2002. *Introduction to Law,* 2nd ed. Upper Saddle River, NJ: Prentice-Hall.

LaFave, Wayne R. 1964. *Arrest: The Decision to Take a Suspect into Custody.* Boston: Little, Brown & Co.

Pound, Roscoe. 1960. *New York University Law Review* 35. "Discretion, Dispensation, and Mitigation: The Problem of the Individual Special Case," pp. 925 and 926.

President's Commission on Law Enforcement and Administration of Justice. 1967. *The Challenge of Crime in a Free Society.* Washington, DC: U.S. Government Printing Office.

Purpura, Philip. 2001. *Police & Community: Concepts & Cases.* Boston, MA: Allyn & Bacon, pp. 93–116.

U.S. Department of Justice. 1988. *Report to the Nation on Crime and Justice,* 2nd ed. Washington, DC: U.S. Government Printing Office.

U.S. Department of Justice. 1972. *Private Police in the United States: Findings and Recommendations.* Washington, DC: U.S. Government Printing

Office. (Study completed by Rand Corporation and U.S. Department of Justice; commonly called *Rand Report 1972.*)

Zalman, Marvin. 2002. *Criminal Procedure: Constitution and Society,* 3rd ed. Upper Saddle River, NJ: Prentice-Hall.

Chapter 8: Arrest Law and Procedures

Bilek, Arthur J., et al. 1981. *Legal Aspects of Private Security.* Cincinnati, OH: Anderson, pp. 17–19, 89–91.

Fischer, Robert, and Gion Green. 1998. *Introduction to Security,* 6th ed. Boston, MA: Butterworth, p. 133.

Gardner, Thomas J. 1988. *Criminal Evidence,* 2nd ed. St. Paul, MN: West Publishing, p. 63.

Inbau, Fred E., Bernard Farber, and David Arnold. 1996. *Protective Security Law,* 2nd ed. Boston, MA: Butterworth.

Inciardi, James. 2002. *Criminal Justice,* 7th ed. Orlando, FL: Harcourt College Publishers.

Lyman, Michael. 2002. *Criminal Investigation: The Art and the Science,* 3rd ed. Upper Saddle River, NJ: Prentice-Hall.

Nemeth, Charles P. 1989. *Private Security and the Law.* Cincinnati, OH: Anderson, p. 77.

Purpura, Philip. 2001. *Police & Community: Concepts & Cases.* Boston, MA: Allyn & Bacon.

Purpura, Philip. 1989. *Modern Security & Loss Prevention Management.* Stoneham, MA: Butterworth, pp. 302–304.

Strobl, Walter M. 1984. *The Investigator's Handbook.* Stoneham, MA: Butterworth, p. 135.

U.S. Department of Justice, Private Security Advisory Council. 1979. *Scope of Legal Authority of Private Security Personnel.* Washington, DC: U.S. Government Printing Office, p. 15.

Young, Kevin. Winter 2000. *Protection News* 15. "10 Tough Tactics To Keep You On Top," p. 3.

Zalman, Marvin. 2002. *Criminal Procedure: Constitution and Society,* 3rd ed. Upper Saddle River, NJ: Prentice-Hall.

Chapter 9: Self-Defense and Weapons

Cope, Jeff, and Kenneth Goddard. 1979. *Weaponless Control.* Springfield, IL: Charles C Thomas.

Finneran, Eugene D. 1981. *Security Supervision: A Handbook for Supervisors and Managers.* Stoneham, MA: Butterworth, p. 230.

Haynes, Richard. October 2001. *Security Management* 45. "Not By Force Alone," pp. 65–68.

Hunter, John. May 1994. *FBI Law Enforcement Bulletin.* "Pepper Spray," pp. 24–26.

Rowland, Desmond, and James Bailey. 1985. *The Law Enforcement Handbook.* New York: Facts on File, pp. 114–116.

Security Equipment Corporation. January 16, 2002. "Frequently Asked Questions." www.sabredefensesprays.com.

Security Watch 3003. February 1, 2001. "What You Should Know Before Arming Your Guards," pp. 1–2.

Shenkman, Frederick A. April 1984. "Police Handgun Training and Qualification: A Question of Validity," *FBI Law Enforcement Bulletin,* pp. 7–12.

Tobin, Chuck. September 2000. *Security Management* 44. "For Every Action," pp. 61–65.

U.S. Department of Justice. 1987. *Equipment Performance Report: .38 and .357 Caliber Revolvers Test Results.* Washington, DC: U.S. Government Printing Office, p. 9.

U.S. Department of Justice. 1987. *Equipment Performance Report: 9mm and .45 Caliber Autoloading Pistol Test Results.* Washington, DC: U.S. Government Printing Office, p. 7.

Williams, Mason. 1977. *The Law Enforcement Book of Weapons, Ammunition, and Training Procedures.* Springfield, IL: Charles C Thomas.

Chapter 10: Combatting Internal Losses

Access Control & Security Systems Integration 43. December 2000. "Background Checks Provide Means to Combat Employee Theft," p. 8.

Baker, Michael A., and Alan F. Westin. 1987. *Employer Perceptions of Workplace Crime.* Washington, DC: U.S. Government Printing Office, p. 12.

Conley, John. November 2000. *Risk Management* 47. "Knocking the Starch Out of White Collar Crime," p. 14.

Corporate Security 27. August 31, 2001. "Employee Theft Flourishes with Innovation," p. 3.

Cunningham, William C., and Todd H. Taylor. 1985. *Private Security and Police in America: The Hallcrest Report.* Portland, OR: Chancellor Press. (Study completed by Hallcrest Systems, Inc., and funded by the U.S. Department of Justice; commonly called *The Hallcrest Report.*)

Garner, Bryan. 2000. *A Handbook of Criminal Law Terms.* St. Paul, MN: West Group.

Purpura, Philip. 2002. *Security & Loss Prevention: An Introduction,* 4th ed. Boston, MA: Butterworth-Heinemann.

Security Watch 3005. March 1, 2001. "Be Alert to Internal Fraud," p. 7.

Shaw, Eric, Jerrold Post, and Keven Ruby. July 2000. *Information Security* 3. "Managing the Threat from Within," p. 62.

Shepard, Ira, and Robert Duston. 1988. *Thieves At Work.* Bureau of National Affairs. Washington, DC: U.S. Government Printing Office, p. 19.

U.S. Department of Justice. 1985. *Crime and Protection in America: A Study of Private Security and Law Enforcement Resources and Relationships.* Washington, DC: U.S. Government Printing Office.

Chapter 11: Retail Loss Prevention

Altheide, David L. 1978. *Crime at the Top.* New York: Lippincott, pp. 114–118.

Brunker, Mike. May 16, 2001. *MSNBC.* "Internet Merchants Fight Back." www.msnbc.com/news/377221.asp.

Corporate Security 28. May 31, 2001. "Retail," p. 2.

Cunningham, William C., and Todd H. Taylor. 1985. *Private Security and Police in America: The Hallcrest Report.* Portland, OR: Chancellor Press. (Study completed by Hallcrest Systems, Inc., and funded by the U.S. Department of Justice; commonly called *The Hallcrest Report.*)

Holland, Thomas. August 1999. *Security Management* 43. "Checks and Balances," pp. 76–82.

Purpura, Philip. 1993. *Retail Security and Shrinkage Protection.* Boston, MA: Butterworth-Heinemann.

Security Technology & Design 12. January 2002. "National Retail Security Survey," p. 20.

Security Watch 2902. January 15, 2000. "How Stores Fight Theft," p. 5.

U.S. Department of Justice. 2000. *Crime in the United States, Uniform Crime Reports, 1999.* Washington, DC: U.S. Government Printing Office. www.fbi.gov/ucr.

U.S. Department of Justice. 1985. *Crime and Protection in America: A Study of Private Security and Law Enforcement Resources and Relationships.* Washington, DC: U.S. Government Printing Office.

Chapter 12: Safety, Fire Protection, and Emergencies

Adams, Walter. October 2001. *Security Technology & Design* 11. "Who, What, When, and Where's the Fire?," pp. 78–84.

Bugbee, Percy. 1978. *Principles of Fire Protection.* Boston. MA: National Fire Protection Association.

Fire Journal. November/December 1988, pp. 25–38.

Grimaldi, John V., and Rollin H. Simonds. 1975. *Safety Management.* Homewood, IL: Irwin, p. 5.

Mroz, Joseph H. 1978. *Safety in Everyday Living.* Dubuque, IA: William C Brown, p. 3.

National Fire Data Center. 2000. *The Overall Fire Picture—1999.* www.usfa.fema.gov. February 16, 2001.

Occupational Hazards 63. January 2001. "Lockout/Tagout," p. 17.

Security Watch 3006. March 15, 2001. "Are Your Fire Extinguishers Properly Maintained," pp. 1, 3–4.

U.S. Department of Health & Human Services. 1975. *Health & Safety Guide for Retail Lumber & Building Materials.* Washington, DC: U.S. Government Printing Office.

U.S. Department of the Interior. 1979. *Fire Safety Manual #13.* Washington, DC: U.S. Government Printing Office.

U.S. Department of Labor, OSHA. 2001. *How to Plan for Workplace Emergencies and Evacuations.* Washington, DC: U.S. Government Printing Office.

U.S. Department of Labor, OSHA. *OSHA Strategic Plan.* www.osha.gov. May 3, 2001.

U.S. Department of Labor, OSHA. 1998. *Chemical Hazard Communication.* Washington, DC: U.S. Government Printing Office, pp. 1–24.

Vendrell, Ernest. Winter 2000/2001. *Protection News* 16. "Responding to a Hazardous Materials Incident," pp. 1, 7–8.

Chapter 13: Medical Emergencies

Acello, Barbara. 1998. *Basic Skills for the Health Care Provider.* Albany, NY: Delmar.

American Academy of Orthopaedic Surgeons. 1987. *Emergency Care and Transportation,* 4th ed. Park Ridge, IL: American Academy of Orthopaedic Surgeons, pp. 396–410.

American Heart Association. 1988. *Basic Life Support.* Dallas, TX: American Heart Association, p. 79.

American National Red Cross. 1981. *Cardiopulmonary Resuscitation.* Washington, DC: American National Red Cross.

American National Red Cross. 1973. *Standard First Aid and Personal Safety.* Garden City, N.J.: Doubleday & Co., p. 11.

Azain, Gail. 2001. *Bloodborne Safety: Universal Precautions, Standard Precautions, and Needlestick Prevention.* Cypress, CA: Medcom, Inc.

Besse, William, and Charles Whitehead. June 2000. *Security Management* 44. "New Tools of an Old Trade," pp. 66–72.

Editors of *Reader's Digest.* 1984. *Family Safety & First Aid.* New York: Berkley Books, pp. 260–263.

Limmer, Daniel, et al. 2001. *Emergency Care,* 9th ed. Upper Saddle River, NJ: Brady/Prentice-Hall.

Longmore-Etheridge, Ann. March 2000. *Security Management* 44. "The Beat Goes On," p. 20.

Purpura, Philip. 1997. *Criminal Justice: An Introduction.* Boston, MA: Butterworth-Heinemann, pp. 189–190.

Purpura, Philip. 1989. *Modern Security & Loss Prevention Management.* Boston, MA: Butterworth.

Rowland, Loyd W., and Robert A. Matthews. 1988. *Aiding People in Conflict.* Alexandria, VA: National Mental Health Association, p. 16.

Security Magazine 37. February 2000. "Shopper Shock," pp. 16–18.

U.S. Department of Justice, National Institute of Justice. 1988. *Precautionary Measures and Protective Equipment.* Washington, DC: U.S. Government Printing Office, p. 3.

Chapter 14: Special Problems

Adams, Carey. February 2001. *iSecurity* 44. "A Partnership to Expose Cybercrim," p. 1.

Albanese, Jay. 2001. *Criminal Justice.* Boston: Allyn & Bacon, pp. 81–82.

Briney, Andy, and Kirk Fretwell. September 2000. *Information Security* 3. "Security Focused," p. 41.

Broughton, Marisa. Winter 2000. *Protection News* 15. "Workplace Violence," pp. 3, 6.

FBI. 1997. *Terrorism in the United States, 1995.* Washington, DC: U.S. Government Printing Office, p. 14.

Freidenfelds, Lauris. January 2002. *Security Technology & Design* 12. "Protection Against Terrorism," pp. 34–39.

Goode, Erich. 1989. *Drugs in American Society.* New York: Alfred A. Knopf.

Harper's Magazine. January 1995. "Pro-Life Terrorism: A How-To," p. 19.

Hughes, Sandra. 2001. *Security Journal* 14. "Violence in the Workplace: Identifying Costs and Preventive Solutions," p. 69.

Ivancevich, John. 2001. *Human Resource Management,* 8th ed. Boston: McGraw-Hill Irwin, p. 464.

Kiyota, Stan. November 2000. *Information Security* 3. "Planning Makes Perfect," p. 104.

Naisbitt, John. 1982. *Megatrends.* New York: Warren Books.

Neeley, Dequendre. May 2000. *Security Management* 44. "Protection Progress Report," p. 34.

Protection News 16. Spring 2001. "Domestic Violence Targets the Heart of American Business," p. 1.

Purpura, Philip. 2002. *Security & Loss Prevention: An Introduction,* 4th ed. Boston, MA: Butterworth-Heinemann.

Risk & Insurance 12. May 2001. "Computer Crime Increases," p. 8.

Sager, Ira, et al. February 21, 2000. *Business Week.* "Cybercrime," p. 40.

Security Watch 2912. June 15, 2000. "10 Tips That Help Security and IT Stop Hackers," pp. 1–3.

Toffler, Alvin. 1980. *The Third Wave.* New York: Morrow.

U.S. Commission on National Security. September 15, 1999. *New World Coming: American Security in the 21st Century.* www.nssg.gov.

University of Iowa. February 2001. "Workplace Violence: A Report to the Nation." www.public-health.viowa.edu/iprc/index.html.

Waxman, Harvey. September 1995. *Security Management.* "Putting Workplace Violence in Perspective," p. 123.

Chapter 15: Career Planning

Beckmann, Gerald. July 1999. *Security Technology & Design* 9. "Security Training: Testing Your Staff's Competency," pp. 22–28.

Bureau of Justice Statistics. 1999. www.ojp.usdoj.gov/bjs (February 20, 2001).

Cunningham, William C., and Todd H. Taylor. 1985. *Private Security and Police in America: The Hallcrest Report.* Portland, OR: Chancellor Press. (Study completed by Hallcrest Systems, Inc., and funded by the U.S. Department of Justice; commonly called *The Hallcrest Report.*)

Purpura, Philip. 2002. *Security & Loss Prevention: An Introduction,* 4th ed. Boston, MA: Butterworth-Heinemann.

Purpura, Philip. 1997. *Criminal Justice: An Introduction.* Boston, MA: Butterworth-Heinemann, pp. 372–383.

Security 37. January 2000. "Law Enforcement Count Dwarfed by Private Security," Page 7.

U.S. Department of Justice. 1985. *Crime and Protection in America: A Study of Private Security and Law Enforcement Resources and Relationships.* Washington, DC: U.S. Government Printing Office.

Whitehurst, Susan. February 2000. *Security* 37. "1980–2000: What a Ride!," p. 14. And, telephone call to Security Industry Association, 703-683-2075 (February 22, 2001).